2

F. Scott Fitzgerald

A BIOGRAPHY

André Le Vot

Translated from the French by William Byron

WARNER BOOKS

A Warner Communications Company

Warner Books Edition
English translation copyright © 1983 by Doubleday & Company, Inc.
English edition published by arrangement with Julliard, Paris,
from the "Vivants" Collection, Editorial Director Camille Bourniquel.
Originally published as *Scott Fitzgerald*
Copyright © 1979 by Julliard, Paris
All rights reserved.

This Warner Books edition is published by arrangement with
Doubleday & Company, Inc., 245 Park Avenue, New York, NY 10017

Warner Books, Inc., 666 Fifth Avenue, New York, NY 10103
W A Warner Communications Company

Printed in the United States of America
First Warner printing: August 1984
10 9 8 7 6 5 4 3 2 1

Cover design by James Laird
Cover photo of F. Scott Fitzgerald courtesy of The Bettmann Archives

Library of Congress Cataloging in Publication Data

Le Vot, André.
    F. Scott Fitzgerald.

    Translation of: Scott Fitzgerald.
    Bibliography: p. 357
    Includes index.
    1. Fitzgerald, F. Scott (Francis Scott), 1896–1940.
2. Novelists, American—20th century—Biography.
I. Title.
PS3511.I9Z68213   1983b   813'.52[B]   83-23573
ISBN 0-446-38065-2 (U.S.A.) (pbk.)
       0-446-38066-0 (Canada) (pbk.)

The publisher thanks the following for permission to quote from the sources listed.
    Charles Scribner's Sons for quotations from books by F. Scott Fitzgerald, i.e., *The Beautiful and Damned*, copyright 1922 Charles Scribner's Sons, copyright renewed

CONTENTS

I. AN AMERICAN EDUCATION

(1896-1917)

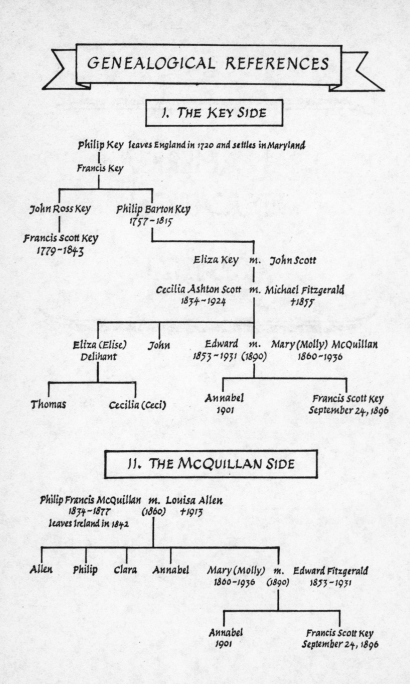

GENEALOGICAL REFERENCES

I. THE KEY SIDE

Philip Key leaves England in 1720 and settles in Maryland

Francis Key

John Ross Key   Philip Barton Key
                            1757 – 1815

Francis Scott Key
1779 – 1843

Eliza Key   m.   John Scott

Cecilia Ashton Scott   m.   Michael Fitzgerald
1834 – 1924   † 1855

Eliza (Elise)   John   Edward   m.   Mary (Molly) McQuillan
Delihant   1853 – 1931 (1890)   1860 – 1936

Thomas   Cecilia (Ceci)   Annabel   Francis Scott Key
                               1901   September 24, 1896

II. THE MCQUILLAN SIDE

Philip Francis McQuillan   m.   Louisa Allen
1834 – 1877   (1860)   † 1913
leaves Ireland in 1842

Allen   Philip   Clara   Annabel   Mary (Molly)   m.   Edward Fitzgerald
                                    1860 – 1936 (1890)   1853 – 1931

Annabel   Francis Scott Key
1901   September 24, 1896

1. THE CHILD AND THE LEGEND

(1896–1908)

Let's begin with the Christian names. Fitzgerald's—Francis Scott Key—constitute a program, point a direction. Not the first name for the father, nor the second for the mother, as is so often the case in the United States, but a jump three generations back for three indissociable names designating the patron under whose aegis the child was to be placed: Francis Scott Key, first cousin of a paternal great-grandmother, Eliza Key Scott. Fitzgerald did not choose them, but he accepted them, assumed and bore them like a flag. And this patronage really was a matter of flags and plumes, as though, the Christian name given, he had then to conquer a last name. Francis Scott Key: four strongly rhythmic syllables, rich in connotations, a prelude after the repetition of the opening *F* to the pyramidal symmetry of the final, still meaningless, trisyllable with its strongly accented middle measure: Fitz-*ge*-rald.

The connection with Francis Scott Key and "The Star-Spangled Banner" would be merely anecdotal if it did not shed light on certain themes and attitudes in both the parents and the son who, we must not forget, would make a lifelong point of his relationship with Key. Perhaps because in his distant ancestor he recognized the admirably symbolic situation, the basic motivation that carried him, too, toward literature: frustrated in his desire to become a man of action, to take an active part in the struggles of his time (he would never cease to regret that he could not fight in the Great War), he in turn found himself, like Key watching the bombardment of Fort McHenry from the deck of a British warship, relegated to the role of spectator and, in a sense, in the losers' camp. And writing seemed, as we shall see, a tempting way to compensate for this feeling of frustration. But Key represented something else as well; his name recalls a culture, a life-style, a survival of ancestral virtues, a way of being that was rapidly disappearing from the business-minded America of the late nineteenth century. Perhaps there was a touch of snobbery in this return to the family's origins, but most of all it betokened a deep nostalgia for values threatened by the mercantilism triumphant when Fitzgerald was born.

Francis Scott Key belonged to a patrician, resolutely Catholic family that had settled in Maryland in 1720. Its members had sat in America's assemblies and advised its governors both before and after the War of Independence. The career of Philip Barton Key, the father of Fitzgerald's paternal great-grandmother, Eliza Key, clearly illustrates the importance and influence of a family that prospered despite the vicissitudes of politics. The son of a rich planter, he had read for law at the universities of Edinburgh and London. A British loyalist during the Revolutionary War, he was wounded in action and pensioned by George III. This did not prevent him from making amends to America after the war, winning his pardon and assuming his place in the community as an American citizen. After marrying the daughter of the governor of Maryland in 1790, he served in Congress before making a career as a talented and successful lawyer specializing in Supreme Court cases. Among the most prominent members of his Washington firm was his nephew, Francis Scott Key.

One of Philip's daughters, Eliza, married John Scott, a Baltimore judge who left no trace in American history, but whose lack of luster was compensated by the distinguished origins ascribed to him in the family's annals: one of his ancestors, twenty-seven generations earlier, was no less a personage than Roger Bigot (1150–1221), Earl of Suffolk and Norfolk, himself a descendant of King Sveid of the Vikings. Bigot married a Plantagenet and was one of the nobles assigned to enforce the Magna Charta.

Around 1850 one of Scott's daughters, Cecilia—Scott Fitzgerald's grandmother—wed a gentleman farmer, Captain Michael Fitzgerald, who soon left her a widow with three children, Eliza, John and Edward, the writer's father. Here again, an ancestor's obscurity is made up for by the fabulous lineage attributed to him: legend has the Fitzgeralds descending from the Geraldini family of Tuscany, from an Earl Fitzgerald who ruled over Ireland in the fifteenth century and from the first Catholic landowners to colonize Maryland in the middle of the seventeenth century, after the British crown ceded the territory to Lord Baltimore in 1632. During Cromwell's dictatorship, Maryland was a haven for Catholics persecuted in England and became a royal colony after the Stuart restoration.

Hardly anything is known of Michael Fitzgerald himself except that his family had lived for generations on Glenmary Farm near Rockville, Montgomery County, some twenty miles from Washington. It was here that Scott's father, Edward Fitzgerald, was born in 1853 "in his grandfather's great-grandfather's house"[1] two years before Michael Fitzgerald's death. With his brother, John, and his sister, Eliza, Edward was raised by his mother and his maternal grandmother, Eliza Key Scott, Francis Scott Key's cousin.

In a piece written on his father's death, echoes of which are found in *Tender Is the Night*, Fitzgerald paid tribute in his fashion to the ethical training those two women gave his father: "What he knew he had learned from his mother and grandmother, the latter a bore to me—'If your grandmother Scott heard that she would turn over in her grave.' . . . He had a good heart that came from another America—he was much too sure of what he was, much too sure of the deep pride of the two proud women who brought him up to doubt for a moment that his own instincts were good."[2]

The writer ended his essay by noting that his father had always been a stranger to his generation—the generation of victors who had distinguished themselves in the Civil War—and remained an eighteenth-century man: "he was of the generation of the colony and the revolution."[3] In 1940, when his aunt Eliza (or Elise, as she called herself) died, he wrote to her daughter, his cousin "Ceci" (Cecilia), the Clara of *This Side of Paradise*, who was sixteen years his senior: "With Father, Uncle John and Aunt Elise a generation goes. I wonder how deep the Civil War was in them—that odd childhood on the border between the states with Grandmother and old Mrs. Scott and the shadow of Mrs. Surratt. What a sense of honor and duty— almost eighteenth-century rather than Victorian. How lost they seemed in the changing world."[4]

During the Civil War Edward had witnessed the Confederate struggles to capture Washington and liberate Maryland, Southern in sympathies but isolated behind the Union lines. He joined in his neighbors' efforts to aid the Confederacy, guiding spies across the Potomac, helping a sniper with Mosby's guerrillas to escape, watching General Jubal Early's troops march past on their final attempt to seize the Federal capital. With the armistice in 1865, tragedy struck the family: the mother-in-law of one of Edward's first cousins, Mary Surratt, was implicated in Lincoln's assassination. Convicted as an accomplice of John Wilkes Booth, she was condemned and hanged. Edward Fitzgerald was to remember that feverish time all his life, and he would enthrall young Scott with stories of those legendary events. In a foreword he wrote to a book on the historic homes of Maryland, Fitzgerald recalled his childhood enchantment with those tales: "the vistas and glories of Maryland followed many a young man West after the Civil War and my father was of that number. Much of my early childhood in Minnesota was spent in asking him such questions as: 'and how long did it take Early's columns to pass Glenmary that day?' (that was a farm in Montgomery County) and 'what would have happened if Jeb Stuart's cavalry had joined Lee instead of coming all the way to Rockville?' and 'tell me again about how you used to ride through the woods with a spy up behind you on the horse,' and 'why wouldn't they let Francis Scott Key off the British Frigate?' "[5]

One of his first short stories, written when he was only fourteen, was called "The Room with the Green Blinds" (published by his school, the St. Paul Academy, in its magazine, *Now and Then*, in June 1911); it gives young Scott's version of the story of Lincoln's assassin. The last long story published in his lifetime was "The End of Hate," based on one of his father's tales (". . . he had only a few, the story of the Spy, the one about the Man Hung by his Thumbs, the one about Early's March"[6]). The Civil War also inspired "The Night at Chancellorsville," an account of the beginning of the battle as seen by a prostitute aboard a train that was briefly held by Confederate soldiers.

The influence of his ancestors' native region is felt in a more diffuse but nevertheless more conclusive way—it is less dependent on picturesque details of local lore and color—in a philosophy of life of which we shall see the importance later on. These patrician forebears' moral heritage, reviewed and revised by a romantic imagination, can be summed up as an idealistic attitude contrasting with America's postwar materialism—the Southern aristocracy's traditional panache, inherited from the English Cavaliers and sharply different from the down-to-earth mercantilism of the Puritans' descendants.

To Fitzgerald, what his father embodied was as much a life-style as a romantic past. In a booming Middle West reaching out toward the future, toward progress, and prizing energy and success above all virtues, he displayed an elegantly courtly nonchalance, exquisite courtesy and a singular capacity for failing in everything he undertook. True, like most of the young men of his generation, he had heard the call of the West. He sought his fortune first in Chicago, then in St. Paul. At the time of his marriage in 1890, he headed a small firm there producing wicker furniture under the pompous name of The American Rattan and Willow Works. His wife bore him two daughters, who were carried off in an epidemic in 1896; a few months after they died, she produced a son, Francis Scott Key Fitzgerald. Ruined by the economic crisis then gripping the country, the family business failed in 1898. Procter and Gamble hired Edward Fitzgerald as a salesman in Buffalo. That didn't last long. In 1901 the family turned up in Syracuse, where it stayed for nearly three years, changing its residence every year. A daughter, Annabel, was born a few months after the Fitzgeralds arrived there. In September 1903 they were back in Buffalo. The elder Fitzgerald really had no talent for business. In March 1908, at the age of fifty-five, he was fired from his job. This was disaster for the Fitzgeralds. Scott, then eleven years old, was deeply affected. When his father telephoned the news, panic filled him. "Dear God, please don't let us go to the poorhouse; please don't let us go to the poorhouse."[7] He returned the quarter his mother had just given him to go swimming.

His father had toppled from his pedestal; he was finished now, and his family's affection for him would henceforth be cruelly mixed with pity: "That morning he had gone out a comparatively young man, a man full of strength, full of confidence. He came home that evening an old man, a completely broken man. He had lost his essential drive, his immaculateness of purpose. He was a failure the rest of his days."[8]

Yet Scott was thinking of his own father when he endowed the fathers of

Nick Carraway in *The Great Gatsby* and Dick Diver in *Tender Is the Night* with human and moral qualities that made them the oracles to whom their sons turn at moments of uncertainty and crisis. Reverend Diver, especially, is painted directly from life. This is clear if we compare a few phrases—among others that are equally meaningful—from the passage in the novel describing Dick's feelings and reminiscences with almost identical lines in the essay Fitzgerald wrote after Edward Fitzgerald's death in 1931: "Dick loved his father—again and again he referred judgments to what his father would probably have thought or done. Dick was born several months after the death of two young sisters and his father, guessing what would be the effect on Dick's mother, had saved him from a spoiling by becoming his moral guide. He was of tired stock yet he raised himself to that effort."[9]

Here is the corresponding passage in the essay: "I loved my father—always deep in my subconscious I have referred judgments back to him, what he would have thought, or done. He loved me—and felt a deep responsibility for me. I was born several months after the sudden death of my two elder sisters and he felt what the effect of this would be on my mother, that he would be my only guide. He became that to the best of his ability."[10]

Despite his failures, perhaps because of them, Edward Fitzgerald long remained a symbol for his son of a concept of life, a moral code that had vanished from post-World War I urban civilization. His public disgrace, however, would have been irremediable had his wife, Mary, not been helped by her family. After the disaster the Fitzgeralds returned to St. Paul and found refuge in the big house owned by her mother, Louisa McQuillan.

In the McQuillan tribe we find the second determining influence in the formation of young Scott's mind and imagination. He was torn between his loyalty to a father who had failed and his admiration for the memory of an energetic grandfather who had carved out a solid fortune in the greedy, brutal years that followed the War of Secession. In 1933, in a period of doubt and introspection, the adult Scott wrote in a letter to John O'Hara of the conflicting influences that marked his childhood: "I am half black Irish and half old American stock with the usual exaggerated ancestral pretensions. The black Irish half of the family had the money and looked down upon the Maryland side of the family who had, and really had, that . . . series of reticences and obligations that go under the poor old shattered word 'breeding.' "[11]

Philip Francis McQuillan was a very model of the self-made man characteristic of the second half of the American nineteenth century. Fleeing the poverty then prevailing in Ireland, his parents had emigrated to the United States in 1842 and settled in Galena, Illinois, a small town on the Mississippi. It was from there that he set out on his progress to prosperity. At twenty-three he started as a bookkeeper for Beaupré & Temple, a wholesale grocery firm in St. Paul; in 1872 he took over the business and by 1875 he owned a five-story store, then the city's biggest building. By age forty he had made his fortune. But his health was precarious: he suffered from Bright's disease and his lungs were affected. In vain he sought relief in Havana, where he remained for several months; he died in 1877 at the age of forty-three, leaving a widow and four children (a fifth was born after his death), the oldest of whom, Mary—"Molly"—was seventeen. But he also left a fortune the newspapers estimated at $400,000 and a thriving business.

Although they never fully joined in a social life in which they would have felt ill at ease, the McQuillans nevertheless always suitably maintained their rank in St. Paul society. As many as five hundred guests sometimes gathered at receptions in the huge Victorian house at 397 East Tenth Street. Annabel, one of McQuillan's three daughters, was maid of honor at the marriage of the daughter of Northwestern railroad magnate James J. Hill. When McQuillan died, the local papers sang the praises of this "pioneer of wholesale grocery": "He came here a poor boy with but a few dollars in his pocket, depending solely on a clear head, sound judgment, good habits, strict honesty and willing hands, with strict integrity his guiding motive. How these qualities have aided him is shown in the immense business he has built up, the acquisition of large property outside, and the universal respect felt for him by the businessmen of the county, among whom probably no man was better known or stood higher."[12]

Clearly, grandfather McQuillan's rapid rise to fortune lent itself to hyperbole; it fit nicely in the mold in which, since the days of Benjamin Franklin, the models were cast that set American imaginations to dreaming. It even recalls the beginnings of his contemporary Andrew Carnegie, who left his native Scotland to seek work in America and founded a kingdom in steel. If McQuillan's success was less resounding, it was because he died prematurely, in full ascension. What he might have achieved is suggested by the career of one of his St. Paul friends who, like Carnegie, founded an empire: James Jerome Hill, builder of the Great Northern Railroad, which linked the Great Lakes with the Pacific Coast. Fitzgerald would allude several times in his work to the Hill legend. In "Absolution," Carl Miller, father of the future Gatsby, works in one of Hill's transport companies, "growing old in Hill's gigantic shadow. For twenty years he had lived alone with Hill's name and God." At Gatsby's funeral we hear the father use Hill's name to evoke the great future that had awaited his son: "If he'd lived, he'd of been a great man. A man like James J. Hill. He'd of helped build up the country."[13]

Fitzgerald, who belonged to a generation of idol smashers and who knew his history, was implicitly condemning the myth as he did explicitly in *Tender Is the Night* in discussing the origins and rapacity of the Warren family of Chicago—a "ducal family without a title," a feudal clan on a par with the Armours, Swifts and McCormicks. In the book it is not the colorless Henry Gatz (alias Carl Miller) whom Fitzgerald contrasts with the legend of the empire builders, but the noble figure of Reverend Diver, repository of America's moral virtues. Behind the relationships of the "obscure" and the "titans" we discern Fitzgerald's own attitudes toward the two branches of his family—toward his father's economic failure and his grandfather's spectacular success.

This dichotomy affected his depiction in the novel of America's geographic space. But the East-West opposition on which *The Great Gatsby* is based ultimately comes down to a deeper and more radical opposition between the great urban centers and the provincial cities where the old traditions survived. During the 1930s Fitzgerald would point out the even sharper differences between the North (including the industrial and commercial West) and the South. He would renounce the McQuillans' moral heritage in favor of that bequeathed him by his father, by another region more cultural than geographic, more mythical than historical: the South. Not Faulkner's violent and bloody Deep South, but the more cultivated and cosmopolitan, more delicate and romantic land of Poe, the moderate South of Maryland, in its origins a royal land, a Catholic land. In a sense he associated the North with the masculine spirit of conquest, the South with the feminine spirit of a quest for happiness, more intuitive, closer to things, to the elements.

The marked partiality in so many of his works did not mean, however, that Fitzgerald idealized his South. We have seen how much on his guard he was against the "exaggerated ancestral pretensions" that seemed one of the characteristics of this land turned toward the past. Ever watchful, he could be ironic about some of his compatriots. Yet through his years of trial, Maryland and especially Baltimore were to remain havens midway between reality and myth, present and past, life and death. In September 1935, during one of his most acute moral crises, he felt a certain comfort in gazing from his hotel-room window at Mount Vernon Place in the heart of Baltimore, where stood a statue of Francis Scott Key: "it is nice to look up the street and see the statue of my great uncle and to know Poe is buried here and that many ancestors of mine have walked in the old town by the bay. I belong here, where everything is civilized and gay and rotted and polite."[14]

After her husband's death Louisa McQuillan sold the big family house, but continued to live on the hills overlooking the Mississippi, near Summit Avenue, in the middle of the city's most exclusive residential district. She gave her children a strict Catholic upbringing and contributed generously to religious charities. The McQuillan family was considered among the most devout in St. Paul, as attests this passage in a letter from the city's archbishop written to obtain a papal audience for Scott in 1921: "I know his family well, none have merited more of the Church in this city than they have through several generations—staunch, devout, generous."[15]

Sometimes the whole family would sail for Europe, chiefly to visit Rome

and the Vatican. Mary McQuillan made four such trips before her marriage. She married late for her time and circle; she was thirty and did not
want to remain a spinster. She wasn't pretty, but she was gentle and romantic. Edward Fitzgerald, seven years her senior, waged a long courtship; he
was Catholic, and though he lacked social stature, he had illustrious forebears
and gentlemanly manners. They were married in 1890 in Louisa McQuillan's winter home in Washington and spent their honeymoon on the French
Riviera, of which Mary retained an enchanted memory. The future, as we
have seen, would not be kind to her; first there was the death of her two
daughters, then her pride was deeply wounded when her husband lost his
job and the family had to ask her mother for asylum. Fitzgerald would later
note her remark at the time: "Well, if it wasn't for him [grandfather] now
where would we be?"[16] Leaving Buffalo forever, the Fitzgeralds took refuge in the family home at 294 Laurel Avenue; they stayed there a year,
with Scott's grandmother and his two unmarried aunts, stern Annabel and
pretty, weak-lunged Clara, who had only a few years to live and who spent
her winters in Arizona. All three ladies were strictly dressed in black and
steeped in piety. Adrift once more, the Fitzgeralds briefly changed
addresses: as in the past, they moved frequently, never inhabiting the same
house more than three years, always on the edge of the residential district
and never very far from its center on Summit Avenue. It was in the attic
atop the narrow, vine-covered facade of a red-sandstone two-family house
at 599 Summit Avenue that Fitzgerald was to write the final version of *This
Side of Paradise* in 1919:

> *In a house below the average*
> *Of a street above the average*
> *In a room below the roof. . .*[17]

St. Paul then was a middle-class city with well-seated traditions. On several occasions Fitzgerald made a point of emphasizing that its leading
families had been established there for three generations, while other Middle
Western cities could at best boast a two-generation past—"just remember,"
says the hero of the story "The Ice Palace," vaunting his city's antiquity to
his Southern fiancée, "that this is a three-generation town. Everybody has a
father, and about half of us have grandfathers."[18]

With its residential districts perched atop a rocky cliff rising some three
hundred feet above the Mississippi Valley, it dominated its plebeian rival,
Minneapolis, a more dynamic, fast-developing city, which tried in vain to
acquire the tone and the reserve that made St. Paul the Boston of the Middle
West. St. Paul had also grown quickly, but too-sudden acquisition of
wealth seemed to have depleted its vitality and changed its former pioneers
into coupon clippers straining toward worldliness and the Victorian virtues.
This was current at the turn of the century. The McQuillans' sudden fortune and slow decline were typical not only of St. Paul at the end of the

nineteenth century but also of those other rich American families, too prompt to deny their origins, whose decadence would be described by Booth Tarkington in *The Magnificent Ambersons.*

Encouraged by his parents, young Scott, fascinated by the mystery surrounding these social circles, burned to enter them and, if he could, shine in them. Later he would keep his distance, would analyze the workings of the social machine and perceive all the maneuvering and snobbery that fixed each member's place. In 1923, in an account of Grace Flandrau's novel *Being Respectable,* he recalled how the social life in St. Paul around the middle of the nineteenth century was stimulated by the arrival of wealthy people with sick lungs who were attracted by the supposed benefits of the city's climate: "These Easterners mingled with the rising German and Irish stock whose second generation left the cobbler's last, forgot the steerage, and became passionately 'swell' on its own account. But the pace was set by the tubercular Easterners."[19]

What is notable in this is the distinction bestowed by tuberculosis, a romantic ailment if ever there was one. (Grandfather McQuillan would be ennobled this way and so, later on, would his daughter Clara. Fitzgerald would never fail to make use of that distinction in portraying victims of this dark disease.) Note also the spirit of emulation that drove immigrants' children to ape the civilized manners of persons of rank. The older of McQuillan's sons, Allen, an excellent dancer, was to distinguish himself in society; even Annabel gloried in having been maid of honor to one of J. J. Hill's daughters. We can see what compensatory profit Edward Fitzgerald could make from the fact that he was an authentic Easterner descended from a long line of patricians.

St. Paul's growth was doubtless as rapid as that of most Midwestern cities after the Civil War. Around 1845 it was still just a hamlet peopled by a mere dozen French Canadian pioneers; twenty years later it was a booming city where steamboats arrived daily loaded with immigrants. Two men specially contributed to the city's particular identity: Archbishop John Ireland and railroad baron Hill. In less than a generation the prelate's tireless efforts made St. Paul a bastion of Roman Catholicism in the United States, a rallying point for thousands of Irish and German Catholics driven from their countries by famine or political upheaval. Such a builder was Archbishop Ireland that local residents gave the name Vatican City to the cluster of schools, religious houses and seminaries around the cathedral built from 1906 to 1915, while Fitzgerald was growing up there.

At about the same time Hill, who in 1873 had been, like Philip McQuillan, simply one more of the town's leading citizens, launched his railroad operations. In 1879 he began building the Great Northern Railroad, which in three decades earned $400 million in profits. St. Paul, where many New England businessmen settled before World War I, became a major financial and trading center, the true capital of the great Northwest that Hill's railroad opened to settlement and cultivation. At the fringe of these growing empires the Fitzgeralds tried as best they could to soften their rancor as people who had missed every train. Edward Fitzgerald was notably lacking in the two qualities, energy and luck, that brought men into step with this march toward expansion. Prosperity's discards, the first victims of depressions that came in series, he and his family lived meagerly, as poor relations do, on crumbs from the feast. True, they lacked for nothing; their children were the best dressed, they went to the best schools, their mother traveled frequently, their father's wardrobe was impeccable, but they owed everything to P. F. McQuillan's estate. Molly had found a husband, but she remained under the tutelage of her mother and her two sisters. Humiliated by this dependence, she renounced any claims to social prominence, gave up trying to preserve appearances. Clumsily, incoherently, overpossessively, she tried to pamper her son, protect him, make him shine, fashion him into a winner whose success would wipe out her disappointment.

But in this too she failed. Scott took his father's side. Edward Fitzgerald, facing up to his situation with the poise of the weak, subscribed to values other than those governing the world that had defeated him. With the materialistic heritage of which he was a dependent he contrasted the cultural heritage of his origins. The vulgar, mercantile present and its shrewd practitioners were confronted with a past of dignity and breeding. This unsuccessful traveling salesman saw himself as representing a higher order, raising his good manners and slightly restrained elegance to the status of rules for living. And the choice of his son's three Christian names was a way of recalling his background, of affirming to the world the permanence of an ideal based not on a quest for riches but on America's old virtues, those of humanistic, idealistic America at the end of the eighteenth century. He probably believed in this deeply, but it was also an effective strategy that saved him from losing face completely. Didn't Molly make a point of telling her son's friends that he was descended from the famous Francis Scott Key? And didn't Scott himself boast of it, at least until he reached his teens?

In St. Paul his father maintained appearances by pretending to be a wholesale grocery broker, but he fooled no one. He didn't even have an office in which to receive his hypothetical customers; he stored his meager stock of samples in a desk in the office of brother-in-law Philip McQuillan's real estate agency. When he bought stamps, he didn't pay for them; he had them chalked up to his wife's account.

Scott's mother, her ambitions disappointed, her emotions lacerated, made a cult of her son. She spoiled him all the more for his fragile health, his susceptibility to colds; she feared he would fall prey to the tuberculosis that afflicted her father and her sister Clara. At the age of one Scott was already a bronchitis sufferer, and his mother took him to spend the winter of 1898 in a Washington hotel, far from the harsh Buffalo climate. But his cough persisted after their return in June, to her alarm. He would be taken on many similar trips away from Buffalo and, later on, from St. Paul.

For several consecutive years he spent long spells in early spring in Maryland, with his grandmother Cecilia in Rockville or his aunt Elise in Randolph. In 1903 he was a page at the wedding of his cousin Cecilia in Rockville; when he returned there two years later, he learned with horror that the other boy who had carried the train of the bride's gown had just died. In July 1905 he spent some time with his aunt Clara in the Catskills. Concerned for his health, she made him swallow a raw egg every morning and then rewarded him with a quarter; every day he used the money to buy another of G. A. Henty's countless historical novels. At age nine he stopped believing in Santa Claus and noted in his diary his suspicion that he was not his parents' son, but a foundling of more exalted origins. That was also the period when he fell in love for the first time, with one of his partners at the Van Arnum dancing school, and he noted her name for posterity: Nancy Gardiner. A year later, in January 1907, he was overcome with admiration for the melancholy grace of a basketball player: "He fell madly into admiration for a dark-haired boy who played with a melancholy defiance."[20] The idea would be picked up, as was often the case with influential events—for example, his notion that he was not his parents' child —in the first version of *This Side of Paradise*, entitled *The Romantic Egotist:* "The Captain of the losing side was a dark, slender youth of perhaps fourteen, who played with a fierce but facile abandon. . . . Oh he was fine, really one of the finest things I ever saw. . . . After I saw him all athletes were dark and devilish and despairing and enthusiastic."[21]

Scott was already drawing the kind of man he would have wanted to be, the one he described briefly in a diary entry in March 1915: "Perfection: black hair, olive skin and tenor voice."[22] Boyish yet masculine grace, but marked, etched by defeat. It was then that his father began to lose prestige. After Scott's evocation of the romantic young athlete, we feel the pathos of a lapidary remark two paragraphs higher in his diary: "His father used to drink too much and then play baseball in the back yard."[23] We can imagine the incongruous spectacle of a drunken old man flailing with a baseball bat at balls pitched to him by a ten-year-old son with sharp and knowing eyes.

Scott had long since distanced himself from his mother by then. Her solicitude exasperated him. She acceded to his whims, while his father already dealt with him man to man, appealing to his pride and dignity. For example, when at age ten he was separated from his family, for the first time, at a boys' camp in Canada and treated rudely by the other boys, he felt desperately unhappy and told his parents how miserable he was. Mrs. Fitzgerald immediately offered to join him. His father sent him some reading matter and a dollar bill along with a few moral admonitions that, however outrageously parodic they may be, appealed to a child's sense of responsibility: "Spend it liberally, generously, carefully, judiciously, sensibly. Get from it pleasure, wisdom, health, experience."[24] Scott understood the lesson, thanked his father and tried as tactfully as he could to dissuade his mother from coming; he reversed the situation, forgetting his own troubles to implicitly present things from Molly's point of view, knowing her to be too concerned with her physical comfort not to regret her decision: "Though I would like very much to have you up here I don't think you would like it as you know no one here. . . . I don't think you would like the accommodation as it is only a small town and no good hotels. There are some very nice boarding houses but about the only fare is lamb and beef." By way of compensation, however, he extorted a dollar from her for pocket money: "Please send me a dollar because there are a lot of little odds and ends I need. I will spend it cautiously. All the other boys have pocket money besides their regular allowance."[25]

From the allusion to "the other boys" and the camp norm, we can guess Scott's real motives for writing his letter: to avoid being made to look ridiculous in the eyes of boys already hostile to him by appearing as a mama's boy. Scott, it must be said, was a little contemptuous of his mother's weakness; she encouraged his vanity, pushed him in among people wealthier than his family, always took his side against everyone else, especially against Aunt Annabel, who was firmer and who was scandalized by the deplorable training he was getting. And he was also a little ashamed of this eccentric chatterbox of a woman whose strange airs made her the laughingstock of the neighborhood: she went around with her hair awry, wearing an old hat with tired plumes; inevitably flanked by her umbrella, she thought nothing of going visiting in shoes that didn't match or weren't laced. He resented her living in a childish fantasy world and spending most of her time reading novels borrowed from the public library instead of attending to her household.

Conversely, he had great respect for Annabel, who did not spoil him. He saw in her "the real matriarch of my family, a dried-up old maid, but with character and culture."[26] He paid tribute to her and to his father's sister, Elise, in a letter to his cousin Ceci: "I was fond of Aunt Annabel and Aunt Elise, who gave me almost my first tastes of discipline, in a peculiar way in which I wasn't fond of my mother, who spoiled me. You were a great exception among mothers—managing by some magic of your own to preserve both your children's love and their respect. Too often one of the two things is sacrificed."[27]

Even after he became famous and independent, Fitzgerald would lack the courage to accept his mother as she was. When she visited him in France some years after the success of *The Great Gatsby*, he warned his friends about her, describing her as a kind of shrew; they were thoroughly surprised to meet a perfectly normal person. It wasn't until her death in 1936, when an accident prevented him from being at her bedside and when a bequest—McQuillan money again—had righted a desperate financial situation, that he paid tribute, in a letter to a friend, to the old woman's unselfishness: "By an irony. which quite fits into the picture, the legacy which I received from my mother's death (after being too ill to go to her death bed or her funeral) is the luckiest event of some time. She was a defiant old woman, defiant in her love for me in spite of my neglect of her, and it would have been quite within her character to have died that I might live."[28]

In his heart, however, Fitzgerald was never very close to his parents. The qualities he lent them were cited after their deaths, out of a kind of filial piety, perhaps of remorse at having so little known and loved them. During their lifetimes, once he had shed the illusions of childhood, he held them responsible for his botched education and, too, for the weaknesses—similar to theirs—he found in himself. In a moment of depression he would even write: "Why shouldn't I go crazy? My father is a moron and my mother a neurotic, half insane with pathological nervous worry. Between them, they haven't and never have had the brains of Calvin Coolidge."[29]

2. THE DISQUIET TEENS

(1908–13)

In September 1908 he entered St. Paul Academy, a private high school he was to attend for three years. Still, it was not until the following year, when his first stories were published, that he really took part in the activities that fascinated him. It was also in 1909 that he made friends with a group of boys and girls he met at the dancing lessons his mother made him take at Ramaley Hall, for she knew that there he would consort with the children of the city's leading families. There he saw some of his friends' liveried chauffeurs arrive in limousines adorned with monograms and bogus crests. Gladys Van Schellinger was one of these familiar yet inaccessible people Fitzgerald would later present in one of his stories, "A Night at the Fair": "A tranquil, carefully nurtured girl who, so local tradition had it, was being brought up to marry in the East. She had a governess and always played with a certain few girls at her house or theirs, and was not allowed the casual freedom of children in a Midwestern city. She was never present at such rendezvous as the Whartons' yard, where the others played games in the afternoons."[1]

Twenty years later the writer would remember his first intrigues and adventures in that small circle. He recalled in that and the other stories devoted to his alter ego, Basil Duke Lee, the warm dusks filled with shouts and laughter, the childhood games, the anxieties and conflicts of adolescence. In these stories we find the sudden gusts of imagination, the doubts and ambitions of a boy teetering on the line between two stages of life: "Fifteen is of all ages the most difficult to locate—to put one's finger on and say, 'That's the way I was.' The melancholy Jacques does not select it for mention, and all one can know is that somewhere between thirteen, boyhood's majority, and seventeen, when one is a sort of counterfeit young man, there is a time when youth fluctuates hourly between one world and another—pushed ceaselessly forward into unprecedented experiences and vainly trying to struggle back to the days when nothing had to be paid for."[2]

Basil is unquestionably a portrait of the artist as a young man. A few thinly veiled biographical details confirm what the character's psychological makeup suggests: "Basil's father had been an unsuccessful young Kentuckian of good family and his mother, Alice Reilly, the daughter of a 'pioneer' wholesale grocer. As Tarkington says, American children belong to their mother's families, and Basil was 'Alice Reilly's son.' "[3]

Indeed, his friends and playmates immediately recognized themselves in the figures peopling Basil's little world.

The group prefigured the circles in which Fitzgerald would travel later, and his reactions to the Summit Avenue microcosm were more or less typical of those he would feel throughout his life. He was then a thirteen-year-old who had been raised by women, subjected to contradictory influences through which he had learned to thread his way. Notable among these were the incomprehensible demands of his grandmother and his aunt Annabel, pious old women on whom his material satisfactions depended, and the tantrum-shot indulgence with which his mother encouraged his weaknesses. In the background was the faded image of a father whose son was his only consolation and his sole ambition, who took the boy's part against the prevailing matriarchal forces and jealously supervised the smallest details of his grooming and public behavior. But his concept of educating a son was limited to this fashionable gentility; when his responsibilities became too burdensome for him, Edward Fitzgerald took refuge in alcohol.

So when Scott ventured outside this warm family enclave into the larger republic of the children of Summit Avenue, he was painfully surprised to learn that there were other people in the world, an outer world ruled by immutable laws against which he savaged his egotism. Gradually he learned the workings of the rigid, ineluctable machinery of others' psychological reactions to him. Repeatedly he confirmed the continuity of causes and effects, passed through the same stages with the same dismayed and impotent indignation; he had an intolerable desire to impress others, to be the center of attention, to win in an indifferent world (its very indifference made it desirable) the privileged position—now emptied of prestige—he held in his family. Sometimes this imperious desire connected with reality, bringing triumph—whether in schoolwork, sports or romance was unimportant—and the admiration of a nucleus of faithful friends. But Basil/Fitzgerald's smugness and condescension soon made him insupportable; then came the wounded pride, the offended looks, desertion, conspiracy, persecution, rending loneliness, true humility, the intolerable yearning to be recognized as the best of them all—the infernal cycle renewed. And, like Mademoiselle de Scudéry's trembling lovers, Scott would set out again along the familiar route across a landscape not of Tenderness but of Vanity toward his unhappy love affairs with the world.

The Basil Duke Lee stories, revealing as they are of the adolescent Scott, were obviously conceived by a man who had surveyed himself and who had known discouragement and success, the extremes of adulation and abandonment. They partly express the Fitzgerald of 1928–29 who, after the success of *The Great Gatsby* and its promises of glory and fortune, saw the situation as it really was: idle, sterile, dissipated. His mind plunged back into a past of simpler problems and unequivocal promises, seeking in the boy he had been potentialities, truths that he had since lost. His attitude was a bit like Gatsby's, who wanted to reverse the past, to set apart and annihilate five "wasted" years, reweld the present to a past rich with possibilities and begin life over again, starting from a magical point from which circumstances had forced him to deviate.

We understand with what interest, what detached and yet passionate curiosity Fitzgerald, like a biologist examining a culture medium, inspected the closed world of a bittersweet adolescence; this was a miniature theater in which eagerness to succeed was transposed and purified in a drama without disasters or lasting penalties, as poignant and unreal as a Marivaux fantasy.

Like Gatsby thinking of the crucial moment when he saw in the frail figure he held in his arms all his dreams of grandeur and beauty, Fitzgerald tried to understand the failure of his own dreams by analyzing the role girls played in Basil's formation. Here there is nothing of that sensual awakening, that churning sexual instinct that sent Joyce's Stephen Dedalus through the hot streets of Dublin. Other imperatives dictated Basil's relations with the opposite sex, even with girls he picked up at a fun fair. A girl's heart and lips were mere symbols for him: more than rewards, they were the tangible signs of a victory over his rivals, even, sometimes, over himself. Will, not the senses, was the motor. Fitzgerald's young heroes had to try to seduce out of duty to themselves. We recall Amory's existential repugnance after he had assigned himself the chore of kissing Myra St. Claire in *This Side of Paradise:* "Sudden revulsion seized Amory, disgust, loathing for the whole incident. He desired frantically to be away, never to see Myra again, never to kiss anyone; he became conscious of his face and hers, of their clinging hands, and he wanted to creep out of his body and hide somewhere safe out of sight, up in the corner of his mind."[4]

From this particular notion of love's adventure stemmed the requirement that amatory conquest be as difficult as possible. Only a girl in whom were joined the superlatives of beauty and social position—or, failing these, the prestige conferred by having a number of suitors—was worth the attention of this buccaneer as chaste as he was Machiavellian. We find these concerns expressed in regard to a first skirmish that had occurred two years earlier, while he was still in Syracuse. The *Thoughtbook of Francis Scott Key Fitzgerald of Saint Paul, Minn., U.S.A.* includes a section entitled "My Girls," which begins with a victory communiqué. Passing rapidly over his first infatuation with Nancy Gardiner ("I was about nine years old, Nancy about eight, and we were quite infatuated with each other"), the diarist soon reaches the important matter, the first conquest worth the name: "Kitty William is much plainer to my memory: I met her first at dancing school and as Mr. Van Arnam [*sic*] (our dancing teacher) chose me to lead the march I asked her to be my pardner [*sic*]. The next day she told Marie Louty and Marie repeated it to Dorothy Knox who in turn passed it on to Earl, that I was third in her affections. . . . I then and there resolved that I should gain first place." The moment of triumph remained sharply etched on his mind: "it was there that my eventful day was. We played postoffice, pillow, clap-in-and-clap-out and other foolish but interesting games. It was impossible to count the number of times I kissed Kitty that afternoon. At any rate when we went home I had secured the coveted first place."[5]

The true American Eve, who refuses to be prey, who turns huntress and defeats men on their own ground, appears in the guise of a Southern girl, Violet Stockton of Atlanta, who spent a summer vacation in St. Paul. She occupies the major part of the *Thoughtbook* and figures in the Basil cycle under the name of Erminie Gilbert Labouisse Bibble of New Orleans; Erminie is the heroine of "He Thinks He's Wonderful," "Forging Ahead" and, especially, "Basil and Cleopatra." In the last-mentioned story the girl's attitude was probably partly inspired by another model, Ginevra King, whom we will soon meet and who was to inspire both the Josephine cycle and the character of Isabelle in *This Side of Paradise*.

How instinctively Fitzgerald understood her heart and motives, how keenly he perceived her game and how cautiously he handled her! For Narcissus sees himself in her, his inaccessible feminine image. She fascinates him as Amory is fascinated by his mirror. In drag, this blond, slender, graceful boy with the long lashes could easily pass for a girl, could understand women with an intuition generally reserved to other women. He was more comfortable with them than with boys his own age; his true rivalries were with girls rather than with those who sought to steal their hearts away from him. The meeting of Isabelle and Amory is a masterpiece of its kind. In the calm ceremoniousness that precedes ritual combat, they observe and gauge each other, estimating their mutual chances like adversaries soon to do battle: "Isabelle had walked with an artificial gait at nine and a half, and when her eyes, wide and starry, proclaimed the ingenue most. Amory was proportionately less deceived. He waited for the mask to drop off, but at the same time he did not question her right to wear it. She, on her part, was not impressed by his studied air of blasé sophistication. . . . But she accepted his pose—it was one of the dozen little conventions of this kind of affair. So they proceeded with an infinite guile that would have horrified her parents."[6]

This was not mere fooling; "amateur standing had very little value in the game they were playing. . . ."[7] The game was a challenge to reputations. Amory breaks with Isabelle when he realizes that she has gained the upper hand: "It wasn't dignified to come off second best, *pleading*, with a doughty warrior like Isabelle."[8]

In Fitzgerald's passionate interest in women, in the affinities of taste and temperament that drew him to them, we discern a curious detour around the tumultuous battle of the sexes to reach a kind of fulfilled peace, a comradeship in love, a reconciliation with the world that might restore the confident warmth and security of his family nest. But until he met Zelda Sayre, he would seek in vain the true sister soul, the ally he needed. He would emerge from most of his escapades hurt, dissatisfied with himself and others. Luckily, he had other means by which to assert himself in the lover's quarrel he waged with the world.

He was particularly anxious to shine in sports. His reading had taught him how popular a good player is at college. He knew the vogue professional athletes enjoyed. Although he had little appetite for rough games—he preferred reading and dreaming—here again he forced himself to violate his instincts. During his second year at the St. Paul Academy he played basketball and football. But he was too short to succeed in the first and too light for the second. His yen to stand out, plus his repugnance at facing opponents more violent and brutal than he, weakened the team. Still, he did derive some prestige from a broken rib suffered in a game. In May 1911, against all logic, he was named captain of the academy's basketball team.

He did better on terrain better suited to his talents and imagination and his penchant for fine phrasing. The first of his stories to appear in print, "The Mystery of the Raymond Mortgage," ran in the school magazine, *Now and Then*, in October 1909; the tale reflects his taste for the mystery stories he devoured then. Three more stories would appear in the magazine. "Reade, Substitute Right Half" is one of those familiar daydreams in which Scott soothed his wounded pride by casting himself as the hero: during a game in which the school's honor is gravely imperiled, a young second-string player, called in when all seems lost, covers himself with glory by bringing home a victory. "A Debt of Honor" again relates a brilliant exploit, this time in a sacred setting in Scott's reveries, the Civil War: a soldier who disgraces himself by falling asleep at his post regains his honor by dying gloriously at Chancellorsville. We have already mentioned "The Room with the Green Blinds"; in it Scott imagines the flight of John Wilkes Booth after he assassinated Lincoln and his life in hiding until he is found and killed. An entry in the author's diary for 1911 notes that he was becoming "an inveterate author and a successful, not to say brilliant, debater and writer."[9]

Winters went by in sleighing parties, bobsledding, skiing. In summertime he was sometimes invited to stay with friends whose parents owned homes on the cool shores of White Bear Lake. He learned to ride and won a first prize dancing the cakewalk with his girl friend of the moment, Marie Hersey. The rest of the year, weather permitting, his crowd gathered in the big, shady gardens that stretched before their houses. Boys and girls played in tree houses, vied at gymnastics, chased each other across the lawns or bicycled along the paths, flirting and falling in love. In bad weather the boys met in each other's homes, but preferably in the attic of Cecil Reed, the Ripley Buckner of Fitzgerald's fiction. It was an ideal place for organizing secret societies; lists were drawn up of real or imaginary people's weaknesses and transgressions and plots laid to dispose of them. The unsuccessful kidnapping of Hubert Blair in "The Scandal Detectives" is based on a real event noted in Scott's diary in April 1911: the victim was his rival Reuben Warner, guilty of having stolen Marie Hersey from him. Usually, however, the attic was a perfect setting in which to relive the action in the stories the boys read. There they could safely impersonate heroes of fiction and of history, cross swords with the three musketeers or play at being men of the world with Arsène Lupin.

Scott's reading, vastly more voluminous and varied than his friends', his always lively imagination and his love of history made him the natural and resourceful leader at these gatherings. Since childhood he had delighted in slipping into the skins of heroic and glorious characters. His *Ledger* reports how, at the age of seven, he came home from a play about the Revolutionary War, wrapped himself in a red scarf and, alone, acted his hero of the moment, Paul Revere. At the home of a friend, Tubby Washington, he was excited by a miniature theater peopled with cardboard cutouts; while Tubby moved the actors around the tiny stage, Scott improvised a scenario.

The stage was his passion; he never missed any of the Saturday vaudeville shows and operettas at the local theater, the Orpheum. But he was not satisfied with the passive role of spectator; he mimed whole scenes for his friends and family, reciting the most dramatic speeches from memory. When, in the summer of 1911, he was given a part in an amateur production mounted at his school by a spinster named Elizabeth Magoffin, he saw in it a way to show off his talent for imitation and invention. He set to work at once and turned out a one-act melodrama called *The Girl from the Lazy J*, which was put on with himself as author, leading man (Jack Darcy of Frisco), director and producer. The company, in honor of its founder, took the name of the Elizabethan Dramatic Club. Every summer for four years, Fitzgerald would write and act in a play for the company, with growing success. Later he would apply his skills at playwriting to the operettas produced by the Triangle Club at Princeton. The stage gave him his first public triumphs and wakened him to the hold his talent gave him on the outside world. In this small, sheltered world of limitless potential where each day brought a new discovery, he lived the happiest years of his youth. It is moving to read in the entry in his *Ledger*, at the foot of page 164, devoted to his fourteenth year, a note added by the writer in 1940, the year of his death: "would begin thirty years ago (1940)."

In that same summer of 1911, Scott was preparing to go East; his parents, disappointed in his grades at the academy, had enrolled him in the Newman

School, a Catholic institution where, they hoped, being a boarder would force him to study harder. They thought of it a little as a disciplinary measure; he saw it as a highly promising promotion. He felt he was no longer a child; he demanded long pants, began smoking in secret. With Tubby Washington he began trying to pick up the docile young girls at the fun fairs. If we believe the version he gives of the expedition in "A Night at the Fair," self-affirmation was his only reason for letting himself be dragged into these escapades; the kiss Basil implants on the cheek of the homely little girl with him on the Ferris wheel gives him no more pleasure than the one Amory steals from Myra St. Claire.

So it was with no regret that he left St. Paul Academy. He had begun to find the ultraprovincial Summit Avenue circle too small for him. His imagination was no longer satisfied with forays into the cosmopolitan settings of his favorite novels; it sought new theaters in which to operate.

To Scott the Newman School, a prep school located less than an hour from New York, represented the fabulous East of his reading and his dreams, the splendor of the great metropolis, proximity to Broadway's dazzling theaters. Newman was also the kind of small community of males, far removed from women's supervision, that Scott had imagined in reading the classics of college life in those days: *Tom Brown's School Days*, of course, as well as the more specifically American books by H. R. Barbour, C. M. Flandrau, W. J. Lynch. He longed to be there, to star there, to become the hero, like Reade, who saves the school's honor during a dramatic game. Here again, Basil's feelings tell us what Scott felt as the time neared to leave his parents: "Basil . . . had lived with such intensity on so many stories of boarding-school life that, far from being homesick, he had a glad feeling a recognition and familiarity."[10]

He was, therefore, unprepared for the reality he found. Newman School was small; a kind of good-natured anarchy reigned there, an unbridled whimsicality that upended all the new boy's preconceived notions. He brought to it a starchy self-importance and seriousness of mind that soon irritated his schoolmates. So he prepared himself to become the Tom Brown of Newman. Within weeks he was ostracized by everyone. He tried to command attention with an insolent ingenuousness that quickly made him detested by the other new boys as well as their seniors. His lack of courage at football was the last straw, damning him in minds already exasperated by his boasting. His dream became a nightmare; his first term at school seemed a never-ending calvary. Two pages in *This Side of Paradise* evoke his beginnings at boarding school. Only a few lines are needed to set the tone: "He went all wrong at the start, was generally considered both conceited and arrogant, and universally detested. . . . He was unbearably lonely, desperately unhappy. . . . Miserable, confined to bounds, unpopular with both faculty and students—that was Amory's first term."[11]

More than fifteen years later, when writing "The Freshest Boy," he would still remember his unhappiness at Newman. For one thing he was made piercingly aware that the world judged him by his actions, not his intentions, that plans are useless without the will to convert them into action. But he also perceived that public failures can be turned into private victories through art. One incident among others showed him the unsuspected power of poetry. He had been accused, wrongly this time, of cowardice on the football field. Bitterly, he wrote a thirty-six-stanza poem in the Kipling manner that more or less duplicated the theme of "Reade, Substitute Right Half," a breathless celebration of a lone hero who wins for his side. The poem, entitled *Football*, was published in the school magazine, the *Newman News*. A sample stanza:

> *Look, he's clear. Oh, gee! don't stumble.*
> *Faster, faster, for the school.*
> *There's the goal, now, right before you,*
> *Ten yards, five yards, bless your name!*
> *Oh, you Newman, 1911,*
> *You know how to play the game.*[12]

The incident, he would write, "inspired me to write a poem for the school paper which made me as big a hit with my father as if I had become a football hero. So when I went home that Christmas vacation it was in my mind that if you weren't able to function in action, you might at least be able to tell about it, because you felt the same intensity. It was a back-door way out of facing reality."[13]

Scott's second term was hard-going. He was often kept after class because his grades were still poor, but he had learned humility and the value of steady effort. He no longer thought he had only to appear on the scene to win people's admiration and affection. He squelched his imagination and accepted the stern realities that govern the outside world.

His only radiant memories of that melancholy year were of all-too-rare excursions to the theater when his schoolwork won him an evening's leave. He discovered the magic of nighttime New York and the enchantment of Broadway musicals. He admired the stars of that sequined world: George M. Cohan in *The Little Millionaire*, Ina Claire in *The Quaker Girl* and Gertrude Bryan in *Little Boy Blue*. He fell in love with both actresses, who merged in his mind into an ethereal image of femininity. And he couldn't wait to be admired, famous, worthy of such splendid creatures. Riding the train back to St. Paul, he wrote an act directly inspired by a whodunit, *Alias Jimmy Valentine*, that he had just seen played. Two months later his play *The Captured Shadow* was put on by the Elizabethan Dramatic Club before a packed and appreciative house. Scott recovered his faith in his destiny, received a photo of Elizabeth Magoffin with a flattering dedication and proudly presented the sum of sixty dollars to the charity on whose behalf the performance was given.

After a consoling Easter vacation with his cousin Cecilia in Norfolk, he finished the school year less ignominiously. His grades were better, he shone in ancient history, to his teacher's surprise, and was the big winner in a track-and-field meet. Meanwhile, he made friends with Charles Donahoe, one of the leading boys at the school, whose erudition had won him the nickname Sap (for Homo sapiens). Sap was from Seattle and, though small, was a football hero at Newman. He and Scott got to know each other better on their long transcontinental trips homeward from New York. Sap's friendliness toward Fitzgerald constituted a general pardon. Scott's errors forgotten, he was accepted by the little community. His second year at Newman went better, but it by no means fulfilled all his hopes. Only by sheer force of will did he overcome the handicap of the previous year.

Still, he did manage to stand out in several sports events, even occasionally replacing the captain of the football team. At the end of the year he again won at track and field. In March he gave a convincing performance as a magnanimous king in a short play written by one of the teachers. And three of his stories were published in the *Newman News:* "A Luckless Santa Claus," telling of the misadventures of a man whose wish to help others brings him nothing but trouble; "Pain and the Scientist," an ironic criticism of Christian Science; and "The Trail of the Duke," on a theme—a millionaire's life—borrowed from such favorite authors as Robert William Chambers, E. Phillips Oppenheim and David Graham Phillips. For Scott read voraciously, but had no patience for what bored him. He still spent little time with the poets. His father had enchanted his childhood by reading aloud the best-known bits by Poe and Byron, but, except for the *Allegro*, which charmed him, only Tennyson's suave cadences and Kipling's stoic couplets held his attention. Among the novelists, aside from the three mentioned above, he was particularly fond of Booth Tarkington, who was to become his favorite at Princeton, and especially of his book *The Gentleman from Indiana*, a satire on Middle Western political customs. Scott kept Owen Johnson's famous *Stover at Yale* at his bedside; from it he learned the science of succeeding as a student that, he thought, would help him avoid at Princeton the mistakes he made at Newman.

At the start of his second school year he met his spiritual guide, the man whose influence over him would be the deepest during the succeeding seven years: Father Sigourney Webster Fay. The attraction was mutual and instantaneous: "He and Amory took to each other at first sight—the jovial, impressive prelate who could dazzle an embassy ball, and the green-eyed, intent youth, in his first long trousers, accepted in their own minds a relation of father and son within a half-hour's conversation."[14]

Sigourney Fay, just turned thirty-seven, was a member of the Newman board and soon to become the school's director. A recent convert to Roman

Catholicism, ordained a priest two years earlier, he had a neophyte's zeal, but his was an intelligent zeal that presented religion not as an arduous road to eternity but as an end in itself, a way of living to the fullest as an individual here on earth. Fay's religion could inspire the most tumultuous feelings as it could the most exalting meditation. Stout, jovial, of a contagious gaiety, his ruddy face haloed with very pale blond hair, he might at first have been taken for Pickwick in a cassock. But behind this heart of gold and child's soul was a man of the world, a polished esthete, friend of Cardinal Gibbons and of Henry Adams, with entrée in Washington through such men as British Ambassador Spring Rice, whose confidant he was. Fay was always about to leave on some special mission, on "trips to all parts of the Roman Catholic world, rather like an exiled Stuart king awaiting to be called to the rule of his land."[15] In 1918 Pope Benedict XV made him a prelate. "Do you know that the holy Father has made me a Prelate, so that I am the Right Reverend Mgr. now," he wrote in an amusing letter to Fitzgerald, "and my clothes are too gorgeous for words. I look like a Turner sunset when I am in full regalia."[16] (Fitzgerald would use the comparison almost verbatim in *This Side of Paradise*.) He was all charm, spontaneity, curiosity; he could listen to anything, understand anything, was sure enough of his own faith to speak of it with wit and detachment. Romantic and enthusiastic, he struck a responsive chord in young Fitzgerald, whom he soon made one of his favorites. Fay later appeared under the name Monsignor Darcy in *This Side of Paradise:* "Children adored him because he was like a child; youth reveled in his company because he was still a youth, and couldn't be shocked. In the proper land and century he might have been a Richelieu—at present he was a very moral, very religious (if not particularly pious) clergyman, making a great mystery about pulling rusty wires, and appreciating life to the fullest, if not entirely enjoying it."[17]

Scott was delighted by so much warmth and understanding. For the first time an adult outside the family circle listened to him attentively and took him seriously. In his visits to Fay's house he discovered a world of refinement that eclipsed anything his reading might have led him to imagine. He was judged worthy of introduction to the Catholic aristocracy: Margaret Winthrop Chanler received him with his mentor in her magnificent Hudson River mansion. Better yet, he was made to feel he was accepted by this prestigious elite, recognized as a peer, a young Shelley whose future was assured. The feelings of inferiority he nourished concerning his Irish ancestry and his religion were senseless given the respect bestowed in such circles on the Roman Church and the Celtic mind.

The indisputable authority Fay enjoyed in Scott's eyes led the boy to reevaluate the Catholicism that had been identified in his imagination with the narrow bigotry of the black-clad women of St. Paul. His feelings about his Irish blood also changed: Fay, whose mother was of Irish ancestry, and his friend Shane Leslie, a young writer, son of an Irish baronet and newly come down from King's College, Cambridge, insistently proclaimed the superiority of Irish Catholicism over Anglo-Saxon Protestantism.

Five years later, in a review of Leslie's novel *The Oppidan*, Fitzgerald recognized how strong the two men's influence had been: they "made of that Church a dazzling, golden thing, dispelling its oppressive mugginess and giving the succession of days upon gray days, passing under its plaintive ritual, the romantic glamour of an adolescent dream."[18] Leslie would confirm this in an article that appeared in 1958: "To him Catholicism meant all that was middle class, dull, unpoetical and fettering in the Middle West. It was with a shock that he realized how romantic and exciting Catholicism could seem to a convert. . . . We encouraged him to believe that he could write the unwritten great Catholic novel—the John Inglesant—of the United States."[19]

When Fitzgerald doubted himself most, then, when his child's dreams broke against fact and the adolescent sought desperately for a new way, Fay opened wide to him the doors to a glittering world. The priest brought him comfort and hope, restored his confidence in his destiny, transposed his naive ambitions to a higher plane and gave him the feeling of belonging to an elite group that expected much of him. Finally, and most important, Fay vivified Scott's wobbling faith, setting it on new foundations, blending it with his philosophic anxieties and his poetic effusions. Even when, in his last years at Princeton, after Fay's death, Fitzgerald strayed from the Church, the flexibility and breadth of his spiritual father's religious concepts enabled him to hang on to what was essential in Fay's message while giving himself over to a fashionable literary paganism. For the rest of his life he would preserve a latent religiosity, would always feel a need to transmute the phenomena of the material world to a higher plane. His way would be a sort of confused Neoplatonism; behind the century's chaotic semblance he would try to find not so much a moral as a luminous oneness, the glittering, lost paradise that haunts the fabric of his great works like a memory.

The dissociation of the sacred and the profane, of spirit and body, seems to have been revealed to Scott at a tender age when, to a boy with a strict Catholic upbringing, it was self-evident that the wonders of the universe could only be of divine origin. The experience we are going to examine seems not to have left any visible trace in his conscious mind. Only through the recurrence in his work of the theme of light can we measure the reverberations of a childhood episode mentioned in a line in his *Ledger* for August 1901: "He attended the Buffalo Exposition, the Pan-American."[20]

Two other details, noted down the same year, can help us understand the effect of contrast produced on his childish imagination by the exposition's marvels. One is the birth in January of his sister Annabel: "His first certain memory is the sight of her howling on a bed."[21] The other is the discovery that certain parts of his body—specifically, his feet—caused him a sort of shame and repulsion. Writing of a visit to Atlantic City, he told of how he avoided showing his bare feet by refusing to go into the water: "Some Freudian complex refused to let him display his *feet*, so he refused to swim, concealing the real reason. They thought he feared the water. In reality he craved it."[22]

Here was a coddled child going on five, the center of his parents' world, who in the space of a few months made two traumatizing discoveries, the second probably precipitated by the first: to start with, that he was no longer the *only* child, the one whose whims were law, and that he would have to share his parents' affection with the howling object named Annabel; next, that he was not pure spirit, that he also had a body the feet of which sum up the situation's full horror. We recall that it was Amory's glance at the apparition's feet in *This Side of Paradise* that told him he had to do with a demon.

His visit to the Pan-American Exposition in Buffalo probably helped unveil an extraordinary world to him in which human weakness was reduced to its proper proportion. No event, however tragic, could have dimmed the brilliance of that fair. In fact, its inauguration was marked by the assassination of President William McKinley, which could only have fixed the memory in the child's mind, even if that memory seems not to have recurred to the adult who in 1922 transcribed the jottings from his *Ledger*.

The exposition—"The Rainbow City"—occupied a square mile in south Buffalo. In a city still a decade away from providing electric light for its inhabitants (the Fitzgeralds had used oil lamps in their two years in a lower-middle-class neighborhood there), visitors to the exposition were dazzled by a glitter of lights like a vision from *The Thousand and One Nights*, dominated by a Goddess of Light whose glow could be seen as far away as Niagara Falls. It was all wheeling searchlights and phosphorescent spouts, cascades of fire, gardens haloed by clusters of colored lights, and fountains glimmering in the summer nights.

Exposition brochures, preserved in the Buffalo Historical Museum, were lavish in their descriptions of visitors' wonder at this riot of light. Could Scott Fitzgerald, who summoned equally enchanting visions in "The Diamond as Big as the Ritz" and so many other stories, have been indifferent to the magical glare in Buffalo?

Especially in "Absolution": Father Schwartz's mystical vision of a brilliant light that captivates the joyous crowds, a light he compares with that of an amusement park sparkling in the night, was obviously inspired by the Buffalo exposition.

Another event, this one much more personal and domestic, was soon to establish a symbolic bond between two hitherto distinct happenings we have mentioned in connection with the exposition: McKinley's murder and the appearance of the Goddess of Light. The event itself seems trivial but, as much as his father's tragic dismissal from his job, was to leave a lasting trace in young Scott's imagination. This was the round spanking he received from his father just before the fireworks display one July Fourth evening. "I ran away when I was seven on the Fourth of July. I spent the day with a friend in a pear orchard and the police were informed that I was missing and on my return my father thrashed me according to the customs of the nineties—on the bottom—and then let me come out and watch the night fireworks from the balcony with my pants still down and my behind smarting and knowing in my heart that he was absolutely right. Afterwards, seeing in his face his regret that it had to happen, I asked him to tell me a story."[23] This close connivance, this mutual compassion, is the product of a harsh but necessary action, one that establishes recognized and accepted limits. It was thus that Roman farmers stamped indelible traces of their hereditary limits on their children's memories.

The relationship of corporal punishment and a fairy vision echoed in Scott's mind two years later in the twinning of the President's assassination and the boy's discovery of a world of splendor. This pairing of the ineffable and the disastrous certainly has something to do with the sensitivity Fitzgerald would show in his work to the beauty of lights in the darkness. It was a moral as well as an aesthetic sensitivity; the appearance of lights is often linked to a feeling of anxiety, a premonition of disaster.

In "Absolution" the festival of lights follows the stern punishment little Rudolph receives from his father and is immediately followed by the death of another, spiritual father, the priest. The festival's brilliance is associated with the boy's rejection—in a sense the murder—of his father and remains a symbol of his resultant guilt. This Oedipal metaphor, this key to Fitzgerald's imaginative process of generalizing from particulars, may explain to us why Fitzgerald's role was so important in forming the sensibility of his time. It may signify the general refusal of daily constraints, the sense of radical liberation from the grip of the past that Americans manifested in the twenties. Fitzgerald identified himself with this rejection of tradition, gave it a voice, a style. He became his generation's spokesman, he raced passionately toward the mirage of festival lights; at the same time he felt remorse at having transgressed his limits, having violated quasi-divine laws—an orphan awaiting his punishment and accepting it.

Newly emerged from a harsh period in his life, a particularly vulnerable Fitzgerald, thanks to Sigourney Fay, acquired the balance and self-confidence he had lost as a small child. He found a second family, the elective one he had dreamed of when he denied his own parents. He thought of himself as a foundling, mysteriously designated as a descendant of the Stuarts, and he would compare Fay to "an exiled Stuart king awaiting to be called to the rule of the land."[24] In Fay he found his mother's attentive solicitude without her importunity, and his father's advice and behavior, but with vastly more breadth and imagination. With Fay, morality became an adventure, and religion, poetry, the joy of writing became the most honorable of ambitions. For the first time the profane blended with the sacred, the will to win with the assurance of fulfilling a mission. These were precarious moments of faith and certitude that would recur only fleetingly, while he was writing *The Great Gatsby*. But by the time he left Newman School, he had undergone a change that henceforth made him a stranger to St. Paul provincialism and the narrowness of family life. He was ready to confront his first great adventure: the conquest of Princeton.

3. PRINCETON

(1913–15)

By the time he was ready to enter university in 1913, then, Fitzgerald had weathered the crisis that had almost ended his studies in the East. His grandmother had just died and left a large estate ($125,000), which gave the Fitzgeralds long-term financial security. Now he could attend any university he chose; he no longer had to go to the University of Minnesota, which would have been cheaper but utterly without prestige. And he could turn down Aunt Annabel's offer to pay for his studies if he would enroll in the Catholic Georgetown University where his father had been a student. He gave several reasons for his choice of Princeton, the most decisive apparently being that his talents would find an ideal outlet in the Triangle Club's theatricals: "Near the end of my last year at school I came across a new musical-comedy score lying on top of the piano. It was a show called *His Honor the Sultan*, and the title furnished the information that it had been presented by the Triangle Club of Princeton University. That was enough for me. From then on, the university question was settled. I was bound for Princeton."[1]

We will see later that his old dream of becoming a football hero also entered into his decision. He was much impressed by the annual Princeton-Harvard game he watched in November 1911, in which Princeton's fullback Sam White sent him wild with a heroic eighty-five-yard run to score the winning touchdown. His preference for the Princeton eleven is analyzed in *The Romantic Egotist* in a way that recalls the melancholy grace of the basketball captain he once noted: "I think what started my Princeton sympathy was that they always just lost the football championship. . . . I imagine the Princeton man as slender and keen and romantic, and the Yale man as brawny and brutal and powerful."[2] Sports and theatricals were the areas in which he wanted to shine at St. Paul and Newman, and it was through them that he would try to stand out at Princeton.

But he still had to pass the entrance exams, and he was a long way from ready for them. He would later admit that he cheated and that he had never forgiven himself. Even so, he failed the written test. He made up for it in an oral exam that allowed him to plead his cause eloquently, and the jury, perhaps more impressed with his possibilities than with his knowledge, gave him the benefit of the doubt. That day was his seventeenth birthday. He immediately telegraphed his mother, asking her to send on his football gear.

The various portraits he drew of Amory coincide with what the photos pasted in his album tell us of his physical appearance around 1913: a boy with blond hair, long lashes and finely chiseled features, slightly shorter than the average American, dressed with studied elegance. He noted several times that he had a lot of charm and that he was not unaware of it. His state of mind was more complex than those fairly conventional photos might suggest, and he showed a self-knowledge that was unusual in a boy of his age. Scott's Catholic education probably fostered his characteristic introspection. He overlooked none of his weaknesses. Having learned the lessons to be drawn from his mistakes at Newman and St. Paul, he could now judge himself with some objectivity. Here is the balance sheet he drew up about himself in *The Romantic Egotist* in a passage that would later be condensed and carried over, with the detachment that the third-person singular confers, to *This Side of Paradise*. First, the good points: "I considered that I was a fortunate youth capable of expansion to any extent for good or evil. I based this, not on latent strength, but upon facility and superior mentality." Physically: "I marked myself handsome; of great athletic possibilities, and an extremely good dancer." Intellectually: "Here I had a free hand, I was vain of having so much, of being so talented, ingenious* and quick to learn."

He clear-mindedly contrasted his social graces with the gaps in his morality: "I was convinced that I had personality, charm, magnetism, poise and ability to dominate others. Also I was sure that I exercised a subtle fascination over women." To balance this, "I had several things on the other side. *First:* morally I thought I was rather worse than most boys, due to latent unscrupulousness and the desire to influence people in some way, even for evil. . . . I had a curious cross-section of weakness running through my character. I was liable to be swept off my poise into a timid stupidity. . . . I knew I was completely the slave of my own moods, and often dropped into a surly sensitiveness most unprepossessing to others. . . . I knew that at bottom I lacked the essential."

In conclusion: "There seemed to have been a conspiracy to spoil me and all my inordinate vanity was absorbed from that. At the last crisis, I knew that I had no real courage, perseverance or self-respect. . . . If I may push it farther still, I should say that, underneath the whole thing lay a sense of infinite possibilities that was always with me whether vanity or shame was my mood."[3]

The only remark that does not figure in the novel's first version is one

---

* "Ingenuous" in the original, which is obviously inappropriate here. Such confusion was typical of a young Fitzgerald more concerned with the sound of a word than its meaning. (A.L.V.)

about sex, an unknown quantity in the equation, "a puzzled, furtive interest in everything concerning sex."⁴ This was the moral baggage with which he had passed through the storms at Newman and which he now readied to confront college life.

When he entered Princeton, the university, although considered one of the "big three" of American higher education after its elders, Harvard and Yale, had only 1,500 students. But it was in the process of growing and changing. For a generation new buildings had been sprouting everywhere. Fitzgerald's Princeton witnessed the final years of what Dean Christian Gauss would call "the Indian summer of the 'College Customs' era in our campus life."⁵

Although founded nearly two centuries earlier, Princeton on the eve of World War I was an almost new university. Except for half a dozen buildings, the campus, with its great trees and ivy-shrouded Gothic towers celebrated in *This Side of Paradise,* was no more than a quarter of a century old.

It is interesting to watch Fitzgerald's imagination at work, bestirring itself to ripen, improve, detach itself in a temporal mist from a too obviously contemporary group of buildings. His desire to re-create a palace worthy of his dreams, to cover Princeton with a venerable and romantic patina, is easily detected simply by checking the construction dates of the halls whose mystery and antiquity he extolls in a descriptive page in his novel. In the following passage the dates are given in brackets: ". . . he wanted to ramble through the shadowy scented lanes, where Witherspoon [1877] brooded like a dark mother over Whig [1893] and Clio [1893], her Attic children, where the black Gothic snake of Little [1899] curled down to Cuyler [1912] and Patton [1906], these in turn flinging the mystery out over the placid slope rolling to the lake.

"Princeton of the daytime filtered into his consciousness—West [1836] and Reunion [1870], redolent of the sixties, Seventy-nine Hall [1899], brick-red and arrogant, Upper and Lower Pyne [1897], aristocratic Elizabethan ladies not quite content to live among shopkeepers, and, topping all, climbing with clean blue aspiration, the great dreaming spires of Holder [1910] and Cleveland [1913] towers."⁶

We see that of the twelve buildings cited, only one, West, dates from before the Civil War; one of the two towers whose spires symbolize the poetry of his campus had been standing for three years at the time of Amory/Fitzgerald's song to them, the other only a few months. In 1927, ten years after he left Princeton, Fitzgerald saw it with the same eye:

"Two tall spires and then suddenly all around you spreads out the loveliest riot of Gothic architecture in America, battlement linked to battlement, hall to hall, arch-broken, vine-covered, luxuriant and lovely over two square miles of green grass. Here is no monotony, no feeling that it was all built yesterday at the whim of last week's millionaire; Nassau Hall was already thirty years old when Hessian bullets pierced its sides."[7]

Despite the allusion to the Hessian mercenaries who fought against Washington, it is clear that Fitzgerald always saw Princeton through a lover's eyes. Here the university is approached from the south, seen from a train window, and it was on the southern side of the campus that the most recent buildings stood. Nassau Hall—cited at the end of the paragraph as though to authenticate the whole setting—is located on a rise that slopes gently toward Nassau Street, the main thoroughfare bordering the campus on the north, and cannot be seen from the train or the station. Besides, whatever Fitzgerald may have thought, most of the buildings owe their existence to the generosity of millionaires whose influence was strongly felt in the university's development.

It is to be noted that Fitzgerald was more receptive to turn-of-the-century neo-Gothic architecture than he was to the severely ordered vestiges of the eighteenth century. It was neo-Gothic that provided the matter of his reverie, and this was extended by the reading of his favorite poets, especially Dowson and Swinburne. Princeton was bemisted in decadent fin-de-siècle poetry, in the mysterious colors of Pre-Raphaelite painting. Its forms were bathed in a religiosity that wholly conformed to the vision Sigourney Fay would have had of the world. And this medieval decor enabled Fitzgerald to identify himself completely with Compton Mackenzie's hero Michael Fane, whose sensual education at Oxford (in the third book, "Dreaming Spires," of *Sinister Street*) gave Scott a cultural model, a lifestyle, a series of poses he would have sought in vain in the American tradition. These stereotypes could only have been authenticated at a Princeton that resembled as closely as possible the Oxford described in Mackenzie's novel, published in 1913, Fitzgerald's freshman year. That he was aware of all this is certain; he saw Princeton as Amory saw it: "The world became pale and interesting, and he tried hard to look at Princeton through the satiated eyes of Oscar Wilde and Swinburne."[8]

We must not, however, neglect the historical factor, the true Princeton legend that combined with the Fitzgerald family's legendary past to confirm a teenaged Scott in his feeling of being different from the friends he had left in the West, of being made of nobler fiber. His arrival at Princeton was, in a way, a return to a lost motherland. The certainty of belonging to an elite, of being heir to a great tradition, the accent he placed on charm, courtesy and courage—all these were, in varying degrees, formative elements in his personality development. He would find illustrations at Princeton for, especially, his concept of a "gentleman," in examples from the past as well as in present reality. Despite his slightly theatrical preference for neo-Gothic architecture, the real spirit of the place lived for him in its vestiges and memories of the Revolutionary period. He skipped over the inter-

vening generations to find men after his own heart, contemporaries of his illustrious Maryland ancestors.

This takes us back to the school's origins. It was founded by Presbyterian
ministers in 1746, over a century after Harvard (1636) and nearly a half
century after Yale (1701). The College of New Jersey, located first in
Elizabeth and then in Newark, moved to its permanent home in Princeton
ten years later, after Nassau Hall was built to house it. It would not take its
present name of Princeton University, however, until its 150th anniversary
in 1896, the year of Fitzgerald's birth. During the Revolutionary War, Nassau Hall was used as a barracks and hospital by the British and American ar-
mies, and it was at Princeton, on January 3, 1777, that Washington won his
first battle. Nine Princetonians, the largest delegation from any American
college, sat in the Constitutional Convention in 1787. In those days the College of New Jersey shared its Southern-aristocracy clientele with William
and Mary College in Williamsburg and with the Philadelphia Academy. In
founding the University of Virginia in Charlottesville in 1819, Jefferson
gave the South the cultural center it needed, but, by tradition, Princeton
would remain the university most popular with students from states south
of New York.

The major building program ended the year Fitzgerald entered, when a
residential graduate school devoted to research, the first such institution in
the United States, was solemnly inaugurated. The decisive influence of an
energetic university president, Woodrow Wilson (1902–10), was making itself felt.

Wilson, the son of a Presbyterian minister and himself a devout Presbyterian, was the first president of the school who was not a churchman. The
board of trustees that hired him saw in him an exceptional man, enthusiastic, resolute and objective, who would accomplish at Princeton what
other dynamic college presidents—Daniel Gilman at Johns Hopkins, Andrew White at Cornell and, especially, Charles W. Eliot at Harvard—had
done for their schools: transform it into a cultural center adapted to the
new demands of an America that was beginning to play a part in international affairs. He was young—forty-six—and had come to know Princeton's
particular problems as a professor of constitutional law there for a dozen
years.

As soon as he took office, he envisaged far-reaching structural changes,
but he began by attacking the most pressing problems: to rouse university
life from the torpor into which it had fallen, to effect a transfusion of new
blood before subjecting the organism to major surgery. His most original
achievement was the formation of a corps of some fifty "preceptors" who
were to transform teaching methods. Until then, instruction had been by
lectures only. Wilson's innovation, inspired by British methods, aimed to
supplement professorial lectures by a seminar system in which small groups
—five or six students—would work under the direction of an assistant, or
preceptor.

For Wilson, however, these changes were merely the prelude to a more radical transformation of Princetonian life. Again borrowing from the British, he set about altering the arrangement of the campus by basing it around quadrangles that would unify Princeton as they did Oxford and Cambridge. Each square would be surrounded by buildings containing classrooms, dining halls and dormitories grouping students in a given branch of studies, their preceptors and perhaps some of their professors. Wilson believed that the quad system would establish organic, homogeneous, harmonious groupings in place of the anarchy that scattered students haphazardly through dormitories and classrooms all over the campus.

Before Wilson's time students' only meeting places were highly selective clubs to which only three out of four students were elected at the end of their sophomore year. It was a time-honored system, though considered undemocratic by students excluded from the clubs. Wilson was shrewd enough to interlace the negative and positive aspects of his reform, eliminating the clubs while instituting the quad system. Obviously, his plan required a sweeping, and costly, building program. And the luxurious clubhouses that lined Prospect Avenue, one of Princeton's noblest thoroughfares, represented considerable capital. Was Wilson, in the name of the school's morale, going to play Henry VIII to Princeton's England, despoiling institutions whose only sin was to own valuable real estate? In his defense it should be noted that a number of student movements aimed at suppressing the clubs had already arisen. During Fitzgerald's last year at Princeton—Wilson was in the White House by then—a rebellion by sophomore students threatened the clubs' existence and divided the campus into enemy factions. It took America's entry into the war to restore peace to the school.

The main charge against the clubs was that they perpetuated the social barriers erected by the students' backgrounds, fostering a debasing snobbery and systematically consolidating distinctions that a properly conceived university community should abolish. For a decade admission to his favorite club had been an undisputed sign of a student's success, and it had become students' prime preoccupation during their first two years at the university. The criteria by which club members chose new pledges were as vague but categorical in their exclusiveness as those governing elections in any nonuniversity club—America's big country clubs, for example; they were designed to maintain a certain tone and an esprit de corps within a given circle. As a system, it had its defenders. "The clubs have been called undemocratic," said Fitzgerald's friend John Peale Bishop, "as if a goosestep method should be applied to choosing one's friends. They have been assailed as snobbish when many a poor but honest student has found that neither poverty nor honesty could keep visitations of upperclassmen and election committees from his door. . . . The trouble with the clubs is that, once in them they matter so little after having seemed to matter so much. During the first two years even quite sane students look upon these formidable buildings on

Prospect Street as having the awesomeness of the College of Cardinals and as having the hereditary privileges of the stalls of the Knights of the Garter."[9]

Rivalry was keen among freshmen and sophomores anxious to be noticed by the influential upperclassmen on whom depended their entrance into the prestigious world of Ivy Club, noted for its aristocratic refinement; Cottage, worldy and stamped with Southern elegance; Tiger Inn of studied, churlish simplicity, the athletes' Olympus; or the unctuous, evangelizing Cap and Gown. Although there were nine clubs extant in the period around 1910—their number would double in the succeeding twenty years—the system's iniquity lay in the fact that one out of four sophomores was refused by all of them and so was exposed to the humiliation of being rejected by the little communities on Prospect Avenue.

This was the situation that Wilson tackled and that subsisted throughout Fitzgerald's college career, to the great prejudice of his studies. Criticized on all sides, the university's new president saw his costly project of replacing the club system by a quad system rejected by donors who lined up behind the no less costly plan to establish a graduate school. Defeated by an influx of massive donations to the moneymen's favorite project, Wilson resigned in 1910 to run—with relief—for the New Jersey governorship. Two years later he was elected President.

Such was the rather sordid little war that ended with the completion in 1913 of the Graduate College on the site where Washington had beaten George III's troops. For the Newman boy who entered that year, its noble architecture, especially the spaciousness of Procter Hall and the tall spire of Cleveland Tower, would symbolize the thrust and fervor of his aspirations. Its program of intensifying and broadening scholarship to give it new dignity would begin bearing fruit even during Fitzgerald's time at Princeton. So did the newly developed preceptor system. And the foreign languages department was growing fast under the direction of Christian Gauss, the most remarkable of the teachers Wilson hired.

If the war generation at Princeton includes so many distinguished names —such as Edmund Wilson, John Bishop, T. K. Whipple, G. R. Stewart and Fitzgerald—the credit belongs largely to the work of this professor of French and Italian language and literature. Gauss began teaching at Princeton in 1905 and was soon entrusted by Wilson with expansion of the embryonic modern languages department. When Edmund Wilson entered the university in 1912, he noted the department's excellence and its popularity with the students. "By the time I came to Princeton, in the class of 1916," he later wrote, "the Modern Language Department was one of the best in the country and had become very much in the fashion with the more intellectual students. This was one of the results of Wilson's administration, but entirely the creation of Gauss, who had not always found it easy to get Wilson to accept his proposals."[10] Edmund Wilson compared the situation in 1912 with what it had been a generation earlier: "My father, of the class of 1885, was drilled in French with more force than finesse by an exiled Polish general who swore at his students as though they were troops."[11]

Gauss was certainly one of the very few Princeton professors to capture Fitzgerald's attention and esteem. He first influenced those students whose minds were already open to the world of ideas, such young men as Bishop and especially Edmund Wilson. Wilson's picture of Gauss's culture and method might very well describe his own critical work: ". . . extreme flexibility and enormous range were, of course, a feature of his lectures. He was able to explain and appreciate almost any kind of work of literature from almost any period. He would show you what the author was aiming at and the method he had adopted to achieve his ends."[12] As Wilson remarked, however, Gauss also reached more frivolous minds, notably Fitzgerald's: "Less directly, perhaps, but no less certainly, the development of F. Scott Fitzgerald from *This Side of Paradise* to *The Great Gatsby*, from a loose and subjective conception of the novel to an organized impersonal one, was also due to Christian's influence. He made us all want to write something in which every word, every cadence, every detail, should perform a definite function in producing an intense effect.[13]

Gauss was austere and shy, seldom outgoing, but always receptive, generous with his time when students came to him with problems. An admirer of Flaubert and Dante, but equally capable of remembering his conversations with Oscar Wilde in Paris and of stressing the importance of Spengler's *The Decline of the West*, he brought more than flawless competence to his courses; he also invested them with a conviction and an enthusiasm that carried his message across to his audience. The long, warm essay Wilson devoted to him nicely conveys how much esteem and gratitude he inspired in his most demanding students: "In his role of the least didactic of sages, the most accessible of talkers, he seemed a part of that good eighteenth-century Princeton which had always managed to flourish between the pressures of a narrow Presbyterianism and a rich man's suburbanism."[14]

The secret of his success was probably that he could make the authors he talked about contemporary with his audience, alive and necessary, not mere subjects for academic exercise. Wilson's most telling tribute to Gauss's flexibility and intelligence was that a man teaching at Princeton during World War I "admirably prepared us for Joyce and Proust."[15] In that atmosphere of absorption in struggles for prestige, in which all that seemed to matter were the tumultuous glories of the stadium, the frippery of the Triangle's operettas and the smug vanity of the big men on campus, this retiring little man quietly affirmed the unarguable superiority of the life of the mind, ushering the best of those young men into a higher culture and igniting their literary ambitions.

Fitzgerald, quick to spot the inadequacies in his English professors, had to be deeply impressed by Gauss's solid teaching, by his tranquil certainty that great writers were the salt of the earth. For the first time in an institutional setting, he saw Sigourney Fay's convictions—of the primacy of the mind and of art—confirmed with incontestable authority. He watched a new code of values take shape, one that ignored hollow textbook formulas to express the conviction of a man he could not help but respect and admire. Had Gauss done nothing more for Fitzgerald than to instill in him a lasting belief in the superiority of the artistic and intellectual ideal over the codes then prevalent on the campus, his achievement would already have been considerable. That influence was extended and reinforced, however, by the efforts of a friendly but merciless and vigilant Wilson. Through many vicissitudes, it would develop what Fitzgerald called his "intellectual conscience," a painful awareness of the struggle between a demanding ideal and the allure of facility. But it raised his best work to the level of excellence Gauss preached. The professor's courses, which Fitzgerald did not follow until near the end of his school career, remained an isolated phenomenon for him, the exception that proved the rule.

It seems that only one other teacher succeeded in interesting him, in a course on the English Romantic poets. But, as he remarked in his article on Princeton, the effect of this professor's lectures was nullified by the assistants assigned to his exercises: "a surprisingly pallid English department, top-heavy, undistinguished and with an uncanny knack of making literature distasteful to young men. Dr. Spaeth . . . aroused interest and even enthusiasm for the Romantic poets, an interest later killed in the preceptorial rooms where mildly poetic gentlemen resented any warmth of discussion and called the prominent men of the class by their first names. . . ."[16]

Fitzgerald's lack of interest and application gave some of his English teachers the impression that he was poor in the subject. One of them, who became head of the department, was so convinced of the young man's weakness in English that he was never to believe that Fitzgerald wrote *The Great Gatsby*. Scott also irritated another member of the department, Jesse Lynch Williams, who might have seemed just the man to understand him. Cofounder with Tarkington of the Triangle Club, Williams had published *Princeton Stories* in 1895, a collection of the kind of tales of student life Fitzgerald loved. In 1917 his play *Why Marry?* won a Pulitzer Prize and became a Broadway hit. Fitzgerald went to see it. Then, in a discussion with Williams, he reversed the student-teacher relationship and analyzed for the author his play's technical weaknesses and structural flaws. Hadn't Fitzgerald, after all, written four plays and three operettas of his own?

Scott found his true mentors in classmate John Bishop and in Edmund Wilson, who was a year ahead of them. These were his elders in age as well as maturity of mind and breadth of culture. It was their example, their encouragement and, often, their frank and unsparing criticism that led him to the education that Princeton, except for Gauss, could not give him. He had always been a voracious reader, indiscriminatingly devouring everything that came to hand. At the age of twelve, he noted in his *Ledger,* he had formed the habit of reading in bed before going to sleep, "a life habit."[17] He might have added that the habit created difficulties for him. He read quickly, assimilated what he read even faster, which meant that he knew infinitely more than his classmates in the various schools he attended. He already knew some of the things his teachers told him, considered the rest uninteresting and was impatient with the torpor of his schoolmates' minds. Hence his dislike for formal schooling. It wasn't until he reached Princeton that he found boys his own age to whom he could talk and whom he could emulate. Scott's first meeting with Bishop in the spring of 1914 is described in *This Side of Paradise:* "They sallied into a discussion of poetry, in the course of which they introduced themselves, and Amory's companion proved to be none other than 'that awful highbrow, Thomas Parke d'Invilliers,' who signed the passionate love-poems in the Lit. He was, perhaps, nineteen, with stooped shoulders, pale blue eyes, and, as Amory could tell from his general appearance, without much conception of social competition and such phenomena of absorbing interest. Still, he liked books, and it seemed forever since Amory had met anyone who did. . . . So he let himself go, discussed books by the dozens—books he had read, read about, books he had never heard of, rattling off lists of titles with the facility of a Brentano's clerk. D'Invilliers was partially taken in and wholly delighted. In a good-natured way he had almost decided that Princeton was one part deadly Philistines . . . and to find a person who could mention Keats without stammering . . . was rather a treat."[18]

Bishop told of the meeting in similar terms: "We talked about books: those I had read, which were not many, those Fitzgerald had read, which were even less; those he said he had read, which were many, many more."[19] This was written over twenty years later, and Bishop placed the meeting in September, a few days after his arrival at Princeton, in a place exquisitely named for such an encounter, the Peacock Inn. He slyly stressed the connection: "The lights came on against the paper walls, where tiny peacocks strode and trailed their tails among the gayer foliations."[20]

Stimulated by the exchange, conscious of his inadequacies, Fitzgerald devoted his nights to discovering a whole realm of poetry that, until then, had been closed to him. His friendship with Bishop had its crises, but it would remain warm and sincere. Bishop, four years older than Fitzgerald (illness had delayed his schooling—tuberculosis again, it has been suggested), belonged to an old Virginia family. With more cause than Fitzgerald, he was proud of his lineage, which went back to the Scottish aristocracy. Passionate about poetry, sensuous and a bon vivant, making no secret of his love affairs, he cut a figure on campus of a graceful aesthete with the blasé air of a young libertine.

Fitzgerald knew that Bishop had a secret that was denied his professors: a fervor for literature that they lacked. It was Bishop who taught him the essence of poetry; it was his example and his criticism that opened the doors of writing to his younger friend. When Fitzgerald tried in 1940 to teach his daughter to love poetry, he used Bishop as his example: "It isn't something easy to get started on by yourself. You need, at the beginning, some enthusiast who also knows his way around—John Peale Bishop performed that office for me at Princeton. . . . He made me see . . . the difference between poetry and non-poetry. After that one of my first discoveries was that some of the professors who were teaching poetry really hated it and didn't know what it was about. I got in a series of endless scraps with them so that finally I dropped English altogether."[21]

Among the poets Bishop loved, Keats was the favorite. The student's sensuality chimed with the carnal sense of life and death the poet expressed in his sonnets and odes; he saw his own sensitivity in Keats's desperate love of the world, a love intensely shared by this young man who felt himself dying and who affirmed his precarious presence in the world in sumptuous and musical language. Bishop transmitted his veneration to Fitzgerald, for whom Keats would remain the most accomplished, the most moving of poets.

Fitzgerald did not find in Wilson the same community of temperaments and tastes, the same brotherly complicity and intuitive awareness of the other's resources and weaknesses that he so valued in his relationship with Bishop. To Bishop's indulgence, his amused tolerance of everything that was superficial and showy in Scott, succeeded Wilson's straightforward and sarcastic reproof. Wilson was the first to admire, perhaps even to envy, Fitzgerald's facility, but we feel in his comments the expert's irritation at seeing an ignoramus succeed by what seemed like luck, or pure intuition, where toil and knowledge failed. He seemed fascinated by Fitzgerald, with an incredulous fascination in a writer of raw talent who could make words evocative and phrases come alive even though his vocabulary was limited and his grammar shaky.

Fitzgerald, on the other hand, admired in Wilson the qualities he lacked in himself: his imperturbably objective judgment, his faculty for abstract reasoning, his easy honesty in handling concepts and a seemingly exhaustive knowledge of literature that was constantly nourished by well-planned reading. The two young men immediately established a master-disciple relationship: humility and submission from Fitzgerald and, from Wilson, haughty irony and biting comments. But there was a balm for the wounds: the admission that this barbarian had talent, that although he committed every imaginable literary sin, there was an unquestionable vital energy in what he wrote. Here is a brief example of Wilson's brand of peremptory criticism, taken from a study he wrote of Fitzgerald five years later. Slyly, he quoted poet Edna St. Vincent Millay: " 'To meet F. Scott Fitzgerald is to think of a stupid old woman with whom someone has left a diamond; she is extremely proud of the diamond and shows it to everyone who comes by, and everyone is surprised that such an ignorant old woman should possess so valuable a jewel; for in nothing does she appear so inept as in the remarks she makes about the diamond.'" Wilson hastened to add that Fitzgerald was far from stupid, that he had a lively, stimulating mind, but that the parable expressed a symbolic truth, and that it was a fact that "Fitzgerald has been left with a jewel which he doesn't quite know what to do with. For he has been given imagination without intellectual control of it; he has been given the desire for beauty without an aesthetic ideal; and he has been given a gift for expression without many ideas to express."[22]

Fitzgerald liked being whipsawed. He needed flogging more than praise, provided the strokes were well placed. He was grateful to whoever uncovered his weak points and hammered at them. We recall his respect for stern Aunt Annabel and his gratitude for his father's rare moments of firmness. He consented to be Wilson's whipping boy without a murmur, contritely. For he recognized a superiority in his friend, an authority he was never to question. He made Wilson his mentor, his "intellectual conscience." Even when he was twenty years out of Princeton, Fitzgerald could still write to him after a brief reunion: "Believe me, Bunny, it meant more to me than it could possibly have meant to you to see you that evening. It seemed to renew old times learning about Franz Kafka and latter things that are going on in the world of poetry, because I am still the ignoramus that you and John Bishop wrote about at Princeton."[23]

4. PRINCETON II

(1915–17)

When a wonder-struck Fitzgerald first entered Princeton's gilded bowers, early in the fall of 1913, the quad system, that dream of scholarly communities wholly consecrated to learning, was forgotten and the clubs were flourishing, stronger than ever. In the years immediately preceding America's entry into the World War, their primacy was unchallenged. It was by unconditional submission to their code of values, far more than by scholarship or respect for university rules, that Fitzgerald, his ambition rekindled, thought to carve out a reputation for himself on campus. Later, when John Grier Hibben, Woodrow Wilson's successor as president of Princeton, complained that Fitzgerald's first novel portrayed only the futile side of university life, the author wrote to him that he saw the school system as having been conceived uniquely for students without talent or imagination.

It is true that his efforts to maintain average grades, undemanding as these were, consisted mainly of cramming for exams. For he had a different notion of what a university was. Like St. Paul Academy, like Newman, Princeton to him was merely a social frame, a meeting place, a source of experience. But it was also an enchanted palace, a refined theater governed by rules as arbitrary as those of chess, where, for four years, the commedia dell'arte of his ambition was to be played out. For the canvas sketched at St. Paul's, enlarged at Newman, he would find the suitable setting, the talented actors and poetic atmosphere that would let him give free rein to his gift for improvisation and his rich imagination. In the dreary suburbia stretching from Trenton to New York, it was a secret and luminous place that seemed to have been imagined by the Shakespeare of *A Midsummer Night's Dream.*

Fitzgerald's Princeton was a community—one is tempted, when reading his stories to call it an order of chivalry—that was, of course, organized to fit the needs of a particular social class. But it really reflected only a stylized image of that class, fragmented and reconstituted according to a very special perspective. It lived by its own rules, which were not always those of the time. It had its heroes and its martyrs, its ceremonies and cults, its scales of values and taboos. Lectures and academic exercises were queer, anachronistic survivals at best, concessions to the outside world's idea of the education of a gentleman. Fitzgerald's remarks to Hibben were corroborated by Bishop, whose article on Princeton showed that while he understood the social polish and worldly veneer the university could give its students in those days, he was skeptical of how much intellectual training a gifted youngster could receive there. "If I had a son who was an ordinarily healthy, not too intelligent youth," he wrote, "I should certainly send him to Princeton. But if I ever find myself the father of an extraordinary youth, I shall not send him to college at all. I shall lock him up in a library until he is old enough to go to Paris."[1]

Princeton manifestly aspired to be something other than the seedbed of knowledge and culture that Harvard was, something other than a test site for success, like Yale. Its specialty, if we are to believe some of its most illustrious alumni, was to encourage its students—more systematically than its great rivals did—to cultivate a particular image of gentility that reached beyond the notion of a Victorian gentleman toward an older aristocratic ideal. To take purely intellectual pursuits too seriously was a breach of taste at Princeton. A love of books could not be openly paraded there as it could at Harvard, nor could competitiveness be flaunted, as at Yale. Both had to be tempered with blasé nonchalance and a cool aestheticism. A young man seeking to get ahead at Princeton had first of all to be a man of the world who had learned to avoid excessiveness and zeal.

Princeton in those days, then, can be defined as a distinctive, homogeneous social grouping united by a community of feelings and principles rather than a consensus of interests and ideas. It seemed to have established ideal conditions for getting to know one's fellows, once the necessary initiation procedure was completed and certain obstacles overcome. What this produced was a society as closed and artificial as the court of Louis XIV, or, rather, to keep things in their proper proportion, as one of those late-eighteenth-century German principalities where even a Goethe could seriously play at being a chamberlain. Life at Princeton had very little to do with what was going on in the world outside; this enclave of lawns and bowers and monuments was a happy island in which the rumblings of the avid, feverish America of industrial trusts and social conflict were not heard. There, education in the sense of breeding, of manners, had priority over the dissemination of knowledge; its aim was worldliness in a very particular world: a princely education. Some minds that naturally tended toward study and reflection—Edmund Wilson's was one—were indignant at the presumptuousness and restrictiveness inherent in such a concept. But it is easy to see its appeal to students less curious about art and literature than about good manners and satisfied egos. Princeton's reputation in the early years of the century was summed up in Amory Blaine's explanation of why it attracted him: "I think of Princeton as being lazy and goodlooking and aristocratic—you know, like a spring day."[2]

In a closed society the importance—indeed, the necessity—of clubs is obvious, as are the importance and necessity of those great group rituals, football games. Not to mention alumni gratitude, pride and generosity toward the shrine of their gilded youth, where they lived intensely their most impressionable years. Equally understandable is the insurmountable nostalgia that stalked them when they left the magic circle to face, alone, the material and psychological realities of a world that had been fashioned without them. Unless there was steel in their souls, they seemed condemned to wander in a vain search for a life as perfect as the one they left behind them, like Tom Buchanan in *Gatsby*, "one of those men who reach such an acute, limited excellence at twenty-one that everything afterward savors of anticlimax."[3] Such men outlive themselves, so to speak, finding no place for themselves in adult life. "Tom would drift on forever, seeking, a little wistfully, for the dramatic turbulence of some irrecoverable football game."

Football was a key element in this social system. The manly Princetonian ideal had long been symbolized, almost parodically, by the statue of D. C. French, the "Christian Student," which stood facing a dormitory with its back to the library. The figure was in football uniform, the powerful torso encased in a jersey with its right sleeve rolled up to accentuate the muscular arm. The other arm, holding a pile of thick books, was half-shrouded in the folds of an academic gown tossed carelessly over the left shoulder like a musketeer's cloak. French's handsome, haughty face was stamped with male self-assurance as he stared blankly and, it seemed, myopically into the distance.

College football got under way with a Princeton-Rutgers game in 1869; by the turn of the century it had acquired an importance it would long hold in university life. (It still draws crowds to the stadia, of course, but it no longer has the sacred status it once enjoyed on American campuses.) Fitzgerald celebrated it at length, pondering its meaning:

"For at Princeton, as at Yale, football became, back in the nineties, a sort of symbol. Symbol of what? Of the eternal violence of American life? Of the eternal immaturity of the race? The failure of a culture within the walls? Who knows? It became something at first satisfactory, then essential and beautiful. It became . . . the most intense and dramatic spectacle since the Olympic games."[4]

In his first novel we see how much of a cult was devoted to members of the football team. They were the community's champions, in the medieval sense, defending its prestige and honor in perilous tournaments. One of the sights that most deeply struck Amory's imagination on his arrival at Princeton was that of a file of white-clad senior-class men singing in the twilight like a phalanx of demigods descended among mortals. At their head was the supreme hero, the captain of the football team. "He sighed eagerly. There at the head of the white platoon marched Allenby, the football captain, slim and defiant, as if aware that this year the hopes of the college rested on him, that his hundred-and-sixty pounds were expected to dodge to victory through the heavy blue and crimson lines."[5]

The passage clearly betrays the author's veneration of his model for Allenby, a boy named Hobey Baker, who was team captain in 1913; the feeling was heir to Fitzgerald's enthusiasm for Sam White's exploit against Harvard in 1911, and it announced a later surge of emotion when he saw "the romantic Buzz Law . . . one cold fall evening in 1915, kicking from behind his goal line with a bloody bandage round his head."[6] So deep was the thrill that the sight of his idol ten years later, when Fitzgerald was at the height of his fame, stirred the old feeling: ". . . on the Champs-Elysées, I passed a slender, dark-haired young man with an insolent, characteristic walk. Something stopped inside me; I turned and looked after him. It was the romantic Buzz Law. . . ."[7]

The team, having survived the grueling selection process, was considered the flower of Princeton's youth, its highest aristocracy, the august caste to which every freshman dreamed of belonging. Football was the surest and most obvious road to glory. Like most of the other boys, Fitzgerald tried his luck, foreshadowing Amory who, "having decided to be one of the gods of the class . . . reported for freshman football practice."[8] It was a foolish hope and soon dashed. Desire alone could no more compensate at Princeton than it had at St. Paul's or Newman for his inadequate physique and lack of real athletic ability. The intensity of his yearning to be a university sports star, and the bitterness of his disappointment when the miracle refused to happen, survived the trivia that bred them to live again in the adult Fitzgerald's daydreams. "As the twenties passed," he wrote, "with my own twenties marching a little ahead of them, my two juvenile regrets—at not being big enough (or good enough) to play football in college and at not getting overseas during the war—resolved themselves into childish waking dreams of imaginary heroism that were good enough to go to sleep on in restless nights."[9]

Although he failed to enter the priesthood in the cult, he nonetheless remained an attentive and enthusiastic worshiper. Until the end of his life he would mingle with the crowds in the big university stadia. "I reveled in football as audience, amateur statistician and failed participant," says the narrator of "The Bowl," a short story about football at Princeton.[10] The team's coach, Fritz Crisler, vividly recalled how Fitzgerald, long after leaving college, would phone him in the middle of the night from some distant city on the eve of a big game against Harvard or Yale to recommend unusual plays that he insisted were infallible winners.

To Fitzgerald, as to his fellow students, a game was far more than just a sports event. It was a chance to unashamedly proclaim his faith in, and love for, his college, to share with other clansmen in a feeling of communion. A football field was an extension of his conscience and the game a proxy for his private combat, a perpetual battle of the Horatii and the Curiatii, with Princeton most often playing the poignant and melancholy role of the losers. Even more than a collective ritual, however, despite the crowds and the cheering, the duel was intensely personal: Fitzgerald the spectator vibrated in unison with the rest of the congregation, but what happened on the field touched him personally in the deepest recesses of his heart:

"The eleven little men who ran out on the field at last were like bewitched figures in another world, strange and infinitely romantic, blurred by a throbbing mist of people and sound. One aches with them intolerably, trembles with their excitement, but they have no traffic with us now, they are beyond help; consecrated and unreachable—vaguely holy."[11] In fact, football's fascination for him was an accurate gauge of his longing to be a man of action. The games were a microcosm in which, with flexibility and clockwork precision, the ballet of his deepest desires transpired. In it he saw "a molding of the confusion of life into form."[12] He experienced the catharsis that Aristotle demanded of drama, and through it, for brief moments, he could exalt his eagerness for a life of action and glory, for the crowd's delirious approval. Football superimposed exalting images on that dark area that his choice of a writing career had left unconquered. It revived the triumphal imaginings of his boyhood, his dreams of a life of public acclaim and, at the same time, his bitterness at his inability to realize his vision of the complete man, an ideal blend of man of letters and man of action. He lost himself fervently in this ceremony, which, in a wholly satisfying way, dramatized the ideas dearest to his heart: winning personal glory in a team fight, fast and spectacular action supported by popular enthusiasm; spontaneous, coordinated use in moments of crisis of his finest qualities—intelligence, courage, decisiveness and a spirit of self-abnegation. As long as the game lasted, Fitzgerald was the man he wanted to be.

His dying thought was for his college's football team. He was annotating an article in the *Princeton Alumni Weekly* when he was struck dead by a heart attack. In his copy of the magazine, a pencil line still runs wildly down a page of a story about the current football season.

After football the fields of activity offering ambitious students the highest degree of self-satisfaction were the theater and journalism. Journalism primarily meant three organs: the *Daily Princetonian*, in which university problems were debated; *The Tiger*, a humor magazine with a more specifically student tone and spirit; and the *Nassau Literary Magazine*, called the *Lit* by the faithful, which published the first poems, stories and essays of budding men of letters.

Fitzgerald chose the easiest of the three to break into, *The Tiger*, besieging it with brief reports, gossip, jokes. It was printing his contributions before the end of his first semester, without credit, to be sure. The theater was more demanding, but it also promised more tangible rewards. Fitzgerald had already savored the intoxication of success on the boards at St. Paul's. At Princeton he first enrolled in the English Dramatic Association, hoping to snare a part in the classic drama it staged every year. But he soon perceived that the company's prestige was pale in comparison with that of the Triangle Club, which offered a much broader scope for his eclectic range of talents. Founded twenty years earlier by Booth Tarkington, one of the literary figures Fitzgerald most admired at the time, Triangle put on an annual show, a musical comedy entirely conceived and acted by the students. This required a wide array of skills: scenario writer, songwriter, librettist, actors, singers, director, stage manager, and so forth. Chosen by a committee from among the manuscripts offered, the book often had to be revised, set to music and adapted before parts were assigned during the summer vacation. Rehearsals began in the fall and went on for three months. The work had to be good enough to be taken on tour by the company at Christmas to a dozen major cities including Baltimore, St. Louis, Chicago, even New York.

Fitzgerald's stage experience with *The Captured Shadow* and *The Coward* seemed to him to legitimize his ambition. He plunged into the contest, feverishly rereading Gilbert and Sullivan operettas and Oscar Wilde's plays and submitting manuscript after manuscript. His perseverance, his brio and, of course, his talent made him a winner over some formidable rivals. In 1914 the Triangle president was named Walker Ellis. He was an elegant junior from New Orleans, nonchalant and witty, the type of man who personified for Fitzgerald—still fretting over St. Paul's provincialism—the brilliant and sophisticated world he hoped to live in. Scott's comedy, entitled *Fie! Fie! Fi-Fi!*, was accepted, revised and signed . . . by Ellis. The alliterative title was in the musical comedy tradition: it would become *Ha Ha Hortense* in *This Side of Paradise*. There had been an *Oh! Oh! Delphine* in 1912, and George Gershwin's first musical joined the parade with *La, La Lucille* in 1919. Vincent Youmans's 1925 musical *No, No, Nanette* was in the same mold. But Fitzgerald's play was generally viewed as different from its Princeton predecessors. It steered strictly away from the student tradition. For one thing it introduced a bold and boyish character, the Flapper, whose freedom of manner and language delighted audiences. For another, it made skillful use of the new ragtime rhythms: short, syncopated verses of heavily stressed comic rhymes. It was an instant hit, and Fitzgerald was asked to write the lyrics for the 1915 production, called *The Evil Eye.* Edmund Wilson had begun writing the book, but he was too intellectual to enjoy such amusements for long; when he grew bored with it, he asked Fitzgerald to help him. "I am sick of it myself," he wrote in a letter to his friend. "Perhaps you can infuse into it some of the fresh effervescence of youth for which you are so justly celebrated."[13]

This took up, feverishly, the first half of 1914. No marchioness would have intrigued more ardently for a place at Louis XIV's feet than Fitzgerald schemed to fill the role that meant success at Princeton. He was always available, always eager, ready to prove his loyalty.

In February 1915 he began to harvest the fruit of his labor. He was elected secretary of the Triangle Club, a post that could provide a springboard to the presidency. His consecration as a Princetonian came a month later, when, along with his old friend Sap Donahoe, he was elected to one of the "big four" clubs, Cottage, of which Walker Ellis was then president. And he had been solicited by several others, including Cap and Gown and Quadrangle, which were chosen by Bishop and the other men of letters in his group. In May he was elected to the staff of *The Tiger*. Meanwhile, he proved he was able to write other things besides musical comedy lyrics and satirical squibs. Before the end of the school year two of his stories were accepted by Wilson, who was editing the *Lit*— "Shadow Laurels," published in the April issue, and "The Ordeal," run in June. The second story was good enough to persuade H. L. Mencken to run a revised version in *The Smart Set* five years later. Life was all smiles, all Fitzgerald's goals were fulfilled. He couldn't know that he was approaching the Tarpeian rock. As spring edged toward summer, his thoughts were all for the girl he was soon going to meet in New York.

For Scott's Princeton triumphs were matched by a romance that gave them their full value. The two enterprises were complementary and interdependent, each helping to promote the other. His certainty of belonging to the elite of his generation gave him the self-assurance he needed to attract and hold the attention of a Chicago society girl. At the same time, to shine in her eyes, he redoubled his efforts to become a Princeton celebrity.

Naturally, the girl he chose was the richest, the most popular in her set. Her reputation alone, the legend surrounding her, won him sight unseen. Ginevra King, sixteen, daughter of the fabulously wealthy Charles Garfield King, was bold and brilliant, uncontested queen of the fashionable places through which she gyrated with her cloud of admirers. She was only a name to Fitzgerald when, during the 1914 Christmas vacation, he decided to make a special trip to St. Paul to meet her. Marie Hersey, Ginevra's roommate at Westover and Scott's source for the fabulous rumors about her, told him she had invited Ginevra to spend the holidays in Minnesota. Here was game fit for the hunter. It pleased him to think she was destined for him, like a distant princess married by proxy to an unseen prince.

He did not meet her until January 4, 1915, the eve of his return to Princeton, at the Town and County Club. It was a memorable encounter; Fitzgerald would describe it in detail in "Babes in the Wood," a story written two years later and in turn incorporated, with a little retouching, into *This Side of Paradise*. In a matter of hours the two youngsters measured, judged and accepted each other. Ginevra knew how much vanity there was in Scott's devotion. He was aware that Ginevra was flighty, forever seeking new adventures. This was confirmed in a letter from his old rival, Reuben Warner, who said she had cozied up to him after Scott left. Despite this, a love story began to unfold that was to go on for two years, a fiction maintained by countless letters from both Scott and Ginevra—an exercise in imagination, an almost perfect illustration of Stendhal's theories about the "crystallization" of love. For they seldom saw each other. Their meetings were always memorable; Fitzgerald would use them later in *This Side of Paradise* and in the Basil and Josephine stories. Their first reunion was in February in the Westover lounge, their second in June in New York, "one night when she made luminous the Ritz roof on a brief passage"[14] before they separated for the long summer vacation, which Ginevra was to spend in Maine and he a continent away, on a ranch in Montana owned by Donahoe's parents. Each of these meetings uncorked a fresh flood of passionate letters—it was an epistolary novel—in which each of them inflated feelings exacerbated and idealized by distance, loneliness and regret to a point where each was really writing to a shadow, an idealized projection defined more by imagination than memory. To Fitzgerald, Ginevra was adorned with every feminine grace. She became a symbol—one that Daisy would embody for Gatsby—of the refined and luxurious elegance of blossoms that can bloom only if they are rooted in wealth. Instead of suggesting the temptations of profane love, her image blended naturally into a resurgence of the mystical movement to which Scott was introduced by Sigourney Fay; in his letters to Ginevra, Fitzgerald of course hinted that he might take Holy Orders.

But Ginevra would not have been all woman—the femme fatale, the Cleopatra who teaches Basil to suffer—had she allowed this love story to become mere polyphony in which each sang in joyful stanza of a disincarnate, purified love. The serene joys of a communion of hearts could not satisfy her for long. More than with any man, she was in love with love. And she had to worry the man she captivated, to make him feel how much her choice had cost her, be sure he knew when anyone else made a play for her. Ginevra thought of love as an auction, a never-ending conflict with an always uncertain outcome. Only recurrent crises, dramatic quarrels, betrayals and reconciliations could keep her restless heart ensnared. Against an adversary who thought he had won her, she used jealousy as a weapon, artfully, never losing control, maneuvering him into indefensible positions, pressing home her advantages until, his dignity utterly lost, he became a suppliant, to be disposed of with a last gesture of scorn. Each of her affairs was a campaign in which she played at being conquered, giving a little to take a lot, bewitching the enemy the better to deceive him. This is how Fitzgerald would portray Josephine, and the portrait bore Ginevra's features. Such women fascinated him; he knew they were forever out of reach despite all their promises and concessions. Ginevra later agreed that he had captured an excellent likeness of her:

". . . at this time I was definitely out for quantity, not quality, in beaux, and, although Scott was top man, I still wasn't serious enough not to want plenty of other attention. . . . I was thoughtless in those days and too much in love with love to think of consequences. These things he has emphasized—and over-emphasized—in the Josephine stories, but it is only fair to say I asked for some of them."[15]

Ginevra King would remain for Fitzgerald his archetypal woman, the Cleopatra whose betrayals were cruelly wounding, and the distant, tenderly romantic princess. She is a cult figure in his books, ambiguous, served by strangely similar priestesses named Isabelle and Josephine, Judy Jones, Daisy Buchanan, Nicole Warren. All of them are rich and fickle, all products of his experience of a world offered and then withdrawn. It was as though in Fitzgerald's first love, in his intense passion for what was hardly more than a smile and a silhouette, the real Ginevra was as much enemy as pretext, the serpent as well as Eve.

She remained an image of hopeless temptation, not sexual—Fitzgerald was no sensualist—but romantic, an image of boyhood fantasies fulfilled. To win her would have been to enter a mysterious and splendid realm, to penetrate the secrets of a world he longed to inhabit, the Walker Ellises' world to which he laid siege at Princeton. Ginevra's personality does not count for much in all this. Yet, by revealing herself, by transforming an abstract passion into a personal attraction that jealousy soon deformed, she brought Gatsby/Fitzgerald face to face with himself and his limitations. This sudden insight coincided with Scott's disgrace at school.

During his first two years at Princeton, Fitzgerald had almost totally neglected his studies to devote himself to his musical comedies. Repeated warnings were ignored, exams squeaked through. In his freshman year he failed mathematics and hygiene, and Latin and chemistry as a sophomore. At the end of his sophomore year his average was too low for him to major in English, as he had wanted to. The English department had accepted him on probation, but in mid-November, after six weeks taken up entirely with rehearsals of his play, he failed his makeup exam miserably. He was banned from all extracurricular activities, including Triangle, which meant he could not join its cross-country tour at the end of the year. Scott had cast himself in the juiciest part, a show girl on whom the whole plot hinged. A photo of Fitzgerald in drag—bare shoulders, coy smile, blond wig and big sunbonnet—had already been sent to newspapers in the cities on the tour schedule. St. Paul, specially included in that year's tour, awaited the event with a curiosity kept lively by a stream of rumors and articles in the local press.

A Triangle delegation tried to persuade the dean to relent; some of the

English professors were asked to intercede in Fitzgerald's favor. Nothing doing. The ban was upheld. Fitzgerald was to spend the rest of the year pumping up his grades.

At that point he came down with a severe fever that put him in the infirmary. Malaria was endemic in the New Jersey swamps then, and this was the doctor's diagnosis. When the patient suffered a later relapse, however, he decided—in Fitzgerald's version, at any rate—that it was really tuberculosis. Whatever it was, the ailment put Fitzgerald out of condition to catch up on his studies. He went back to St. Paul to convalesce. When Triangle put on its long-awaited production of *The Evil Eye*, he was in bed. He hoped that, under the circumstances, the school authorities would indulgently allow him to make up his grades by doubling up in the following semester so that he could complete his junior year in the clear. His friends saw through the scheme. In cruelly ironic couplets that parodied Fitzgerald's songs, Bishop and Wilson jeered at him in the January 1916 issue of the *Lit*:

> *I was always clever enough*
> *To make the clever upperclassmen notice me . . .*
> *No doubt by senior year,*
> *I could have been on every committee in college,*
> *But I made one slip:*
> *I flunked out in the middle of junior year.*[16]

On his return to Princeton Fitzgerald was informed that he would not be allowed to complete his junior year until he made up his earlier failures, beginning in the following semester, and that because of his poor grades he was ineligible to run for any campus office. Good-bye Triangle presidency. To add to his woes, his pride was kicked in its most vulnerable spot: Triangle turned down the scenario he proposed for the following year in favor of one by a friend, John Biggs, called *Safety First*. Fitzgerald did write the song lyrics for it, however.

In March 1916 he learned that Ginevra had been expelled from Westover; she had been caught with a date in a compromising situation. Fitzgerald's lingering illusions about her collapsed, along with his dreams of a brilliant career at Princeton. Coming together, the disappointments coagulated into despair. Once, in March, he sought relief in what he thought of as a symbol of his degradation: the sins of the flesh. "It seemed, one March afternoon," he later recalled, "that I had lost every single thing I wanted—and that night was the first time that I hunted down the spectre of womanhood that, for a little while, makes everything else seem unimportant."[17]

Fitzgerald's months of forced retirement in the Midwest healed his wounds. He reconsidered his position, examining more objectively the value of the honors he had gathered at school. There seems even to have been a fleeting thought of dropping out of Princeton and trying to make a career writing song lyrics, perhaps even becoming an actor. The press clippings in his scrapbook include rave reviews of *Fie! Fie! Fi-Fi!* The Baltimore *Sun* said that what made the show were Fitzgerald's lyrics. The Brooklyn *Citizen* compared "this delicious little vehicle" with Broadway musicals that had "less vivacity, less sparkling humor and less genuine music."[18] The Louisville *Post* seemed to point toward his future: "the lyrics of the songs were written by F. S. Fitzgerald, who could take his place right now with the brightest writers of witty lyrics in America." His photo as a show girl ran in a number of newspapers—even the New York *Times* used it—and brought him floods of mail; a few legitimate offers were mixed in with the more inflamed propositions. Broadway impresario Charles Bornhoupt guaranteed him vaudeville bookings: "If you get in town in May I shall be very pleased to meet you, and secure an engagement for you immediately."[19]

At the end of his life Fitzgerald wrote a sad letter to his daughter from Hollywood, where he was turning out scripts that were every bit as lightweight as his college musicals: "Sometimes I wish I had gone along with that gang (Cole Porter, Rodgers and Hart), but I guess I am too much a moralist at heart and really want to preach at people in some acceptable form rather than entertain them."[20]

That spring and summer of 1916 was a thoughtful time for Fitzgerald, a turning point in his college career. The tranquilizing atmosphere of his provincial home and family had its effect. As it had after his return from that first, disastrous term at Newman, his love of life revived. Those around him swallowed the fiction that his illness was to blame for his low grades, and he was received everywhere with solicitude and understanding. He basked in Princetonian prestige. To his friends he was still the local boy who had made good in the East, whose elegance and easy grace made him one of the city's most talked-about young men.

Fitzgerald cultivated his reputation, working hard at being a decadent dandy. He drank too much and he grandstanded, even if it created a scandal. He had a fine time tricking the students at the local college by attending a school ball, in company with his old friend Gus Schurmeier, dressed in his Princeton transvestite costume. The illusion was perfect. Young men crowded around the unknown belle, the daring and provocative beauty who shocked people by smoking in public and lifting her skirt to pluck a compact from her garter. Not until the following day did an indignant newspaper article expose the hoax, under a fat headline complaining that "Local College Men Have No Fear of Going Effeminate."[21] More conventionally rakish was his invitation to a pair of road-show actresses then performing in St. Paul to dine with him at the University Club, to the other members' disapproval—or envy. Not that he was attracted to loose women, as some of his fellow Princetonians were; in life, as in his books, he generally avoided sexual promiscuity except at times of crisis:

"The New York of undergraduate dissipation, of Bustanoby's, Shanley's, Jack's, had become a horror, and though I returned to it, alas, through many an alcoholic mist, I felt each time a betrayal of a persistent idealism. My participance was prurient rather than licentious and scarcely one pleasant memory of it remains from those days."[22]

When Fitzgerald returned to Princeton in September 1916, he doubled up on his junior year. He was now free of the twin handicap of a love affair he recognized was over and a stock of campus ambitions that he knew could never be realized. With nothing more to hope for in the way of social prominence, he lost almost all his interest in what had seemed, the year before, to be his reason for living. "Years later," he would write, "I realized that my failure to be a big shot in college was all right—instead of serving on committees, I took a beating on English poetry; when I got the idea of what it was all about, I set about learning how to write. On Shaw's principle that 'if you don't get what you like, you better like what you get,' it was a lucky break—at the moment it was a harsh and bitter business to know that my career as a leader of men was over."[23]

He watched from the sidelines when some of his friends leagued with about a hundred sophomores in an attempt to end the club system. Among them were Alexander McKaig, editor of the *Daily Princetonian;* Richard Cleveland, former President Grover Cleveland's son; David Bruce, who would become the American ambassador to Paris, Bonn and London. Above all there was Henry Strater, a follower of Tolstoy and Thoreau and greatly admired by Fitzgerald (he appears in *This Side of Paradise* as Burne Holliday). They were no more successful than Woodrow Wilson had been; the only result—short-lived—of their revolt, which was interrupted by America's declaration of war on Germany, was to reduce by a fourth the number of sophomores joining clubs.

Fitzgerald shared a room in Little Hall with Paul Dickey, Triangle's first-string composer; they had once collaborated in writing a martial hymn to the glory of Princeton football. He thus continued to work unofficially for the club despite the official ban, contributing lyrics to Dickey's songs for Biggs's *Safety First.* Although he was still turning out items for *The Tiger,* Fitzgerald's interest was turning increasingly toward serious writing. He was eager to have his work accepted by Wilson for the *Lit.* His friendship with Bishop, Wilson and Biggs was fruitful. In December 1916 Fitzgerald and Biggs wrote almost the whole of one *Lit* issue as a parody of straitlaced *Cosmopolitan* magazine called the *Chaopolitan Number.* Bishop maintained his love of poetry throughout his college career, and this inspired Scott to cultivate his poetic vein. "I had decided," he explained, "that poetry was the only thing worth while, so with my head ringing with the meters of Swinburne and the matters of Rupert Brooke, I spent the spring doing sonnets, ballads and rondels into the small hours. I had read somewhere that every great poet had written great poetry before he was twenty-one. I had only a year, and, besides, war was impending. I must publish a book of startling verse before I was engulfed."[24]

That year he had a total of four poems, six stories and five book reviews published. He plunged into the reading of the English aesthetes—Walter Pater, Ernest Dowson, Swinburne, Wilde—but he discovered that his deepest affinity was with the work of Rupert Brooke, who had died in the army two years earlier. After his break with Ginevra in January, he found in Brooke's work consolation and even enlightenment about the real nature of his feelings for her. He had made of Ginevra a symbol of the religiosity his wavering faith could no longer fully satisfy. He had made the mistake Gatsby would also make, of enclosing his highest aspirations in the frail vessel of a perishable creature who was subject to the law of her world of appearances. Fully aware of the limitations of human love, he would carry over into *This Side of Paradise* the solemn warning contained in a letter from Fay a year later: "You make a great mistake if you think you can be romantic without religion.... Beware of losing yourself in the personality of another being, man or woman."[25]

Brooke's poems revealed to Fitzgerald, in a usable, assimilable form, an aspect of Platonism that supplied his current needs. Especially, the poem *Tiare Tahiti*—from which he took the title of *This Side of Paradise*—seems to have crystallized in him certain poetic notions of God and the universe that were confirmed by careful reading of Keats's poetry. The revelation served an immediate purpose: to conciliate quest and failure, to explain his disenchantment by the impossibility of attaining an absolute that could only be reached yonder, on the other side of paradise.

Along with his discovery of Brooke, who brought him a seductive system for interpreting his problems, Fitzgerald found Bernard Shaw and H. G. Wells, the great popularizers of socialism, who gave him a sense of evolution in history, only the anecdotal side of which had held his attention before. He perceived a new kind of hero in Strater, one of the promoters of the sophomores' revolt. Strater, like Edmund Wilson, was one of those individualists, so rare at Princeton, who were ready to defy the unwritten laws of the campus and to proclaim their personal beliefs. For Fitzgerald he set an example of moral force and unshakable integrity based on purely intellectual convictions.

So the spring of 1917 went by in a ferment of new ideas and poetic effusions. In June Fay proposed that Fitzgerald go with him to Russia at the head of a Red Cross delegation. Being very mysterious, the priest told his young friend what the mission's secret purpose was: to bring Russia back into the Roman Catholic Church now that the country's spiritual leader, the Czar, was deposed. Fitzgerald grasped joyfully at the unexpected chance to forget the present, to bring to real life the games he once played in the attics of St. Paul. He and Fay plotted happily, gravely discussing the cut of the uniform Scott would wear, exchanging letters heavy with double meanings. Then, in September, the Bolsheviks took power and the trip was called off. Fitzgerald, who had undergone officer training at Princeton, was now seriously thinking of enlisting in the army, as most of his friends had. He took a test in St. Paul and, early in September, was notified that he had passed it; this meant he could hope for a second lieutenant's commission when he turned twenty-one.

Meanwhile, he spent a month with Bishop's family in the mountains of West Virginia. Influenced by his recent contacts with Fay, he announced his plan, already mentioned in his letters to Ginevra, of becoming a priest. For a while Mrs. Bishop worried that he might convert her son to Catholicism. At the time John was busily preparing for the publication of a volume of his poems, to be entitled *Green Fruit*, before he went off to the army. His example prompted Scott to express his mystical impulses. The period was one of intense fervor; under the influence of Brooke and John Masefield, he wrote poem after poem, guided and criticized by young Bishop. One of these poems, *The Way to Purgation*, was the first to be accepted and paid for, but not published, by a poetry magazine called *Poet Lore*.

Fitzgerald returned to Princeton to await his army call-up. In Campbell Hall he shared a room with Biggs, who was no more interested than Scott in his college courses and who, like his friend, devoted most of his time to the *Lit*. Scott kept Wilson, who was about to sail for France, up to date on campus doings:

"The *Lit* is prosperous—Biggs and I do the prose—Creese and Keller (a junior who'll be chairman) and I the poetry. . . . I'm rather bored here but I see Shane Leslie occasionally and read Wells and Rousseau."[26] In the same letter he hints at other possibilities suggested by Fay: "I can go to Italy if I like as private secretary of a man (a priest) who is going as Cardinal Gibbon's representative to discuss the war with the Pope (American Catholic point of view . . . forty per cent of Pershing's army are Irish Catholics)."[27]

Six weeks later, at the end of October, he received his commission and left Princeton, without a diploma, for good.

II. SUCCESS AT
TWENTY-FIVE

(1917-22)

5. A WAR, A NOVEL AND LOVE

(1917–19)

With America at war, patriotic fever ran high on the Princeton campus. Playing fields became drill grounds where students and professors learned the rudiments of weaponry and military discipline. But Fitzgerald was one of those who kept their heads, refusing to be carried away by martial propaganda. He did think of enlisting, as an officer, but this mainly because he saw in the war another possible chance to fulfill the old dream he had not been able to realize at school or on the football field. He was unencumbered with excess patriotic baggage when he reported at Fort Leavenworth, Kansas, for three months' basic training, so he could maintain a detached, aristocratic attitude toward the war. He ordered a well-cut uniform from Brooks Brothers and, before joining his unit, admonished his mother against displays of sentiment. In all ways he conformed to the proud code Fay urged on him in a letter written on December 12, 1917: "You went to war as a gentleman should, just as you went to school and college, because it was the thing to do. It's better to leave the blustering and tremulo-heroism to the middle classes; they do it so much better."[1]

Before leaving Princeton, he had shown an enthusiastic Fay and a more reserved Gauss a first draft of a novel that already had the basic characteristics of *This Side of Paradise*, blending his autobiographical notes and some of the poems and stories written for the *Lit* into a more or less fictionalized account of his life at Princeton.

Convinced he was going to be killed in the war, he was anxious to make fullest use of his winter months in the Kansas snow to rewrite the book: "I had only three months to live—in those days all infantry officers thought they had only three months to live—and I had left no mark on the world."[2] He wanted to leave a piece of work behind him, a kind of testament of his generation, he wrote to Wilson, in what he felt was the only meaningful form in which to show it. He fought against time—or, rather, time and space no longer existed for him. He was completely absorbed in creation, and the rest—the training, the hiking—was as unsubstantial as a dream. Pulling his old Newman-Princeton trick when he was bored in class, he scribbled during training lectures, hiding his notes behind his military manual. Caught at it, he was left with only his weekends in which to write in the noise and smoke of the officers' club. Luckily, two of his barracks mates were Harvard men who were also interested in literature; one of them edited a poetry magazine and the other was adapting *War and Peace* for the stage. When his basic training ended in February, Fitzgerald used his furlough to go to Princeton and complete the last of the twenty-three chapters of *The Romantic Egotist*.

Of this long narrative—120,000 words, according to Fitzgerald—only the first five chapters remain, the heavily corrected chapters he sent to his friend Donahoe, which were never returned to him (Donahoe kept them and later donated them to the Princeton library). But we can get an idea of what it was about from the author's letters to his friends. It was a first-person story by a narrator named Stephen Palms, or Delius—evidence that Fitzgerald remembered *A Portrait of the Artist as a Young Man*. He never cited Joyce among his sources, however, seeing his own work rather as "a prose, modernistic *Childe Harold*"[3] than the tale of an upbringing like that of Stephen Dedalus in Clongowes Wood. Nevertheless, aside from the love stories—probably the ones used for stories published in the *Lit* and transposed with only minor changes to the final, published version—the manuscript includes "three psychic adventures including an encounter with the devil in a harlot's apartment";[4] their supernatural content recalls some of Dedalus' mystical perceptions. A single, ambiguous reference to Joyce's novel is found in *This Side of Paradise:* "He read enormously. He was puzzled and depressed by *The Portrait of the Artist as a Young Man*."[5]

With Fay in Europe, his friend Shane Leslie functioned as Fitzgerald's guide. Leslie would have liked to see him stick to poetry, and at first he opposed the plan to write a novel. But he soon changed his mind when he saw the carbons of the chapters Fitzgerald sent him as fast as they came out of the typewriter. "I like the idea of your book," he wrote his protégé on January 1, 1918. "Conceit is the soul or germ of literature and of course 'egotism' is the long sought synonym for 'style.' . . . Put your utmost into your writing while the furor of youth, its cynicism and indignation, is upon you."[6]

Encouraged, Fitzgerald went to Washington to hand the poet the completed manuscript he had just revised at Princeton. Leslie corrected the spelling and syntax and sent it to his publisher, Charles Scribner. Despite a shrewd letter of recommendation that pictured Fitzgerald as a kind of Rupert Brooke in prose who, like his elder, was doomed to vanish soon ("though Fitzgerald is still alive it has a literary value. Of course when he is killed it will also have a commercial value."[7]), the manuscript was returned to its author in August. He made the changes recommended by Scribner readers and submitted it again. In October came the final rejection. Only one of the editors, Maxwell Perkins, tried in vain to defend it.

Meanwhile, his furlough over, Fitzgerald was assigned to Fort Taylor, Kentucky, near Louisville, where he was reunited with Bishop, who had been there for several months and whose *Green Fruit* had just appeared. Bishop was about to ship out for France, and he would fight in the war's final battles. The two talked about Princeton, where Biggs alone of their group remained to carry on their tradition; about Wilson, who was already with an ambulance unit in France, but whose war experience would be confined to the boredom of garrison towns. They explored the streets of Louisville together; Fitzgerald associated the city's beauty with that of its girls and was charmed by it. There he had his introduction to the South, and it was in Louisville that he would place Jay Gatsby's meeting with Daisy Fay.

After a month in Kentucky, Fitzgerald's unit was transferred to Camp Gordon, Georgia; then, two months later, to Camp Sheridan, Alabama, in the heart of the Deep South. The camp was just outside Montgomery, the first capital of the Confederacy. Both these camps, and the lazy life in the towns around them, would be described in *The Beautiful and Damned*. After his stimulating winter months in Fort Leavenworth, Alabama's subtropical summer dulled his energy and ambition; he succumbed to the languor of this new land where the climate brought out new facets of his personality.

His assignment to a staff company gave him the right to wear boots and spurs, a privilege he was the only officer in camp to claim. Military life and the authority it gave him fostered autocratic tendencies in him that could be alarming. On one occasion, for example, he forced a conscientious objector at revolver point to go through the regular training course. Another time he almost caused a rebellion in the ranks by making his men double the length of a hike as punishment for their complaints about the food. And he brought so much pressure to bear on them during a Liberty Bond drive that they each—in violation of military regulations—subscribed two months' pay.

Fitzgerald's irresponsibility was legendary in the camp. Given command of a mortar company, he mistakenly directed the unit's fire—the ammunition, it's true, was blank—on another unit on the firing range. He came off better, however, when a ferry sank during an amphibious landing exercise across the nearby Tallapoosa River, organizing the rescue operation and managing to save most of the men from drowning. "I Didn't Get Over," a story he wrote in 1936, describes the incident and ties it in with the mortar-practice fumble. There is a veiled feeling of guilt in the story: the narrator, theoretically impartial, nonetheless defends Lieutenant Danzer, who redeems himself on the river. The sinking is blamed on Captain Hibbing, whose headstrong zeal has already caused the mortar incident and who takes his vindictiveness out on Danzer. At the end of the story the narrator is revealed as Hibbing himself. The perspective allowed the author to be simultaneously witness, defendant and judge of his own mistakes. Years later, in *The Beautiful and Damned*, he would take a strongly hostile attitude toward the army, denouncing the absurdity of its system and the stupidity of its regular officers, "men with the mentality and aspirations of school-boys."[8] The least inhuman among them, Lieutenant Kretching, turns out to be a heel who makes off with the unit's cash box. Camp life is described from the viewpoint of a private victimized by the lack of understanding in his superiors—in whom, with his habitual honesty, Fitzgerald condemns his own blindness.

It was at a country club dance in Montgomery that he met Zelda Sayre. He had gone through several affairs that summer. A girl named May Steiner, in particular, was so important to him that he kept a photo of her draped in an American flag. She may have been the model for tiny, touching Dorothy Raycroft in *The Beautiful and Damned*.

In June he learned that Ginevra was to be married in September to an Army Air Service officer. The past was decidedly dead. Yet, for the first time since his idyll with Ginevra ended, the word "love" reappeared in his *Ledger*. On the same line was written a name: Zelda. In a July entry the name is coupled with the news of Ginevra's engagement. It crops up again after the second mention of May Steiner: "May and I on the verandah."[9] Both names return in August, but this time Zelda's is mentioned first, after notice that Fitzgerald had begun revising the second version of *The Romantic Egotist*: "Revising novel. Zelda and May."[10] And the entries for September begin, "Fell in love on the seventh."[11] This would seem to invalidate the romantic tale of love at first sight recounted by their biographers; two months apparently went by before Scott and Zelda decided they were in love. The young officer had certainly been attracted at once by the golden-haired girl he met at the club on a Saturday evening in July. She had just finished high school, where she shone in her dancing classes. In a show that evening she had performed her favorite number, "The Dance of the Hours." He asked to be introduced to her, and they went on seeing each other.

Zelda Sayre, born July 24, 1900, was just eighteen then. She was the youngest of the five Sayre children—her three sisters, Marjorie, Rosalind and Clothilde, all much older than she, and a brother, Anthony Jr. Her mother, Minnie Sayre, was nearly forty when Zelda was born, and her father, Judge Anthony D. Sayre, was forty-two; the child was and remained her parents' pet. Minnie had once hoped to be an opera singer in Philadelphia, but her father, a former United States senator from Kentucky, vetoed the plan. Although she was resigned to sacrificing her dream, Minnie's romantic streak and her lively imagination remained intact; her poems were even printed occasionally in the local newspaper. She was sufficiently impressed by her reading to name her youngest daughter Zelda, after a Gypsy queen in a novel.

Zelda's father, a justice of the Alabama Supreme Court for over twenty years, also came from a distinguished family. His uncle, John Tyler Mor-

gan, was a United States senator for three decades. The novel Zelda wrote
in 1932, a few months after Judge Sayre's death, showed how important her
father was in her life, not directly, but through the unshakable dignity and
Olympian assurance he always incarnated for her. His was the only authority for which she had any respect, even if she did make a game of disobey-
ing his orders, of defying him and pitting her will against his. It is
significant that in her novel she always refers to her heroine's father as the
Judge. Throughout her life Zelda would regret the lost orderliness, the reassuring stability her father's authority provided.

When Fitzgerald met her, she was already famous in Montgomery for
her wild escapades and her contempt for convention. Other girls her age
admired and envied her, voting her the prettiest girl in her class at Lanier
High School. But she had long since grown bored with them. Zelda craved
action, the clash of rivalries, the heat of competition. She could not be
satisfied to remain within the bounds convention set around proper young
ladies. She had the nonchalant charm, the love of finery and conquest, the
ready retort and provocative mockery typical of the belle we meet in so
many novels about the South. She had, moreover, a strong sense of the con-
sideration due her and a belief that this ought to take the form of dashing
action as well as romantic speeches.

Her resemblance to fictional Southern heroines, stoutly encamped in their
tradition and propriety, ends here, however. Zelda did not belong to the
world of the great plantations, but to a middle class that was solid, respected, but not notably wealthy. Her notion of honor owed nothing to the
chivalric code of the Southern aristocracy. The responsibility she felt was
to herself alone, and she could not tolerate curbs on her expression of her
zest for life. Not for her the classic Southern belle's passivity. She hated
boredom; good manners left her indifferent and so did the conventions, and
she flouted both without remorse or reservation. And she got away with
this blithe disdain because of her graceful naturalness and poise and a dignity born of her deep conviction that her way of doing things was always
the right way.

Toward men she was as demanding as she was generous, refusing to be
just another pretty pushover. Zelda was determined to live dangerously.
Bold and energetic, she looked for boldness and energy in the friends she
chose. Nothing annoyed her so much as conformity and pale reason-
ableness. She piqued her admirers' pride, expected the impossible of them,
was a constant challenge to them. If she rode behind on a motorcycle, she
insisted that the driver take risks he would never take alone. A fearless
diver, she expected her friends to match her daring. She smoked in public
when this was still scandalous, and she drank as hard as boys her age did.
Wherever she went, Zelda Sayre disconcerted, stimulated, excited or
shocked people.

She had a cat's fluid and dangerous grace. Beauty she had, but it was more in manner than in feature. What was charming about her gray-blue eyes was the bold, mocking, provocative look in them. Well-boned face, thin, bird-of-prey nose, a mass of golden hair and a supple, boyish body: Diana the Huntress.

By the time the United States entered the war, Zelda had already run through all the possibilities available at parties in Montgomery and dances at Alabama State University in Montgomery and at nearby Auburn University. When the aviators took over Camp Taylor and an Ohio regiment moved into Camp Sheridan, she was seventeen and delighted with this new contingent of males. She shone at parties given for officers who vied for her attention and for invitations to the Sayre home on Pleasant Avenue. Pilots flew stunts over the house until their commander forbade flights over the neighborhood.

Zelda plunged into a round of flirtations and intrigues, avowals of love and moonlit walks, old waltzes and the latest hit tunes. In "The Last of the Belles," Fitzgerald perfectly caught this frothy summer-festival atmosphere, a sort of Departure for Cythera, in which a foreboding of death intensified the pursuit of love, a whirl of loving, cruel and witty belles and beaux incognito in their dress uniforms, moving with the dark grace of men marked for battle. People ignored the fact that these young Northern soldiers were yesterday's enemies, entertaining them as doomed men just as, over half a century earlier, they had given at least one splendid ball for Confederate officers about to leave for the massacre. In this frantic festival atmosphere, prejudice, social barriers, all the customary restraints disappeared. People tried to fulfill the promise of a lifetime in a single summer.

The game had already been going on for a year when a young staff officer, slim and proud in his Brooks Brothers uniform, blond and handsome as a summer deity and stepping lightly, as though on winged feet, approached Zelda at the country club. He was twenty-two, she eighteen, and the love born that evening was to become legendary in American literary lore. Time slowed for them and stopped; by the end of that summer they would bring a burning love story to life. The memory of those two late-summer months in 1918 would become the heart of Fitzgerald's writing, inspiring stories in which every heroine would have Zelda's audacity and vivacity and verve and Zelda's smile. "The most important year of life," he wrote in his *Ledger*. "Every emotion and any life work decided. Miserable and ecstatic, but a great success."[12] At a time and place in which passions were brief and unions fleeting—among their friends, Wilson and Hemingway would each marry four times—Scott and Zelda would give the world of the Roaring Twenties, despite their incessant quarreling, a lesson in anachronistic constancy, of a love that was forever threatened, forever reborn.

Each of them confusedly hoped that through marriage they could escape their surroundings and enter a social sphere they liked to think was free of provincial, middle-class contingencies, a lavish and liberal world. This was the sense of Fitzgerald's boyish fixation on Ginevra King, the love of a relatively poor young man for a richer girl through which we glimpse his fascination with the opulent society in which she lived.

To Zelda, too, marriage implied escape to an elegant life in the big northern cities and a blossoming forth of her personality in worldly, luxurious surroundings. Scott fully approved of her dream; in such stories as "The Ice Palace," "The Jelly Bean" and "The Sensible Thing" (it was Zelda who had the ideas for the first two), he endorsed the motivations that make their heroines refuse to marry men they love but who could not open to them the doors to a more glamorous life. Yet Scott, dreaming, like Gatsby, of a king's daughter, fell in love with a shepherdess, and Zelda, awaiting the marvelous prince who would take her out of her ordinary world, gave herself to an impecunious cavalier who could build castles only in the air.

Having recognized themselves in each other, they abandoned their illusions. Each had seen the other's eagerness to live life fully, to reject any impediment to unfettered development. Who better than Zelda could understand Scott's inordinate ambition to cash in richly on a romantic life-style? Who more indulgently than Scott could ignore Zelda's frivolity and her apparent flaws and see only her basic nature, her intense feeling for life, her perfect freedom of spirit and her disdain for whatever is not felt and experienced acutely? Each was reflected in the other's impulses, anticipated the other's thoughts, encouraged the other's most secret potentials, confirmed the other's intuitions, rivaled the other's boldness in their parallel conquest of their inner freedom. Zelda confessed her most sordid adventures, gave him her diary to read, as he gave her his novel. Even more than lovers, they were accomplices, twins going hand in hand to confront the world around them.

For the moment their love seemed a gift from the gods, made more precious and poignant still by their certainty that it was doomed. During that first phase they lived in the present, with no plans, no future. Scott pressed her for a firm commitment, but she backed away, making herself more precious by absence, indifference, responsiveness to his rivals. For she had not dismissed her other admirers, and she made sure that Scott knew it when she encouraged them. Clusters of students from Auburn surrounded her; five members of the football team even formed a new fraternity, Zeta Sigma; according to a newspaper clipping in Zelda's scrapbook, they were "noted for their almost rabid devotion to the principles of their fraternity."[13] The rival of whom Scott was proudest and most jealous was Francis Stubbs, a football hero of the kind he had admired at Princeton, adored by the crowds, proud and nonchalant, as befitted an Auburn star.

Zelda, sure of herself and of Scott, played off his jealousy against her desire. He was invited to dinner by her parents, spent long evenings with her on the Sayres' clematis-shaded porch talking endlessly of love through the hot evenings, analyzing their feelings, tripping all the levers of charm and enticement. Later he would remember that after their hours of communion, she liked to tease him, calling him "an educational feature; an overture to romance which *no* young lady should be without."[14]

One incident provides a rousing illustration of her irresistible need to push those she most loved to the limits of their patience. The first time Scott was invited to dinner at the Sayres', Zelda's teasing so enraged her father that he grabbed a carving knife—so, at least, the story goes—and chased her around the table. Just a little lesson in natural history that Scott may not have taken sufficiently to heart.

On October 26 Scott left Montgomery with his unit for Long Island to sail to France. He had just learned of his novel's final rejection, and the girl he loved and who loved him was left behind, but he was ready for battle, ready to die like a gentleman. He had lived fully, had known fierce love. Like Alan Seeger and Rupert Brooke, he had a presentiment of death.

But fate denied him the romantic apotheosis of a glorious end: while his regiment waited to embark for Europe, the armistice was signed. A crushing disappointment: the war had passed him by. He would have to learn to live again. As in March 1916, when all his hopes were frustrated and the tension that had carried him so far had suddenly broken, Scott went to pieces. He let everything go, deserted his post and, for what he later felt were a few despairing, abject days, lived through a nightmare haunted by boozing and whoring. His regiment, meanwhile, was ordered back to Camp Sheridan for demobilization. He just managed to catch up with it in Washington, where his buddies found him at the station, with a bottle in his hand, sitting between two prostitutes. He said he had requisitioned a locomotive by pretending he had a message to deliver to the White House. Despite the escapade, in early December he was appointed aide to General J. A. Ryan, in charge of relations with civil authorities.

Scott no sooner returned to Montgomery than he quarreled with Zelda. "My affair still drifts," he wrote in a December 4 letter to old friend Ruth Sturtevant. "But my mind is firmly made up that I will not, shall not, can not, should not, must not marry—still she *is* remarkable."[15] When they made up, the intoxication of a present without tomorrows gave way to a sober awareness that the tomorrows were all-important, since he was still rich in nothing but plans and promises. Nor did his aura of heroic martyrdom blind Zelda to what she owed herself as well as Scott. She was extremely cautious about sharing her life with him—and he was the first to approve of her realism. "She was wise enough," he later noted, "to be rather reluctant."[16]

He was discharged from the army on February 14. When he left Montgomery a few days later, he knew Zelda had been invited by Stubbs to spend the following week in Auburn. But Scott was confident. He was sure as soon as he arrived in New York that he would succeed, and he was wildly elated. Reinforced by his love, he would conquer the world for her. His first telegram to Montgomery sounded like a victory communiqué: "DARLING HEART AMBITION ENTHUSIASM AND CONFIDENCE I DECLARE EVERY-THING GLORIOUS THIS WORLD IS A GAME AND WHILE I FEEL SURE OF YOUR LOVE EVERYTHING IS POSSIBLE I AM IN THE LAND OF AMBITION AND SUCCESS AND MY ONLY HOPE AND FAITH IS THAT MY DARLING HEART WILL BE WITH ME SOON."[17]

Reality, heightened by the abrupt halt in the American war effort and equally hasty demobilization, soon dented his fine enthusiasm. The unprecedented prosperity of the previous four years collapsed in a few weeks when the government canceled most of its military contracts. A grim recession following hard on the boom threatened not only the war industries but the structure of a whole production system that had grown too fast. Two million discharged soldiers were looking for jobs in a recession-lamed economy. Without contacts, with nothing to recommend him but his manner, his army rank and his undistinguished record at Princeton, where his only "diplomas" had been his musical comedies, Fitzgerald made the sterile rounds of the newspaper city rooms looking for a job as a reporter. When seven papers declined his services—he had hoped, he wrote, "to trail murderers by day and do short stories by night"[18]—he began to lose some of the self-assurance that had borne him through college and the army: "All the confidence I had garnered at Princeton and in a haughty career as the army's worst aide-de-camp melted gradually away. Lost and forgotten, I walked quickly from certain places—from the pawn shop where one left the field glasses, from prosperous friends whom one met wearing the suit from before the war, from busy, cheerful offices that were saving the jobs for their own boys from the war."[19]

He was discovering the other side of the coin of which, in his cloistered life at Princeton and in the training camps, he had seen only the shining face. There was, he found, a sordid city hidden behind the white skyscrapers and twinkling lights of the radiant New York he knew as a teenager.

He had not stopped writing, however. From April to June, again putting his novel aside, he wrote nineteen short stories that were inexorably rejected by the magazines to which he sent them; rejection slips, 122 of them, were pinned in a frieze around the wall of his room. He met Paul Dickey, the Princeton composer, and suggested that they collaborate on a musical, but Dickey was a businessman now. Scott tried everything: "I wrote movies. I wrote song lyrics. I wrote complicated advertising schemes. I wrote poems. I wrote sketches. I wrote jokes. Near the end of June I sold one story for thirty dollars."[20] But the story, "Babes in the Wood," was one that had been published in Princeton two years earlier.

Fitzgerald's panic, his horror of the poverty stalking him, of being lost in the crowd, are recalled in a story called "Dalrymple Goes Wrong" and in

The Great Gatsby. Through Jay Gatsby and Bryan Dalrymple he described the bitterness of ex-soldiers thrust jobless into civilian life with no way to survive except crime. One of them turns burglar, the other hires out to the gangster Wolsheim; both, in short, use the honors they won in battle to serve crooked politicians.

Fitzgerald had to make do with a ninety-dollar-a-month job writing billboard advertising slogans for the Barron Collier Advertising Agency. He rented a cheap room at 200 Claremont Avenue, in New York's Morningside Heights district, and began the gray existence of the office workers he would write about so compassionately in *Gatsby*. The young Princeton dandy was now so broke that he had to paper the insides of his shoes against the holes in the soles. He learned about the subway at rush hours, the endless, insipid days at the office, about lonely meals hastily gobbled. For the first time in his life he was poor, and he simply could not get going again on his novel. A certain reluctance appeared in the letters he received from Montgomery. Fitzgerald's bitterness was only intensified by the fact that he continued to see some of his richer friends—Porter Gillespie, for example, with whom he spent a tumultuous night at a ball in Delmonico's that he would re-create in some detail in "May Day."

For four months he lived a miserable life, disappointed in love, doubting his talent, struggling desperately to resolve the dilemma that paralyzed him: winning fame as a writer without losing the job that gave him a chance, however slight, to persuade Zelda to join him in New York. It was a painful time, but profitable; it considerably broadened his knowledge of other people and of himself.

On his arrival in New York he had told his parents that he wished to marry Zelda and had asked his mother to write to her. This mark of interest pleased Zelda, but the letter she wrote him in response to it alarmed him: "I am acquiring myriad wrinkles pondering over a reply to your Mother's note—I'm so dreadfully afraid of appearing fresh or presuming or casual—Most of my correspondents have always been boys, so I am at a loss—now in my hour of need—I really believe this is my first letter to a lady. . . ."[21] He, meanwhile, wrote to Mrs. Sayre although, on Zelda's advice, he held off writing to the judge.

When Zelda received a discouraged letter from Scott, she tried to reassure him: "Please, please don't be so depressed—We'll be married soon, and then these lonesome nights will be over forever. . . . I love your sad tenderness—when I've hurt you—That's one of the reasons I could never be sorry for our quarrels. . . . Scott, there's nothing in all the world I want but you—and your precious love—All the material things are nothing. I'd just hate to live a sordid, colorless existence—because you'd soon love me less—and less—and I'd do anything—anything—to keep your heart for my own. . . . Why don't you feel that I'm waiting—I'll come to you, Lover, when you're ready—Don't—don't ever think of all the things you can't give me. . . ."[22]

Moved by her letter, appeased and reassured, Fitzgerald asked his mother to send him her own engagement ring, which he mailed to Zelda at the end of March. With it went a letter for her to give to Judge Sayre. Fearing her father's reaction, she did not show it to him ("He's so blind, it'll probably be a terrible shock to him"[23]). But she was delighted with the ring and wore it to a dance at the country club. "You can't imagine," she wrote to her fiancé, "what havoc the ring wrought—A whole dance was completely upset last night. . . ."[24] Because he wanted to know how she spent her time, she described in detail such enterprises as her partnership with another girl: ". . . we're 'best friends' to more college boys than Solomon had wives. . . . I have always been inclined toward masculinity. It's such a cheery atmosphere boys radiate—And we do such unique things—"[25] Fitzgerald, champing at the bit, asked Zelda's sister Clothilde, who was living in New York, to help him find an apartment.

On April 15 he took a few days of vacation to go to Montgomery—the first act in a comedy of errors. He thought he would take her back to New York with him, but he returned alone. A note in his *Ledger* reads: "Failure. I used to wonder why they locked princesses in towers."[26] Back in New York, he unburdened himself in a letter to Ruth Sturtevant in Washington, ignoring the fact that he had once assured her he would never marry Zelda.

Zelda, however, was comforted by Scott's visit. "I'm so glad you came," she wrote him, "like Summer, just when I needed you most—and took me, back with you. Waiting doesn't seem so hard now."[27] Nevertheless, she was soon up to her old tricks. She sent Scott a stern note her mother had written after finding a wine spot on her dress: "Zelda: If you have added whiskey to your tobacco you can subtract your Mother. . . . If you prefer the habits of a prostitute don't try to mix them with gentility. Oil and water do not mix."[28]

Act Two: On May 15 Fitzgerald was back in Montgomery and again he left without furthering his plans. And Zelda had had enough of the stream of letters, questions, sentimentality: "I'm so damned tired of being told that you 'used to wonder why they kept princesses in towers'—you've written that, verbatim, in your last *six* letters! It's dreadfully hard to write so very much—and so many of your letters sound forced—I know you love me, Darling, and I love you more than anything in the world, but if its going to be so much longer, we just *can't* keep up this frantic writing."[29]

At the end of May, with Scott's third visit, Act Three put an end to four months of steady correspondence. The South bathed in its sensuous springtime; dance followed dance at the colleges, and Zelda was spending more time in Auburn than in Montgomery. She dallied with a young man from Georgia Tech who was in Montgomery for a golf tournament. Nothing was withheld from Scott; she told him she was planning to spend a long weekend with the young man in Atlanta. But when she returned home, she realized she had gone too far with the Georgian. She had accepted his fraternity pin; in those days, being pinned had a perfectly clear and binding meaning. Zelda sent it back with an affectionate note—which she slipped (inadvertently, she said) into an envelope addressed to Scott.

Furious, despairing, he sent her a letter asking her never to write to him again; this was followed by a telegram announcing his imminent arrival. He demanded that she marry him at once. She refused. Tears, scenes, pleas; Zelda wept in his arms, but she would not give in. She returned his ring and he took the first train north. Fitzgerald would relive those hours in his story "The Sensible Thing," which, he told Maxwell Perkins in a letter on June 1, 1935, was the "story about Zelda and me, all true."[30] In the story's version, "He seized her in his arms and tried literally to kiss her into marrying him at once. When this failed, he broke into a long monologue of self-pity, and ceased only when he saw that he was making himself despicable in her sight. He threatened to leave when he had no intention of leaving, and refused to go when she told him that, after all, it was best that he should."[31]

On his return to New York, Fitzgerald quit his job and went on a three-week binge that ended only with the beginning of Prohibition on July 1. He decided to leave the city and go to his parents' house in St. Paul. There he would try to take his last chance: to rewrite the novel he had put aside nine months before.

On the train he read Hugh Walpole's latest novel, *Fortitude*, which gave him new hope. He thought that " 'if this fellow can get away with it as an author I can too.' His books seemed to me as bad as possible. The principal thing he did was to make unessentials seem important, but was one of the near best-sellers. After that I dug in and wrote my first book."[32]

In the second version of *The Romantic Egotist* he had specifically taken Compton Mackenzie and H. G. Wells as his models, aestheticism and spontaneity as his principles and, as his subject, the thinly disguised events of his boyhood and adolescence. A diffuse prologue announced these rules with slightly smug impertinence: "I am informed that the time has come for a long, rambling picaresque novel. I shall ramble and be picaresque. I shall be intellectual and echo H. G. Wells, and improper like Compton Mackenzie. My form will be very original for it will mingle verse and prose and not be vers libre."[33] This was the version, a first-person narration by Stephen Palms, that Leslie warmly praised, but that Donahoe and Bishop, who had read part or all of it, disliked. In the light of their criticism, Fitzgerald found his own way, abandoning the confessional recital for a truly novelistic form.

Donahoe had been especially critical of Fitzgerald's self-satisfied and tedious cataloging of his juvenile romances. These were presumably taken from his diaries, especially the *Thoughtbook* he kept when he was fourteen. Fitzgerald took the reproach to heart and combined several of these affairs into a single episode—Amory's romance with Myra St. Claire, which ended with a disastrous first kiss—that captured their spirit effectively and economically. Instead of an aimless, static catalog, we get an alert and meaningful scene that advances the action and marks an important stage in the character's development.

Bishop's criticism centered on the book's very structure and its overall conception. He thought the long first-person monologue slowed the dramatic action by so leveling a string of episodes that none of them stood out particularly. "I have a theory novels should be written in scenes," Fitzgerald had once informed Bishop citing Dostoevski and Anatole France as examples.[34] That the lessons his friends taught were absorbed is clear in the final version. Discarding his prologue and his statement of intent, Fitzgerald moved straight into the heart of his story with hilarious portraits of his protagonist's parents. He eliminated a number of minor biographical details. Most important, he adopted a strictly objective point of view by shifting from a first-person narration to a series of scenes in which his hero, Amory Blaine, is seen from outside with a critical detachment that is colored at times with humor, at others with irony. Fitzgerald was no longer content simply to mention events; he makes us see and hear them. He had acquired a sense of dramatic action, of stage direction, making good use of his theatrical experience; his instinctive feeling for dialogue does wonders in the love scenes. He fragmented his book, stressing this fragmentation with subtitles mostly borrowed from Shaw's "Prefaces." This gives *This Side of Paradise* the appearance of a mosaic into which were set older pieces already published in the *Nassau Lit*, poems and bits from his friends' letters, especially four of Fay's letters. His description of the priest's funeral[35] was inspired by a letter Leslie wrote on that occasion. Finally, a letter from Zelda gave him a page at the end of the novel, in which he describes an old Confederate cemetery.

His manuscript, then, was thoroughly revised and radically shortened; its original title, *The Romantic Egotist*, was now the title of the first part of *This Side of Paradise*. A second part, "The Education of a Personage," contains most of the things that had happened since Scribner's final rejection of the manuscript and his meeting Zelda a year earlier—or, if not the events themselves, their reverberations on the author's sensitivity. There are allusions to most of Fitzgerald's tribulations after his discharge from the army, his discovery of New York's seamy side, his break with Zelda, his three-week bender.

All the material in "The Education of a Personage" was new except for the first and third chapters, the third had been written a year before, as can be seen from an August 1918 letter in which Fay expressed his surprise to find that the Eleanor episode was based on an incident from the priest's youth: "I seemed to go back twenty-five years. . . . I never realized that I told you so much about her. . . . How you got it in I don't know. . . . Really the whole thing is most startling."[36] Only the heroine's name is changed, and she reads Brooke instead of Swinburne. The episode is so frantic, especially Eleanor's attempt at suicide by riding her horse off a cliff, that unless the author altered the story, Fay had let his imagination run away with him. A girl Fitzgerald met during his stay with the Bishops in Charles Town in July 1917 alleged that the chapter had been taken from her life. "J. B. told me that Scott had said I was his model for Eleanor in the section called 'Young Irony,'" she would write. "I saw a vague resemblance to myself in the description of Eleanor's 'green eyes and nondescript hair,' and there were A's-E's horseback rides through mountain paths together, and the rural setting which was so obviously inspired by the country around Charles Town."[37] On the eve of his departure Fitzgerald gave her a sonnet dedicated "to Fluff Beckwith, the only begetter of this sonnet."[38] That "only" was obviously suspect, but it was not until after his death that, to her surprise, she saw the poem published with the title *For Cecilia*.

Fitzgerald's first chapter in the section, "The Debutante," picks up the title and setting of a story inspired by his break with Ginevra King and published in January 1917. The situation is the same, but the narrative was much changed and Zelda is the model for the version in the novel; even her style is caught in a passage taken from one of her letters. The breaking off of Amory's engagement (he is too poor for the girl) to Rosalind, who is too aware of her needs to accept him as a husband, poignantly evokes the last meeting of Zelda and Scott in Montgomery. His two defeats in love, though two years apart, were blended in a common experience that would remain at the core of Fitzgerald's sensibility. This is the only episode from his recent past to be treated so intensely and in such detail in the novel. Few direct autobiographical allusions are found to his four months in New York, except for Amory's job with an ad agency and his unhappiness at being a poor man lost in the crowd. This slice of Fitzgerald's life would not be exploited until later, in such stories as "May Day," just as his army experience remained buried until he wrote his second book, *The Beautiful and Damned*.

What happened next reads like a fairy tale. His manuscript, sent to Scribner September 3 under its new title, *This Side of Paradise*, was accepted on September 16. Fitzgerald, who had hired on as a member of a railroad labor gang, immediately quit the job. So much for his experience of proletarian life in New York and St. Paul.

In his reply to Maxwell Perkins, his editor at Scribner's, he urged that the book be issued soon, before the end of the year if possible; he hoped to get married on his royalties. And he announced that he had started work on a new book, *The Demon Lover*, which would take him about a year to complete. When he was told a few days later that the novel would not appear before spring and that he had better be under no illusions about how much he might earn from it, Fitzgerald turned to a source of more immediate income, the short-story market. He wrote new ones. He returned to old ones that had been widely rejected and, in the light of his new experience, revised their structures, altered details, changed their titles and resubmitted them. Some were accepted by the same people who had previously turned them down. That fall and winter, before *This Side of Paradise* came out, he sold fifteen stories and began seriously to think of himself as a writer: "While I waited for the novel to appear, the metamorphosis of amateur into professional began to take place—a sort of stitching together of your whole life into a pattern of work, so that the end of one job is automatically the beginning of another."³⁹

That he was starting to reap the fruit of his perseverance reinforced his feeling of professionalism. In October *The Smart Set* sent him a check for $215 in payment for six stories. In November came another for $300 for two stories bought by *Scribner's Magazine*. With the money he could return to Montgomery and try to patch things up with Zelda. When he had written to her a month earlier to tell her that his novel had been accepted and that he wanted to see her, she had answered eagerly. "I'm mighty glad you're coming," she wrote him. "I've been wanting to see you (which you probably knew) but I *couldn't* ask you. . . . It's fine and I'm tickled to death."⁴⁰

He took with him a copy of his manuscript and the bottle of gin Zelda had asked for. A letter she wrote after his visit showed how well the reunion had gone: "I am very proud of you—I hate to say this, but I don't *think* I had much confidence in you at first. . . . It's so nice to know that you really *can* do things. . . . I believe if I had deliberately decided on a sweetheart, he'd have been you—"⁴¹ By the time they separated, they had agreed to marry after the book came out.

Back in New York he learned that *The Saturday Evening Post,* one of the hardest of the mass-circulation magazines to crack, had bought his story "Head and Shoulders" for $400. This breakthrough he owed to Harold Ober, who worked for the Paul Reynolds literary agency, recommended to Fitzgerald by St. Paul novelist Grace Flandrau. After payment of the agent's fee, Fitzgerald's work earned a net total of $879 in the last three months of 1919. Every time he sold a story, he wired Montgomery; four pages of Zelda's scrapbook are filled with these victory bulletins. There was no more doubting now: he could live by writing.

Fitzgerald invited some Princeton friends to help him celebrate. They found him in his room at the Knickerbocker Hotel, already a little drunk and surrounded by valets helping him get ready for the party; twenty- and fifty-dollar bills were crammed partway into his pockets with enough left showing to let everyone see he was rich. He insisted on escorting everyone to the man he called "his" bootlegger, who would supply each of them with a bottle of illegal whiskey, courtesy of F. Scott Fitzgerald. When he left the hotel, he forgot to turn off the taps in the bathtub and the room was flooded. This was how he celebrated his entry on a literary career, naively, arrogantly, ostentatiously, as though, like a vindictive child, to efface the humiliation he had suffered. Three months earlier this twenty-four-year-old man could not have bought a pal a Coca-Cola; now, with money that seemed to have fallen from heaven, he was as disoriented and scatterbrained as a shoe clerk who suddenly comes into a fortune. His crude drinking aside, this Princetonian behaved as foolishly as H. G. Wells's newly rich Kipps.[42]

Fitzgerald wrote to Perkins that when he returned to St. Paul, he was in a state of nervous exhaustion from boozing. This did not prevent him from churning out a story in one eleven-hour stretch and then spending nine hours more correcting and recopying it; he began writing it at eight o'clock one morning and mailed it at five o'clock the following morning. Five hundred dollars. In four hours he revised two others that had been rejected the previous spring; a week later Reynolds sold them to the *Post* for $1,000. By mid-January Fitzgerald felt prosperous enough to rest up in New Orleans. He may have been worried about his health, too. He had caught a chill in New York that left him with a persistent cough, and he told Perkins he was afraid he had tuberculosis. He nevertheless went South with the plan for his new novel, and he asked his editor what the deadline would be for fall publication. For the first time he wondered if he could finish it without interruption; the problem would recur often. "Do you think a book on the type of my first one would have any chance of being accepted for serial publication in any magazine?" he asked. "I want to start [the novel], but I don't want to get broke in the middle and start in and have to write short stories again because I don't enjoy it and just do it for money."[43] He also wondered about the possibility of publishing a collection of his stories in book form.

New Orleans is not far from Montgomery and he went there twice, picking up again with Zelda. On his second visit they informed the Sayres of their engagement. Although her parents were Episcopalians, they did not object to their daughter's marrying a Catholic; Mrs. Sayre wrote as much to Fitzgerald. "A good Catholic," she assured him, "is as good as any other man and that is good enough. It will take more than the Pope to make Zelda good: you will have to call on God Almighty direct."[44]

Film rights to "Head and Shoulders" were sold for $2,500, and Fitzgerald spent the money on a platinum-and-diamond wristwatch for Zelda; it was one of the luxury items in the Fifth Avenue shopwindow described in "May Day." But he did not like New Orleans, where he lived in a boardinghouse on Prytonia Street. He could not get his creative juices flowing, and after a month in the South he put his novel aside and went back to New York. On February 11 he moved into the Allerton Hotel on 39th

Street and began work on two stories, "The Jelly Bean," based on his impressions of Alabama, and "May Day." The latter work, probably distilled from the manuscript of his aborted novel, was completed in the Cottage Club at Princeton, where he went in March to await Zelda. They still had not set a wedding date. On the day Fitzgerald received the first copy off the press of *This Side of Paradise*, he ran across Lawton Campbell, a Princetonian from Montgomery, and asked him for news of Zelda. "I phoned her long distance last night," Scott told Campbell. "She's still on the fence and I may have to go to Montgomery to get her but I believe this will do the trick."[45] He was right: the wedding was officially announced for March 20 and Zelda went to New York with her sister Marjorie.

Her other two sisters, Clothilde and Rosalind, and their husbands attended the wedding, but neither the elder Sayres nor the Fitzgeralds turned up. Only one friend of Scott's was invited: Ludlow Fowler, who acted as best man. The marriage took place at around noon on Easter Saturday, April 3, in the rectory of St. Patrick's Cathedral. After concluding the ceremony, the officiating priest, prompted by the same ecumenical spirit that had moved Mrs. Sayre, told them, "You be a good Episcopalian, Zelda, and Scott, you be a good Catholic, and you'll get along fine."[46]

Nancy Milford, in her biography of Zelda, portrays her heroine this way: "Zelda wore a suit of midnight blue with a matching hat trimmed with leather ribbons and buckles; she carried a bouquet of orchids and small white flowers. It was a brilliantly sunny day and when they stepped outside the cathedral Zelda looked for all the world like a young goddess of spring, with Scott at her side as consort."[47] To complete the picture, we have the impression Scott had made a few days earlier on a writer to whom he delivered a copy of his book: "He looked exactly like an Archangel, and he had the strange aloofness and evasiveness you associate with Archangels. He was beautiful and a little eerie."[48] Later on, Zelda would recall her first meeting with Scott in similar terms: "There seemed to be some heavenly support beneath his shoulder blades that lifted his feet from the ground in ecstatic suspension, as if he secretly enjoyed the ability to fly but was walking as a compromise to convention."[49]

The goddess and the archangel. This was more than the priest could have imagined, but it was how, in this century's springtime, Zelda and Scott entered this side of paradise.

6. SUCCESS, LOVE AND MONEY

(1920)

In six months Fitzgerald had reversed a seemingly desperate position, situating himself as a writer whose stories appeared in such high-voltage literary magazines as *The Smart Set* and *Scribner's Magazine* as well as the mass-audience *Saturday Evening Post*. His book was selling extraordinarily well for a first novel, far better than his publisher had hoped, exceeding even his own expectations in its first week out. "I told the Scribner Company that I didn't expect my novel to sell more than twenty thousand copies and when the laughter died away I was told that a sale of five thousand was excellent for a first novel," he later wrote. "I think it was a week after publication that it passed the twenty thousand mark, but I took myself so seriously that I didn't even think it was funny."[1] The book sold 40,000 copies in its first year, a genuine success, though not to be compared with Sinclair Lewis's best-seller *Main Street*, published the same year, which sold 180,000 copies in its first six months. Fitzgerald's earnings—and, remember, he wrote for a living—were relatively disappointing. "The book didn't make me as rich as I thought it would nor as you would suspect from the vogue and the way it was talked about," he commented some years later.[2] In 1920 his novel brought him just over $6,000, a third of that year's income. It earned a little less the following year, and from then on the royalties from it declined steadily; four years after its publication, 50,000 copies of *This Side of Paradise* had been sold, bringing its author a total of under $12,000. Now he faced a choice: to write for the big weeklies, which would be far more lucrative, or devote himself to his art, obey his deepest impulse, and live in comparative poverty. The dilemma had already arisen in 1920, when he had to interrupt work on his new novel for lack of cash. He had accordingly dismembered his early chapters and turned them into stories he tried to sell to *The Smart Set*. "May Day" is probably one of these; its style is much more polished than that of the usual run of Fitzgerald's magazine pieces. But it was too realistic, too gloomy to qualify for the popular magazines. So the choice was not only between novels and short stories but also between the kinds of stories magazine editors would buy and those he enjoyed writing. Because of Zelda's demands, his own taste for high living and his private certainty that he could bet and win on both wheels, he increasingly spent more than he earned. He was almost constantly in debt. This forced him to write stories he was the first to despise. A trivial piece like "The Camel's Pack," written in one twenty-four-hour go, was sold to the *Post* for $500, but the magazine turned down the immensely superior "May Day," which finally brought Fitzgerald a mere $200. Banking on his talent and his facility, he earned more in 1920 than he could have hoped for ($18,850) and ended the year over $1,200 in the red. His bank turned down his application for a loan. He was incapable of writing the commercial novel expected of him and for which he had been paid a substantial advance. In a letter to Perkins he confessed, "I've made half a dozen starts yesterday and today and I'll go mad if I have to do another Debutante, which is what they want."³ The letter ended with a plea for a further advance of $1,600 on the novel to come. This was the start of a process that would be repeated as long as he lived.

As a writer, Fitzgerald had to live by the pendulum because as soon as he stopped grinding out pulp for the big magazines and turned to serious writing, he found himself on the brink of financial disaster. His independence was measured by the number of stories he had to produce each year. But his dependence increased with his needs, which grew grander by the year; the temptation to take the easy way was reinforced by the rapidly rising fees he commanded, especially from the *Post*. His first story for the magazine had brought him $400; two years later, thanks to Ober's efforts, Fitzgerald was getting $1,500 for a story, and this went up to $2,000 in 1925, to $3,000 in 1927, to $4,000 in 1929, a rate that was maintained into 1932, in the trough of the Depression. And it was all in constant dollars because the cost of living remained practically stationary throughout the twenties.

The *Post* was his first source of big money; it ran six of his stories in 1920. Then Ober began playing publications against each other, establishing a precedent by offering a story to several magazines at once. Such organs as *Metropolitan Magazine, Collier's, Hearst's International* were constantly outbidding each other in the hope of bringing Fitzgerald into their permanent stables. His name, however, was to become a fixture in the *Post*, to which he sold his whole story output after 1927. The relationship, clearly, had nothing to do with literature. It was basically the result of editor-in-chief George H. Lorimer's drive to make the *Post* America's leading weekly magazine.

Lorimer was fifty-one when he bought his first Fitzgerald story, and he had been running the *Post* for twenty years; even before the war he had doubled the magazine's circulation to two million. The *Post*'s nearest rival was Edward Bok's *Ladies' Home Journal*, the world's most widely read magazine, which, like the *Post*, belonged to Philadelphia's Curtis Publications.

At Bok's retirement in 1919 the two magazines had sharply different readerships. The *Journal* was addressed chiefly to a decidedly conventional family clientele still living by Victorian standards. Bok's skill lay in choosing and eliciting the kind of editorial matter that would sell the wares advertised in the magazine, a brilliance that boosted the *Journal*'s advertising revenue to $12 million a year. The *Post* appealed mainly to men: financial, economic and sports sections, action stories by such illustrious contributors as Rudyard Kipling, Jack London and Stephen Crane. When Bok left, Lorimer adopted his policies and set out to win his market.

The Ladies' Home Journal had not kept pace with the rapid changes in manners that shook postwar America. Its notion of the family rested on generations-old values and prejudices. The new fashions, new products, especially cosmetics, were echoed only faintly in its pages. Lorimer was shrewd enough to see the importance of the changes that would create a new generation of consumers with needs totally different from their elders'. Wartime prosperity had given these young people a buying power that only older people had wielded in the past. Lorimer's whole effort was now concentrated on capturing this new advertising market. So the *Post* adapted its editorial policy to the new demands being heard on every side. This in turn converted the magazine into a major influence on a whole generation of new readers, intensifying and spreading the changes in habits, contributing mightily to the new atmosphere in the postwar United States. Historian Elizabeth Stevenson, a specialist in the period, stresses the *Post*'s influence and, through it, that of advertising in general. "It has become a commonplace notion," she wrote, "that an uncritical, ambitious, rising culture becomes itself through imitating the life of advertisements. In the Twenties in such a typical magazine as *The Saturday Evening Post*, one can see it begin to happen. . . . This was probably the first time that on a giant scale a society developed a set of manners, a provision of wants and needs, and a faith from the selling and buying of goods."[4]

In the same month in which Bok resigned, Lorimer received a Fitzgerald manuscript that expressed the new spirit; it was exactly the kind of story to attract young readers whose reading matter until then could have been written by their grandparents. Jazz and dancing vibrated in its pages. The story was written in the language the new generation was speaking; its characters paraded the clothes young people were wearing or longed to wear, the hairdos and makeup they dreamed of wearing, the romantic situations that matched their imaginings. To the magazine flocked advertisers who were finding few other mass-circulation outlets in which to vaunt products specially conceived for a clientele that had been born with the century. Within months advertising volume grew, and its message came increasingly in tune with the manners and demands depicted in Fitzgerald's stories. In May 1920, for example, "Bernice Bobs Her Hair" appeared and scandalized parents who were indignant at the thought that their daughters might wear their hair short; only two years earlier this had still been a sign of dangerously subversive ideas.* Letters of protest cascaded down upon Lorimer, but he stood his ground, convinced that he was moving with history. The cover girl in the November issue wore her hair in a boyish bob. Cosmetics ads had already run in the previous issue, and the new dances had made their appearance.

Lorimer was taking risks, but he knew precisely how far he could go; he perceived that borderline of controlled audacity that could attract new readers without alienating old ones. His strategy was based on respect for the American Way of Life. To encourage individual initiative in the young, in businessmen and admen was at once honorable, moral and profitable. But his approach cried "No!" to subversion. The American dream could not accommodate license or pessimism. Love that did not aspire to marriage, stories with unhappy endings had no place in the *Post*. "May Day" and "The Jelly Bean," chaste as they are, were deemed undesirable. The stories Lorimer wanted had to be light, witty, modish enough to please teenagers, but moral enough to appease parents—the tone of the day's hit musical comedies. This was exactly what Fitzgerald's first stories offered. In him *The Saturday Evening Post* found a writer who could help make it America's leading magazine. In 1925 it had nearly three million readers, and every issue earned $5 million from its advertising.

As his story price rose, however, Fitzgerald knew that the stories' quality suffered from the constraints imposed on him. He complained to Ober, who could not get a fifth of the price for so excellent a story as "The Diamond as Big as the Ritz" that he could for the trashy "The Popular Girl," which the *Post* bought. But, he concluded, "by God and Lorimer, I'm going to make a fortune yet."[5] Alluding to "The Popular Girl," published in 1922, he remarked to his agent that he was now merely reworking the subjects of his early stories, but that they had lost their old vitality. It was all coming down to a question of skill: "I've learned the tricks better and am technically more proficient."[6]

Lorimer asked nothing more of him. To the editor Fitzgerald was simply a well-paid professional like his other advertising men. And if he insisted on writing subversive stories, there were plenty of others like him who had also learned the tricks, who were equally good technicians and were ready to replace him without missing a step. He was preferred because his name was a kind of trademark, a label of quality on his products. But lesser brands also sold well.

Similarly, one of the reasons for the success of *This Side of Paradise* was that, for the first time, a talented novelist had dared to describe the real morals of the new middle-class generation instead of the fictitious version

---

* In November 1918 the manager of the Palm Garden in New York rented the place to a lady of fashion who wanted to stage a political rally. The participants turned out to be pro-Bolshevik, and the meeting broke up in a riot. The manager admitted that if he had noticed the woman's short haircut, he would never have rented the hall to her.

bequeathed by literary tradition. All the piously preserved Victorian illusions about pure and modest girls carefully reared to be good wives and mothers were shattered by the eruption on the literary scene of young bacchantes who smoked, drank, used makeup and danced, no longer to the music of romantic violins but to the cacophony of barbarous saxophones. The old model of elegant, vaporously—curvaceous young womanhood had been captured by Charles Dana Gibson, whose Gibson Girl, born the same year as Fitzgerald, remained the popular ideal until the war; now she was rapidly vanishing behind the image of the flapper portrayed by John Held, Jr., whose caricatures celebrated the new woman: boyish, flat-chested, flat-hipped, her hair cut short under a cloche hat, her arms and knees bare, a cigarette held in one hand, a glass in the other.

Manners that were at first limited to a wealthy and self-indulgent class—the one Fitzgerald wrote about—were propagated throughout the country by the press, radio (the first public broadcast took place in November 1920) and the movies (in 1920 Fitzgerald sold the film rights to four of his stories). Rapid development of the automobile, especially the cheaper, mass-produced Model T Ford, enabled young people to escape family supervision and neighborhood gossip. The growing vogue for sedans encouraged petting in cars, a typically American sport that moved one judge in a small Midwestern city to deplore the automobile as a "house of prostitution on wheels."

This revolution in manners brought about corresponding changes in industry. Beauty products were booming, but other lines were reeling. Cotton fabrics, for example, were out, rayon and silk were in; rayon production rose from eight million pounds in 1920 to fifty-three million pounds five years later, and by 1926 only 33 percent of women's clothes were made of cotton. Makers of slips and corsets were becalmed. From 1913 to 1928 the annual yardage of fabrics needed to clothe a woman dropped from eighteen to six and one-half. Skirt lengths became a thermometer showing the symbolic degree of a modern woman's liberation. In 1919 a hem could be no more than eight inches from the ground, which supposedly represented 10 percent of a woman's height. By 1920 the figure was 20 percent. In 1923, under the influence of French fashions marketed by American manufacturers but accepted only reluctantly by American women, it dropped to 10 percent again, but it climbed back up to more than 20 percent in 1925 and was finally stabilized at around 25 percent—above the knee—until 1929. As skirts and hair shortened, women stripped off layer after layer of the clothing that had enshrouded them. Flesh-colored silk stockings (even working-class schoolgirls were soon refusing to wear the traditional cotton stockings) showed off their legs, emphasizing the trend toward lightness and exposure.

All these changes converged. They aimed at the destruction of a quasi-oriental notion of Woman, the violin-shaped woman, full-breasted, wasp-waisted, lavishly hipped, a pizzicato creature, languorous and swooning, reclusive, idle, living only for the moment when marriage and maternity at last brought out her true self. Now she was being replaced by the clarinet woman: youthful, strident and boyish, a little piping, a little acid, unmysterious and disillusioned; she vied with and matched men in sports, at work, in love, expecting nothing from them but confirmation of her independence. In love duets it was she who chose the key and sounded the A. The new woman rejected boredom and monotony. She wanted to be entertained, and her partner had to turn wizard, change the humdrum into something magical, transform life itself.

Zelda is surely recognizable in this composite portrait, she being both inspiration for this new feminine image and inspired by it in building her own personality. And the readers of *This Side of Paradise* and the *Post* stories, those who made them successful, also saw themselves, saw the kind of people they wanted to become, in the female characters drawn from Zelda. In his first stories, from "The Offshore Pirate" to "Rags Martin-Jones," wildly exuberant stories written, we sense, with the jubilation, the joy of invention, Fitzgerald turned his young swains into impresarios, stage directors, organizers of impromptu celebrations to amaze and charm their girls. Jaded and indifferent, the girls seem to say, "Amuse me! Surprise me!" They have turned themselves into spectators of some frenetic comic opera that must prove its worth through movement, that works only if it sweeps its audiences up in its dynamism and jollity. Convince, amuse, bewitch: the very image of the role the author must play to the *Post*, to its readers and to Zelda. A mass-media Scheherazade, he indeed had to surprise and amuse—to sell ads, sell his stories, sell himself, too, on the idea of writing them when the game began to pall.

And then it was his turn to judge. In Fitzgeraldian society the women are the great predators, consumers on a dizzying shopping spree through his stories. It's as though, in keeping with Thorstein Veblen's *Theory of the Leisure Class*, they had to keep buying to demonstrate their husbands' social status; this was their function, as earning money was a man's. Freely accepted at marriage, this function became a burden after a few years: "We make an agreement with children that they can sit in the audience without helping to make the play . . . but if they still sit in the audience after they're grown, somebody's got to work double time for them, so that they can enjoy the light and glitter of the world."[7] At the end of the twenties, in a story entitled "The Swimmers," whose accomplished heroine is a worthy sister to Rosalind and Gloria, Fitzgerald summed up his conclusions concerning the American woman's unquestionable supremacy in the battle of the sexes: "In her grace, at once exquisite and hardy, she was that perfect type of American girl that makes one wonder if the male is not being sacrificed to it, much as, in the last century, the lower strata in England were sacrificed to produce the governing class."[8]

This was his judgment of a model he did not invent, but which he helped create and which, as a good adman, he sold by the millions. Pygmalion is subjugated and dispossessed by the statue he carves—this is also the subject of the story in which the protagonists are named Scott and Zelda Fitzgerald.

In 1920 the chrysalis became a butterfly. Zelda was out of her usual element—where violin-women still maintained prewar traditions and fashions—and, despite her quickness, her frills and flounces jarred a bit on New York elegance. Scott contacted Marie Hersey, his old friend from St. Paul, who had gone to Vassar and knew New York well. He asked her to steer Zelda through the chic shops and tactfully persuade her to change her wardrobe. The first thing bought was a Patou suit, which, feeling strange, she charged to Scott for the first time. Thirteen years later she came across the suit, badly moth-eaten, in a trunk; Scott noted that "we are glad—oh, so relieved, to find it devastated at last."[9]

Her apprenticeship was brief; she did not have to put up for long with another woman's advice. Soon she had shed her provincial excesses and set out to conquer New York with nothing but her velvety Southern accent, the dissonances in her line of chatter and a coarse, roughneck bluntness. Other guides were more willingly accepted because she met them by chance and because they did not try to proselytize her; they were young writers introduced by Scott; by poking fun at her, having fun with her and, finally, being made fun of by her, they gave her the big-city gloss she lacked.

Within a few months she and Scott were thought to embody the spirit of New York. Not Edith Wharton's aristocratic New York, nor the poor man's New York of Stephen Crane and Theodore Dreiser, but a brand-new, luxurious, postwar New York, its face changed by a building boom, peopled by a new generation come from all over the country with money and ambition but without preconceived notions, showing the cultural tint daubed on them by the universities. This was the New York of the great eastward rush so shrewdly analyzed by Nick Carraway in the opening pages of *Gatsby*, a city of big hotels and small cliques, Successville, whether on Wall Street or Broadway or in Greenwich Village. Scott later recalled it in his essay "My Lost City": "Then, for just a moment, the 'younger generation' idea became a fusion of many elements in New York life . . . . For just a moment, before it was demonstrated that I was unable to play the role, I, who knew less of New York than any reporter of six months' standing . . . was pushed into the position not only of spokesman for the time but of the typical product of that same moment. I, or rather it was 'we' now, did not know exactly what New York expected of us and found it rather confusing. . . . Actually our 'contacts' included half a dozen unmarried college friends and a few new literary acquaintances. . . . Finding no nucleus to which we could cling, we became a small nucleus ourselves and gradually we fitted our disruptive personalities into the contemporary scene of New York."[10]

The newlyweds spent their honeymoon at the Biltmore Hotel, which was favored by Princetonians. Old college chums soon began dropping into room 2109. These included Fowler, their best man, as well as Lawton Campbell, the Montgomeryite who was a friend to both Scott and Zelda. There was also Alexander McKaig, former editor of the *Daily Princetonian*, who was now living with his mother and working in advertising. A short, baby-faced man with curly hair parted in the middle, McKaig liked to rub shoulders with his more gifted friends in the hope of someday making a name for himself in literature. The diary he kept at that period provides valuable glimpses of the Fitzgeralds, to whom he paid assiduous court. His first entry concerning them, written a few days after their marriage, is hardly flattering to Zelda and not at all optimistic about the couple's future. "Called on Scott Fitz and his bride," he noted. "Latter temperamental small-town Southern belle. Chews gum. Shows knees. I don't think marriage can succeed. Both drinking heavily. Think they will be divorced in three years. Scott write something big—then die in a garret at thirty-two."[11]

Edmund Wilson, meanwhile, had fallen in love with Edna St. Vincent Millay. He shared an apartment with three friends, and one of them was terribly shocked the day he saw her emerge naked from their bathroom. Wilson left this minicommune and moved in with Ted Paramore, an ex-Princetonian Don Juan; the layout of his huge apartment allowed each man to receive his mistress in private. Soon after his return from France in the summer of 1919, young Wilson had gone to work for the literary review *Vanity Fair*. When his friends Dorothy Parker and Robert Benchley quit the magazine and he became its managing editor, he hired John Bishop, who was also back in New York. Both were soon interested in Edna Millay, who contributed an occasional poem to the magazine. Bishop sometimes stayed in the opulent bachelor apartment of another college friend, Townsend Martin, a globe-trotter who was well established in international society. The place suited John's aesthetic tastes; he liked to receive friends there swathed in one of Martin's damask dressing gowns against a backdrop of Japanese screens and a canopied Renaissance bed. He blossomed in its atmosphere of Regency libertinism.

When Wilson and Bishop called on Fitzgerald and saw Zelda for the first time, she was lying languidly—and very prettily, Wilson reported—on a divan. They were served fashionable orange blossom cocktails and promised to come again.

Marriage had not instantly squelched Zelda's flirtatiousness. She immediately made plays for the most attractive of the bachelors, Bishop, the mysterious sensualist, and Martin, the elegant man of the world. When she subsided in their arms and offered her lips to be kissed, Fitzgerald, magnanimously, made no objection. They had not been at the wedding, he

volunteered, and they at least had as much right as the others to a share of
the kissing. But, Wilson observed, "when Zelda rushed into John's room just
as he was going to bed and insisted that she was going to spend the night
there, and when she cornered Townsend in the bathroom and demanded
that he should give her a bath, he began to become a little worried and even
huffy."[12] She told Bishop: "John, I like you better than anybody in the
world: I never feel safe with you! I only like men who kiss as a means to an
end. I never know how to treat the other kind."[13]

Wilson, who doted on racy details (in his memoirs he gave a full account
of Paramore's technique of seduction) and loved nonsense, was delighted by
the things Zelda said. For example, he cited her explanation of how her
confidences to Bishop, McKaig and Martin differed: "When I'm with John,
I say, 'Well, John, you and I are the only real artists,' and when I'm with
Alex, I say, 'You and I are the only ones who understand the common man,'
and when I'm with Townsend, I say: 'Well, Townsend, you and I are the
only ones who are really interested in ourselves,' but when I'm alone, I say:
'Well, Fitz, you're the only one!' "[14]

Wilson was too infatuated with Edna Millay to flirt with Zelda. McKaig
had this to say about *that* affair: "Bunny evidently much in love with her.
Not much chance to get impression from her myself, though I think from
her verse she must be a genius. Modern Sappho. Eighteen love affairs and
now Bunny is thinking of marrying her."[15] Bunny nonetheless tolerated her
cuddling with Bishop. Here is how he describes their farewell evening before his departure for France on a story assignment for *Vanity Fair:* "After
dinner, sitting on her daybed, John and I held Edna in our arms—according
to an arrangement insisted upon by herself—I her lower half and John her
upper—with a polite exchange of pleasantries as to which had the better
share. She referred to us, I was told, as 'the choir boys of hell' and complained that our both being in love with her had not even broken up our
friendship."[16]

Millay—we remember her image of Fitzgerald as a diamond in a stupid
old woman's hands—was nevertheless the only member of the group to recognize a "Byronic trait"[17] in Scott, doubtless a temperamental affinity in the
woman four years his senior who had championed nonconformism in
Greenwich Village. She was, after all, famous for a quatrain that summed
up her approach to life:

> *My candle burns at both ends;*
> *It will not last the night;*
> *But, ah, my foes, and, oh, my friends—*
> *It gives a lovely light.*[18]

Another person who respected Fitzgerald's talent, if not Fitzgerald himself, was Edna's lover, Wilson. McKaig noted this in his diary; the entry for

August 31, 1920, tells of "discussing with John the fact that of entire group of eight or ten only one man believes in another—Wilson in him."

Three weeks after they were married, Scott proposed that Zelda get to know Princeton. But it was Princeton that got to know Zelda. She somersaulted down sacrosanct Prospect Avenue and had her omelet flamed in brandy at the Cottage Club. Scott introduced her to his friends as his mistress; the joke fell flat and Fitzgerald got drunk, started a fight and wound up with two black eyes.

On May 1 he went back to the college with Wilson and Bishop for a *Lit* dinner. Intent on celebrating the rites of spring and of Literature, they came equipped with props borrowed from a theater: lyre, gilded wings, laurel wreaths. They went looking for Gauss and crowned him on the central green after a long verse speech improvised by Fitzgerald. Then, while his two friends went to their clubs, Scott, tootling on a shepherd's pipe, danced his way toward the Cottage, a wreath askew on his brow, wings fixed to his shoulders, looking "like a tarnished Apollo with the two black eyes," Wilson wrote in a poem he sent to Millay. ". . . But looking like Apollo just the same, with the sun in his pale yellow hair."[19] When the slightly sozzled Apollo entered the Cottage Club, its president barred the way and informed him that the members, outraged by his conduct the previous week, had decided, in agreement with university authorities, to expel him. When Fitzgerald tried to defend his actions, he was seized by the shoulders and tossed out through a rear window. Furious and humiliated, he marched to the railroad station without seeing Wilson and Bishop and took the seven o'clock train to New York; he was not to set foot in Princeton again for seven years.

Gauss was shocked by what had happened; after all, those who clamored for Fitzgerald's expulsion had also been drinking that day. Nearly ten years later, when he too was having his troubles at Princeton, the teacher recalled the incident with a kind of wry nostalgia: "I remember with a good deal of feeling how a number of years ago a number of respectable evangelists in the cause of letters came down to Princeton crowned with laurels to reestablish the cult of Apollo and what a scandal this was to bluenosed respectability. Yet the aim was a worthy one."[20]

What shocked Princeton delighted the New York gossip writers. Anecdotes galore detailed how Fitzgerald, that "disruptive little nucleus" launched into orbit in the big town's nightlife, had very quickly acquired the notoriety generally reserved up to then for publicity-hungry actors. Scott, they reported, undressed in the theater while attending a musical; Zelda dived fully dressed into the Pulitzer fountain, naked into the one on Union Square, and danced on a cabaret table; Scott blanked out on a drunken brawl and came to the next morning to see a headline reporting that "Fitzgerald Knocks Officer This Side of Paradise."[21] The couple's first meeting with Dorothy Parker was typical. She had already met Scott the previous fall, and he had told her "he was going to marry the most beautiful girl in Alabama *and* Georgia!"[22] But even Mrs. Parker was surprised to see Zelda riding down Fifth Avenue astride the hood of a taxi with Scott sitting on the roof. She decided they had a childish need to shock people, but that they had to be forgiven for their natural grace. "They did both look as though they had just stepped out of the sun," she said; "their youth was striking. *Everyone* wanted to meet him."[23] Mrs. Parker thought Zelda attractive when she was caught up in her own whirlwind of words and gestures, but that her face at rest was ordinary: "I never thought she was beautiful. She was very blond with a candy box face and little bow mouth, very much on a small scale and there was something petulant about her. If she didn't like something she sulked; I didn't find that an attractive trait."[24]

Asked to leave the Biltmore, where they upset a clientele unaccustomed to seeing a man walk the halls on his hands, they moved to the Commodore; there too they caused talk when they bought their first car. "A man sold us a broken Marmon," Scott recalled, "and a wild burst of friends spent half an hour revolving in the revolving door."[25]

Still, the city's pleasures no longer satisfied Zelda's vitality. She was used to an outdoor life; she loved to swim and dive, and Scott thought it was time to get back to work in a quiet country retreat. Always helpful, Ruth Sturtevant organized a stay for them on the shores of Lake Champlain. On the way there, however, they heard that the water in the lake was icy and impossible to swim in. They veered off toward the coast and in Westport, Connecticut, found a rustic cottage near a beach. Charmed by it, they immediately signed a five-month lease, unpacked their bags and hired a very small Japanese houseboy. That was on May 14. Unfortunately, Westport was an easy train ride from New York, and the temptation to invite friends down for weekends was hard to resist. Fowler, for example, soon received a letter from Zelda informing him that "we have a house with a room for you and a ruined automobile because I drove it over a fire-plug and completely deintestined it . . . and much health and fresh-air which is all very nice and picturesque, although I'm still partial to Coney Island."[26]

A month later, bored with rural tranquillity, they plunged back into an interminable round of parties that lasted for days and left them exhausted, disgusted with themselves and quarrelling. McKaig wrote in his diary on June 13, 1920: "Visit Fitz at Westport. . . . Terrible party. Fitz and Zelda fighting like mad. Say themselves marriage can't succeed."

That summer Zelda added a prize catch to her bag of admirers: theater critic George Jean Nathan, coeditor with H. L. Mencken of *The Smart Set*. Dark and suave, with burning, cynical eyes, he was some fifteen years older than Scott, who admired his urbanity and wit. Nathan at once paid ardent court to Zelda, who responded in her usual lively manner, under Scott's approving eye if we are to believe Nathan's testimony. "While Zelda and I were accustomed to engage publicly in obviously exaggerated endearing terms," he later wrote, "which Scott appreciated and which were in the accepted vein of Dixie chivalry, our close friendship was never interrupted."[27]

On the evening of July 4 Zelda thought the party was going cold and turned in a fire alarm, bringing three fire trucks and the fire chief's wrath down upon them. When he asked where the fire was, Zelda pounded her breast melodramatically and replied, "Here!" They were summoned to court a week later, but the case was dismissed for lack of evidence. Scott grandly offered to pay the cost of the trucks' run.

When visitors grew scarce, the Fitzgeralds went to New York. Nathan described these forays: "When in his cups, it was his drollery to descend upon my working quarters in company with his friends Edmund (Bunny) Wilson, . . . Donald Ogden Stewart, Ed Paramore and Edna St. Vincent Millay, all in a more or less exalted state, and to occupy his talents in applying matches to the rubber bindings on the pillows on my sofa. Their howls of glee when the rubber started to stench up the place could be heard a block away and were matched by my less gleeful ones."[28]

One morning when the revelry continued into the dawn, Nathan hid in the cottage cellar in hopes of finding a little peace. He came across Zelda's diary. Struck by its psychological and literary quality, he offered to publish it in his magazine. Scott refused to allow it, saying he had already been inspired by it and planned to use it again in his stories and in his next novel. An exchange of letters soon became a Nathan-Zelda duet. A few lines from it give the tone. At one point, having annoyed her by informing Scott about one of his warmer notes, he wrote: "Dear misguided woman: Like so many uncommonly beautiful creatures, you reveal a streak of obtuseness. The calling of a husband's attention to a love letter addressed to his wife is but a part of a highly righteous technique. . . . It completely disarms suspicion."[29]

Mencken sometimes accompanied Nathan to Westport. Both had a taste for crude humor and they liked to pretend that they had a kind of Laurel and Hardy friendship. Mencken, the fat, grumpy one, acted as the persecutor, a role he assumed naturally in American letters. In Westport the pair picked on Tana, the houseboy, insisting that his real name was Tannenbaum and that he was a German spy. They pestered him with letters written in an undecipherable pseudo-oriental script, and even with German newspapers. Mencken sent Tana a postcard asking him to make sure the foundations of Fitzgerald's house were firm enough to support the weight of a two-ton cannon. "Let me know," he then wrote to Nathan, "if Fitzgerald is killed when the Westport American Legion raids his house."[30]

Most of that summer's events, the visits, benders, quarrels, would filter into the novel Fitzgerald had in progress. He considered making Nathan its protagonist, but his marital problems soon became the book's subject. He discussed it with Nathan, to whom he had spoken of his earlier plan. The critic's recollection points up how impossible it was for Fitzgerald to develop any characters but Zelda and himself. "He came to me somewhat apologetically," the critic wrote, "and explained that he had tried, but could not lionize me in his novel. He said that he found himself unable to write a heroic character other than himself and that he had to be the hero of any novel he undertook. So I duly discovered that what he started as heroic me resulted in a wholly minor and subsidiary character not distinguished for any perceptible favorable attribute."[31]

The analysis was confirmed by a note in McKaig's diary: "Fitz made another true remark about himself—draw brilliant picture of Nathan sitting in chair but how Nathan thinks he cannot depict—cannot depict how anyone thinks except himself and possibly Zelda. Find that after he has written about a character for a while it becomes just himself again."[32]

Relations between Fitzgerald and Nathan had nevertheless cooled during the summer. Zelda showered marks of affection on the critic that, for all their burlesque quality, probably denoted a real attraction, and this contributed to the two men's estrangement. Scott realized that he could not completely trust Zelda, and this made him touchier about her flirtatiousness with other men. His irritation is visible in his novel in Anthony's dismay at the growing intimacy between Gloria and Bloekman, a rich and elegant Jew whose meteoric rise in the motion picture industry provides a counterpoint to Anthony's failure. Perhaps Nathan, after supplying some of Anthony's physical traits, then suggested a rivalry in which he figured as the tempter offering Gloria everything her weak husband could not give her. And this came at a time when Fitzgerald himself despaired of doing right by his second novel.

He and Zelda decided that a change would clarify the situation, and in mid-July they left Westport for Montgomery. The story of their odyssey was published in *Motor* magazine, illustrated with their own photos showing them in twin, white-knickered suits registering the various states of perplexity into which their 1917 Marmon's whims plunged them. After many trials—breakdowns, flat tires, flooded roads, inhospitable hotelkeepers—they did reach the end of their 1,100-mile journey to the city where they first met. Their sentimental pilgrimage had drawn them together and they could now review how far they had come together since the summer of 1918.

For Zelda, especially, this was a return to the land of insouciance and happy love affairs. Scott noted that "in every town which we passed" after crossing the Alabama state line, "Zelda would declare enthusiastically that she knew dozens of boys who lived there if she could just remember their names." Auburn and the university there: "Here Zelda had known the greatest gaiety of her youth." Then Montgomery: "Suddenly Zelda was crying, crying because things were the same and yet were not the same. It was for her faithlessness that she wept and for the faithlessness of time."[33] The Marmon, faithful despite the abuse it had suffered, finally refused to go any farther; it expired near the Sayre doorstep and was sold for junk. After two weeks of rest and family life, the Fitzgeralds took the train back to New York, feeling relieved.

The trip did have one beneficial effect: Fitzgerald returned resolved to set seriously to work on his novel. He really had to do it, because before leaving he had signed a contract with *Metropolitan Magazine* for serialized publication of the book, and he had told Ober he would give him the manuscript in October. That meant he had barely three months in which to deliver a book he had not written and for which he was to collect $7,000. He had already described his project to Charles Scribner: "My new novel called 'The Flight of the Rocket' concerns the life of Anthony Patch between his twenty-fifth and thirty-third years (1913–1921). He is one of the many with the tastes and weaknesses of an artist but with no actual creative inspiration. How he and his beautiful young wife are wrecked on the shoals of dissipation is told in the story. This sounds sordid but it's really a most sensational book and I hope won't disappoint the critics who liked my first one. I hope it'll be in your hands by November 1st."[34] Fitzgerald overestimated his capacity for work and concentration. The manuscript, renamed *The Beautiful and Damned*, would not be delivered to the publisher until late April, eight months later.

The Sayres returned their visit in August, but Zelda was already feeling febrile at the idea of being alone while Scott worked. Again she called on Fowler for help. "Please come out to see us," she wrote him. "Scott's hot in the midst of a new novel and Westport is unendurably dull but you and I might be able to amuse ourselves. . . . Mamma and Daddy are here this week and I can't tell you how glad I was to see them—however I feel very festive and I guess it's hardly conventional or according to Hoyle to take one's family on a celebration of the kind I feel in dire need of."[35] These were the conditions in which Fitzgerald tried, despite constant interruption by his recriminatory wife, to get on with his work. One day in mid-September, with things at their lowest ebb, a drunken Zelda decided to leave Scott. The incident provided material for a chapter in *The Beautiful and Damned*, the details of which were corroborated by an entry in McKaig's diary. She fled to the railroad station, pursued by Scott, who just managed to leap aboard her train. But he had left home without money or identification, and the conductor had wanted to put him off until he realized that this was a lovers' quarrel and let Fitzgerald stay aboard. "Fitz should let Zelda go & not run after her," McKaig reflected on September 15. "Like all husbands he is afraid of what she may do in a moment of caprice." Not surprisingly, the diarist would note twelve days later that the "new novel sounds awful—no seriousness of approach. Zelda interrupts him all the time— diverts in both senses." And on October 12: "Usual problem there. What shall Zelda do? I think she might do a little housework—apartment looks like a pig sty. If she's there Fitz can't work—she bothers him—if she's not there he can't work—worried what she might do."

So ended the first summer of their life together. They rented a small apartment at 38 West Fifty-ninth Street, near Central Park and the Plaza Hotel, which served as a kind of annex for them and sent in their meals. McKaig's complaint about the disorderliness of the place was confirmed by Lawton Campbell, who was invited to lunch and found them in the bedroom; a breakfast tray perched on the unmade bed and vestiges of the previous evening were everywhere: half-empty glasses, ashtrays overflowing with cigarette butts and manuscript pages scattered around the room.

Zelda sometimes visited Campbell, occasionally escorted by McKaig. "She would stretch out on the long sofa in my living room," Campbell reported, "with her eyes to the ceiling and recount some fabulous experience of the night before or dream up some strange exploit that she thought would be a 'cute idea.' . . . If her remarks were occasionally *non sequitur* one didn't notice it at the time. She passed very quickly from one topic to another and you didn't question her. It wouldn't occur to you to stop her and ask what she meant."[36]

While his friends attended to Zelda, Fitzgerald made great strides on his book, sometimes writing as much as 15,000 words in three days. On October 17 McKaig remarked that Fitzgerald had not had a drink in eight days. But he had not written a single short story all summer, either, and the couple's bank balance was beginning to shrink. Money vanished mysteriously. Back in June Scott had noticed that Zelda had hidden $500. In November a note in the *Ledger* mentioned that she had done it again, but this time with $100 belonging to Dorothy Parker. The $500 advance he got from Scribner's for a volume of short stories, *Flappers and Philosophers*, which appeared in August 1920, barely kept them going. This was the moment Zelda chose to open her campaign to persuade Scott to buy her a $700 squirrel coat. In a November 7 letter to Perkins, he asked for immediate payment of his outstanding royalties on *This Side of Paradise*, which were not due until January, explaining that he did not want to interrupt his work and, besides, "my family seems to need a fur coat."[37] The fur coat episode was used in *The Beautiful and Damned* to point up the growing lack of understanding between Gloria and Anthony: "Throughout the previous winter one small matter had been a subtle and omnipresent irritant—the question of Gloria's gray fur coat. At that time women enveloped in long squirrel wraps could be seen every few yards along Fifth Avenue. The women were converted to the shape of tops. They seemed porcine and obscene; they resembled kept women in the concealing richness, the feminine animality of the garment. Yet—Gloria wanted a gray squirrel coat."[38]

In November Zelda and Scott took another apartment at 381 East Fifty-ninth Street. They had picked up again with Nathan, who sometimes went with them to theatrical first nights. Meanwhile, McKaig had fallen hopelessly in love with Zelda; his old antipathy toward the capricious little hick he had met seven months earlier had now vanished. "I spent the evening shaving Zelda's neck to make her bobbed hair look better," he told his diary on November 27. "She is lovely—wonderful hair—eyes and mouth." But he would not betray Scott. When she asked him to kiss her in a taxi taking them back to the Fitzgeralds' on the evening of December 4, he couldn't do it: "I couldn't forget Scott—he's so damn pitiful." But he became their closest friend at the time when Fitzgerald quarreled with Townsend Martin and stopped seeing him.

Appearances notwithstanding, the couple felt lonely in New York, and when most of the little group's bachelor members went off to spend Christmas with their families, they found themselves alone, feeling that "we had not one friend in the city, nor one house we could go to. . . . later I realized that behind much of the entertainment that the city poured forth into the nation there were only a lot of rather lost and lonely people. The world of the picture actors was like our own in that it was in New York and not of it. It had little sense of itself and no center: when I first met Dorothy Gish I had the feeling that we were both standing on the North Pole and it was snowing."[39]

Their isolation, so painful to Zelda, was complicated by fresh financial difficulties. At the end of December Fitzgerald asked Perkins for a $1,600 advance on his novel, which he thought he could finish in two weeks. We know what his promises were worth; *Metropolitan Magazine* had already been waiting for the book since October. This time, however, he kept his word—within two weeks: the book was completed late in January, after six months' work. But the work had been interrupted so often, had been so rushed, especially at the beginning, that he had to put in three more months' work on it before he could release it to *Metropolitan*. The novel was to appear in serial form before publication by Scribner's.

In mid-February Zelda discovered she was pregnant. A month later she went to Montgomery to see her parents before the European tour she and Scott had promised themselves when the book was finished. He negotiated a $3,400 loan to pay for the trip, joined her three days later and spent much of his time in the South revising the book's last chapter, which he did not like. Zelda prattled with her old friends and took part in a show they had mounted for the annual *Les Mystérieuses* ball. Lawton Campbell also happened to be visiting his family then and attended the ball. It was a lesson in how lively an image of Zelda remained in Montgomeryites' memories.

Zelda was one of a group dancing masked in a Hawaiian pageant. The audience, Campbell later wrote in his unpublished memoirs of the Fitzgeralds, "began to notice that one masker was doing her dance more daring than the others. . . . Finally the dancer in question turned her back to the audience, lifted her grass skirt over her head for a quick view of her pantied posterior and gave it an extra wiggle for good measure. A murmur went over the auditorium in a wave of excitement and everybody was whispering 'That's Zelda!' It was Zelda and no mistake! She wanted it known beyond a doubt and she was happy with the recognition."[40]

Campbell saw his friends again at the end of April, a few days before they sailed for England, in a speakeasy called the Jungle Club. Scott had drunk too much and was having a row with the bouncer, who was trying to dissuade him from going back to the bar. Campbell stepped in and persuaded Scott to join him at his table. Then Zelda appeared, complaining that her husband had left her alone. She refused to listen to Campbell's explanation, took Scott by the arm and steered him toward the bar, announcing that no mere bouncer was going to keep him from going where he wanted to go. The bouncer let Zelda by, but tried to stop Scott from entering the bar. Fitzgerald loosed a few feeble punches at him, whereupon the man lost his patience and gave him a shove that sent him crashing into a table.

Campbell ran to him, picked him up and pleaded with him to leave. Zelda had disappeared, and Campbell was going to put Scott into a taxi and then look for her. At that moment she dashed out onto the sidewalk and yelled, "Scott, you're not going to let that so-and-so get away with that." He waded stoically back into the fight and received one of the severest beatings of his life.

The following day, when Campbell went to inquire after him, he found Scott in bed with his head bandaged, one eye blackened, his body covered with cuts and bruises and absolutely no memory of what had happened. He did have the presence of mind to add spice to the drama by pretending to his visitor that they were supposed to leave for Europe that day and that Zelda had gone to postpone their departure.

7. A NOVEL OF MARRIED LIFE

(1921–22)

On Tuesday, May 3, they boarded the *Aquitania*, which deposited them seven days later on a quay at Southampton. They went to London, where they stayed at the Cecil. The British edition of *This Side of Paradise* was soon to appear, and Perkins had given Fitzgerald letters of introduction to a number of writers, including John Galsworthy, whose books were published in the United States by Scribner's. Shane Leslie happened to be in London and, knowing Scott's interest in Mackenzie's novel *Sinister Street*, took the Fitzgeralds on a tour of the slums described at the end of the book. The tourists rigged themselves out in caps and work clothes to explore the dock area where, they fancied, there were no taxis and no police, and where Jack the Ripper had made his reputation. Zelda was tickled to be disguised as a man and exposed to a doubtless imaginary danger. Galsworthy received them in his Hampstead home in company with several playwrights and novelists and was slightly embarrassed by Fitzgerald's excessive deference: the American insisted that, along with Anatole France and Joseph Conrad, Galsworthy was the writer he admired most.

Scott refurbished his wardrobe, they visited Oxford, danced at the Savoy and dined with Lady Randolph Churchill and her son Winston, a memorable evening that Scott would recall twenty years later in a letter to Zelda. Ten days after their arrival, they left for Italy via a brief and disappointing stay in Paris. First Venice, "in a gondola feeling like a soft Italian song,"[1] then Florence in early June, and finally Rome, in a flea-infested Grand Hotel, and the inevitable visit to the Vatican, where grandmother McQuillan had gone so often. Fitzgerald did not mention in his *Ledger* the papal audience arranged for him by the bishop of St. Paul, merely noting two impressions: "the woman weeping in Vatican" and "the loot of twenty centuries."[2]

On June 22 they were back in Paris for a deeply disappointing week. Because neither of them knew French, the only person they spoke to was Edna Millay, there on an assignment for *Vanity Fair*. With her they searched for Wilson, who had arrived in Paris two days before they had without giving them his address; he was at the Hôtel Mont-Thabor, only a few minutes' walk from their hotel. Anatole France had just received the

Nobel Prize, and they stationed themselves before his house, the Villa Saïd, in the hope of catching a glimpse of the great man. An evening at the *Folies-Bergère*, a day at Versailles and Malmaison, the purchase of a poorly tanned sheepskin that stank up their room in the Hôtel de Saint-James et d'Albany, and a reprimand from the management because Zelda blocked the elevator door at their floor—these were the paltry memories of their first contact with a city to which they would return in good times and bad.

They were at Claridge's in London on June 20, and they visited Cambridge, which, with Oxford, gave them their only lasting impression of their trip, probably because of the universities' evocation of *Sinister Street*, which had so inspired Fitzgerald in his description of Princeton in *This Side of Paradise*. They had considered staying in Europe until the autumn, had even told Wilson they would remain in Italy for a year. But they were weary of traveling, Zelda's pregnancy tired her and Scott was disappointed by the unfavorable reception given *This Side of Paradise* in Britain; they cut short their stay and sailed July 9 aboard the *Celtic*, two months after their arrival in Europe. New York and the Biltmore were welcomed with relief.

From London Fitzgerald had written a long letter to Wilson in which he frankly voiced his disappointment: "God damn the continent of Europe. It is of merely antiquarian interest. . . . The negroid streak creeps northward to defile the Nordic race. Already the Italians have the souls of blacka-moors. Raise the bars of immigration and permit only Scandinavians, Teutons, Anglo-Saxons and Celts to enter. France made me sick. Its silly pose as the thing the world has to save. I think it's a shame that England and America didn't let Germany conquer Europe. It's the only thing that would have saved the fleet of tottering old wrecks. My reactions were all philistine, anti-socialistic, provincial and racially snobbish. I believe at last in the white man's burden. We are as far above the modern Frenchman as he is above the Negro. Even in art! Italy has no one. When Anatole France dies French literature will be a silly jealous rehashing of technical quarrels. They're thru and done. You may have spoken in jest about New York as the capital of culture, but in 25 years it will be just as London is now. Culture follows money and all the refinements of aestheticism can't stave off its change of seat (Christ! what a metaphor). We will be the Romans in the next generations as the English are now."[3]

This fit of chauvinism obviously denotes deep frustration. Fitzgerald, a constant center of attention in New York's yellow press, celebrated in literary circles, had been whittled to the ungrateful status of an actor without an audience. Or, if there was an audience, its reactions were unpredictable, different from those his effects were aimed at producing. From Princeton to the Jungle Club, even if an incident ended badly, there was a community of feeling, a common logic that allowed one to achieve effects that were expected, perhaps even sought. We feel a sort of vague longing for the intense relationship of a victim to his executioner in this enigmatic little note on a street scene in Venice: "Man kicked in stomach because he wasn't a Roman."[4]

A whole cause-and-effect relationship is missing here. A spectator who wishes he were an actor feels excluded from a symbolic occurrence. What at the Jungle Club had been a cultural commonplace ("Man beaten up because he tried to drink too much") here becomes an act of barbarism. During his second stay in Italy five years later, some obscure compulsion would push Fitzgerald into a situation that would end with his being beaten up by a clutch of taxi drivers.

After his few contacts had been made, he also suffered from the humiliation of being just another sheeplike tourist driven from monument to monument without ever meeting anyone. Finally, there was the disappointment of finding that the brilliant young novelist who had just written the key book to the new America was accorded only polite disdain by British critics. Fitzgerald noted their lack of enthusiasm in his letter to Wilson: "Of 20 reviews about half are mildly favorable, a quarter of them imply that I've read '*Sinister Street*' once too often!' "[5] For the first time as a published author, he felt dull, provincial, shut out of a system of behavior whose meaning he did not understand. He was anxious to rid himself of these feelings of inferiority, to reassure himself, and in his distress he stooped to racist arguments of the vilest kind.

In a reply sent July 5, Wilson showed he had perceptively diagnosed the wound that was festering in Fitzgerald's vanity. He began by describing how happy he was to be in Paris, which he artfully compared with his happiness in Princeton. "Paris," he wrote, "seems to me an ideal place to live: it combines all the attractions and conveniences of a large city with all the freedom, beauty and regard for the arts and pleasures of a place like Princeton. I find myself more contented and at ease here than anywhere else I know." He went on to discuss the relativity of fame in American cultural life, alleging that "it is too easy to be a highbrow or an artist in America these days" and warning artists against "the ease with which a traditionless and half-educated public . . . can be impressed, delighted and satisfied; the Messrs. Mencken, Nathan, Dreiser, Anderson, Lewis, Dell, Lippmann, Rosenfeld, Fitzgerald, etc., etc. . . . owe a good deal of eminence to the flatness of the surrounding country!" Wilson explained what had led him to rub against a richer and less razzle-dazzle culture, to measure his illusory superiority by the yardstick of an ancient tradition. His reasons reversed all his friend's arguments: "In America I feel so superior and culturally sophisticated in comparison to most of the rest of the intellectual and artistic life of the country that . . . I am obliged to save my soul by emigrating to a country which humiliates me intellectually and artistically by surrounding me with the solid perfection of a standard arrived at by way of Racine (etc.)." Fitzgerald, he advised, should profit from his example: "Settle down and learn French and apply a little French leisure and measure to that restless and jumpy nervous system. It would be a service to American letters; your novels would never be the same afterwards."[6]

The reasons for Wilson's travels were not quite so loftily disinterested as he pretended they were. In fact, he wanted to see Edna once more. She was broke, but thoroughly at ease in the Left Bank avant-garde, close to Sylvia Beach and on terms of the greatest intimacy with a British newspaper correspondent. Wilson's knowledge of French enabled him to appreciate the subtleties in Yvette Guilbert's songs as well as the epigrams of Jean Cocteau, with whom he lunched. Edna wanted to go to the Riviera with him, but his passion for her had cooled. He knew that she would ditch him without a second thought if she met someone who pleased her more. Besides, while she was away he had taken up with an actress with the Provincetown Players named Mary Blair, who was supposed to join him later in Europe. So he lent Edna some money and went south alone. In Cannes he happened across the girl who had initiated him in the subtleties of the French language while he was an ambulance driver in Vittel. Her name was Ninette and her quick impulsiveness enchanted him again this time. In his *Memoirs* he quoted in French her retort when he remarked that her nose was cold: "*Comme les petits chiens qui se portent bien. Il me faut deux ans pour digérer les baisers. Après, je vais recommencer.*"[7] Happy Bunny! Despite his difficulty in communicating with the French, he was as comfortable or more so in France as in the streets of New York. It was his love of books that had opened human nature to him.

The rest of his trip—interrupted in Florence when his money was stolen—showed the same curiosity, the same sympathy for alien cultures, qualities of which Fitzgerald had no trace. One sentence in Wilson's July letter neatly analyzed his friend's antipathy to Europe: "The lower animals frequently die when transplanted; Fitzgerald denounces European civilization and returns at once to God's country."

The lesson took. Back in New York, after rereading his manuscript in his room at the Biltmore, Fitzgerald knew he would have to rewrite it. He and Zelda decided to flee the temptations of the great city and settle in peaceful Montgomery while waiting for the baby to be born. They looked for a house there, but Zelda, then in her sixth month of pregnancy, could not stand the damp heat of an Alabama summer. After a week there they agreed that the child would be born in Scott's native city of St. Paul, where the more invigorating climate would better suit both of them. Off they went, and after two weeks in which they traveled more miles than separate America from Europe, they finally came to a halt in a rented house in Dellwood, on the shore of White Bear Lake, in the outskirts of St. Paul.

When *Metropolitan Magazine* began serializing *The Beautiful and Damned* in its September 1921 issue, Fitzgerald noticed that the text had been radically changed by the deep cuts the magazine's editors had made. It was not that the magazine had been shocked by the realism of some of the book's scenes; the idea was simply to keep the story moving, with everything else considered superfluous. There was nothing the author could do about this because the contract he had signed under pressure of financial need had authorized such cuts. With the excised material vanished all the pictures of manners, all the meaningful episodes for which the badly strung plot was merely a support. The book, which aimed to portray an atmosphere of revelry and dissipation, was reduced to mere anecdote. Its satiric thrust and its power of evocation were weakened, and its technical flaws stood out all too clearly. A quarter of the book was dropped from the six installments that ran from September through February.

It was a bitter lesson for Fitzgerald, who wasted no time in warning his friends against judging the book on the basis of this truncated version. Yet, despite his determination to rework the novel before its publication, he was having trouble reviving the creative surge that had swept him along earlier in the year. Three months of ceaseless travel had blunted his faculties. The only intellectual effort he had made in Europe had been the writing of a movie script he intended to sell on his return. In a new climate and a new setting, he despaired of regaining the previous winter's work pace.

As soon as he arrived in Dellwood, he communicated his gloom to Perkins. "I'm having a hell of a time because I've loafed for 5 months and I want to get to work," he wrote in a letter on August 25, 1921. "Loafing puts me in this particularly obnoxious and abominable gloom. My third novel, if I ever write another, will I am sure be black as death with gloom. I should like to sit down with ½ dozen chosen companions and drink myself to death, but I am sick alike of life, liquor and literature. If it wasn't for Zelda I think I'd disappear out of sight for three years. Ship as a sailor or something and get hard—I'm sick of the flabby semi-intellectual softness in which I flounder with my generation."[8]

The obvious flaws in his novel further blackened his mood. *This Side of Paradise* had been written over three years and rewritten three times; *The Beautiful and Damned*, twice as long as its predecessor, had been hurriedly written in six months. The opening, especially, suffered from the emotionalism of the Fitzgeralds' previous summer in Westport. Three months had been set aside for revision, but this was not enough time to improve it as much as he had hoped. Only the euphoria of knowing that the book was nearly finished and the prospect of a trip to Europe could have so blinded Fitzgerald to the weakness of parts of his novel. Then his European experience had dispelled his optimism and his arrogance, and Wilson's letter had forced him back to reexamine his ideas. So, reluctantly, he went to work to revise a manuscript in which he no longer believed. He informed Wilson in November that he had "almost completely rewritten" his book.[9] In fact, comparison of the *Metropolitan Magazine* version with the one Scribner's published shows that most of his work went into the first part of the book; changes were fewer and farther between in the second part and there were none at all in Book III, which was, it's true, the most polished.

Book III, depicting Anthony's months in an army camp, his discharge and his attempts to find a job in postwar New York, is certainly the novel's most endearing and most successful section. It functions as a follow-up to the closing chapters of *This Side of Paradise,* in which the author's military and advertising experience had not been used. The picturesque bender scenes sketched in at the end of the first novel are exhaustively examined here. Did Fitzgerald use passages from his aborted novels of the autumn and winter of 1919, as he had already done with "May Day," the atmosphere and style of which prefigure the last quarter of *The Beautiful and Damned?* Some of the titles he had proposed to Perkins do seem to cover the same ground. *The Demon Lover* (September 1919) and *The Darling Heart* (January 1920), both of which are about a girl's seduction (they may even be two versions of the same story) could very well be the sources for Anthony's affair with Dot. And *The Drunkard's Holiday* (December 1919) could be an early version of the scenes of Anthony's degradation. A fourth project, *The Diary of a Literary Failure* (October 1919), was to include a fifty-page episode entitled "The Diary of a Popular Girl," based on Zelda's diary, which Nathan had thought fit to publish; this closely matches the passages describing Anthony's fruitless efforts to make a name for himself in literature. And there are the passages directly inspired by Zelda's letters, which are attributed to Gloria. The *Diary* would also explain the presence in the novel of Richard Caramel, the successful hack writer and author of . . . *The Demon Lover;* Caramel is Fitzgerald's caricature of himself as a writer whose talent wanes as he prospers.

Such borrowings would help us understand the inconsistencies of tone and atmosphere that make *The Beautiful* a bastard work from which a number of episodes, brilliant as they are—the love story of Anthony and Dot, for example—could have been eliminated without harming the whole. As in his first book, Fitzgerald had resorted to dishing up his leftovers. His idea of a novel resembled that of H. G. Wells, for whom the sole criterion was effectiveness. Wells considered that if a book delights and instructs, the novelist has done his job; to him a novel's form was open, functional, able to accommodate all the author sought to express. In his famous dispute with James, which grew up around 1914, he stubbornly defended his notion of a catchall novel based on a principle of saturation. James, on the other hand, preached selection aimed at forging a minutely dovetailed work in which each part must contribute to the effectiveness of the whole.

Fitzgerald was not yet artistically mature enough to conceive of a novel as anything but a series of incidents, of episodes juxtaposed without artfully machined interlocking. Not until *The Great Gatsby* would the stern

Jamesian aesthetic prevail over the pleasant indiscipline of the Wellsian journalistic novel.

What is striking about *The Beautiful,* aside from its lack of structure, is its lack of unity. Two subjects and two approaches coexist in it without always meeting. First there is a sprightly comedy of manners, in a Wildean vein, that picks up the rollicking spirit of *This Side of Paradise* and of the short stories and allows room for social satire and contemporary caricatures. It is also a roman à clef that recalls the transparent portraits of the first novel. Nathan, Wilson, Fowler, Paramore and others were immediately recognized by those who knew them. Fitzgerald appears in the parodic character of Caramel and in some of Anthony's characteristics (although, as we have seen, Nathan was the model for Anthony's physical appearance). There is even a lot of Zelda in Gloria. When W. E. Hill, who had designed the book jacket for *This Side of Paradise,* prepared a cover for the new book, he naturally drew the fictional couple as looking like Zelda and Scott. This annoyed Fitzgerald, not only because the illustrator had forgotten that Anthony was six feet tall and dark, but also because, he complained, the portrait made him look like "a sort of debauched edition of me"[10] and his slightly short legs showed up all too clearly.

"I wish 'The Beautiful and Damned' had been a maturely written book because it was all true," he wrote in a later moment of depression.[11] This was modified by another observation in a letter to his daughter: "Gloria was a much more trivial and vulgar person than your mother. I can't really say there was any resemblance except in the beauty and certain terms or expressions she used, and also I naturally used many circumstantial events of our early married life. However, the emphases were different. We had a much better time than Anthony and Gloria did."[12]

Parallel with—or consecutive to—this sometimes comic, sometimes lyric portrayal of contemporary life and love as Fitzgerald lived or observed them runs a second subject, a conjugal tragedy. It scarcely appears until the middle of the book, and when it does, the tone changes completely and Zola replaces Wilde. One is suddenly immersed in the style and atmosphere of the naturalists' dramas of misunderstanding and drunkenness. The dandy of the earlier chapters becomes a derelict whose ineluctable degradation recalls that of Hurstwood in Dreiser's *Sister Carrie.* From this point on, the very concept of the character of Anthony no less irresistibly evokes the protagonist of naturalist Frank Norris's novel *Vandover and the Brute.* Oddly, Fitzgerald turned to realism just when he stopped drawing for inspiration on the reality he knew. Literary models replaced direct observation, bringing with them their burden of pessimism.

This is no literarily natural psychological shift, but a radical change of perspective. All the characters of naturalistic novels are here, along with the quasi-scientific approach that gives fiction a documentary, even didactic, tone. Man is pictured as an animal driven by his lowest instincts, which are determined by his environment. There is a predilection for sordid surroundings and debauchery, an affinity for the declining curve and a fascination with degradation, decrepitude and death. By recklessly violating probability, Fitzgerald succeeded in transforming Anthony from a brilliant aesthete into a drunken tramp in an advanced stage of decay. (Hurstwood, whom Fitzgerald considered one of the most successful characters in contemporary fiction, gasses himself in a tenement; Vandover ends up running around on all fours, naked and howling like a wolf.)

The influences are evident and, as we shall see, Fitzgerald freely owned to them. But does a wish to conform to admired models in itself justify such a change in style and substance? Why this sudden eruption of unrelieved misery, of pessimism at its blackest, that forced Fitzgerald to abandon his own register, to renounce the light and witty tone that prevailed in the first part of the book? What he was doing, in a paradoxical way, was using the aesthetics of naturalism, founded on clinical observation of reality, to depict a purely imaginary situation. A second paradox: materialism in society is assigned the same task here as mystical spiritualism was given in *This Side of Paradise:* to make tangible and objective the tenacious obsessions that lodge in experience like a worm in a fruit. Fitzgerald extrapolated reality to disclose a hideous future in which the worst fears of the present are fulfilled. In the earlier book it was sexual obsession and its concomitants, sin and damnation, that caused the demon's three appearances. The sexual threat was exorcised in *The Beautiful and Damned,* but the reality of married life is portrayed in it as being equally threatening and destructive. Pathological anguish no longer takes the form of devastating damnation, but of erosion, of a more insidious corruption of body and mind. And alcoholism objectifies this resignation and degradation.

Fitzgerald appears to have made conscious, organized use of naturalistic techniques to achieve psychological, not literary, ends. All the theatrical melodrama inherent in these techniques was perfectly suited to his purpose. With bold strokes it blackens the warped, pathetic image the author tried to project, had to project on his future to protect his present. We know this effort at exorcism did not accomplish much for Fitzgerald's moral well-being; the least that can be said is that it was no more successful artistically. There is a kind of continuity between the two nominals in the title of *The Beautiful and Damned:* the beautiful grow ugly, the happy become unhappy, the elect are damned. But the hidden springs of these changes are never uncovered. The antithetical terms are never joined in a revealing dialectic; the two panels of the diptych remain irreconcilable: two ways of living, two styles, two techniques that were never meant to cohabit.

Nevertheless, this incursion into a hitherto unexplored realm, unfortunate as it may have been for the novel's design and structure, had a positive result, if only *a contrario:* it forced Fitzgerald to acknowledge his limitations and the nature of his own genius. At least it was symptomatic of a desire for expansion and renewal through which Fitzgerald tried to escape the role into which he was being forced as the new generation's chorister, as advance man for the flapper. As far as this went, his readers' demands were as precise and as narrow as Lorimer's. Fortunately, just when he was feeling locked into the stereotypes that had made him famous, new standards and new demands offered new openings to his longing for approbation. The instrument of this liberation was Henry Louis Mencken, of whom Fitzgerald said in 1921 that he would rather have him like a book of his than anyone else in America.

The program Fitzgerald tried to carry out in *The Beautiful and Damned* in direct opposition to the forced optimism required by the *Post* is explicitly outlined by Mencken in an essay called "The National Letters." In it he laments that the typical hero of American novels was not "a man of delicate organization in revolt against the inexplicable tragedy of existence, but a man of low sensibilities and elemental desires yielding himself gladly to his environment, and so achieving what, under a third-rate civilization, passes for success." A true hero, he said, is not a man who bows to social pressure and succeeds, but one who resists and fails. "Character in decay," he confidently concluded, "is thus the theme of the great bulk of superior fiction."[13] This was the viewpoint Fitzgerald adopted in writing "May Day," which Mencken published in July 1920, and in *The Beautiful and Damned*. This was the direction in which, confusedly, he would have wished to move after completing his first novel had the *Post*'s attraction been weaker. In December 1919 he had asked Ober about the possibility of finding other outlets for his work that were more in sympathy with what he wanted to write: "Is there any market at all for the cynical or pessimistic story except *Smart Set* or does realism bar a story from any well-paying magazine no matter how cleverly it is done?"[14]

Coeditor with Nathan of *The Smart Set* since 1914, Mencken had made the magazine into the organ of nonconformism in the United States, a sort of anti-*Saturday Evening Post* that set itself the task of denouncing the stupidity, ignorance, pretentiousness and hypocrisy of the powers that be, whether in government, the press, religion or literature. His favorite whipping boy was the average American, representative of the smug and ignorant "booboisie" that Sinclair Lewis would immortalize in *Babbitt* in 1922. Especially marked for scorn were the bigots and fanatics who, he charged, had turned the South into a "Sahara of Bozarts." *The Smart Set* was open to anything that might broaden its readers' horizons, and it called on the period's most stimulating writers, from W. B. Yeats to Dashiell Hammett, from D. H. Lawrence to Eugene O'Neill.

Mencken had another forum in the Baltimore *Sun,* and he used it as a pulpit from which, in his role of prophet of a new age, he crushed the squalid ignoramus under the weight of his sarcasm. A master of invective, crusader against cant, contemner of the American Way of Life, he had become the mentor of the country's young intellectuals, earning the loyalty and respect of minds as dissimilar as Wilson's and Fitzgerald's. Of German ancestry, violently opposed to the Great War, he had promoted Nietzsche as early as 1908 and took pleasure in contrasting German culture with what he insisted was the vast lack of culture reigning in the United States. An American intellectual, he fumed, was like a man surrounded by animals in a zoo.

The extent of his influence can be gauged from an exchange of letters between Fitzgerald and Wilson in the early summer of 1921. Fitzgerald unquestioningly adopted Mencken's views on Nordic superiority while Wilson echoed the master's contempt for American culture, although he was independent enough to prefer Racine to Nietzsche as his model. Both men were obsessed with Mencken then. In March Fitzgerald had reviewed his latest book for *The Bookman*, and Wilson had contributed an essay about him to the June *New Republic*, which earned Mencken's praise. Fitzgerald's letter to his friend from London began with an allusion to this mark of favor: "Of course I'm wild with jealousy! Do you think you can indecently parade this obscene success before my envious disposition with *equanimity?*" It went on to allude to Mencken's popularity in Britain, where *The Times* had just published a dithyrambic article about one of his books. And the great man reappears indirectly in the letter's last paragraph: "We sail for America on the 9th and thence to the 'Sahara of Bozart' (Montgomery) for life."[15]

Fitzgerald's review of Mencken's collection of essays, *Prejudices: Second Series* (which included "The National Letters"), was headed "The Baltimore Anti-Christ" and was so solemn it might have been an account of the destruction wrought by a horseman of the Apocalypse: "Will he find new gods to dethrone, some eternal 'yokelry' still callous enough to pose as intelligentzia before the Menckenian pen fingers [it]? . . . Granted that, solidly, book by book, he has built up a literary reputation most to be envied by any American, granted also that he has done more for the national letters than any man alive, one is yet inclined to regret a success so complete."[16]

Mencken's name first appears in *This Side of Paradise* linked with the works of three naturalistic novelists, Frank Norris, Harold Frederic and Theodore Dreiser, whom Mencken had revealed to Amory: "He was . . . rather surprised by the discovery through a critic named Mencken of several excellent novels: *Vandover and the Brute*, *The Damnation of Theron Ware* and *Jennie Gerhardt*." Significantly, he contrasted these titles with the constellation of British authors he had until then used as models: "Mackenzie, Chesterton, Galsworthy, Bennett had sunk in his appreciation from sagacious, life-saturated geniuses to merely diverting contemporaries."[17] This is still nothing more than a list of titles aimed, as is frequently done in novels, to identify the hero as a with-it intellectual. Mencken was hardly more than a name to Fitzgerald then, one of the editors of *The*

Smart Set who had published his first short story in September 1919. "It was not until after I had got the proofs of my book back from the publisher that I learned of Mencken," the author told St. Paul reporter Thomas Boyd in an interview in Dellwood in the summer of 1921. "I happened across *The Smart Set* one day and thought: 'Here's a man whose name I ought to know. I guess I'll stick it in the proof sheets.' "[18]

Mencken's influence, added to that of the naturalists, stimulated Fitzgerald's consciousness of the problems of his time. It dominates the part of *The Beautiful and Damned* that deals with the contemporary scene. Later he would write that the Jazz Age "was an age of miracles, it was an age of art, it was an age of excess and it was an age of satire."[19] But he seemed chiefly inspired by the excess and the miracles in writing his first novel and his short stories. He did indeed reproduce the verve of Wells in *Kipps* and *Tono-Bungay* when he described the follies of his day, but he lacked the conviction, the contempt, the sovereign insolence that are the mark of the true satirist and are brought to their peak of intensity in Mencken's essays. It was Mencken's influence, combined with that of Wells, that gave Fitzgerald a firmer voice, that spurred him to widen his field of observation and perceive more clearly the possibilities postwar America offered to a novelist with his talent. It enabled him to judge the weaknesses of his earlier models, the decadent British poets and such sentimental novelists as Mackenzie and Tarkington, and to adopt more robust ones. At this point Mencken became his mentor, a function he retained for the next three years. "The sage of Baltimore," sixteen years older than Fitzgerald, now succeeded Sigourney Fay as his spiritual father, persuading him to write "significantly" about contemporary problems.

The Beautiful and Damned attests to the breadth of Mencken's influence; few American institutions or activities escape attack in the book in varying degrees of sarcasm and virulence. The army and advertising are ridiculed and so are Wall Street, religion, puritanism, American justice and literature, sometimes giving Fitzgerald an opening for a well-minted aphorism or a boldly drawn scene. Pure Menckenian outrage rings, for example, in Anthony's picture of American politics: "He tried to imagine himself in Congress rooting around in the litter of that incredible pigsty with the narrow and porcine brows he saw pictured sometimes in the rotogravure sections of the Sunday newspapers, those glorified proletarians babbling blandly to the nation the ideas of high school seniors! Little men with copybook ambitions who by mediocrity had thought to emerge from mediocrity into the lustreless and unromantic heaven of a government by the people."[20]

Generally speaking, such bravura passages are not integrated into the novel's action and could have been omitted, as they were in the *Metropolitan* version, without noticeably affecting the overall impression the book makes. Satire and the romantic imagination clearly walk divergent ways, and Fitzgerald's indictments do not always coincide with the objects

he sought to lambaste. His invective does not suggest a liberated indignation, a free-ranging rancor, as Mencken's usually does; Fitzgerald seems
merely to be playing scales, reciting without conviction a lesson he has not
quite learned.

His style here is, finally, that of a writer more concerned with the problems of his art than with an impromptu mobilization of a journalist's or satirist's creative faculties. In *The Beautiful* he was seeking new registers on
which to deploy and diversify his talent. The novel can be seen as a test-bed
on which, while perfecting his old manner, he acquainted himself with new
styles. From his life and times he mined pretexts for testing, experimenting
with types of material, styles, tones whose effectiveness he had measured in
the work of other writers.

But he had to recognize the incompatibility of his approach to novel
writing with Menckenian satire. He would turn next to the theater and
would increasingly try to purge his fiction of the heterogeneous elements
that burdened his second novel. Essays would be his chosen form for voic-
ing his didactic opinions; in the following three years he would publish ten
such articles in various magazines. His mistakes in *The Beautiful*, then, were
tonic because they forced him to think about what a novel specifically is
and to envisage a type of fiction as removed from polemics as from social
realism. Conrad's example, especially, would gradually lead him to abandon
the three determining influences that had turned *The Beautiful and Damned*
into a hybrid compounded of Wells, the naturalists and H. L. Mencken.

Conscious of his failure, recognizing the uselessness of trying to patch up
a botched job, Fitzgerald nevertheless continued to look after his interests.
As a former advertising man, he had closely followed Scribner's efforts to
promote his first book, and they had not satisfied him. Chagrined by the
failure of *Paradise* in Britain, he complained to Perkins about it on his return to Montgomery. Fitzgerald had just learned that Floyd Dell's novel
Mooncalf, published around the same time as *Paradise* and which he considered greatly inferior to his own book, was still being pushed by Knopf
while Scribner's had practically stopped promoting *Paradise*. Fitzgerald
protested that his book had sold on its reputation without the proper support of Scribner's marketing service. No advertising at all had been done in
Montgomery itself—yet fifty copies were sold there—or in St. Paul, where
the campaign consisted of three advertisements and where the local papers
had been far more effective in publicizing the native son. The book had
been a best-seller in Chicago for eighteen weeks, although only a dozen
newspaper ads had appeared there. Whereas the sales of *Mooncalf* had been
swollen in all three cities by a promotion drive that went on for months. As
a result, Dell's novel, which had enjoyed neither the critical success nor the
vogue of *This Side of Paradise*, had been a much bigger seller and was still

doing well. It was not just the quantity of advertising that Fitzgerald criticized, but its quality, which the author ascribed to a lack of imagination on the part of those responsible. He particularly accused them of failing to exploit the praise of such famous writers as Mencken and Sinclair Lewis. Hadn't Lewis declared in the *Tribune* that "in Scott Fitzgerald we have an author who will be the equal of any young European"?[21]

The analysis was professional and backed by accurate figures, and Perkins was impressed by it. He promised that the complaints would be borne in mind in conducting the advertising campaign for Fitzgerald's next novel, but that the author would be asked to take a hand in it, especially in writing the copy for newspaper ads. Proofs of the book began arriving in October, Zelda was approaching her term and requests for advances on the book became more pressing. It is true that Fitzgerald hoped the advertising would sell 60,000 copies of his new book, 20,000 more than *Paradise*.

Most of his correspondence with Perkins in the first quarter of 1922 bore on the best tactics to attract readers. Fitzgerald paid attention to the smallest details, kept a close eye on the advertising copy, calculated the effect of reviews on sales, grumbled about the cover design (Zelda proposed another showing a naked woman kneeling in a champagne glass, but it was rejected), kept track of orders from St. Paul bookstores. When the novel went on sale March 3, he must have been just as nervous as Richard Caramel, the fashionable writer in his book: "The author, indeed, spent his days in a state of pleasant madness. The book was in his conversation three-fourths of the time—he wanted to know if one had heard 'the latest'; he would go into a store and in a loud voice order books to be charged to him, in order to catch a chance morsel of recognition from clerk or customer. He knew to a town in what sections of the country it was selling best; he knew exactly what he cleared on each edition, and when he met anyone who had not read it, or, as it happened only too often, had not heard of it, he succumbed to moody depression."[22]

Like his personage, Fitzgerald kept a febrile finger on market fluctuations. He reckoned that to reimburse Scribner's for the $5,643 he had received in advances, he would have to sell exactly 18,810 copies. Six weeks after publication sales had reached 33,000, and Perkins warned him that the book was unlikely to be a big success. In the first full year 43,000 copies were sold, about the same number as *This Side of Paradise*.

We recall that after completing his first novel, Fitzgerald realized that he had imperceptibly progressed from amateur to professional. But until the publication of his second book, he had left his financial interests in the hands of Perkins and Ober, simply delivering his work and asking them to fatten his bank balance in return. Now the Fitzgeralds were spending heedlessly, debts were mounting and the writer found he was not working to earn his living, but to repay his loans. This was when he began to take a personal interest in the publishing industry's advertising and sales methods so as to earn as much as possible from his work. This was also the point at which he began to ask himself seriously where the money was coming from; only a bit later would he wonder about its important corollary: where was it going?

To find an answer, he resolved to begin, like any shopkeeper, keeping exact accounts of his output and his income. He accordingly bought a large ledger from a St. Paul stationer, Brown, Blodget & Sperry, a boxed volume nine and a half by fifteen inches, containing 200 numbered pages. This *Ledger* he would keep until the end of his life, recording his income, if not his outlay. He reserved the first fifty pages as a catalog of his fiction, writing across two pages, a total of nineteen inches, which he divided into sixteen columns. Each story was listed with the date on which it was written, the names of magazines and dates of publication, first in the United States, then in Britain. Similar records were kept for his novels and volumes of short stories, his theater and movie scenarios, translations and reprints in anthologies. The last column detailed each story's ultimate fate, whether it was judged worthy to appear in a collection (publication of each novel would be followed by a volume of short stories) or too weak to be picked up. In the latter case there were two further possibilities: if the piece was irrecuperable, it was "definitely buried"; if parts of it could be reused, it was "junked"—phrases and paragraphs were salvaged from it and filed in notebooks for possible inclusion in a future novel. Eight double pages were devoted to this history of the approximately 130 works published between 1918 and 1937.

A second section of the *Ledger*, beginning with page 51, was devoted to the purely financial aspect of this huge output. Income for each year was itemized down to the smallest payment and totaled at the foot of the page. Included were royalties on full texts and adaptations, fees for each item published in periodicals and his advances on royalties. This accounting, like the rest, ended in 1937, when Fitzgerald went to Hollywood and, he thought, gave up the writer's trade.

Finally, a third section complements the first, listing his published nonfiction pieces, mainly poems and articles. The volume is a mine of valuable information, a kind of autobibliography that provides an accurate chart of the author's production rhythm and his popularity in terms, for example, of printings, reprintings and prices paid by magazines.

What gives the *Ledger* its inestimable value and makes it unique of its kind, at least in American literature, is another kind of accounting that fills thirty-eight pages beginning on page 151. In this section, too, each year gets a separate page, but the material is autobiographical. Experiences, events, encounters, places visited follow the résumé of professional accomplishments. This is not, strictly speaking, a diary but a kind of *aide-mémoire*, very selective, written in a telegraphic style, which month after month records the events Fitzgerald did not want to forget. It is here that he summed up the meaningful experiences in his boyhood notebooks (notations from the *Thoughtbook* are found in a sort of dehydrated form). And it was from here that he resurrected memories his imagination brought to life as fictional material. For example, the brief entry in which he records having once lied in confession could provide a subtitle for his story "Absolution." Throughout his life Fitzgerald referred to his *Ledger;* witness a penciled note at the foot of page 162: "Red underlines on this page indicates possible use (1940)."

The last page, on which he broke off in March 1936 but in which the names of the months until September are entered in the left-hand margin, seems to indicate that he prepared a monthly calendar he filled in later. Scraps found among his papers show that he made notes for his *Ledger* that he did not always use, as we see from notes dated 1934, 1935 and 1936, in which the wording and even the contents are very different from the *Ledger* entries for the corresponding dates. Some entries are very brief—only half a line, for example, for April 1922: "Coached Junior League play" and, for the following month, "Parties with the Herseys. Bought car."[23]

Even the longest entries seldom exceed half a dozen lines. The style is lapidary, impersonal; Fitzgerald alludes to himself in the third person. Beginning with his fourteenth year, there is an annual summary. For 1922, the author's twenty-fifth year—for the monthly pages begin in September, his birth month—the summary reads: "A bad year. No work. Slow deteriorating depression with outbreak around the corner."[24]

Two types of notations, then: a kind of datebook in which the author records his encounters with life, mostly the names of women, men, cities, countries, hermetic names bursting with events and feelings experienced, so that verbs and complements are often useless; and the other filled with the traces left by the huge body of work he turned out, work published and money earned, almost incidentally to the events, one might think in leafing through the *Ledger,* so fleeting are the writer's allusions to his work. Two concurrent, opposed areas, their contradiction reflected in the spareness of the writing. Fitzgerald's continuing need to write is expressed in the *Ledger* chiefly by the dry arithmetic and the severely ordered columns of the tables. In tension with these are the evidences of chance, the new names sounding like calls wresting the man from his work and finally subsiding on half-empty pages on which, in the space allotted to each month, there is only silence. Two orders shared the man as they shared the *Ledger*'s pages: the permanent and the ephemeral, the spirit of meditation and the spirit of dispersion and—let us say so frankly because they are the real subjects—the sacred and the profane.

But, for Fitzgerald, sacred and profane were deeply marked by the Protestant ethic of success, embedded in the American mythology that contrasted a twin heritage: that of the Northern Puritan building his New

Jerusalem, and the Southern cavalier's, whose kingdom was on earth. In the *Ledger* we first meet the thrifty Puritan who stores his harvest and thinks to prove his membership in the Elect with the marks of his success. Only later comes the libertine cavalier who squanders his heritage and, knowing he is damned, perseveres in his folly. It is all summed up, perhaps, in Fitzgerald's provocative epigram in *The Beautiful and Damned:* "The victor belongs to the spoils."

III. A MEETING WITH THE ERA

(1922-23)

8. THE JAZZ AGE

(1922–23)

After a summer at Dellwood the Fitzgeralds returned to St. Paul October 21, moving into the Commodore Hotel to await the birth of their baby. The delivery occurred October 26 and it was difficult, but Fitzgerald, despite his nervousness, professionally noted Zelda's incoherent maunderings as she came out of the anesthetic; they would be attributed almost verbatim to Daisy in *Gatsby*. For the time being they were consigned to the *Ledger*: "Oh God, goofo I'm drunk . . . Mark Twain . . . isn't she smart . . . she has the hiccups . . . I hope it's beautiful and a fool . . . a beautiful little fool."[1]

The baby girl was named Frances Scott and was christened in November, with Father Joe Barron, a McQuillan family familiar whom Fitzgerald had befriended, acting as godfather. This was probably a conciliatory gesture toward Scott's parents, whom he seldom saw and whom he regarded with embarrassment and irritation. Zelda lost no love on Mrs. Fitzgerald; she still had as much trouble communicating with her mother-in-law as she did when answering her first letter. Besides, grandmother was too lacking in common sense to look after the baby. It was Xandra Kalman, the friend of Scott who had found them the Dellwood house and who was the only person in town with whom Zelda was on any sort of terms, who took responsibility for the child, hired a nurse and bought everything needed for the baby. She also rented an apartment for them at 625 Goodrich Avenue, to which they moved after Zelda's convalescence.

To work in peace, Scott rented an office in the city. He had revived a number of boyhood friendships and became friendly with Tom Boyd, the reporter who had interviewed him in Dellwood and who was also co-owner of the Kilmarnock Bookshop. On his way home from the office Fitzgerald would spend hours ensconced in a comfortable chair before a wood fire in the store's back room, leafing through the new books, chatting with Boyd and his wife, Peggy, whose novel had just been published, with Father Barron, a regular at the shop, and such visiting writers as Joseph Hergesheimer, a pop novelist whose sales Scott envied. It was there that he first heard of the *Ulysses* that had just appeared in Paris and of which he obtained a contraband copy.

Boyd, younger than Fitzgerald, had nevertheless seen active service with the Marines during the Germans' final push in the war; he was writing a novel based on his wartime experiences. He was one of the first to speak enthusiastically of John Dos Passos's novel *Three Soldiers*, which Fitzgerald had reviewed no less enthusiastically for the St. Paul *Daily News* soon after his arrival in Dellwood. Fitzgerald encouraged Boyd to write and mentioned him to Perkins, who published the book, *Through the Wheat*, a year later. Scott reviewed it in the New York *Evening Post* in May 1923, calling it a better war novel than Dos Passos's and ending the review on an even more eloquent note: "To my mind, this is not only the best combatant story of the Great War, but also the best war book since *The Red Badge of Courage*."[2]

Boyd, for his part, did all he could to bolster the success of *The Beautiful and Damned*. According to Fitzgerald himself, his name was mentioned by Boyd more than forty times in the *Daily News*. The Kilmarnock Bookshop put in a hefty order for the book and organized a sales campaign that included a promotional film to be shown in all the city's movie theaters.

Fitzgerald, meanwhile, had gone to work on a play in the satiric line inspired by Mencken. In November he described it as a play about politics. Early in January he said it would be finished in three more weeks. Full of optimism, he wrote to Perkins: "I am writing an awfully funny play that's going to make me rich forever. It really is. I'm so damned tired of the feeling that I'm living up to my income."[3] Only days later, however, he confessed that he was having difficulty wrapping up the third act, although he persisted in thinking that "my play is a gem."[4]

It was finished in February 1922, but no producer cared for it. All Scott's correspondence with Perkins and Wilson in that late winter and spring revolved around the play.

The winter nevertheless seemed long and the city asleep. Scott and Zelda set about rousing St. Paul from its provincial torpor. At parties Zelda devoted as much zeal to shocking the dancers as Scott had once done by appearing at a dance in drag. Xandra Kalman said "she and Scott were always thinking up perfectly killing things to do. You know, entertaining stunts which were so gay that one wanted to be in on them." But, she added, Zelda wasted no effort making friends. "She was not at all interested in going out with the girls, and when Scott wanted to remain at home, Zelda stayed with him. Certainly she enjoyed being different. . . . But there weren't many people whom she liked. I won't say she was rude, but she made it quite clear. If she didn't like someone or if she disapproved of them, then she set out to be as impossible as she could be."[5]

On Friday, January 13, 1922, they and a few friends organized a "bad luck ball" in a room hung with black crepe at the University Club. The idea probably came from *The Undertaker's Garland*, a funny-macabre book Bishop and Wilson had just jointly written. During the ball copies were distributed of the first and last edition of the St. Paul *Dirge*, "mortuary edition," with a headline that occupied the whole of the front page proclaiming that "Cotillon Is Sad Failure"; it dripped subheadings in the vein of "Frightful Orgy at University Club" and "Business Better, Says Bootlegger."[6]

Not even these sophomoric farces kept the Fitzgeralds occupied. February saw both of them ill and drinking too much. Scott had written to Wilson in November that "Saint Paul is dull as hell" and, in January, that "I'm bored as hell out here."[7] Zelda sang the same tune in a letter to Fowler: "We are both simply mad to get back to New York. . . . This damned place is 18 below zero."[8] She was in a situation she had imagined in December 1919 and on which Scott had based "The Ice Palace." It was that of a Southern girl who follows her fiancé to a snowy Northern city (St. Paul) and languishes for the human warmth and sunny days of her little town until the day she comes near death in a labyrinthine ice palace.

A chance to get away from St. Paul came when *The Beautiful and Damned* went on sale March 3, 1922. They stayed at the Plaza in New York for a disappointing month, through most of which they were drunk. It was so bad that Scott failed even to find the time to talk to Wilson about his play, as he had hoped to do. "I was sorry our meetings in New York were so fragmentary," he wrote. "My original plan was to contrive to have long discourses with you but that interminable party began and I couldn't seem to be sober enough to be able to tolerate being sober. In fact the whole trip was largely a failure."[9] He had nevertheless left his script with Wilson, whose affair with Mary Blair had brought him into the theater (he also wrote a play) and who offered to get it read by a company.

Back in St. Paul the Fitzgeralds were absorbed by rehearsals of a musical comedy Scott had written in his spare time for the Junior League. It was called *The Flappers of Midnight;* Zelda was to play the title role in her own likeness. Scott was resuming the tradition of his college days when he put on an amateur production every summer of which he was author, star and director. This play was a typical Jazz Age commodity, set in a nightclub and displaying the period's types: the flapper, the sheik, the night owl, the vamp, the Prohibition cop, and so on. The cast featured St. Paul's most prominent society girls, including Arditta Ford, the model for the heroine in Fitzgerald's story "The Offshore Pirate." This, then, was a social event that would confirm the popularity of America's postwar cultural models. The new wave rising from New York had swept over the middle-class bastions of the Middle West; what had been daring in 1919 was accepted in proper provincial households in 1922. The show was given on April 17, after which Fitzgerald began writing a new version of that other play, the one he thought would revolutionize Broadway and make his fortune.

Zelda, meanwhile, sought relief from her boredom by breaking into the newspaper business. The New York *Tribune*'s book critic, Burton Rascoe, suggested that she review *The Beautiful*. When she did, her lively and wholly personal style of discussing her husband's novel brought her fresh offers. She was asked to state her feelings about the new woman she so authoritatively embodied, the flapper. Zelda performed this task honorably, producing four articles, three of which were published in *McCall's* and in *Metropolitan Magazine*. Fitzgerald devoted a special section on his 1922 *Ledger* page for "Zelda's Earnings," which came to $815.

"Eulogy on the Flapper," "The Super-Flapper" and "Where Do Flappers Go?" make up a kind of passionate yet ironic commentary on the character who had made Scott famous and who, in the character of Gloria, had just made her last appearance on the literary scene. The "Eulogy" was illustrated with a picture of its author—the proud, pure profile of a Jazz Age figurehead, her Amazon features accentuated by the puff of short hair at her neck. It was a cameo that might also have illustrated Bishop's comparison of Gloria and her model. *The Beautiful*'s hero, he wrote, "has put away all emotions but one. This last illusion is a Fitzgerald flapper of the most famous type—hair honey-colored and bobbed, mouth rose-colored and profane. . . . Even with his famous flapper, he has yet failed to show that hard intelligence, that intricate emotional equipment upon which her charm depends, so that Gloria, the beautiful and damned lady of his imaginings, remains a little inexplicable, a pretty, vulgar shadow of her prototype."[10]

In the few articles she published then, Zelda showed how sound this judgment was. Gloria could never have written them. Of them all, it was the book review, the first article published and signed by Zelda Sayre, that best displayed her acid, airy wit. She began it by explaining to the reader her first reason for wanting him to buy the book: she coveted a gold lamé dress that a shop on Forty-second Street was offering for a mere $300. Then, if enough people bought the book, she would buy a platinum ring. And if it was a smash success, her husband could replace the old overcoat he'd been wearing for the past three years. After all, hadn't she unwittingly collaborated on the book? It seemed to her, she wrote, "that on one page I recognized a portion of an old diary of mine which mysteriously disappeared shortly after my marriage, and also scraps of letters, which, though considerably edited, sound to me vaguely familiar. In fact, Mr. Fitzgerald—I believe that is how he spells his name—seems to believe that plagiarism begins at home." She concludes in her own style with a comment on the book's melodramatic end, when a thoroughly crushed Anthony finally inherits his grandfather's fortune. It was not Anthony's fate that interested Zelda, but Gloria's: "The book ends on a tragic note, in fact a note which will fill any woman with horror, or, for that matter, will fill my furrier with horror, for Gloria, with thirty million to spend, buys a sable coat instead of a kolinsky coat. This is a tragedy unequaled in the entire works of Hardy. Then the book closes on a note of tremendous depression and Mr

Fitzgerald's subtle manner of having Gloria's deterioration turn on her taste in coats has scarcely been equaled by Henry James."[11]

In June they left with the baby and her nurse for White Bear Lake, where they had spent the previous summer. To simplify the housekeeping, they moved into the Yacht Club, where Zelda could swim, play golf and water-ski while Scott again revised his play and gave it a title, *Gabriel's Trombone*. This was a time of conflicting demands on him. For one thing he was anxious to exploit his literary and paraliterary gifts as much as he could to settle his financial problems, he hoped, once and for all. It was in this spirit that he labored on a musical designed to please Broadway audiences, a show that was in a direct line from the musicals he had written at Princeton. He even considered cashing in on his talent as an actor. Around mid-July, to Perkins's dismay, he seemed ready to accept the producers' offers to him and Zelda to play the leads in a movie version of *This Side of Paradise*. The project fizzled out, but that Fitzgerald even considered it is significant, despite his assurances to Perkins that it would have been his "first and last appearance positively" on the screen.[12]

At the same time he still dreamed of making, or remaking, a name for himself as a novelist. In May he had mapped out a new novel on which he furnished some details: "Its locale will be the middle west and New York of 885 I think. It will concern less superlative beauties than I run to usually and will be centered on a smaller period of time. It will have a catholic element."[13] This was not followed up, but he probably spent part of the early summer working on it. This was probably a first sketch for *Gatsby*. When he got down to serious work on his third novel, he lifted out a planned prologue describing his hero's childhood and turned it into a short story, "Absolution." The story shows the characteristics outlined above, is set in late-nineteenth-century Minnesota and has a strong Catholic element, since the whole story revolves on the relationship of young Rudolph Miller (alias Jay Gatz) with the priest Augustus Schwartz.

His return to the scene of his childhood, his talks with Father Barron about religion (the priest, convinced that Scott's faith would revive, told him that his disaffection was good riddance for the Church), all his home-town memories, especially of grandfather McQuillan and the empire builders, may have given Fitzgerald a desire to call up a world wholly different from the St. Paul of *The Flappers of Midnight*. "Winter Dreams," the only short story he wrote in 1922 after his novel came out, is about the unhappy love of a poor young man, Dexter Green, for Judy Jones, a St. Paul heiress. Dexter, who starts out in life as a caddie at the Yacht Club on White Bear Lake, gets ahead fast and becomes one of the city's richest men, but he abandons his pursuit of Judy: "The dream was gone. . . . He wanted to care, and he could not care. For he had gone away and he could never go back any more. . . . Even the grief he could have borne was left behind in the country of illusion, of youth, of the richness of life, where his winter dreams had finished."[14] This is another forerunner of *Gatsby*.

Wilson had clearly perceived how important the Middle West had become in Fitzgerald's imagination. In preparing an essay on his friend that was to run in *The Bookman* when *The Beautiful* appeared, he stressed three major influences that could explain Fitzgerald's work: his Irish Catholic lineage, St. Paul and excessive drinking. Wilson had been strongly influenced by the works of Hippolyte Taine, and he bore down on Taine's theory of the importance of environment. He contrasted Fitzgerald's Middle West of big commercial cities and country clubs with Sinclair Lewis's Middle West of small prairie towns like the one in *Main Street*.

"What we find in him [Fitzgerald] is much what we find in the more prosperous strata of these cities," Wilson wrote: "sensitivity and eagerness for life without a sound base of culture and taste; a structure of millionaire residences, brilliant expensive hotels and exhilarating social activities built not on the eighteenth century but simply on the flat Western land. And it seems to me rather a pity that he has not written more of the West: it is perhaps the only milieu that he thoroughly understands. When Fitzgerald approaches the East, he brings to it the standards of the wealthy West—the preoccupation with display, the appetite for visible magnificence and audible jamboree, the vigorous social atmosphere of amiable flappers and youths comparatively untainted as yet by the snobbery of the East. . . . Surely F. Scott Fitzgerald should some day do for Summit Avenue what Lewis has done for Main Street."[15]

Fitzgerald's special qualities, the critic maintained, owed little to Anglo-Saxon solidity and much to Irish lightness. Still following in Taine's wake, Wilson ventured a few theories on national psychology that may be debatable but that, on a pragmatic level, do fairly precisely define some psychological characteristics peculiar to Fitzgerald: "Like the Irish, Fitzgerald is romantic, but also cynical about romance; he is bitter as well as ecstatic; astringent as well as lyrical. He casts himself in the role of playboy, yet at the playboy he incessantly mocks. He is vain, a little malicious, of quick intelligence and wit, and has an Irish gift for turning language into something iridescent and surprising." Wilson concludes by citing "a great Irishman," Bernard Shaw, on the Irish: "'An Irishman's imagination never lets him alone, never convinces him, never satisfies him; but it makes him that he can't face reality nor deal with it nor handle it nor conquer it: he can only sneer at them that do . . . and imagination's such a torture that he can't bear it without whisky.'"[16]

When Wilson read his first draft of the article to Fitzgerald, the subject conceded the rightness of its diagnosis. "Needless to say," he wrote Wilson in January 1922, "I have never read anything with quite the uncanny fascination with which I read your article. It is, of course, the only intelligible and intelligent thing of any length which has been written about me and my stuff. . . . I am guilty of every stricture and I take an extraordinary delight in its considered approbation." Fitzgerald nevertheless feared that the article's emphasis on his drinking would damage his reputation, and he asked Wilson to eliminate it, denying he wrote when he was drunk: "As a matter of fact I have never written a line of any kind while I was under the glow of so much as a single cocktail and tho my parties have been many it's been their spectacularity rather than their frequency which has built up the usual 'dope-fiend' story. Judge and Mrs. Sayre would be crazy! And they never miss *The Bookman*." Referring to the three influences listed in the article, he told Wilson he had missed the most important one: "I feel less hesitancy asking you to remove the liquor because your catalogue is not complete anyhow—the most enormous influence on me in the four and a half years since I met her has been the complete, fine and full-hearted selfishness and chill-mindedness of Zelda."[17]

Fitzgerald spent the final weeks of his stay in St. Paul reading the proofs of the volume of short stories he had entitled *Tales of the Jazz Age*. He had found it difficult to put together a collection worthy of appearing in book form. Only three stories had been written since the summer of 1920, and he chose to use only one of these, "The Diamond as Big as the Ritz," which had been published in *The Smart Set;* the other two were "The Popular Girl" and "Two for a Cent," and although he had been well paid for them, he considered them inferior. Most of the collection, then, had been written before he began work on his second novel; and some of these, such as "The Camel's Back," had already been rejected as unfit for his first volume of stories. To flesh out the new book, Fitzgerald even added "Tarquin of Cheapside," first published at Princeton in 1917 and later picked up in *The Smart Set*. The collection was designed, the author admitted cynically, to please "those who read as they run as they run as they read."[18] As with *The Beautiful*, he had stopped worrying about quality; it was sales that concerned him now. But he was airily good-humored about it. Each of the titles in the table of contents was preceded by a winning little commentary, which seemed to warn his readers that this stuff may not be great literature, but it was entertaining.

There is a touch here of the insolence of Zelda's book review. Of "The Camel's Back," for example, he commented, "I suppose that of all the stories I have ever written, this one cost me the least travail and perhaps gave me the most amusement. . . . it was written . . . with the express purpose of buying a platinum and diamond wrist watch which cost six hundred dollars. . . . I like it least of all the stories in this volume."[19] Of "Jemina," written at Princeton and revised for *The Smart Set*, he remarked: "I have laughed over it a great deal, especially when I first wrote it, but I can laugh over it no longer. It seems to me worth preserving a few years—at least until the ennui of changing fashions suppresses me, my books and it together."[20]

That last line may be related to his rather surprising dedication of the book, "Quite inappropriately, To My Mother." Defiance, or pathetic mark of affection? On the gaudy cover of this book dedicated to the unloved Molly Fitzgerald, whom he had hardly seen during the year just spent in St. Paul, writhed dancers as frantic as those in a John Held cartoon. Through her, his mother, Fitzgerald was peering back at his lost childhood with a sense of both regret and guilt at a time when a chapter of his life was ending. This book was a kind of farewell to his pink-and-blue, bittersweet period of tenderness and jubilation. With few exceptions his stories—increasingly devoted to keeping food on the table—would never again show the giddy spontaneity, the burlesque fantasy of his early work. The next book of stories, published after the appearance of *Gatsby*, would tap the realistic, sociological vein mined in *The Beautiful and Damned;* the stories would chiefly reflect the Fitzgeralds' marriage problems. This would be the end of the commedia dell'arte period; the book's very title, *All the Sad Young Men*, would testify to its author's feeling that the ball was over.

That the haughty Wilson had been enchanted by his friend's unfettered inventiveness was clear in his *Bookman* article in which, tucked in among the critical barbs, is his confession of sheer pleasure at the show: "His characters—and he—are actors in an elfin harlequinade; they are as nimble, as gay and as lovely—and as hardhearted—as fairies: Columbine elopes with Harlequin on a rope ladder dropped from the Ritz and both go morris-dancing amuck on a case of bootleg liquor. . . . Just before the curtain falls, Harlequin puts on false whiskers and pretends to be Bernard Shaw; he gives reporters an elaborate interview on politics, religion and history. . . . Columbine nearly dies laughing; Harlequin sends out for a case of gin."[21]

The Fitzgeralds left St. Paul at the beginning of September to be in New York when *Tales of the Jazz Age* appeared. They arrived in the midst of a heat wave that made them long for the cool shade of White Bear Lake. Tuesday, September 6, was one of the hottest days of the year and their suite at the Plaza was suffocating. A few days later, rainstorms flooded the city; an inch and a half of rain fell on September 12 alone. These meteorological details would be gratuitous had they not been converted into drama in the final chapters of *Gatsby*. The scene at the Plaza in which Daisy rejects Gatsby, who is defeated by the steamy dampness, is described as taking place in September 1922, on "almost the last, certainly the warmest [day] of the summer."[22] Gatsby is murdered a few days later and he is buried in a downpour six days after his defeat. The coincidence is really too strong to be accidental; this was Fitzgerald's imagination distilling the effective essence from these climatic vagaries. We should not forget that like his narrator and witness Nick Carraway, Fitzgerald viewed that summer's events through the moral glass of the Midwest he had just left.

For the Fitzgeralds, however, the fall of 1922 took another turning: the Manhattan of Park Avenue and Broadway rejoiced at their return; they resumed their place among the celebrities vital to maintaining New York's idea of itself. A newspaper clipping from one of their scrapbooks gives an excellent summary of what was expected of them: "We are accustomed enough to this kind of rumor in regard to stage stars, but it is fairly new in relation to authors. The great drinking bouts, the petting may be what the public expects of Fitzgerald, whose books told so much of this kind of life."[23] Decorator Reginald March gave them a prominent place on the curtain of the Greenwich Village Follies among the artists who had recently become famous; shown aboard a truck rolling to glory were the Princeton trio, Wilson, Bishop and Fitzgerald, and two newcomers, Gilbert Seldes and John Dos Passos. But it was Zelda, diving into the Washington Square fountain, who was the center of attention.

Dos Passos had not forgotten that Fitzgerald had been among the most ardent defenders of *Three Soldiers*. Wilson introduced him to the Fitzgeralds, and they invited him to lunch at the Plaza. In his *Memoirs* he recalled the impressions left by that first contact. He was charmed by Zelda's beauty and grace, but struck by a strange gleam in her eyes. When lunch was over, it was suggested that they all go to Long Island, where the Fitzgeralds were about to rent a house. The expedition landed at the home of Ring Lardner, for whom Scott had recently developed a liking, but Lardner was drunk and very sad, and the group went on to spend the evening at Coney Island, which had always fascinated Zelda. Dos Passos found himself alone with her in a Ferris-wheel car. At the top of the circuit she said something that struck him: "I don't remember any more what it was, but I thought to myself, suddenly, this woman is mad. Whatever she had said was so completely off track; it was like peering into a dark abyss—something forbidding between us. She didn't pause as I recall, but went right on. I was stunned. I can honestly say that from that first time I sensed that there was something peculiar about her."[24]

Dos Passos, a poor dancer, was surprised at how flatly she told him so. She became aggressive in a very personal way, and despite the tone of acid wit the group affected, he found it hard to tolerate her sarcasm. "You see," he explained, "there was a lot of banter between all of us; it was the period of the great wisecrack. Her humor was good about minor things, but she'd go off into regions that weren't funny anymore."[25]

Gilbert Seldes, who had made a name for his analyses of the new popular arts—comic strips, musical comedies, movies and jazz—was then the managing editor of *The Dial*, a magazine that embraced the new literary movements. He met the Fitzgeralds at the end of a party in Townsend Martin's bachelor apartment. Seldes was tight and he had stretched out on Martin's sumptuous bed when, he later recounted, "suddenly, as though in a dream, the apparition, the double apparition approached me. The two most beautiful people in the world were floating toward me, smiling. It was as if they were angelic visitors. I thought to myself, 'If there is anything I can do to keep them as beautiful as they are, I will do it.' "[26]

This recalls the report of Van Wyck Brooks, whose biography of Mark Twain showing the devastating effect of puritanism on an American artist's development had been praised by Fitzgerald. He was present at a dinner party at which the Fitzgeralds arrived an hour late and promptly dozed off at the table. Scott pulled himself together to explain that they had spent the previous two nights carousing. "Someone gathered Zelda up, with her bright cropped hair and diaphanous gown, and dropped her on a bed in a room near by. There she lay curled and asleep like a silken kitten. Scott slumbered in the living-room, waking up suddenly again to telephone an order for two cases of champagne, together with a fleet of taxis to take us to a night club." Even before the period's excesses were generally associated with madness and tragedy, Brooks thought that the incident represented the spirit of the twenties. And the Fitzgeralds, he decided, were "so obviously, romantic lovers."[27]

In early October they took a house in Great Neck, Long Island. It was on the southeastern shore of the peninsula, at the foot of Manhasset Bay, near the town and station of Great Neck. In *Gatsby*, Great Neck became West Egg, and another peninsula across the bay became East Egg, where Daisy and Tom Buchanan and the old moneyed families lived. This in fact was where the Guggenheims, the Astors, the Van Nostrands and the Pulitzers had their summer homes.

As at Westport, the Fitzgeralds hoped to remain apart from the feverish life of New York, and they had resolved to stay sober. Shane Leslie had introduced Fitzgerald into the great estates on the shores of the strait separating the island from the continent, and Scott was dazzled by them. Since then the area had been taken over by theater people, newspapermen, songwriters and musicians, along with a few rich bootleggers. Among the Fitzgeralds' neighbors were Florenz Ziegfeld, of *Follies* fame, and his lieutenant, Gene Buck, who lived across the bay in a house with a living room that Ring Lardner said was like the Yale Bowl; George M. Cohan and his partner Sam Harris, who was to stage Fitzgerald's *The Vegetable, or, From President to Postman.* Lillian Russell lived there too, and so did Ernest Truex, who would play the lead in *The Vegetable;* caricaturist Rube Goldberg; polo champion Tom Hitchcock; Basil Rathbone; Groucho Marx; and financier Edward Fuller, whom Fitzgerald remembered in mapping out Gatsby's financial frauds.

This was the type of society that flocked to Gatsby's parties and that is so suggestively evoked in the guest list that opens chapter 5 in *The Great*

Gatsby. Compared with the luxurious homes around them, the big house the Fitzgeralds rented for $300 a month at 6 Gateway Drive was a shack. They hired a Swedish couple as servants, and a nurse for Scottie. A police dog named Fritzie brought the number of occupants to seven. As usual when she moved into a new home, Zelda began issuing invitations. This was the college football season, and she wrote to the Kalmans, the only friends she had made in St. Paul: "Are you coming east for the football games? If you are you *must* come stay with us in our nifty little Babbitt-home at Great Neck. We seem to have achieved a state of comparative organization at last and, having bought loads of very interesting flour sieves and cocktail shakers, are in a position to make a bid for your patronage on your next trip."[28]

So began a round of parties that sometimes went on for several days. Just as Gatsby's house was a target for gate-crashers, so "it became a habit with many world-weary New Yorkers," Scott observed, "to pass their weekends at the Fitzgerald house in the country."[29] He wrote out a series of house rules for importunate guests: "Visitors are requested not to break down doors in search of liquor, even when authorized to do so by the host and hostess. . . . Weekend guests are respectfully notified that the invitation to stay over Monday, issued by the host-hostess during the small hours of Sunday morning, must not be taken seriously."[30]

In a satire entitled "The Delegate from Great Neck," in the form of a dialogue between a frivolous Fitzgerald and a sententious Van Wyck Brooks, Wilson lists the visitors to whom Fitzgerald promises to introduce Brooks if he accepts an invitation to Great Neck: Gloria Swanson, Sherwood Anderson, Dos Passos, Marc Connelly, Dorothy Parker, Rube Goldberg and Lardner. The two men's discussion revolves around Brooks's refusal to accept the pretension of Fitzgerald and his friends to having freed American letters from the taboos that paralyzed the creativity of such men as Twain and James. To which Fitzgerald, confessing his ignorance, replies: "The Puritan thing, you mean. I suppose you're probably right. I don't know anything about James myself. I've never read a word of him."[31] Brooks, who is used here as Wilson's mouthpiece, points out that the work of the young generation of which Fitzgerald claims to be the delegate smacks strongly of journalism; it seems to him that the generation unwittingly reflects the spirit of capitalist ideology, especially in these writers' obedience to the laws of advertising. "Did you realize," Brooks asserts, "when you used that expression [the man who made America Younger-Generation-conscious], that you had dropped into the language of advertising? In describing your literary activities, you could not avoid the jargon of business; and it strikes me that the production of books by the younger generation has become an industry much like another." To which Fitzgerald can only reply, "I knew that what I said about making America Younger-Generation-conscious sounded like advertising. I was just making fun of the way that the advertising people talk."[32] All this very neatly summarizes the position of a Fitzgerald who was immersed in the mercenary milieu of show business—which, like him, pleased to think itself distinguished by its irony toward, and satire of, the zeitgeist of the period.

The ambiguity of Fitzgerald's position is illustrated by his close relationship with Lardner, who was also fascinated by the lights of fame, but repelled by the Great Neck circle that he called a "social sewer." As soon as he moved to Long Island, Fitzgerald conceived a liking for this man, nine years his senior and a Midwesterner like himself, whose ambition was also to see his work staged on Broadway.

Until then, Lardner had been a sports writer who had used his baseball lore in the Twain-style stories he sold to *The Saturday Evening Post*. He was also known for his satiric poetry and for his lyrics to a few show tunes. In 1922 the *Ziegfeld Follies* had presented one of his skits, *The Bulls' Pen*, but he had about given up hope of writing a play that the great Cohan would produce. Most of his sizable income was earned from journalism. The huge house on East Shore Road, in which he lived with his wife and four sons, may have been the model for Gatsby's. Despite his prosperity, Lardner was a restless, pessimistic man who, even more than Fitzgerald, tried to drown his anxiety in drink. In appearance he was tall, dark, skinny, almost bald, with an aquiline profile and bulging eyes; there was something in his face of the infinite distress one saw in Buster Keaton's features. And, like the Keaton persona, he was fearless, taciturn and hypnotic, the living antithesis of blond, pink Fitzgerald, who was always exclaiming, always bouncing, never at rest.

What attracted Scott to Lardner, he would later recall, were the man's impregnable dignity—he was always impeccably polite, always imperturbable whatever the circumstances—and the crushing contempt he heaped on the society around him, the gloomy ferocity with which he pilloried the absurdities of his time. In the harshness of his invective he resembled Mencken, but he was a somber, lanky Mencken, lacking the older man's plump joviality and gluttonous appetite for life. "The special force of Ring Lardner's work," wrote critic Clifton Fadiman, "springs from a single fact: he just doesn't like people. Except Swift, no writer has gone further on hatred alone. I believe he hates himself; more certainly he hates his characters; and most clearly of all, his characters hate each other. But of this integral triune repulsion is born his icy satiric power."[33]

Scott could not help being flattered by his exemption from this universal condemnation; perhaps, too, as unlike each other as they were physically, he was fascinated to find his double in Lardner, a projection of his own death instinct. He could feel only respect and a kind of terror for this man who was slowly and deliberately drinking himself to death and who, stoically compounding with absurdity, wrote song lyrics and doggerel verse while he dreamed of writing the surpassingly, impossibly fine play that would bring him release.

Lardner took so little interest in what he wrote that he never bothered to keep a copy or a clipping of the stories he published, which outraged Fitzgerald, who saved everything. Impressed by some of Lardner's stories, Scott persuaded him to collect and publish them in book form. As he had done for Boyd, he enlisted Perkins in his crusade, dug out other pieces and, with Lardner's very reluctant help, put together a book he called *How to Write Short Stories (with Examples)*. Published by Scribner's, it sold well and was hailed by Mencken as a masterpiece.

When Lardner died ten years later, Fitzgerald wrote a sad, grave tribute, one of his finest pieces. At that point he was in the same situation his friend had been in when they met—alcoholic and despairing and sinking all his hopes in the novel he was then completing. His sense of their brotherhood in disaster had already permeated the early versions of *Tender Is the Night*, in which Abe North, modeled on Lardner, precedes Dick Diver in failure and degradation.

Yet this hypochondriac, this sad clown, this emaciated wit who seemed to have come straight out of the pages of *The Undertaker's Garland*, could make others laugh even if he could not laugh himself. Fitzgerald said Lardner's work was "the most uproarious and inspired nonsense since Lewis Carroll."[34] His black humor and incisive wit delighted the Fitzgeralds, especially Zelda, who had never before been courted with such a mixture of burlesque petulance and touchy gravity. He wrote funny poems to her; at times he shed his moroseness and became sociable in her presence, all without a trace of sentimentality.

Lardner was not averse to playing practical jokes or joining in an occasional escapade. One night in May 1923, learning that Joseph Conrad was visiting his publisher, Nelson Doubleday, at the latter's home on Oyster Bay, not far from Great Neck, Fitzgerald persuaded Lardner to join him on Doubleday's lawn. There they were to do a dance in Conrad's honor in the hope of attracting his attention and showing American writers' esteem for him. This turned out no more successfully than Fitzgerald's tribute to Apollo had a few years earlier: they attracted no one's attention but the caretaker's, who threw them off the place. Scott must have remembered the incident a year later on learning of Conrad's death. Seldes remembered having seen him that day standing motionless on his balcony overlooking the Mediterranean, unable to say anything but, over and over, "Conrad is dead."

Ring became Scott's confidant, the solitary companion of nightlong discussions that went on until, at daylight, Lardner would stretch to his full height, yawn and say, "Well, I guess the children have left for school by this time. I might as well go home."[35] But the Fitzgeralds saw crowds of people; the stories are legion about their stay in Great Neck. Like everything touching on the Fitzgerald legend, these tales are to be handled with care, thought of not as objective reports, but as signs of the fascination the couple exerted on those around them. The stories are of documentary value only if we remember that they are not candid snapshots, but scenes reconstituted from memory.

A montage of these shots in eight-millimeter black and white might, for example, show: Fitzgerald, with a bottle of champagne clamped under his arm, escorting screenwriter Anita Loos into the Plaza in search of Zelda and a friend, only to be chucked out for being too drunk; sharing the warm champagne with the three women in the taxi taking them to Great Neck; interrupting dinner to show out a woman admirer who had forced her way into the house; being so annoyed at a remark by Zelda that he pulls at the tablecloth, sending dishes and glasses crashing to the floor, whereupon the ladies retire to the living room; falling asleep under a tree and waking to join them at tea, whereupon the evening proceeds in the coziest affability.

Fitzgerald giving a dinner in honor of novelist Rebecca West, but forgetting to give her his address. Setting an effigy in her place at table in the form of a pillow painted with a grotesque face and crowned with a feathered hat. Spending the evening insulting the pillow. Rushing to answer the doorbell and being heard loudly declaring, "No, Miss West, you can't come in. We don't want you now."[36] It was only a deliveryman. In counterpoint, Miss West's impression when she finally met Zelda: "I had been told that she was very beautiful, but when I . . . saw her I had quite a shock. She was standing with her back to me, and her hair was quite lovely, it glistened like a child's. . . . Then she turned round and she startled me. . . . There was a curious unevenness about [her face], such as one sees in Géricault's pictures of the insane. Her profile seemed on two different planes. . . . There was something very appealing about her. But frightening. Not that one was frightened from one's own point of view, only from hers."[37]

Fitzgerald, Lardner and Goldberg, all a little drunk, with Goldberg yawning and protesting that it was late, but that he had to find a barber because he had to be presentable for an important dinner. So his two friends accompany him to the barbershop. He falls asleep; when he awakes, he is alone and his hair has been cut in checkerboard fashion.

Fitzgerald dropping to his knees before beautiful actress Laurette Taylor, grasping her hands and, gazing into her deep brown eyes, repeating like an incantation, "My God! You beautiful egg! You beautiful egg!" And she, returning home in distress, sobbing to her husband, "I have just seen the doom of youth. Understand? The doom of youth itself. A walking doom."[38]

Fitzgerald driving Perkins to Long Island, missing a downhill turn and driving his Rolls-Royce axle-deep into a pond. He and Zelda floundering among the water lilies, trying to push the car out of the water.

Zelda trying to phone the Kalmans at the Ritz, anxious not to miss them on their way through New York. Scott hears her talking to the operator and reminds her that she had seen them the previous evening and had left their room in a basket of laundry.

Fitzgerald, an admirer of Edith Wharton's novels, interrupting a conference in Mr. Scribner's office to throw himself on one knee at her feet and declaim, like a subtitle in a movie comedy, "Could I let the author of *Ethan Frome* pass through New York without paying my respects?"[39]

And, in the same tone, but without the subtitle, Fitzgerald attending one of the rare parties given by Theodore Dreiser, to which the veteran of naturalism had invited everyone who was anyone in literature in New York. There are half a dozen contradictory versions of this scene reported by some of those present—Sherwood Anderson, Burton Rascoe and Llewelyn Powys, among others. The only point on which they agree is that Dreiser had provided no refreshment, introduced no one to anyone and remained absolutely silent while his guests, sitting on chairs lined up along the walls, waited for something to happen. Fitzgerald, excited as usual at the idea of meeting a great writer and, as usual, ready to rise to the occasion with a grandiloquent gesture or a rousing declaration, arrives bearing a bottle of excellent champagne. Some of the guests ascribe the expected declaration to him ("I consider H. L. Mencken and Theodore Dreiser the greatest living men in the country today"[40]); others maintain that he was too drunk to get through the door; still others, that he went from chair to chair until he found out which person was Dreiser. In all the versions the bottle is gravely presented to the host, who puts it in his icebox and returns to his seat, allowing the gathering to fall back into its former lethargy. After a seemingly endless wait, despairing of seeing the champagne again, bored with decorating the walls like tapestries, the men of letters leave, one by one.

These short films, a little fuzzy, a little scratched and jumpy, sometimes superimposed, end with the clear, sharp still picture of the couple that appeared on the cover of *Hearst's International* in May 1923 and was picked up by most American newspapers and magazines. It was, in a way, the official photograph that immortalized their status as movers and shakers in New York's postwar nightlife. He was twenty-six years old, she twenty-three. They were at the peak of their social career; they already had a past and still had a future. They were sure of themselves and, especially in Zelda's case, confident that money would be increasingly easy to come by; Scott still hoped to write a novel that would make him the best writer of his generation.

There they were, suspended for an instant at the crest of the wave, posing for posterity, with Zelda in front standing straight and impassive in her ermine-trimmed dress and pearl necklace, her wavy hair puffed out at the sides, parted in the middle. Her long, almond-shaped eyes and neatly chiseled mouth perfectly fitted her oval face. This was her great-occasions face, her "Elizabeth Arden face," as she would say. Scott stood slightly behind her, bending slightly to the left, his cheek lightly brushing her hair and his right hand resting carelessly on two of her fingers. His brushed-back blond hair was also parted. He wore a light-colored striped jacket open over a dark vest and a flowing checked tie. They did not smile; there was just a hint of a faintly ironic pout. They stared into the camera with veiled eyes, Scott's a little dreamy, Zelda's a shade disdainful.

9. THE UNDERSIDE OF PROSPERITY

(1923)

The cover photo of *Hearst's International* was not designed merely to celebrate the young couple. Fitzgerald had just signed an exclusive contract with the magazine, and the puff was basically aimed at signaling his entry into the Hearst stable with its thirty-two newspapers, nine magazines and nine million readers.

The egocentric, exhibitionistic, megalomaniac Hearst depicted by Orson Welles in *Citizen Kane* was distinguished from the austere nabobs of the preceding generation—Rockefeller, Carnegie, Ford and the rest—by a new attitude toward money that was the trademark of the time. Although he was immensely rich—he battered his way into the newspaper business with the seven and a half million dollars he inherited from his mother—Hearst spent lavishly and was always short of money, sometimes having to dip into his newspapers' tills for ready cash.

He could be wryly aware of his profligacy: to a visitor who remarked that there was money to be made in the movie business, he replied shortly, "Yes, mine!" But this hardly sobered him; biographer W. A. Swanberg estimated Hearst's personal expenses at fifteen million dollars a year. The ostentation of his "follies," from his patronage of his actress mistress, Marion Davies, to his movie-set California castle, San Simeon, and his extraordinary art collection, may have frustrated the political ambitions he cherished. Doughty trustbuster, fierce foe of the Republican party (he was wrongly accused of collusion in McKinley's assassination), he had also made enemies among the Democrats, especially in New York, where his rows with Al Smith and Tammany Hall had kept him from running for the mayoralty and governership he coveted. He had to settle for powering the election of his own man, John Hylan, mayor of New York from 1917 to 1923.

Hearst's personality and career typify the mentality of the men who held power in postwar America. An era of prosperity, the era of "the seven fat kine," began in 1923 and ended with the crash of 1929. After a period of inflation and unemployment in 1919, marked by riots and a wave of antisocialist repression ("May Day" exactly catches the climate), the national economy perked up in 1920; there was a brief recession in 1921–22, then it resumed its climb. Industrial production doubled in ten years and average income rose by 40 percent. From 1920 to 1929 stock market indices tripled, which meant that Americans were borrowing against the future in the same way that, encouraged by advertising, they were forming the habit of installment buying. So strong were the come-ons that Americans' debts outstripped their earnings. In their constant need of money, though on very different scales, Hearst and Fitzgerald were not isolated examples but reflections of most Americans' state of mind.

People were impatient to live fully in the present, trusting to the future to pay the bills. What was important was to get rich as quickly as possible, wealth being its own justification for the means used to acquire it. Government was not immune to the fever. After his election in 1921, President Warren G. Harding, chosen by the Republican party precisely for his mediocrity, surrounded himself with politicians equally lacking in scope and scruples. This was "the Ohio gang" that was to discredit his administration.

Two examples show the tone of political life under the successor to Woodrow Wilson, who was disavowed for his excessive idealism. Charles Forbes, head of the Veterans Administration, was convicted of signing fraudulent contracts that cost the government some two hundred million dollars. Interior Secretary Albert Fall was also guilty, with the Secretary of the Navy, of secretly leasing drilling rights to private interests in oil fields owned by the navy. All this in return for munificent bribes. The Elk Hill and Teapot Dome scandals, named for the pirated oil fields, were the major contributions to Harding's disgrace. Soon afterward the President died mysteriously while touring the country to appease public wrath.

The same corruption was rife in the big cities. New York had long been in the grip of Tammany Hall's Irish politicians, who controlled the police, largely made up of Irish cops, and turned a profit on the underworld by collecting a tithe on its operations. One example of this, interesting because Fitzgerald used it directly in *Gatsby*, concerned the then undisputed czar of the underworld, Arnold Rothstein, who appears in *Gatsby* as Meyer Wolfsheim and who maintained his supremacy until his murder in 1928. He bought Tammany's protection with election campaign contributions that gave him virtually complete freedom to extend his hold over prostitution and gambling.

One of his friends, Herman Rosenthal, was less skillful, or less lucky. He fell out with Lieutenant Charles Becker, in charge of police on New York's East Side, who laid claim to the payments Rosenthal had been making to political boss Tim Sullivan. Threatened by Becker, Rosenthal made the mistake of complaining to New York *World* reporter Herbert Bayard Swope. He lost no time in breaking the story. On July 13, 1912, the *World* denounced corruption in the police and Tammany Hall. Two days later Rosenthal was murdered at the door of the Metropole by Becker's killers in circumstances reported to Gatsby by Wolfsheim. Tammany immediately disowned Becker; he and his henchmen were arrested, tried and sent to the electric chair.

Rothstein carried on smoothly, functioning as go-between for the underworld and the politicians, and in the years that followed, no major scandal troubled the peace of Tammany Hall. With his political rear covered, Rothstein engineered his biggest coup of all, the Black Sox fix of the 1919 World Series. This was the exploit that showed the narrator of *Gatsby* how big a man "Wolfsheim" was: "It never occurred to me that one man could start to play with the faith of fifty million people with the single-mindedness of a burglar blowing a safe."[1]

Even his Black Sox take was small change compared with the huge profits Rothstein was to make from bootlegging. The start of Prohibition in 1920 opened realms of enterprise to him he had never dreamed possible.

Rising out of the moralizing fever that swept America on its entry into the war, the Eighteenth Amendment was accepted without protest at first. It fit the ideal of health, efficiency and productivity that animated the war effort; besides, most of the big brewers at whom the legislation was chiefly aimed were of German origin. By the time the Volstead Act was passed in 1919, America was in a laissez-faire mood and Congress was not anxious to increase the power of the federal government. Only 1,500 ill-paid ($1,000 to $2,000 a year) agents were assigned to enforce Prohibition, with special emphasis on patrolling the roughly 25,000 miles of coastlines and borders across which liquor could be smuggled. Almost at once, bootlegging was organized on a large scale.

Of all the fads that marked the Jazz Age—Mah-Jongg in 1923, the Coué method ("Every day, in every way, I am becoming better and better.") in the same year, crossword puzzles in 1924—drinking was the most durable and the most pernicious. Spurred by a streak of snobbery, people who had never before touched alcohol made it a duty to lay in a stock of liquors, to offer them to their friends, to patronize their favorite speakeasies, where men and women now guzzled on an equal footing. The bootlegger entered American folklore with as much public complicity as the outlaws of the Old West had enjoyed. The law's absurdity, federal agents' inability to enforce it (in 1925 they managed to intercept only 5 percent of the illegal traffic) fostered a spirit of skepticism and revolt against the law and traditional morality. What had been thought in 1917 to be the best intentions in the world were seen in 1923 as mere hypocrisy. The borderline between what was legal and what was not became more and more blurred. It was a paradox of Prohibition that the effect of this attempt to legislate virtue finally weakened Americans' civic sense.

In the context it is understandable that Fitzgerald, seeking a character that would best represent his era, made Gatsby a hoodlum accepted, if not by the East Egg "aristocracy," at least by the floating population of West

Egg, the environment in which Fitzgerald circulated. His interest in this type of person was evident, and his neighbor, Swope of the *World*, must certainly have supplied much of the information he needed when he went seriously to work on his novel. Nathan remembered how insistently Fitzgerald had pressed him for an introduction into a sphere of activity that was still largely unfamiliar to him.

Even after *The Great Gatsby* was finished and the manuscript sent to Perkins, Fitzgerald continued to study his subject with an eye to correcting the proofs: ". . . after careful searching of the files . . . for the Fuller Magee [sic] case," he wrote Perkins, "and after having had Zelda draw pictures until her fingers ache I know Gatsby better than I know my own child."[2]

Edward Fuller was a neighbor in Great Neck who had headed a brokerage firm of which William McGee was vice-president. In June 1922 he had filed for bankruptcy with a deficit of six million dollars, and the two men were convicted of having gambled away their customers' money. Unknown a few years earlier, Fuller had mysteriously become a force on Wall Street with the aid of a leading stockbroker, C. A. Stoneham, who had ceded part of his interests to him in 1921. Stoneham lived high and owned a racetrack, a casino and a newspaper; he was also the majority stockholder of the New York Giants baseball team. He raided the Giants' cashbox to try to salvage Fuller's firm, maintaining that he was acting at the behest of Thomas Foley, a former New York City sheriff and a mover in Tammany Hall. Like Gatsby, Fuller had pull on the highest police levels and, like him, had been one of the first residents of Great Neck to own a plane and fly it himself. In the paternal Stoneham's benevolence to Fuller we see a model for millionaire Dan Cody's affection for, and generosity to, Gatsby.

Fuller knew his way around the law and managed through four trials to drown his indictment in the general turmoil of his business affairs. Incriminating papers vanished during the investigation, key witnesses were bought off or kidnapped; when Fuller and his accomplices were finally convicted, it was years before he actually began serving his five-year prison sentence. And he was out of jail a year later.

The case became public two months after the Fitzgeralds moved to Great Neck, and the newspapers covered it assiduously. On the eve of his third trial, Fuller and his accomplices were arrested on a fresh charge of hawking nonexistent stocks by telephone and preparing to form a new firm to issue worthless shares. Again, the prosecution failed to come up with conclusive proof of guilt. The yellow press, led by Hearst's *American*, took over the case. Fuller openly credited his close contacts with Tammany Hall for his impunity, and the *American* pressed its own investigation to learn who his protector was. Patient digging through countless files at last led an American reporter to a check for ten thousand dollars issued by the Fuller-McGee company to Foley, a personal enemy of Hearst in New York Democratic circles. This unleashed a violent press campaign; during the third trial in the spring of 1923, the *American* revealed that Fuller's attorney, William Fallon, had suborned a member of the jury. Fallon was formally charged, whereupon he threatened to reveal details of Hearst's private life, and the case frittered out. Arnold Rothstein, with whom Fuller frequently gambled, was also accused of complicity in the case, but, as usual, he wriggled clear of the legal net.

We could go on cataloging cases of corruption in the period, but we have already seen enough to be sure that the criminal annals of the twenties were amply used in Fitzgerald's new novel, often as mere allusions, since the facts were familiar to his readers. There is no part of Gatsby's career that cannot be linked to one of the cases we have mentioned. The Veterans Administration scam is mirrored in one of Gatsby's guests, P. Jewett, former head of the American Legion. Wolfsheim insisted that his protégé join the Legion: "when he told me he was an Oggsford I knew I could use him good. I got him to join up in the American Legion and he used to stand high there."[3] One critic based his study of the origins of Gatsby's fortune on such clues as "I was in the drug business and then I was in the oil business."[4] The "drug business" is seen as designating the speakeasies to which Tom refers in the Plaza scene, while the "oil business" was an allusion to the more resounding Teapot Dome scandal. In Gatsby's mysterious phone calls all over the country, in young Parker's arrest when he attempts to sell his spurious stocks, we can read a recall of the Fuller case. And so on.

Hearst's munificence, Rothstein's hidden power, Fuller's audacity all certainly helped highlight Gatsby's portrait and fill in the background of sensational rumors, scandal and violence. But Fitzgerald stopped short of mere anecdote, simply suggesting the atmosphere through composite facts authenticated by occasional specific allusions. A number of details in his manuscript and proof corrections disappeared in the printed book, along with the whole section concerning Gatsby's childhood.

In *The Great Gatsby* Fitzgerald avoided dealing directly with the picturesque or repugnant ills of his time, reined in the satiric glee with which he had excoriated public life in *The Beautiful and Damned* and in *The Vegetable*. For the first time he resisted the temptation to spatter his work with bravura passages or Menckenesque diatribes. He tried to go beyond these surface mannerisms to a profound explanation of why, for Gatsby, for himself, for all America, sudden accession to a way of living that was free of the old material and moral constraints had degenerated into license, disorder and corruption. Why, with the promised land in sight, did the dream become a nightmare? But, paradoxically, through the mist of degradation surrounding himself and his protagonist, he also perceived hope that a sense of purpose, of mission, could survive and be revivified.

The year 1923 was pivotal both to the twenties and to Fitzgerald's career. "The uncertainties of 1919 were over," he would write. "There seemed little doubt about what was going to happen—America was going on the greatest, gaudiest spree in history and there was going to be plenty to tell about it. The whole golden boom was in the air—its splendid generosities, its outrageous corruptions in the tortuous death struggle of the old America in Prohibition. All the stories that came into my head had a touch of disaster in them; the lovely young creatures in my novels went to ruin, the diamond mountains of my short stories blew up, my millionaires were as beautiful and damned as Thomas Hardy's peasants."[5]

Fitzgerald's photo in *Hearst's International* was far more symbolic of what he had been than of what he was soon to become. The event it marked—his signing of an exclusive contract—was soon forgotten. Unable to supply the stories he had contracted to write (the summer was spent working on his novel), he canceled the contract, returned his $1,500 advance and bought back the two stories he had delivered to the magazine. He had indeed arrived, he had succeeded, he belonged now to New York society; but his success forced him to conform to the role he was expected to play and to keep his winning formula intact in the magazines. "By this time," he wrote in "My Lost City," "we 'knew everybody'—which is to say most of those whom Ralph Barton would draw as being in the orchestra on an opening night. But we were no longer important. The flapper, upon whose activities the popularity of my first books was based, had become *passé* by 1923, anyhow in the East. I decided to crash Broadway with a play, but Broadway sent its scouts to Atlantic City and quashed the idea in advance, so I felt that, for the moment, the city and I had little to offer each other."[6]

Fitzgerald's play was his swan song to his early manner; its failure wrecked his theatrical ambitions, which, from his boyhood efforts in St. Paul to his Princeton musicals, had seemed to him an alternative to novel writing and a shortcut to glory. With this illusion dissolved, he could devote himself entirely to completing his third novel.

Scribner's had published *The Vegetable* in April 1923, since no producer had yet seen fit to stage the play. The dedication reads: "to Katherine Tighe and Edmund Wilson Jr., who deleted many absurdities from my first two novels, I recommend the absurdities set down here." John Held again designed the book jacket, depicting the characters in Fitzgerald's phantasmagoria: Jerry Frost, the vegetable, and his shrewish wife, Charlotte; her sister Doris, a no-holds-barred flapper; Doris's lover, Joseph Fish, the "sheik of Idaho"; an octogenarian father; General Pushing; Judge Fossile; and Mr. Snooks, the bootlegger. This was a distillation of guignol, an absurdist treatment of the American Dream, 1923 version, revised and corrected by Mencken and Lardner.

Begun in November 1921, the play had been reworked several times and refused by such influential men of the theater as Gilbert Miller, Arthur Hopkins and George Selwyn; actor Frank Craven, whom Fitzgerald pictured in the lead, also backed off. But, encouraged by praise from Wilson and Nathan, who read the various versions, the author persevered. Wilson, more respectful of the fantasist and fantastic vein in Fitzgerald, the *Evil Eye* streak, than he was of his talent as a novelist, for once emerged from his usual reserve: "So far as I am concerned, I think it is one of the best things you ever wrote . . . no doubt the best American comedy ever written. . . . I think you have a gift for comic dialogue even though you can never resist a stupid gag, and should go on writing plays."[7] Nathan, delighted by the sketches he had run in *The Smart Set*—"The Debutante," "Mister Icky," "Porcelain and Pink"—and secure in his reputation as a drama critic, declared in 1921 that Fitzgerald certainly had a gift for playwriting. "I hope," he wrote, "that young F. Scott Fitzgerald will turn from the one-act form to the three-act form one of these days; I feel that he will confect a genuinely diverting comedy. He has a good sense of character, a sharp eye, a ferocious humor, and an aptitude for setting down adolescent dialogue that Tarkington has rarely matched."[8] It was this feeling for contemporary life, especially the flapper role, that persuaded producer Sam Harris to stage the play shortly after its publication.

The title *The Vegetable* was explained in a bogus quotation supposedly taken from a newspaper story: " 'Any man who doesn't want to get on in the world, to make a million dollars, and maybe even park his toothbrush in the White House, hasn't got as much to him as a good dog has—he's nothing more or less than a vegetable.'—From a current magazine."[9] This lapidary expression of the American Dream of success echoed a passage in a Mencken essay published in 1922 in the *Third Series* of *Prejudices*. It was surely in this that Fitzgerald found the title for the play he had originally planned to call *Gabriel's Trombone*. "This is a country in which all political thought and activity are concentrated upon the scramble for jobs," Mencken had written. ". . . Here is a country in which it is an axiom that a businessman shall be a member of the Chamber of Commerce, an admirer of Charles M. Schwab, a reader of *The Saturday Evening Post*, a golfer—in brief, a vegetable."[10]

In the play it is Charlotte, the unhappy vegetable's wife, who nags her husband to climb the ladder to wealth and prominence, although his sole ambition is to be a mailman some day. The first and third acts, realistic in tone and acutely boring, deride the goals and trials of the American lower middle class. True satire emerges in the second act, and it is dramatically effective. Yet this very dramatic impact counteracts Fitzgerald's critical intent because the entire act bathes in an atmosphere of dreamy farce in which his genius for fantasy skillfully exploits characters and situations. Jerry Frost, elected President of the United States, puts his cronies in key posts, more or less as Harding did after his inauguration in 1921. All the political corruption and scandals of the day, beside which Watergate seems merely a peccadillo, are alluded to in the play. But the outlandish plot robs the work of credibility and significance. Jerry's senile dad, appointed Secretary of the Treasury, cleans out the cashbox and cannot remember if he buried the money or threw it into the ocean; Jerry's bootlegger winds up ambassador to Irish Poland, from which Jerry buys certain islands while General Pushing arranges a declaration of war against it. Etcetera, etcetera. Fitzgerald's sense of absurdity, carred to its logical conclusion, produced scenes as surreal as those in *Ubu roi,* but it lacks the barbarous grandeur and tightness of plot and characterization that might have made *The Vegetable* a memorable play.

When rehearsals began in October 1923, Fitzgerald stopped work on his novel and even passed up the Harvard-Princeton game, so absorbed was he in watching his play take shape on the stage. Although sale of the movie rights to *This Side of Paradise* had brought him $10,000, he was still $3,500 in debt to Scribner's; early in November he was again appealing to Perkins for a loan of $650, which, he said, would spare his having to sell off his furniture. But he was convinced his play would be a hit and would earn him a small fortune. "We knew what colossal sums were earned on play royalties," he would write, "and just to be sure, we asked several playrights what was the maximum that could be earned on a year's run. I never allowed myself to be rash. I took a sum halfway between the maximum and the minimum, and put that down as what we could fairly count on its earning. I think my figures came to about $100,000."[11]

The play opened November 20 in Atlantic City before a glittering audience that included Mayor Hylan of New York. Fitzgerald later recalled this long-awaited evening: "It was a colossal frost. People left their seats and walked out, people rustled their programs and talked audibly in bored, impatient whispers. After the second act I wanted to stop the show and say it was all a mistake, but the actors struggled heroically on."[12]

Now it was time for Fitzgerald to take stock of his finances. Going back to work on the novel was out of the question. As heroically as his actors had struggled with his play, Fitzgerald spent the winter mending his financial fences by writing instantly salable short stories. For four months he quarantined himself in a room over his garage, and with the energy he had expended four years earlier in conquering the magazine market, he manufactured eleven stories and earned $17,000, which wiped out his debts and left him with a substantial sum. He labored like a prisoner digging a tunnel under the wall. For he had decided to end his wandering, to flee the temptations of Great Neck, to leave America in the spring for another go at Europe. It took him nearly a year to recover from the strain of those months of production. Not until October 1924 could he report to Wilson that he was in the clear: "I have got my health back—I no longer cough and itch and roll from one side of the bed to the other all night and have a hollow ache in my stomach after two cups of black coffee. I really worked hard as hell last winter—but it was all trash and it nearly broke my heart as well as my iron constitution."[13]

It is symptomatic of the Fitzgeralds' situation that many of the stories he wrote that winter deal with marriages threatened by the wife's selfishness. She is forever demanding more than her overworked husband can give; while he, at the brink of a nervous breakdown, exhausts himself to earn more money, she tries to flirt her way—dangerously—out of boredom. This was a way for Scott to clarify his relations with Zelda while contributing to the sociology of the middle class. But it was also a technique of self-examination, a review of a destructive way of living. In his *Ledger*, as we have seen, he had answered one of the questions hanging over him: where did the money come from? Now its corollary pressed for a reply: where did the money go? During this period he wrote the apparently comic essay published by the *Post* in April 1924, "How to Live on $36,000 a Year"; it might have been subtitled "The Balmy Bookkeeping of Francis Scott Fitzgerald." For the first time he pondered the paradox that the more he earned, the deeper into debt he sank.

He began by recounting a typical situation, one that would occur again later: "After we had been married for three months I found to my horror that I didn't have a dollar in the world, and the weekly hotel bill for two hundred dollars would be due next day." A sudden surge of anxiety was quickly squelched. "I knew there was nothing to worry about. I was now a successful author, and when successful authors ran out of money all they had to do was to sign cheques. I wasn't poor—they couldn't fool me. Poverty meant being depressed and living in a small, remote room and eating at a *rôtisserie* on the corner, while I—why, it was impossible that I should be poor. I was living at the best hotel in New York!"[14]

The move to Great Neck is described, along with his determination to budget carefully so as to end the year with money in the bank "to buy safety and security for our old age." He adds up the servants' wages; his wife buys a notebook in which she will record all the household expenses so as to keep track of them and trim them if need be. The trouble is, they live in one of those small towns near New York "which are built especially for those who have made money suddenly but have never had money before." The couple is caught in a kind of gold rush by tradesmen who are also newly disembarked and who turn Great Neck into one of the world's most expensive towns.

Knot by knot he unravels the snarled skein of causes and effects that make the couple victims of an order of things over which they have no control. Humbly, candidly, he exhibits his bills, makes inventories, compares his profits and losses, calculates average monthly household budgets, estimates extraordinary expenses, all in minute detail, omitting neither "barber and hairdresser: $25" nor "charity and loans: $15," adding and re-adding and finding that some $1,000 a month, $12,000 a year, mysteriously disappears. At that moment a neighbor rings their doorbell.

" 'Good heavens!' I announced. 'We have just lost $12,000!'

'Burglars?' he inquired.

'Ghosts,' answered my wife."

Thirty-six thousand phantom dollars have thus been frittered away, leaving no trace but debts. But the author's wife is resourceful. " 'The only thing you can do,' she said finally, 'is to write a magazine article and call it How to Live on $36,000 a year.'

" 'What a silly suggestion!' I replied coldly."

Writing this article just before leaving Long Island was a way for Fitzgerald to confess, to examine his conscience, to beat his breast. A public confession, recited to a jazz rhythm. But there is a shadow of alarm behind this comic pirouetting; from under the careless tone and the wry moralizing peer real anxiety and an ill-disguised sense of guilt. The blurred face of the penitentiary vaguely seen behind the confessional grille looks strangely like grandfather McQuillan. Scott must show his figures, must bare his scandalous prodigality, shine a bright light on his bad management. Here the parable of the talents[15] takes on its full meaning: how has he multiplied his gifts? How has he profited from his patrimony, from the talent that distinguished him among men? Fitzgerald tried to answer these theological questions with the resources of his time, in terms of household budgets. This was a way for him to evade the real problem, to shift responsibility from morality to the marketplace, to insinuate an anonymous and urbane jury of his contemporaries into the implacable tribunal of his conscience. He knew he had already won plenary indulgence; his graceful style and sincere tone would have seen to that. But he also knew that he would lose on appeal: his pseudo confession was merely one more attempt to delay the moment of true absolution—the absolution he would earn by realizing his potentialities, achieving the edifice he knew he had to build outside his century and its temptations.

IV. A CHOREOGRAPHY OF THE IMAGINATION

10. THE COLORS IN THE CREST

On May 3, 1924, the Fitzgeralds left New York for France aboard the *Min-newaska*. It was more as though they were fleeing than embarking on a pleasure trip. Only Perkins and Lardner had been let in on the secret, Ring having been entrusted with subletting their Great Neck home, on which the lease had not yet expired. Scott and Zelda left on the anniversary of their first sailing, but this time they were set on seeking a favorable climate for creation in Europe, as though Wilson's remarks on the stimulation afforded by a different culture had finally sunk in. In April Scott had finished writing the last of the stories that would enable him to start a new life; the story was called "John Jackson's Arcady," and its author was now heading for an Arcady of his own. "We were going to the Old World," he would write, "to find a new rhythm for our lives, with a true conviction that we had left our old selves behind forever."[1] In his *Ledger* he wrote, "Out of the woods at last and starting novel." Mention followed, as though parenthetically, of two parties, Gloria Swanson's and George Kaufman's, and then the note, "Decision on the 15th to go to Europe."[2]

The two items are closely linked: departure and novel combine to push aside everything that had hitherto fostered idleness and mediocrity. In the same week he wrote a long letter to Perkins to assure him of his determination to get out of the impasse he was in. He believed, if not too confidently, that he could complete his novel in two months. But he added that even if it took him ten times as long to finish it, he was resolved to outdo himself. "I cannot let it go out unless it has the very best I'm capable of in it, or even, as I feel sometimes, something better than I'm capable of. Much of what I wrote last summer was good but it was so interrupted that it was ragged and, in approaching it from a new angle, I've had to discard a lot of it."[3]

From the material he eliminated, he said, he had salvaged the material for his story "Absolution," which was to be published in the June issue of *The American Mercury*, a magazine newly founded by Mencken and Nathan. When the story appeared and Perkins congratulated him on its excellence, Fitzgerald added a detail: "I'm glad you liked 'Absolution.' As you know it was to have been the prologue of the novel but it interfered with the neatness of the plan."[4] Ten years later he would amplify this to a critic in response to an analysis of the character of Gatsby. "It might interest you to know," he wrote, "that a story of mine, called 'Absolution,' in my book *All the Sad Young Men* was intended to be a picture of [Gatsby's] early life, but that I cut it because I preferred to preserve the sense of mystery."[5]

From the start of his work on the novel, Fitzgerald lost interest in everything else (the sole exception being the rehearsals for *The Vegetable*). A letter Zelda wrote to Xandra Kalman in July 1923 confirmed his absorption in his new work: "Scott has started a new novel and retired into strict seclusion and celibacy. He's horribly intent on it and has built up a beautiful legend about himself which corresponds somewhat to the old fable about the ant and the grasshopper. *Me* being the grasshopper."[6] Indeed, in his letter to Perkins two weeks before leaving for Europe, Fitzgerald lamented that he had played the grasshopper too long, and he confessed his "bad habits":

"1. Laziness.

"2. Referring everything to Zelda—a terrible habit; nothing ought to be referred to anybody until it's finished

"3. Word consciousness and self-doubt, etc., etc., etc., etc."[7]

He was nevertheless optimistic. "I feel I have an enormous power in me now," he told the editor in his letter, "more than I've ever had, in a way, but it works so fitfully and with so many bogeys because I've *talked so much* and not lived enough within myself to develop the necessary self-reliance." His writing up to then had been taken directly from personal experience. Now, for the first time, his imagination was taking command: "So in my new novel I'm thrown directly on purely creative work—not trashy imaginings as in my stories but the sustained imagination of a sincere yet radiant world. So I tread slowly and carefully and at times at considerable distress. This book will be a consciously artistic achievement and must depend on that as the first books did not."[8] The letter ended on a note of contrition and humility: "If ever I win the right to any leisure again, I will assuredly not waste it as I wasted this past time. Please believe me when I say that now I'm doing the best I can."

When he began to write the novel with the almost religious ardor Zelda described, he worked in a spirit of exorcism and purification. He was afraid of being swallowed up in the orgy of interminable parties in which he had dissipated his energies for the past two years. In describing Gatsby's childhood, he was returning to his own: the meaningful episode of the lie told in confession gave his hero occasion to relive intensely his own first moral crisis. Like the adult Gatsby, Fitzgerald was seeking the crucial moment, the crossroads in his life at which he had taken a wrong turn: "His life had been confused and disordered since then, but if he could once return to a certain starting place and go over it all slowly, he could find out what that thing was. . . ."[9] He wanted to be born again, to become the man he should have been. Fitzgerald lived on two planes, in himself and in the alter egos he called up in the holy moments of creation. For little Rudolph Miller in "Absolution," the search for—and choice of—a personality also involves living a double life, although his attempt at liberation takes another tack: disavowal of his father, rebellion against family constraints, rejection of a stifling religion. Miller, whose German name reveals his social status, at the time only slightly above that of the Irish, invents a double with a magic name, Blatchford Sarnemington, whose polysyllables he thought clanged with a patrician English sound.

In the same way in the novel, Jim Gatz, a poor farmer's son, denies his name and family to build an identity as Jay Gatsby. The splitting process here was complicated for Fitzgerald by the fact that Nick, his narrator, and Gatsby, his hero, share certain essential traits that, in the last analysis, are borrowed from their creator. Nick, cowardly and erratic, recalls a Rudolph who is terrified by his violation of tribal laws. Gatsby, who has a Blatchford's aristocratic and romantic nature, can transform his dreams into action, can coincide with the archetypal ideal he wants to live up to. He wills himself to be the "son of God," that is, of himself, of his imagination and will, absolved of the blemishes of his birth, immaculate, miraculously saved.

This had been a childhood dream of Fitzgerald's that had taken naive shape in *The Romantic Egotist*, in which Stephen Palms imagines himself a foundling who turns out to be a descendant of the royal Stuarts—a dream the author associates in an essay with other syndromes, with "my first childish love of myself, my belief that I would never die like other people, and that I wasn't the son of my parents, but a son of a king, a king who ruled the whole world."[10] Similarly, Nick, who does honor his father, pretends to descend from the Dukes of Buccleuch (thus recalling Fitzgerald's insistence on his connection with Francis Scott Key). Gatsby feels his parents are unworthy of him, "his imagination had never really accepted them as his parents at all."[11] Fitzgerald's heroes cannot come to life until they shake off parental law. Even Amory Blaine's weak, insignificant father has to die before his son can come into his own; Amory's literary career begins with a sarcastic oration at the funeral. In *The Beautiful*, Anthony is indeed orphaned at eleven (Rudolph's age, too), but power over him rests with old Patch, his grandfather, who embodies the worst aspects of puritanism. Anthony's youth is spent in a sort of purgatory while he awaits the vast fortune he is to inherit. Only through this fabulous heritage can he be synchronized with his Platonic self-image. But the long wait for metamorphosis is more than his soul can stand. By the time the chrysalis is ready to open, the moment of mutation is long since past: pupa he was and pupa he remains.

The temptation to see in this a parable of the blighted author is irresistible. Everything points to it: Fitzgerald's smug expectation when he rewrote *The Beautiful and Damned*, his shilly-shallying, his compromises, his subterfuges, the alibi he gave himself about making a fortune from his play. His creativity suspended, he drifted—lolled, rather—responding to offers as they came in, a shifty manager of a talent exploited for immediate gain. In *Gatsby*, haunted as it is by a sense of Sin and Fall, Fitzgerald assumed to himself all the weakness and depravity of human nature. He deliberately blackened the image he then held of himself, identified himself with the object of his repugnance and mirrored his horror in his character's fate.

Another protagonist had already been tried out as a scapegoat to exorcise his creator's specters: Gordon Sterrett, the empty, debauched artist in "May Day," who tries in vain to turn his talent into money. This shadow play would be reenacted again in *Tender Is the Night*, in which Dick Diver and Abe North prefigure the failure of creative power Fitzgerald feared in himself. So, even, does the foolish Pat Hobby, the unsuccessful, drunken, flabby screenwriter who, during Fitzgerald's Hollywood days, would be contrasted in *The Last Tycoon* with a noble man of action and imagination, Monroe Stahr, in whom Fitzgerald was to celebrate the virtues of a hero after his own heart. In his first novel, his first stories, Fitzgerald's protagonists were handsome, young, overflowing with energy and charm. They could confound the law, defy opinion with impunity, as though they enjoyed some extravagant extraterritorial right. They chose their own reality, free of contingency and custom, in a realm far removed from daily routine, where their every action proclaimed that "the King is dead, long live the King!"

In short, the author sometimes identified himself with a prestigious double, found himself by disavowing a mutilating, humiliating lineage, asserted that he was a self-made man in the true sense of the term: the son of his works, who had broken loose from his moorings, burned his ships and striven to outdo himself. At other times Fitzgerald tried to dispel his worst fears by miring his character in impotence and renunciation.

In *Gatsby*, these two antithetical and heretofore alternating attitudes are juxtaposed, confronting each other in a dialectical relationship. No longer does the author identify with one or the other, shifting with the wind from fair to stormy. For the first time he is not speaking in his own name, in reaction to the events of the moment. He is detached, looking down from above, so distant from his immediate preoccupations that they become mere landmarks in a panorama that embraces his whole era, that stretches to the very horizons of America's history. Fitzgerald does not do this topically and anecdotally, as he did in *The Beautiful and Damned*, in which he thought he was meaningfully addressing the problems of his generation, but serenely and objectively, abandoning the half-truths of social realism to reach the symbolic truth of a global vision.

This vision relies for its effectiveness on a coexistence of contrasts, on their simultaneous operation. To register this new depth of field, this dual aim missing from his earlier work, Fitzgerald had to stretch his own limits, to venture into unexplored novelistic terrain. And there he built an intricate palace of echoes and mirrors, a meticulous architectonic complex, all in trompe l'oeil that traps, refracts, fragments, reconstructs a reality in which he is invisible, but which reflects better than all his autobiographical writing the heart of the problems he and his generation faced.

He begins by creating a fundamental split between the character who is watching and judging and the one who dreams and acts. The first task is assigned to Nick Carraway, his narrator. Nick, newly arrived from his native Midwest in the spring of 1922, is skeptical, seemingly blasé but, at bottom, incurably romantic. He is fascinated by New York life and dreams of making his fortune. As an underpaid stockbroker, he comes into contact with the tremendously rich Buchanans, his cousin Daisy and her husband, Tom, whom Nick knew at Yale. They live in a posh mansion in East Egg, Long Island. Nick has rented a rundown cottage across the bay, in West Egg, where he is invited to the wild parties of his flamboyant neighbor, the enigmatic Jay Gatsby. This early experience in the world of the rich excites his caustic wit, toward the Buchanans, especially the proud and brutal Tom, and toward Gatsby, whose absurd lies and pathetic man-of-the-world pose Nick penetrates.

Thus is defined, in the book's first three chapters, the psychology of the man who will recount that summer's events. He has an objective observer's unflagging curiosity and a humorist's quick perception of the ridiculous. He sees himself as detached, cultivated, unprejudiced. In short, he presents a picture of a man with a sense of proportion and prides himself on a faintly amused tolerance for other people's follies. He makes a point of obeying the rules of propriety and is driven by his social inferiority to maintain a constant vigilance. The secrets he discovers or that are entrusted to him confirm his notion of his own importance and moral superiority.

These, however, are mere appearances. This flattering self-portrait is soon wiped away by Nick's constant lack of assurance and his immaturity. His true nature emerges as the story unfolds. Irresolute, timid, manipulated by those around him, he is a Middle Western cousin of those young people of good family who wander through nineteenth-century novels in search of an identity without ever really learning about love. Incapable of realizing his dreams or of loving wholeheartedly, he tries to give substance to his deepest aspirations by living vicariously. In Gatsby he finds a man who, despite his social sins, is richly endowed with all the qualities Nick lacks: creative imagination, tenacity, boldness, passion. Through Gatsby he will achieve a kind of grandiose romantic destiny that his withered soul and middle-class pretensions could never otherwise reach. In Gatsby, whom he'd have invented had he been a novelist, he recognizes the hero he wished to be and never will be. His sense of his own life is submerged, his potentialities flower, the superman's adventure becomes his own.

This identification is similar in many ways to what a reader or movie viewer feels, with the difference that Nick never suspends his critical judgment. Faithful to his character, he maintains his conventional moralist's reserve as long as he can. "Gatsby," he says, represents "everything for which I have an unaffected scorn."[12] He is won over to him only after a long and reluctant revision of his values. What is ridiculous about the man, his affected manner of speaking, his dandyish clothes, his ostentatious acts, all irritate and wound Nick's sense of reserve and sobriety, but they are informed with a dignity that commands respect.

In any case, these are only questions of manners. Nick finds it more difficult to accept the fact that Gatsby is an unscrupulous gangster, the alarming Wolfsheim's right arm. The narrator's respect for the proprieties has not prepared him to associate mystical flights of love with an outlaw's criminal behavior. Yet when he reaches his moral maturity, he takes Gatsby's side. The corrupt means Gatsby uses to achieve his ends have not altered his fundamental integrity, his spiritual intactness. His means reflect the corruption of the times; they are the only ones available to an indigent cavalier seeking his fortune. True corruption, Nick discovered, lies in the hearts of those who despise Gatsby, especially in Tom's.

The complete reversal of Nick's attitude toward Gatsby, from an amused disdain that Tom could share to a wholehearted, militant identification that blames Tom and those like him for his hero's death, this cross-current of judgments and feelings, provided Fitzgerald's talent with a broad compass that he exploited to the fullest. The whole gamut of comic effects comes into operation as the gap between subject and object narrows. Seen from a distance, when Gatsby is simply a ridiculous stranger, he is treated as a caricature. But when Nick shares his feelings, trying to keep his emotions under control, the humor is tender and compassionate, which still allows the narrator to stand off a bit. And when this reserve becomes impossible to maintain, when the subject identifies with the object of his interest and Nick, so to speak, blends with Gatsby, becomes Gatsby—for it is Nick alone, speaking with Gatsby's voice, who tells Gatsby's love story—the tone changes completely. What was at first grotesque is now sublime, mocking rejection has become passionate loyalty, ironic understatement has changed to lyric hyperbole. From then on, Fitzgerald brought to bear all the resources of his evocative and iridescent prose. Here again, the situation lends itself admirably to stylistic variations, modulations of tone, from fervor to nostalgia.

Fitzgerald had already experimented with these various modes in a fragmented, isolated way. In *Gatsby*, for the first time, inspired by his subject, he found a simple, effective technique for joining them, combining them within a single narrative, setting the changes in his narrator to them like the movements of a piece of music. More generally speaking, two modes, satiric and lyric, dominate the book, expressing its two major themes, which contrast with and complement each other. The first records the failure and inadequacies of an unsatisfied, disquiet, disoriented society in search of something in which to invest its unused energy, a society unable to realize its eagerness to live intensely without disorder and violence. Tom, Daisy, Myrtle, Wolfsheim and, in the background, the people who crowd into Gatsby's parties, embody this new world-weariness. The book's second theme celebrates a vision that transfigures the world and gives meaning and direction to these disappointed hopes and unsatisfied yearnings. His conversion accomplished, Nick exalts Gatsby's creative imagination, his "extraordinary gift for hope, a romantic readiness such as I have never found in any other person and which it is not likely I shall ever find again."[13]

Something of the disorganized sterility of Fitzgerald's own recent history is in these scenes of manners. And it is the revival of his creative power, the liberation of his imagination that he was celebrating in exalting a hero who, despite his weaknesses, embodied that power and freedom: "There was something gorgeous about him, some heightened sensitivity to the promises of life, as if he were related to one of those intricate machines that register earthquakes ten thousand miles away."[14]

The aim that emerges from the opposition of two forms of reality, two modes of expression, is not merely abstract or didactic. It is woven into a web of existence that is in itself profoundly meaningful and functional; its extraordinary poetic richness modulates, accompanies, deepens the writer's purpose.

Light and color were used to maximum effect in creating these secret atmospheres that are more climates of the soul than of places or events. Among these, as distinct in their natures and connotations as any other natural duality, the colors yellow and blue are the most significant; it is they that best reflect the fundamental duality of Fitzgerald's imaginary world. They are usually linked in such a way that their contrast underlines the nature of a given situation or moment. Their conjunction seems to be the sign of a fleeting instant of harmony and beauty, whereas their dissociation suggests disorder or latent conflict. There is nothing pat or preestablished about the effects they engender. Blue can be cold or tender or sentimental, yellow ardent or powerful or destructive, and these are just some of the associations that seem obvious. But their "meaning" is never frozen into an allegorical hierarchy. Glowing within a constellation of other symbols, a color can serve as a leitmotiv. For example, Gatsby, whose innermost nature is stamped by the influence of the moon, of water, of night, is associated with blue, the blue of the grass in his lawns and of his servants' uniforms. But the image he shows the world, a false one, is deliberately given a golden, sunlit gleam, as in his luxurious yellow automobile. Tom Buchanan is subject to no such ambiguity: he is determinedly sunny, aggressively sure of his power, a sturdy, straw-haired man of thirty who is first seen in the book standing booted and solid before his French windows as they glint with the gold of the setting sun. Fitzgerald's use of color could be purely descriptive, but rarely did he fail to aim at another reality beneath the surface. If there is one area in Fitzgerald's work in which realism is no more than a facade, it is in his use of color and light.

The story's realistic background is merely a prop. Blue is, of course, the color of water, the sky, twilight; whiskey, wheat and straw are golden. But these colors are concurrently literary qualities that draw the deep meaning of their relationships not only from this individual artist's imagination, but also from the collective imagination of a country, a history.

In American history, for example, yellow is the symbolic color of a deep cultural schism dating from the nineteenth century: the beneficent yellow of harvests, a color of fertility and abundance, and yellow gold, sterile and tyrannical. It was in 1896, the year of Fitzgerald's birth, that William Jennings Bryan, warmly supported by Hearst, thundered his warning that "you shall not crucify mankind upon a cross of gold" in defending rural America against capitalism, banks and the gold standard. It was also the year in which the yellow press was born and the period in which Frank Norris wrote *McTeague*, a gold-washed novel if ever there was one. Yellow was the color of corrupting and destructive gold as well as of a sort of vulgar, raucous vitality, but it was also the color, for the turn of the century's intellectual anglophiles, of the aestheticism and decadence associated with Oscar Wilde and Aubrey Beardsley's *The Yellow Book*. For those who could read the contemporary French novels then bound in yellow paper, it was the color of passion and eroticism. This was a cultural sign effectively used by Henry James, for example, when he put three French books, two in pink covers and one in yellow, in little Maisie's hands to suggest how mature, quantitatively and qualitatively, her upbringing had made her. In one of his short stories, "The Story in It," he summarized a woman's intellectual status by picturing her reading a book "covered in lemon-colored paper." Later, to please a visitor who held that such books should be burned, she displayed another book covered in reassuring blue, "a pretty, candid blue."[15]

Fitzgerald was now using such calculated effects, nimbly and economically. We have noted that the May 1923 issue of *Hearst's International* marked the end of an era for him. It was an artistic turning point for him as well. In it was a highly inferior story, "Dice, Brass Knuckles and Guitar," in which he waltzed through a wholly gratuitous exercise in pure virtuosity based on the color yellow: "There was something enormously yellow about the whole scene. There was this sunlight, for instance, that was yellow, and the hammock was of the particularly hideous yellow peculiar to hammocks, and the girl's yellow hair was spread out upon the hammock in a sort of invidious comparison."[16] The hero's car is painted yellow, and in describing the girl, he is struck by the "particular yellowness of her yellow hair."

In a review of Aldous Huxley's novel *Crome Yellow*, Fitzgerald could not resist a similar temptation to play variations on a theme: "The book is yellow within and without—and I don't mean yellow in the slangy sense. A sort of yellow haze of mellow laughter plays over it. The people are now like great, awkward canaries trying to swim in saffron pools, now like bright yellow leaves blown along a rusty path under a yellow sky."[17] Better than such laborious eccentricity are the brief, expressionistic threads that sometimes glitter in Fitzgerald's pre-*Gatsby* texture, like the "yellow sobbing" of soldiers' wives on a station platform in *The Beautiful and Damned*,[18] a notion that prefigures the "yellow cocktail music"[19] of the parties in West Egg.

Close to this type of usage is the synesthesia by which a color in *Gatsby* is not only seen but felt, touched, tasted, savored in its density and weight. The specific density of yellow is as well a moral factor here as a physical one. In the heroic days of the pioneer settlements west of the Alleghenies, farmers who found it too difficult and costly to haul their crops over the mountains converted their grain into alcohol, which was lighter and less bulky; the alcohol was easily exchanged for gold, or replaced gold in local barter arrangements. Metamorphoses of yellow, its conversion from one form to another, the concentration of its substance that transforms its nature and distorts its original meaning: here we have a new and central metaphor in Fitzgerald's imagination.

The process is clearly perceived in the vegetable kingdom: in it, yellow appears as a ripening and perversion of green. The shoot eventually becomes grain, what is juicy becomes dry, what is flexible hardens from vegetable to semimineral. A bluish sprout turns green, then, as though by combustion, goes yellow. Temporally, blue and green are the colors of growth, yellow that of fructification. On the one hand we have a fluid *span of time*, on the other an *instant*, intense and concentrated. Yellow is a point of culmination, a state, a substance, whereas blue and green are merely hope, surge, change. Realization of green's promise implies loss of substance—sap —and the dynamic and creative thrust of growth. Potentialities shrink in the transmutation; this is an immense reduction of dream to experience.

And experience, the actual series of events, tastes of ashes and death. For wheat's fate is to be reduced to flour, just as a mineral crumbles into dust. Vegetation's opposite is parodied in the Valley of Ashes, on the road from West Egg to New York, which sits like a gigantic memento mori, a Dantesque spectacle of nature ravaged and reduced to dust, a "desolate area of land. This is a valley of ashes—a fantastic farm where ashes grow like wheat into ridges and hills and grotesque gardens; where ashes take the forms of houses and chimneys and rising smoke and, finally, with a transcendent effort, of men who move dimly and already crumbling through the powdery air."[20]

Gatsby's whole story and, behind it, that of a grand dream gone awry center on this symbol of contemporary America and its companion vision, on the book's last page, of a Long Island imagined in its primitive splendor, as the first navigators must have seen it: "as the moon rose higher the inessential houses began to melt away until gradually I became aware of the old island here that flowered once for Dutch sailors' eyes—a fresh, green breast of the new world. Its vanished trees, the trees that had made way for Gatsby's house, had once pandered in whispers to the last and greatest of all human dreams; for a transitory enchanted moment man must have held his breath in the presence of this continent, compelled into an aesthetic contemplation he neither understood nor desired, face to face for the last time in history with something commensurate to his capacity for wonder."[21]

The collapse of Gatsby's dream is implicitly paralleled in the next paragraph with the failure of the American dream: "And as I sat there brooding on the old, unknown world, I thought of Gatsby's wonder when he first picked out the green light at the end of Daisy's dock. He had come a long way to this blue lawn, and his dream must have seemed so close that he could hardly fail to grasp it. He did not know that it was already behind him, somewhere back in that vast obscurity beyond the city, where the dark fields of the republic rolled on under the night."

A new world's green freshness, the green light shining in the night: symbols of hope gone dry in the sun's heat. When wheat is ripe, its stalk, deprived of sap, goes to straw. Straw is sterile, inflammable, dangerous. When Nick takes the train to see the Buchanans on the hottest day of the year, his presence foretells the sun's victory, the conflagration that will disperse the book's characters; "the straw seats hovered on the edge of combustion."[22] He and Gatsby wear straw hats when they go to visit Daisy, an admirable touch in a story that generally ignores men's headgear; nothing else could quite so well have connected the desiccating powers of gold and straw. A quatrain in the epigraph defines Gatsby's relationship with Daisy as that of a "gold-hatted, high-bouncing lover," and Fitzgerald had briefly considered calling his novel *Gold-Hatted Gatsby*. The iconographic and symbolic nature of the detail is reinforced a few pages farther on when women's hats are seen as helmets of metallic thread. A fairy-tale touch is introduced in Gatsby's remark that Daisy's voice is golden; the remark is immediately linked to fable by Nick's evocation of the musical clinking of gold, his vision of a princess in a white palace, "the king's daughter, the golden girl."[23]

These few touches are enough to call up a legendary background. The two rivals, Buchanan and Gatsby, are competing in a tournament, and when they switch cars, it is meaningful because the machines then designate their drivers' real natures. Tom, the knight of the sun, the "sturdy, straw-haired man,"[24] takes the wheel of Gatsby's yellow car while Jay, the straw-hatted schlemiel, appropriately drives his adversary's blue convertible coupe.

Fitzgerald had for a time thought of giving the straw-and-harvest motif considerably greater thematic importance. Proofs survive among his papers of an earlier version of the party in chapter 6 that clearly shows his intention. The festivities unfold in a bucolic setting of shafts of wheat, ears of corn and crossed rakes. Straw covers the ground thickly, and the bar is set up at the foot of a windmill with moving sails. "For those who came without country costumes, straw hats and sunbonnets were provided at the door."[25] Many of the guests wear similar costumes (Nick rigs himself out in a false beard that so irritates him throughout the evening that he finally rips it off), which results in a general confusion of identities. Who is hiding behind the masks and beards? How distinguish truth and falsehood?

All this parallels Gatsby's flaunting of his wealth on Daisy's first visit. The motive then was to compete with the past, to equal, even surpass in mystery and magnificence the charms of Daisy's cool house in Louisville. Now, at the rustic festival, it is the present that Gatsby is trying to vanquish, Tom's solar power that he seeks to eclipse. By a final effort of metamorphosis, he wants to establish himself as the conquering summer, keeper of the seal of abundance, haloed in life-giving harvest yellow.

The entire, instructive incident was eliminated from the proofs in favor of a version that is more sober, more elegant, but deprives the narrative of a certain thematic richness in the development of the pastoral motif. This motif was already central in Fitzgerald's thinking when he had Rudolph Miller, Gatsby's forerunner in "Absolution," grow up in wheat country. His final version of *Gatsby* eliminates the contrapuntal effect to be obtained by linking the rustic party to two other metaphors that are also handled as parody and are also based on nostalgia for a fake pastoral order. One concerns the Trianon-Gardens decor of Myrtle's apartment; the other is the story of the former owner of Gatsby's palace, who died of chagrin because the villagers refused to reroof their houses with thatch. Both of these imply absurd efforts to connect with a bogus, pseudo-bucolic tradition, to identify with a vanished historical order. In all three incidents, disguising a physical setting betrays a desire for more encompassing camouflage. These homes are as much a part of the fancy-dress party as the people who live in them. No more proof is needed than the appearance of Gatsby's palace, a "factual imitation of some Hôtel de Ville in Normandy," which, like Nick at the party, also wears a false beard: it is "spanking new under a thin beard of raw ivy."[26] With the disappearance of the harvest ball, a chance was also lost to deepen the harmonics sounded by the Valley of Ashes, another mockery of fertility. Dust from the valley does not filter into Gatsby's house until after the disaster of the party. Doesn't the dying Gatsby see himself threatened by a shadow from the valley, an "ashen, fantastic figure gliding toward him through the amorphous trees"?[27]

We can see how ably Fitzgerald worked rhythms and contrasts, this counterpoint in which yellow straw diverges from, and blends with, gray dust and ash. But we can also see how right he was to eliminate the scene; this proliferation of dryness and yellowness would certainly have upset the book's balance. For in *Gatsby* the glare of this golden drought is perceived in a dialectical relationship with its opposites, blueness and wetness. Gatsby's secret, nocturnal aspect might have been eclipsed by his daytime persona, which is all sham and make-believe.

The static scene would also have weakened the dynamism of the yellow, which everywhere else in the book bespeaks a Dionysian élan. During the first evening of partying, "two girls in twin yellow dresses"[28] drift to the strident sound of yellow music, their appearances punctuating the swirling movement of the bacchanal. Set clearly apart from the other guests (they are always designated by the color of their dresses), the girls nevertheless reflect the endless variety of entertainments devised for the party. They are really the spirits of the evening; by their vitality, gaiety and unfailing readiness to join in the fun, they emphasize the party's innocent, naive side. It is symptomatic that they disappear when the discordant people from East Egg corrupt its mood. Their presence, like their absence, is an index to the naturalness and spontaneity of the festivities.

The many roles played by the two girls in yellow reveal the color's instability, its perpetual changes in pigment, density, substance. During the preparations for the party, hundreds of oranges and lemons liquefy at the press of a thumb, roasted turkeys turn to burnished gold. A similar transformation occurs to Gatsby's Rolls-Royce. When Nick first sees it, he thinks of it as cream-colored, more white than yellow. When it is involved in an accident, Michaelis sees it as pale green. Only one other witness, the black, is precise and objective: "'It was a yellow car,' he said, 'big yellow car. New.'" Early that afternoon, when Tom stops for gas, Wilson is also sure of the color; "'It's a nice yellow one,'" he affirms.[29] In the brilliant sunlight the car's Olympian splendor and vibrant color cannot help but strike the ailing Wilson, vegetating in the gray dust of the valley. With its winged form and glittering windshield, it symbolizes for him the difference between his world and that of the demigods. It combines the attributes of what is needed to win Daisy: the color of gold and the wings of success. It is the instrument by which Gatsby hopes to achieve the program proposed in the epigraph:

> *Then wear the gold hat, if that will move her;*
> *If you can bounce high, bounce for her too. . . .*

Another gold object functions as mediator between Gatsby's fears and Daisy's embarrassment during their first meeting at Nick's apartment; once she recognizes a gold brush as a mark of success and of belonging, Gatsby regains his poise.

It is a precarious poise, however. The color gold is indeed the sign of an irresistible impulse, of a seemingly inexhaustible and almost supernatural superabundance. But its energy can become repolarized and generate destructive power at the very source from which benefaction was thought to spout. Its suggestive power is such that even when it is seen in the valley's desolation, it triggers Nick's imagination. When he drives Tom to Wilson's yellow-brick garage, he cannot accept the obvious reality. "It had occurred to me," he muses, "that this shadow of a garage must be a blind, and that sumptuous and romantic apartments were concealed overhead."[30] This yellow, shining in the surrounding grayness, is a clear reference to Myrtle, whom Nick has not yet met. His description of her and the image he uses to suggest her sensuality are a kind of commentary on a color contrast: "There was an immediately perceptible vitality about her as if the nerves of her body were continually smoldering."[31] The last time he sees Myrtle, the "romantic" apartment has turned for her into the prison in which Wilson is holding her. It is from there that she escapes when the yellow car reappears with her lover, she believes, at the wheel—a final illusion. The winged chariot, emblem of freedom and power, becomes the death car in a newspaper headline.

Almost always, the juxtaposition of blue and yellow signals a state of balance and euphoria. The girls in yellow, for example, sound the trumpets of happiness in Gatsby's blue gardens. The two colors are sometimes allied in smiling landscapes that are simply colored projections of the characters' joyousness. The opening scenes of *Tender Is the Night* unfold under the twin signs of sea and sun, the dark yellow sand dissolving into the pale blue sea. This dichromaticism recurs in Fitzgerald's description of his characters, with a few touches of pink and red added. The surging of the sea and the contours of the landscape extend, for example, to the portrait of Rosemary, with her blue eyes and ash-blond hair; they are present in the juxtaposition of Abe North's blue bathing suit and golden, leonine mane. This is a moment of harmony and happiness, indicated by the consonance of characters and elements. Blond Rosemary longs only to live in this blue and gold paradise, to lose herself "in the bright blue worlds of (Dick's) eyes."[32]

This special image of juxtaposed blue and gold occurs again and again in flashes of gold on windows in the blue twilight. What is important here is the relationship of values rather than specific differences in pigmentation. Blue's tendency, as we shall see, is to darken, yellow's to brighten. Even when the two related colors pull away from each other, the blue toward a dull black and the yellow toward shining white, as they do in *Tender Is the Night*, the effects of their association are unchanged. The verb "to bloom," frequently used in conjunction with them, reveals the secret nature of colors that glow only at night, against a shadowy background, but are dried and withered by sunlight. This is why it is important to see yellow, the sun's prevailing color, apart from the sun's other two attributes, its heat and light. It reaches all its varnished intensity, its gleaming clarity, only when it is shielded from the light around it, contrasted with dark blue or displayed like a jewel against the velvety blackness of night. Daytime yellow is intolerably strident.

Removed from this night-colored casket, which demarcates it and serves as a foil for it, yellow glares, grows hostile. Its light burns and cracks what it touches, becomes the color of disintegration and chaos. It is beneficial only at a distance. A spectator must also stand off from it, in creative shadow; if he nears the light, it bursts into flame. The tyranny of the senses overwhelms the fervor of contemplation. But if proper precautions are taken, then yellow, resplendent in the darkness, becomes the emblem of a mystical vision. In "Absolution" Fitzgerald came closest to formulating an aesthetic—even an ethic—of yellow, merging it with the festival spirit, but carefully distinguishing its sacred and profane aspects. He speaks in the voice of the priest urging Rudolph to visit an amusement park:

> "Go to one at night and stand a little way off from it in a dark place— under dark trees. You'll see a big wheel made of lights turning in the air . . . and everything will twinkle. But it won't remind you of anything, you see. It will all just hang out there in the night like a colored balloon —like a big yellow lantern on a pole."
>
> Father Schwartz frowned as he suddenly thought of something. "But don't get up close," he warned Rudolph, "because if you do you'll only feel the heat and the sweat and the life."[33]

This may have been the lesson Gatsby learns. Hadn't Nick told him that his brilliantly lighted house resembled a fairground? At his parties he always remains aloof from his guests, never joining in their games, their dancing; he stands alone in the moonlight on the top step of the marble stairs leading to his door. This separation in space reflects a distancing in time as well. Removed from the present, he lives in memory a love reduced to its essence, for it too is sheltered from "the heat and the sweat and the life."

A whole connotative system is thus erected in climates and seasons of the spirit. A thorough study could bring out the isomorphism of yellow, the sun, heat, dryness and shrillness, for example, in contrast with their opposites, blue, the moon, coolness, moisture and depth. The qualities of day and night, of dawn and dusk, summer and winter are subject to the attraction of these magnetic poles dissociated from their alternation in time, making their influence felt not only in clock and calendar time but in interior space. In the last resort, the countless elements in these two constellations can only be identified by what is most immediately visible in them, the yellowness or blueness of their brightest stars, which thus take on the status of ultimate, indivisible meanings, of the grand, antithetical system that pervades Fitzgerald's universe. Finally, yellow and blue become primary elements, essential qualities toward which gravitate the material and spiritual principles on which the specific character of Fitzgerald's work is based. They can rightly be considered the monads of his imaginary cosmos.

11. AN AMERICAN-STYLE GOD

Among the theoreticians of color, Goethe—who attributed substantial qualities to it—could best have realized its specificity in Fitzgerald's aesthetic, rather than Newton, who saw in color merely a superficial optical effect. For color is seldom merely a surface tinting in *Gatsby;* it is an intimate part of what seems to be the book's substance, its structure. Color is not just paint applied over form. Nor is it a dye that penetrates the fibers of Fitzgerald's aesthetic and brings out its essence. Color is that essence itself, just as perfume is. A rose is rose-colored, and that rose color is the rose: its color, perfume and form are indissolubly linked in each species; to name any one of these qualities is to evoke the others. Thus, in an exemplary synesthetic series, Fitzgerald suggested the yellowness of jonquils and the whiteness of hawthorn simply by mentioning their smell, which in turn evokes the visual impact of their petals: "Daisy . . . admired the gardens, the sparkling odor of jonquils and the frothy odor of hawthorn and plum blossoms and the pale odor of kiss-me-at-the-gate."[1]

Declension of the substances it impregnates reveals a color's whole paradigm. Certain properties of yellow, for example, emerge from the different materials it infuses: it is dry and combustible matter (straw), or ardent (whiskey) or metallic (gold). Infinite variations are possible and these are made still more complex and subtle by their combination with other colors, other substances. A single example will show the flexibility of this grammar of signs. It is an extreme example, because the yellow in it is no longer simply associated with blue but is paradoxically mixed with it, although their specific pigmentation is neither altered nor blended, as might be expected, to form green. It is extreme also because of the fact that blue, when it stands alone, can be reflected in the surface of yellow.

During the evening he spends with Myrtle, Nick's thoughts wander several times to escape the vulgar cacophony around him. His mind drifts above the cackling of a woman telling him about her disagreeable trip to the French Riviera, and he dreams of traveling on his own. He stops listening in order to bring his vision into focus: instead of the routine Riviera of tourists and casinos, he sees a sun-washed sea that he imagines reflected in the windows overlooking it: "The late afternoon sky bloomed in the window for a moment like the blue honey of the Mediterranean."[2] This might merely be a picturesque detail were it not for the important connotation of the word "honey." In the hierarchy of Fitzgeraldian substances, honey is the opposite of straw. Its unctuousness and suaveness lend themselves to metamorphosis. It softens and moistens yellow's brilliance; blue can be mirrored in its surface without changing its essence or diminishing its vital force. Nick's vision is a symbol of divinity, a symbol confirmed here by the fact that it is miraculously imbued with both azure and gold at the same time.

Nick's reverie is thus revealed as more than an escape toward distant horizons. It constitutes a judgment on the stupidity and chaos surrounding him. The honey that he associates with the Mediterranean is not a contemporary image; his imagination is moving not in space but in history. This honey is as much a property of Mount Hymettus as it is of the sea; we are truly dealing here with the quintessence of classical antiquity and its distillation of wisdom and harmony. Through this unexpected association of two contrasting colors, this "blue honey," we see a longing for that Grecian order so often evoked by Keats, a longing for a balance between action and meditation, which were so sharply dissociated in Fitzgerald's society.

But isn't their very combination a snare, a final illusion granted to souls in search of an absolute? The theme of illusion, central to *The Great Gatsby*, is introduced by the green light that shines in the night, green being a blend of blue and yellow. This theme is repeated and developed in the book's dominant symbol, in which the two principal colors continually operate in dialectical opposition. It is the billboard in the Valley of Ashes, showing two blue eyes framed in yellow glasses, the eyes of Dr. Eckleburg, whose description immediately follows the one we have already cited of the desert the characters must cross on their way to New York:

> But above the gray land and the spasms of bleak dust which drift endlessly over it, you perceive, after a moment, the eyes of Doctor T. J. Eckleburg. The eyes of Doctor T. J. Eckleburg are blue and gigantic—their retinas are one yard high. They look out of no face, but, instead, from a pair of enormous yellow spectacles which pass over a non-existent nose. Evidently some wild wag of an oculist set them there to fatten his practice in the borough of Queens, and then sank down himself into eternal blindness, or forgot them and moved away. But his eyes, dimmed a little by many paintless days under sun and rain, brood on over the solemn dumping ground.[3]

Fitzgerald took this image, which would become the book's focal point, from a cover design showing two big blue eyes shining out of a dark face, gazing at a nighttime New York stylized in the form of an amusement park. The artist F. Cugat, may have remembered a D. W. Griffith movie, *Enoch Arden*, in which the screen is filled by a close-up of Lillian Gish's eyes. In an August 1924 letter informing Perkins that the book was almost finished, Fitzgerald implored, "For Christ's sake, don't give anyone that jacket you're saving for me. I've written it into the book."[4]

demiurge, new deity, idol of a new age, or simply an advertising billboard —Dr. Eckleburg's eyes may simultaneously represent all these, mutually exclusive as they seem to be. They seem simultaneously to be the eyes of the material world and of the hereafter.

Dr. Eckleburg's spectacles are a striking prefiguration of pop art in their linear simplification, lack of relief and perspective, and contrasting primary colors. They are a product of contemporary commercial civilization. This idol of the twenties planted in a desert of ash, as strange as Shelley's *Ozymandias* lost among the sands, stands midway between the cool greenery of West Egg and the mineral whiteness of New York; and it marks the geometric intersection of failure, degradation and death. The failure of the American Dream, which could only be materially realized at the cost of this debasement of nature. The failure, too, of the people who live there, whose physical and moral decay are exemplified in George Wilson. And, as well, of the desperate attempt by Myrtle, the only person really alive in this no-man's-land, to escape from it: the blood from her horribly mutilated body is drunk by the dust. In this hell, human sacrifice brings neither redemption nor remission.

In this devastated land, under a leaden sun, huge eyes contemplate the swirling dust and the equally vain attempts of humankind to revel—an impenetrable look, which, like the Sphinx's, implies a riddle to which the answer is sometimes Man and sometimes God.

It is significant that the anonymous artist responsible for the billboard illustration used the same method that Byzantine artists used to represent a new concept of holiness: a frontal gaze, dominant, omnipresent, impossible to escape because it sweeps across every corner of space. The billboard's colors are the basic colors of Byzantine mosaics, azure and gold, but they do not have the mosaics' brilliance, their spiritual radiance. Just as a mosaic, lacking perspective, dominates the holy place beneath it, being one with the curve of the vault, so these eyeglasses are the dominant element in the landscape, inaccessible, always remote from the viewer, always hanging over him. In Greco-Roman art a god was sculptured as a body, an object around which a worshiper could move, which he could touch, could contemplate in all its aspects. Nor were those aspects themselves permanent. They varied with the time of day and the play of light. The god participated in man's attributes; his space and time were man's space and time. In the Valley of Ashes, on the other hand, as in Byzantine art, man is no longer the spectator of a deity that exalts humanity's image; he is himself a spectacle contemplated by an immutable and disincarnate gaze. Man no longer delves familiarly into the mystery of a god who resembles him; it is God, prodigiously remote and strange, whose omniscient eye pierces to the heart of man's mystery. The relationships are reversed: the creature loses his status as the subject who contemplates and is relegated to that of a scrutinized object. This is the transcendental equation that explains the hypnotic power of Dr. Eckleburg's eyes. Their height forces humans to look up to them, inspires in people a confused awareness of their obsessions, their guilt, their fear, their lust for vengeance.

Dr. Eckleburg's eyes, a pop version of the eyes of the Byzantine God, share with them the power to transform subject into object, to force it into an awareness of its own insignificance and frailty. The eyes suffer, however, from an ambiguity that is brought out by the different tones the narrator uses in describing them, an ambiguity clearly summarized by the antithetical attitudes of George and Michaelis when we see them for the last time (it's God/it's an advertisement). This duality disappears if we think of them not in relation to the book's characters but from a distance, thus bringing into clear focus the cultural panorama they contemplate. The reversed relationship between creator and creature postulated by the Byzantine aesthetic has its counterpart here in the reversed relationship between the individual and society that became so glaringly obvious at the start of the twenties. These eyeglasses can thus be thought of in their materiality as an advertising device—indeed, as the very symbol of advertising triumphant, ironically appearing in a place where ruin is the sole residue of industrial prosperity.

Here is realized a prophecy by the Goncourts of a new iconography that would express the new nature of the deity in industrial societies: "Sometimes I think that a day will come when modern peoples will be blessed with an American-style god . . . his image no longer elastic and adaptable to painters' imaginations, no longer floating on Veronica's veil, but caught in a photographic portrait. . . . Yes, I picture a god who will appear in photographs and who will wear glasses."[9]

The god imagined by the Goncourts did not have the face of Carnegie or Rockefeller, but the features of the anonymous Advertising Man. There was no longer a place in the national imagination for the pioneers of production in this period of abundance in which the great problem, the new myth, concerned marketing. Now the new hero of daily life was the seller, the hustler, the ad man. The only real tragedy written by an American playwright, the only one deeply rooted in his people's mythology, is in fact Arthur Miller's *Death of a Salesman*.

Rivaling the expressive force of colors and icons were other, more imponderable images, perhaps the most effective of them all: those that extended the suggestive power of forms through the language of music. Or, rather, through a language half made up of the obsessive lyrics of popular songs, through dance tunes floating in a diffuse area in which the words took on a new meaning, irrefutable, incantatory, made more persuasive by the fact that one's whole body, in dancing, received and assimilated their messages. Countless love scenes were set to these songs, engraved in people's memories by the words and music.

Along with movies, the press and advertising illustrations, songs are among the surest pointers to the popular attitudes of an era—the songs we hear a hundred times, that we know without ever having learned them and that mark particular periods in our lives. Fitzgerald seized music's incomparable power to fix special moments in our memories, to revive in us feelings we thought were dead but that flood back into our minds in all their poignant nostalgia when we happen to hear an old melody again. Vinteuil's sonata, in which Swann and Odette heard "the national anthem" of their love, is to the cultivated world in Proust's *Remembrance of Things Past* what pop tunes are to Fitzgerald's less refined world.

Few of his stories do not contain at least one such song title as a milestone and commentary for his readers. To us today this is a language stripped of its basic associations, but we can still translate its meaning by noting how it affected Fitzgerald's characters. When Basil, for example, hears "his tune of tunes, 'Chinatown,' " he is filled with real emotion; "his heart quickened, suffocating him."[10]

The language of popular songs is, moreover, often the only one in which characters can articulate their feelings or, rather, the accepted, codified, cataloged feelings of which the songs' titles and lyrics are the repertory. Josephine, for example, is a master strategist in love, but she cannot express herself on paper. Her letters are childish; the seeming maturity of her language is "snowed under by ineptitude." She makes out by "much quoting of lines from current popular songs, as if they expressed the writer's state of mind more fully than verbal struggles of her own."[11] Nicole uses the same device in *Tender Is the Night* in declaring her love for Dick to elude the constraints of more formal language that is harder to handle and more easily misunderstood. Communicating through song lyrics gives the partners a common system of references, with the added advantage of conveying the message in such a way that it can be taken as a meaningless joke. Nothing these frothy words say is irreversible; the speaker can be the composer or the girl singing the words, as circumstances require. Old love affairs blend and fuse with the new one aborning, "holding lost times and future hopes in liaison,"[12] functioning as models, insistent, affirming the primacy of romantic love. A secret monologue made up of bits of current tunes pleads for Nicole when Dick joins her to hear the latest records from the States: "They were so sorry, dear; they went down to meet each other in a taxi, honey; they had preferences in smiles and had met in Hindustan, and shortly afterward they must have quarreled, for nobody knew and nobody seemed to care — yet finally one of them had gone and left the other crying, only to feel blue, to feel sad."[13] The system's efficiency is shown at the end of the chapter by Dick's mute emotion when he recognizes this medley as "the essence of a continent."[14]

In a short short story, "Three Acts of Music," published in 1936, we see two people wholly identified with three songs heard at three different moments in their love affair. It's all in dialogue, and only the songs' titles and the names of their composers are given, each evoking a different period and mood. The songs are "Tea for Two" by Vincent Youmans, Irving Berlin's "Blue Sky Overhead," and Jerome Kern's "Lovely to Look At." Significantly, the lovers' names are not mentioned, nor are we told why their affair is doomed. All that matter here are the emotions relived through, and identified with, the songs. "You're all those things in the song," the man says fifteen years later. "Let's not say anything about it," the woman replies. "It was all we had and everything we'll ever know about life."[15]

Thus emotion flows into a musical mold, appropriates music to itself. Music gives emotion its language and its durability. Words here are merely mnemonic devices, as rhyme first was in poetry, which need not mean anything as long as they perform their mnemotechnical duty. What is missing, and what counts, is the music itself, without which the lyrics lose their expressive power. So that what these characters feel, whatever emotions they share, are visible to us only as ripples, as the wakes that intense moments leave going by; attitudes remain to us, silences, unimportant phrases that reflect still earlier attitudes confirmed by other arts and repeated until their very familiarity made them seem real and essential.

The incommunicability of such feelings is avowed at the end of chapter 6 in *Gatsby* when Nick, having described the events on the November night that sealed Gatsby's fate, admits that he cannot understand them. Yet he had participated in his hero's mystical visions, had heard as Gatsby did the music of the infinite, the lights buzzing in the darkness and, after a long wait and a long silence, "the tuning-fork that had been struck upon a star."[16] But the core of the events' meaning, vaguely hinted, almost recognized as a memory, remains elusive, inexpressible. "I was reminded," Nick says, "of something—an elusive rhythm, a fragment of lost words, that I had heard somewhere a long time ago. For a moment a phrase tried to take shape in my mouth and my lips parted like a dumb man's, as though there was more struggling upon them than a wisp of startled air. But they made no sound, and what I had almost remembered was incommunicable forever."[17]

In this we spy the writer pondering his problems, precisely measuring how much to say and how much not to say, reaching to the limits of the expressible to give the reader more of a chance to supply the inexpressible, to help him make the jump from trivial circumstances to the spiritual meaning they generate. Not that Fitzgerald tried to express the inexpressible. The paragraph quoted above is all that remains of six pages added in the galley proofs. Between the first and penultimate paragraphs of this extensive insert he had written a dialogue between the two men in which Gatsby made some interesting revelations. When Nick tells him that Daisy was "a pretty satisfactory incarnation of anything," a disillusioned Gatsby replies, "She is . . . but it's a little like loving a place where you've once been happy." Most striking in this lesson is the way Gatsby admits and analyzes his essential hollowness: " 'But the truth is I'm empty and I guess people feel it. . . . Daisy's all I've got left from a world that was so wonderful that when I think of it I feel sick all over.' He looked around with wild regret. 'Let me sing you a song—I want to sing you a song!' "[18] Gatsby's song, written when he was fourteen and quoted in its entirety, confirms Nick's opinion of Gatsby's appalling sentimentality. This is all the man adds up to, an imitation of a popular song of which he confesses that "the sound of it makes me perfectly happy. But I don't sing it often because I'm afraid I'll use it up." It is after this sequence that Fitzgerald wrote the final passage cited earlier, one that is far more suggestive and effective in its very inability to penetrate Gatsby's secret than all the explanations given in the pages that were later deleted.

This journey into aesthetics is also a voyage through appearances, an effort to reach an essential core. Written here, beyond the world of phenomena, is Fitzgerald's spiritual biography. *Gatsby* is his climactic statement of a twin vision: the world's temptations displayed, offered and refused, and conscience's retreat into its own valley of ashes. What is denied on the one hand is affirmed on the other. The old Janus mask contrasting a lust for life with despair at what has not been accomplished is seen here in a new disguise. It is at this point, when language admits its inadequacy and when colors fade, that jazz—or, rather, two of its harbingers, ragtime and blues— is heard. It was already there, in the background, but it could not be heard because it blended as intimately with the arabesques of language and color as the beating of a heart does with the writhings of imagination. And yet, unconsciously captured on the ear and mimed by the body, that music anticipates, perhaps promotes, the polychrome festival we actually see.

This is another language, immediately perceptible, hard to separate from the noise of his century, that Fitzgerald recognized without having learned it. A primary language of emotion, however, for the rage for ragtime and the popular dances it engendered coincided, as we shall see, with the first flutterings of Fitzgerald's emotions in his teens. This was the music that won its prestige by dethroning the waltz and the mazurka, music that belonged to the flowering twentieth century and its young Americans, not just heard, but sung and danced to in a dialogue with its listeners' voices and bodies. It's no wonder that in its rhythms we find the acoustic and dynamic equivalent of the dialectical play in *Gatsby*.

In ragtime a pianist alone replaces a full dance band, maintaining a fast base beat with the left hand while the right works out syncopated variations on a theme. Thus the left hand does the work of the rhythm section, especially the drums vital to Afro-American music, while the right hand replaces the strings, improvising in the high notes on familiar violin and banjo tunes.

In this use of two registers, two series of contrasting and complementary tones, we find structures like those on which Fitzgerald built *The Great Gatsby*. The two great, antithetical magnetic fields wheeling around blue and yellow correspond in tone to the two registers of ragtime: the left hand plays a grave blues rhythm, its throbbing beat like a call, or, rather, a wistful recall, of the inaccessible. It was this call that summoned Gatsby, with his "instinct toward his future glory," to leave his parents and the small college where he found only a "ferocious indifference to the drums of his destiny" and to make instead for Lake Superior. Destiny was waiting for him there. Dan Cody's yacht, which symbolized to the young man "all the beauty and glamour in the world," convinced him to change his name: henceforth he would be Jay Gatsby, and Cody gave him an initiate's vestments: a skipper's cap, blue blazer and white trousers. This was when "he invented just that sort of Jay Gatsby that a seventeen-year-old boy would be likely to invent, and to this conception he was faithful to the end." It was born of the Platonic notion he had of himself and was made to serve "a vast, vulgar, and meretricious beauty."[19] This projection of an adolescent ideal was crystallized in the image of a diurnal Gatsby to whom Fitzgerald assigned the emblematic color of the sun, and of gold.

The rag pianist's right hand gives a striking musical equivalent of the gamut of sharp, hyperactive yellows when it runs to the end of the keyboard to improvise on familiar themes. But the rolling base is always behind it, testifying to the durability of the music's primary impulse, an immense nocturnal yearning that is trying to realize its form and so satisfy itself, an impatient beat that throbs, recalls, returns to send the agile fingers fluttering off again in search of sparkling new variations. It is as though this yen were trying to exhaust itself, to fill an intolerable emptiness, to appease its anguish with offerings of interminably varied arabesques, each nimbler and more explosive than the last, in the hope of finding, suddenly and miraculously, the form it was meant to take.

In 1896, the year Fitzgerald was born, when crowds were flocking to the first films and pictures from *The Yellow Kid* frowned from a thousand walls, a black pianist named Ben Harney, who played in a nightclub on New York's Fourteenth Street, first sounded the obsessive ragtime rhythms that were to sweep America over the next fifteen years. Until then rag had been known only to blacks, played by the pickup bands in black honkytonks. Two years later ragtime was being heard throughout the country; in 1899 Scott Joplin wrote his classic "Maple Leaf Rag," which sold by the hundreds of thousands of copies. White composers took up the beat, and in 1911 Irving Berlin wrote his famous "Alexander's Ragtime Band."

The song is mentioned in Fitzgerald's *Ledger* for August 1911 and repeated in September of the same year, just before he began at Newman. He was fifteen then, about to leave the family circle for the first time and, the following winter, to begin going to the Broadway theaters. In May 1913 he attended a performance of *Sunshine Girl*, in which Vernon and Irene Castle introduced the Castle walk; they popularized the new, syncopated rhythms composed for them by black bandleader Jim Europe, who also invented the fox-trot and the turkey-trot for them around 1914.

In his essay "Echoes of the Jazz Age," Fitzgerald recalled the dance craze that gripped America then: "We graybeards . . . remember the uproar when in 1912 grandmothers of forty tossed away their crutches and took lessons in the Tango and the Castle-Walk."[20] The whole country sang ragtime and blues tunes, and this musical atmosphere saturated Fitzgerald's teens.

Blues, a basically vocal musical form, emerged from obscurity a few years after ragtime, around 1902. It proposed a new attitude toward life's hard knocks. Instead of finding satisfactions for one's longings, finding diversions to still the heartache, the approach now was to sublimate affliction, to make it tolerable by plunging deeper into it. Blues is melancholy and disillusioned; it knows the vanity of all things, knows that there is no life without pain. But it can also stand back and mock the cause of heartache. Its favorite form is dialogue, an appeal-response technique that fathers humor both black and tender and brings a note of redemption to its elegiac complaint: however tough the breaks are, a man can always overcome them.

When William Christopher Handy came out with "The Memphis Blues" in 1912, the vogue he launched thrust ragtime back into the shadows. Two years later his "St. Louis Blues" made him world-famous, and other blues tunes were adapted for dance orchestras, especially the "Beale Street Blues" (1917), which conquered America during the war years.

These are the poignant rhythms that comfort a doleful Daisy while Gatsby is at the front: "Orchestras . . . set the rhythm of the year, summing up the sadness and suggestiveness of life in new tunes. All night the saxophones wailed the hopeless comment of the *Beale Street Blues* while a hundred pairs of golden and silver slippers shuffled the shining dust. At the gray tea hour there were always rooms that throbbed incessantly with this low, sweet fever, while fresh faces drifted here and there like rose petals blown by the sad horns around the floor."[21]

The two attitudes united in jazz are in this paragraph, "sadness" and "suggestiveness." The music's "hopeless comment" by the "sad horns" sets up a counterpoint to the dancing feet and the faces drifting in time to the beat. Dancing is a median condition between the soul's sadness and the body's demands. Daisy moves in this "twilight universe" that combines renunciation and hope, the coordinated attractions of the day and the night. She wanted to escape this uncertainty, this ambiguity. " . . . something within her was crying for a decision. She wanted her life shaped now, immediately—and the decision must be made by some force—of love, of money, of unquestionable practicality—that was close at hand."[22]

There was no satisfying Daisy's impatience for life with the mournful delights urged by the blues. She was not made to watch the party from afar, in the blue distance of memory. She had to break the circle, find new rhythms, live in the present. And that is what happens. "Daisy began to move again with the seasons." In "Echoes of the Jazz Age," Fitzgerald says jazz became popular because it was a way to dissipate this vast restlessness, this enormous, objectless hope. He saw the reasons for his own success in this, too: "It bore him [the present writer] up, flattered him and gave him more money than he had dreamed of, simply for telling people that he felt as they did, that something had to be done with all the nervous energy stored up and unexpended in the War."[23] He went on to link the music to sex and dancing: "The word jazz in its progress toward respectability has meant first sex, then dancing, then music. It is associated with a state of nervous stimulation, not unlike that of big cities behind the lines of a war."[24]

Fitzgerald saw dancing as a circular movement with no beginning and no end, closed as a merry-go-round, an image of life itself. This carousel vision is briefly suggested in a paragraph in *Gatsby* in which Daisy tries to break out of the circle into another sphere in which she is no longer an object but a subject, no longer a spectator of her own yearning but an actress again, improvising on her longings; in this sphere she could react to the "suggestiveness of life," could leave the "sad horns" of memory behind her. The "Beale Street Blues," then, stands for a time gone by, a time of weary waiting, a harking back to old pain. Daisy's life will pulse to the same new rhythms that beat in the nation's altered attitudes at the end of the war.

This is when jazz, a fusion of ragtime and blues, was born. The Original Dixieland Jazz Band made its name at Reisenweber's Café in New York in 1917. Like blues, jazz is essentially vocal; jazz instrumentalists tried to imitate a singing style, mainly in dialogue form in solos or in solo rides against a band's group harmonies. Jazz adopted ragtime's principle of improvisation on what was usually a short theme, as in blues, that is repeatedly picked up throughout the number. It also borrowed ragtime's accentuated syncopation, with stress on the unaccented beats in its four-four time. The piano is still there, but its function as the basic rhythm section is largely usurped by the drums, banjo and bass, while the right-hand work is taken over by the standard instruments of the New Orleans marching bands. Jazz's polyphony also distinguishes it from ragtime; now everyone in the band could improvise simultaneously instead of just the soloist.

Gatsby's orchestra typifies the form jazz took from 1920 on. It is a big band, "no thin five-piece affair, but a whole pitful of oboes and trombones and saxophones and viols and cornets and piccolos, and low and high drums."[25] It played dance music, but could obligingly switch beats and begin improvising when one of the guests started singing. The band could also play more ambitious pieces, notably an experimental work that had made a sensation at Carnegie Hall, Vladimir Tostoff's "Jazz History of the World."

In the novel's final version, only the title of this piece is mentioned because, just as the symphony begins, Nick's attention is caught by the solitary figure of Gatsby. The manuscript and proofs, however, contain a long passage, with amendments, on the music. Here, Nick's remarks on this new music, which both disconcerts and seduces him, seem oddly appropriate to the very method Fitzgerald was then developing, working feverishly even on the proofs, which he told Perkins would be the costliest since Flaubert's. The duality of ragtime's rhythms can be seen in the Tostoff work; so can the dialogues of blues in its infinite complexity of notes that blend and separate and pop up in unexpected places. There is nothing linear about the piece despite its title; its structure is always changing, reversing relationships and developing themes and their accompaniments in space, not in time.

Fitzgerald's passage is not entirely successful; the many corrections he made show that he did not feel completely at ease as a music critic. He might nevertheless finally have done a satisfactory job on it had he not lost interest, probably because it would have slowed down the fast pace of chapter 3, sitting in it as a kind of long, static pause amid a series of brief and lively scenes. This descriptive passage really stands apart from the novel's structure. It is not a miniaturization of the whole work, as the play within a play is in *Hamlet*. Instead, it is like a buried preface, an anamorphic projection of the book's operative principle. It even estimates readers' probable reaction to its structural novelty:

It [the music] started out with a weird spinning sound that seemed to come mostly from the cornets, very regular and measured and inevitable, with a bell now and then that seemed to ring somewhere a great distance away. A rhythm became distinguishable after a while in the spinning, a sort of dull beat, but as soon as you'd almost made it out it disappeared. . . . The second movement was concerned with the bell, only it wasn't the bell any more, but a muted violincello and two instruments I had never seen before. . . . You were aware that something was trying to establish itself, to get a foothold, something soft and persistent and profound and next you yourself were trying to help it, struggling, praying for it—until suddenly it was *there*, it was established rather scornfully without you and it seemed to look around with a complete self-sufficiency, as if it had been there all the time.

I was curiously moved, and the third part of the thing was full of even stronger emotions. I know so little about music that I can only make a story of it . . . but it wasn't exactly a story . . . there would be a series of interruptive notes that seemed to fall together accidentally and colored everything that came after them until, before you knew it, they became the theme and new discords were opposed to it outside. But what struck me particularly was that just as you'd got used to the new discord business there'd be one of the old themes, rung in this time as a discord, until you'd get a ghastly sense that it was a preposterous cycle after all, purposeless and sardonic. . . .

The last was weak, I thought, though most of the people seemed to like it best of all. It had recognizable strains of famous jazz in it—*Alexander's Ragtime Band* and the *Darktown Strutter's Ball* and recurrent hints of the *Beale Street Blues*.[26]

A significant passage in *The Last Tycoon* would add a dimension to this aesthetic of the unsayable. It removes the last obstacle to our understanding, the intervention of a narrator. For the first time we see into the character's soul at the crucial moment when the musical message is about to take form. This is the only long description of interiorized music to be found in all Fitzgerald's published works. It functions very much as Vinteuil's *Septet* does in *Remembrance of Things Past* when it develops themes that are only sketched in the sonata:

Winding down the hill, he listened inside himself as if something by an unknown composer, powerful and strange and strong, was about to be played for the first time. The theme would be stated presently, but because the composer was always new, he would not recognize it as the theme right away. It would come in some such guise as the auto horns from the technicolor boulevards below, or be barely audible, a tattoo on the muffled drum of the moon. He strained to hear it, knowing that the music was beginning, new music that he liked and did not understand. It was hard to react to what one could not entirely encompass—this was new and confusing, nothing one could shut off in the middle and supply the rest from an old score.[27]

This music is only imminent, however, not yet heard. Its silence subsumes the whole experience of the search in Fitzgerald's work for the present, an unshakably convincing present that no apparent fulfillment can thrust into the past as a thing achieved. It admirably illustrates the message of *Ode on a Grecian Urn*, which locates happiness on the curved flanks of the urn, in the pursuit of desire and not in its realization, in imagination rather than reality—in short, in a silence more eloquent than any music.

All Fitzgerald's work seems to aspire to these instants of suspension and equilibrium in which the search for a hero and a style tend to blend, in which the action's silence seems to reply to another silence of inner music that destroys itself if it is heard. The slow movement that, from rejection to rejection, bears a hero to transcendence matches the writer's progress. More poet than novelist, he evokes a world of sound and fury only to make more audible the murmur of another, more distant world, one that is inaccessible except through forms perceptible solely to those who, like Gatsby, no longer hear the tumult of existence.

V. WHAT HAVE YOU DONE
DONE
WITH YOUR YOUTH?

(1924-30)

12. A KNOWLEDGE OF FOREIGN PLACES

(May 1924–May 1925)

After riding through "the pink carnival of Normandy,"[1] the Fitzgeralds arrived at the Saint-Lazare station in Paris on a May evening in 1924 under more promising auspices than their first visit had offered three years earlier. Many of their friends knew the city well, and their address book was full of the names of expatriates who were thoroughly at home there. They moved into the Hôtel des Deux Mondes, on the Avenue de l'Opéra, where, still unfamiliar with French customs, they took the bidet for a baby's bathtub and proceeded to bathe Scottie in it. She celebrated her arrival in Paris by inadvertently guzzling a gin fizz instead of her lemonade.

Among the Americans they were to look up was the older brother of elegant New Yorker Esther Murphy, whom they had entertained at Great Neck. Gerald Murphy, his wife, Sara, and their three children lived on the Quai des Grands-Augustins, near the Boulevard Saint-Michel on the Left Bank. They were deeply involved in the French capital's artistic life. The two couples hit it off together, and the Murphys strongly urged the Fitzgeralds to go to the Riviera, where they themselves were planning to spend their second summer.

John Bishop, who had married an heiress and lived in baronial ease near Paris, invited them to lunch in the Bois de Boulogne. They talked about literature, and Bishop suggested that they read the biographies of Byron and Shelley by André Maurois. Everywhere they went, the Fitzgeralds ran across old acquaintances. While strolling up the Champs-Élysées one day, they were recognized by Lawton Campbell, who was impressed by their elegance and distinction. When he complimented Zelda on her well-cut, military-blue dress, she told him she had designed it herself and was wearing it that day for the first time. "This, Lawton, is my Jeanne d'Arc dress," she told him.[2]

The train ride south was a voyage of discovery, of the springlike green of the Burgundian and Rhone Valley countryside that Zelda would later call up in her novel *Save Me the Waltz*, the varnished roofs and bell towers of Dijon, "the high terraces of Lyon . . . the white of Avignon . . . the scent of lemon, the rustle of black foliage."[3]

They stopped at Hyères, perhaps because Edith Wharton owned a house there, a gauge of the city's hospitality. But they were disappointed with the Grimm's Park Hotel, where there was never anything but lamb on the table d'hôte menu and where the Fitzgeralds were received with hostility by the British tourists who seemed to have made the hotel their private preserve. The city's stifling heat drove them to look elsewhere for a place to light. Leaving Scottie with an English nanny used to service with the English gentry, Zelda and Scott went off in search of a summer villa. In Cannes, in Monte Carlo, they were taken in taxis that were invariably driven by exiled Russian aristocrats to inspect lavish homes. Either the places required too many servants, or the plumbing was defective, or . . . The tale of their troubles made a funny story designed as a sequel to "How to Live on $36,000 a Year," entitled "How to Live on Practically Nothing a Year." At last, weary of it all, they stepped out on the tiny station at Saint-Raphaël. An hour later an efficient housing agent showed them their dream villa nestled in a pine woods high above the sea in Valescure, "a clean, cool villa set in a large garden on a hill above town. It was what we had been looking for all along."[4]

Huge and well laid out, Villa Marie had two bathrooms and windows opening on big blue-and-white-tiled balconies, pleasant places to breakfast in the sun. A terraced garden where palms, lemon trees and olive trees grew was studded with rocky outcroppings that gave it a forest-primeval look—even though you could see a summer house through the trees. When he spied the Fitzgeralds, the gardener doffed his straw hat and addressed Scott as "milord." The deal was closed on the spot.

In her autobiographical novel Zelda recalls the euphoria that flooded them when they found this earthly Eden. On taking possession of the villa, her heroine, Alabama, exclaims, "Oh, we are going to be so happy away from all the things that almost got us but couldn't quite because we were too smart for them!"[5] But life's problems weren't outside them, they were inside, mixed up with the Fitzgeralds' impatience to live.

Scott could satisfy this need of intensity by plunging wholeheartedly into his novel, protected by the enchanted silence of his estate. There he was once again possessed by the strength and fervor of his most creative hours; he was again the young man who had written *This Side of Paradise* in a few summer weeks. To give this renascence a new look, he grew a mustache, like the Henry James who grew a beard when he began writing the great novels of his last period.

But Zelda? Nanny looked after Scottie, the servants took care of the house and the meals. What was she to do with all the time on her hands? How was she to fill the summer hours when carnival sounds drifted up from the shore below? This is what Alabama asks a David absorbed in his painting: " 'What'll we *do*, David,' she asked, 'with ourselves?' "[6] It was Daisy's question, too, in *The Great Gatsby* as she saw the promising moments go sterile and disappear. As the first day of summer neared, she asked,

"Do you always watch for the longest day of the year and then miss it?"[7] And, a few chapters later, she anticipates Zelda's complaint: "What'll we do with ourselves this afternoon. . . . And the day after that, and the next thirty years?"[8]

To give her more freedom of movement, Scott bought Zelda a Renault car, and while he worked alone, she spent hours on the beach with Scottie and Nanny. Scott went down to the beach with them in the evening, sometimes had a quick swim, and then they dined together to the music of an orchestra that went heavy on American tunes, especially the sempiternal "Yes, We Have No Bananas!," the rage of New York the year before. The owner of the casino introduced them to a group of young officers from the French naval air station at nearby Fréjus. They liked each other, they danced, they discussed the world's future in fractured French-English supplemented with sign language when the words wouldn't come.

This was the Fitzgeralds' first contact with foreigners of their age and class. Moreover, a neighboring villa was inhabited by bachelors. Obviously, the Fitzgeralds had to give a party. Zelda perked up, and Scott was relieved to see her surrounded by people again. Being with these young aviators gave him the feeling of belonging in France. He wrote a page then that radiated all his satisfaction, his delight in being one with the spirit of the place: "It is twilight as I write this, and out of my window darkening banks of trees, set one clump behind another in many greens, slope down to the evening sea. The flaming sun has collapsed behind the peaks of the Estérels and the moon already hovers over the Roman aqueducts of Fréjus, five miles away." He was waiting for his guests to arrive. "In half an hour René and Bobbé, officers of aviation, are coming to dinner in their white ducks. . . . Afterward, in the garden, their white uniforms will grow dimmer as the more liquid dark comes down, until they, like the heavy roses and the nightingale in the pines, will seem to take an essential and indivisible part in the beauty of this proud gay land."[9]

"René" was René Silvy, the son of a Cannes notary public; René had literary ambitions and he wrote, he told the Fitzgeralds, for his own satisfaction. "Bobbé" was the group's veteran: he had fought at Verdun in the Great War. He too was a lover of literature. The most endearing of the bunch was Edouard Jozan, a lieutenant, son of a middle-class family in Nimes with a long military tradition. He was to make a fine career for himself in the navy, would become a vice admiral in 1952, would command France's Far Eastern fleet and wind up with the Legion of Honor and the Grand Cross of the Order of Malta.

All the young men were attentive to the beautiful American. Being surrounded by officers vying for the favor of dancing with her carried Zelda back to her carefree years in Montgomery. As the pilots from Camp Taylor had done there, Jozan here buzzed the Villa Marie in his plane. "Do you think he actually *is* a god?" Alabama asks David in Zelda's novel. "He looks like you—except that he is full of the sun, whereas you are a moon person."[10] With his blond hair, a face like something on a medallion, and his bronzed, well-modeled body, Jozan really did look like a god of Summer.

The group dissolved and re-formed as camp duty dictated. There were auto excursions, picnics, rides on the merry-go-rounds at fun fairs, dancing at the casino in the evenings. Zelda made a habit of swimming with the bunch, but more and more often with Jozan alone. She bought the year's best-seller in France, Raymond Radiguet's *Le Bal du comte d'Orgel*, and a dictionary to help her learn the language. *Save Me the Waltz* shows clearly the magnetism of the good-looking, ardent and available young Frenchman who brought a nick-of-time answer to the question "what'll we do with ourselves this afternoon?":

> He drew her body against his till she felt the blades of his bones carving her own. He was bronze and smelled of the sand and sun; she felt him naked underneath the starched linen. . . . She felt as if she would like to be kissing Jacques Chèvre-Feuille on top of the Arc de Triomphe.[11]

Everyone knew about the affair, even the Murphys, who had come visiting from Cap d'Antibes and who could not mistake the relationship of Zelda and Edouard when they saw them on the beach together, or dancing at the casino. Only Scott, working with a joy he had rarely felt before, seemed unaware of what was going on. He was used to seeing Zelda flirt, but she usually did it so outrageously and so innocently that the very exuberance she brought to it absolved her of any guilty intent.

Then, in mid-July, things went sour. Scott's first *Ledger* entry for July 1924 reads, "The Big Crisis—13th of July. . . ."[12] Exactly what form the crisis took seems impossible to reconstruct now; all that's certain is that Fitzgerald was terribly upset to learn of Zelda's infidelity and that their married life was deeply marked by that summer's events. A remark by Ernest Hemingway gives us an idea of how manipulated and, in effect, fictionalized the "crisis" was to be. "He told me . . . about something tragic that had happened to them at Saint-Raphaël about a year ago," Hemingway reported. "The first version that he told me of Zelda and a French naval aviator falling in love was a truly sad story and I believe it was a true story. Later he told me other versions of it as though trying them for use in a novel, but none was as sad as this first one and I always believed the first one, although any of them might have been true. They were better told each time, but they never hurt you the same way as the first one did."[13]

We might be tempted to question the accuracy of Hemingway's report if his first wife, Hadley, who can hardly be suspected of wanting to slight Fitzgerald, had not confirmed her husband's account in a conversation with Nancy Milford. Indeed, she went even further, turning Scott's remarks into a kind of ritual in which Zelda took part. "It was one of their acts together," she said. "I remember Zelda's beautiful face becoming very, very solemn, and she would say how he had loved her and how hopeless it had been and then how he had committed suicide. . . . Scott would stand next to her looking very pale and distressed and sharing every minute of it. Somehow it struck me as something that gave her status. I can still see both of them standing together telling me about the suicide of Zelda's lover. It created a peculiar effect."[14]

Admiral Jozan did not remember the incident in detail. To him, after all, his affair with Zelda was just another summer flirtation on the beach. A transfer to Hyères put a prosaic end to his contacts with the Fitzgeralds. He was unaware of the drama that was to resound so loudly in Zelda's imagination. In her novel she simply has Chèvre-Feuille leaving for Indochina; of all the possible versions, she chose the soberest. How, then, should we take the tale Fitzgerald later told a relative? He said Zelda had come to him, had confessed that she loved Jozan and asked him for a divorce. Scott allegedly then delivered an ultimatum: Zelda and Jozan were to face him together for a showdown. This never happened, and Zelda was confined to Villa Marie while Scott resumed work on his novel.

In his notes, under the heading "Ideas," was the remark, "That September 1924, I knew something had happened that could never be repaired."[15] This was probably written long after the event. For in August 1924 he noted in his *Ledger*, "Zelda and I close together" and in September, "Trouble clearing away."[16]

Was this irreparable "something" Zelda's transgression, her violation of an unstated code of complicity, of constant connivance that cemented their marriage together? The lateness of that September dating suggests that it wasn't Zelda's infidelity itself that troubled them, but its resonance in their memories. Two months after the event Scott noted an improvement in his relationship with Zelda; indeed, in early August they had shown a serenely united front to the Seldeses, who spent a few days with them. All along, however, Scott knew how deeply shaken Zelda had been. Two weeks after the Seldeses left, the Fitzgeralds went to stay with the Murphys, and Zelda attempted suicide with an overdose of sleeping pills.

What was irreparable was the crack spreading in Zelda's mind, the feeling of sacrilege and guilt that would mark her forever. The marriage was cracked, too, but even more irreparable was the rift in Zelda's self-image, her awareness that without Scott she had no life of her own. That he could not live without her, either, that they were part of each other. And that the focal point of their common identity, the hinge on which their lives swung, was a badly healed wound that ached anew with the slightest strain. Little was needed henceforth to fan in Zelda a feeling of interdependence at blissful moments, or to damp it in more sober ones, but she was always now to be self-conscious, aware of her need and her vulnerability.

When she was placed in a psychiatric hospital in 1930, she wrote an autobiography for her doctor revealing that the two most important emotional events in her life were her marriage, which thrust her into a world "for which I was not qualified or prepared, because of my inadequate education," and her affair with Jozan, "a love affair with a French aviator in Saint-Raphaël. I was locked in my villa for one month to prevent me from seeing him."[17]

The affair was central to *Save Me the Waltz,* which Zelda wrote eight years later, and to the unfinished novel called "Caesar's Things," which occupied the last six years of her life, after Scott's death. It is obsessive in that second work. Chèvre-Feuille reappears in the book, along with an artist husband still absorbed in his work. In it Zelda stressed the similarity between them she had already noted in her first novel—two sides of the same coin, one solar, the other lunar—by giving them similar first names, Jacques and Jacob. Even the heroine's name, Janno, places her in this anaphoric community. Jacob and Janno are "twins," just as Gloria and Anthony were in *The Beautiful and Damned,* too much alike; in fact, their very similarity invites temptation by Another, who is merely a third image of the same person. And Jacques is another Jacob, the one Janno wants, whose work is not a rival to her and who is free to give her as much as she longs to receive. With him she enters existence, breaks out of the purgatory in which Jacob has confined her. For this is her prime grief: being dispossessed by the paintings to which Jacob gives all his vitality; she merely sits and waits; cloistered in his personality and cut off from the source of life, she withers. Even when Jacob learns of her betrayal, he postpones dealing with the problem, simply shuts her in, a concrete metaphor for their relationship. "I'll get out of here as soon as I can," he tells her. " 'In the meantime you are not to leave these premises. You understand?' Of course she understood, a locked door is not difficult of comprehension. So she told her husband that she loved the French officer and her husband locked her up in the villa."[18]

Fitzgerald notes somewhere that a bone is strongest at the point of an old fracture. Perhaps he was thinking of the break that occurred that July. Until then he had never questioned the inviolability of his marriage. He had raised his conviction that only monogamy is moral to a kind of credo. "Upon the theme of marital fidelity his eloquence has moved me to tears," wrote Ernest Boyd in a book published in that very year, 1924. ". . . when so many others are conscious only of sex, he is conscious of the soul. . . . His Catholic heaven is not so far away that he can be misled into mistaking the shoddy dreams of a radical millennium as a substitute for Paradise."[19]

Scott had been hit hard by the Jozan incident, but he felt too close to Zelda, too much like her not to understand and absolve her. With his strongly proclaimed belief in marital fidelity went an awareness of what made Zelda try to seduce all their close friends. There was a sort of connivance, too, as though with his consent, she took on the dangerous job of shaking their alliance to prove how sturdy it was. In the same section of

Scott's notebooks as his remark about the "something . . . that could never be repaired" are two other phrases that certainly refer to the same situation, since they are part of a paragraph devoted to the year 1924 that begins, "Going to the Riviera." The first expresses compassion for the moral anguish Zelda will experience: "He was sorry, knowing how she would pay." The other is more devious; it reflects the ambivalence that kept Fitzgerald from ever feeling wholehearted reproach or pity. Zelda's dereliction had not occurred independently of him, it concerned him directly, as though in his imagination he took her place, or Jozan's. He too was the tempted or the tempter, seducer or seduced, perhaps the procurer, if not in fact, then in passing impulse. When we relate it to the crucial events of July 1924, this sibylline notation brings us deep into the labyrinth of a conscience that was at once detached and ravaged: "Feeling of proxy in passion; strange encouragement."[20]

Nearly twenty years later, with a still irresistible need to confess her part in what had happened, Zelda made this "encouragement" explicit in "Caesar's Things": when Janno and Jacob meet Jacques for the first time, he is standing apart from a group of officers, and it is Jacob who insists, despite her reluctance, that she strike up a conversation with him.

This is the kind of transference and permutation that, applied to fiction, gave the ring of truth to the stormy scenes in *The Great Gatsby* in which Tom Buchanan learns of Daisy's affair with Gatsby. Instead of distracting Fitzgerald's attention from his work, his personal crisis gave him the stuff, the passion that would electrify the end of his novel. He never complained of being interrupted that summer; in fact, he thought of what happened as beneficial and dynamic to his creativity. The flare of that July passion fit into his plans; the crisis echoed a fictional situation that had already fed on his relations with Zelda. Experience and creation converged: Fitzgerald's effort to finish his book and the isolation this imposed on him encouraged the progress of the intrigue toward its painful denouement. Fitzgerald quickly gained control of the situation, diverting it from his private sphere and channeling it toward his work.

"The author would like to say that never before did one try to keep his artistic conscience as pure as during the ten months put into doing it," Fitzgerald would write in the preface to a new edition of *Gatsby* ten years later. Gatsby's idealized love of Daisy was partly Scott's for Zelda, which no sexual adventure could stain. Yet through Tom, the novelist projects his own astonishment, his own indignation and his determination to force a showdown; Buchanan is intent on breaking off Daisy's affair, on making her confess that she never really loved Gatsby, that she had merely felt a passing attraction to him for which Tom bore some of the responsibility. Daisy's vacillation was a bit Zelda's as she waited for someone to make up her mind for her. The showdown that never happened was felt as something lacking, and it finally took place in Fitzgerald's novel. He put into

Gatsby's mouth the words he himself dreaded to hear, and he would give them again later, word for word, to Nicole's lover Barban in *Tender Is the Night:* "Your wife doesn't love you. . . . She's never loved you. She loves me." Jozan, Buchanan, Barban—the three names rhyme, the three men are of the same breed: conquerors, heroes of the sun. That the second is the heroine's husband and the third her lover (for "she" is always Zelda) only emphasizes the "feeling of proxy in passion."

A letter dated August 25 informed Perkins that the novel would be completed the following week, but that another month would be needed for revision. Three short sentences summed up Fitzgerald's stay at Valescure: "It's been a fair summer. I've been unhappy but my work hasn't suffered from it. I am grown at last."[21] In a previous letter, written on July 10, three days before the "big crisis," he told his editor he had begun reading *War and Peace;* in the second he recommends *Le Bal du comte d'Orgel,* which he was halfway through. It was a strange coincidence that he should be reading that story of love and renunciation; if he looked at the final pages, in which Mahaut d'Orgel tells her husband of her love for François de Séryeuse, Fitzgerald must certainly have been struck by their pertinence to his situation. Would he have seen his own attitude mirrored in the Count of Orgel's? "Unlike other men who give in to their feelings and think only later of how to forestall scandal, the Count of Orgel proceeded professionally to do what was most urgent, that is, he exploited his shock, his stupor and, beginning at the end, kept his heartache for later, when he was alone."[22]

Fitzgerald, too, put his heartache in parentheses and worked feverishly to finish his novel. When that was done, he spent a few days in Avignon with Zelda; then they both settled down to rereading and correcting the manuscript. Their money was running out, and Scott wrote a story for the *Post;* Zelda, meanwhile, read Henry James's *Roderick Hudson* and, enticed by its descriptions of Rome, persuaded Scott that they should go to Italy from Valescure. The fact that the currency exchange rate was more favorable in Italy than in France, making living costs lower there for tourists, helped convince him.

Ring Lardner and his family came to visit in October, breaking the chain of long workdays. The Lardners were winding up a tour of Europe that Ring had also seen as a way to break away from the destructive life of Long Island. Scott's efforts to get Ring's work published had borne fruit; Lardner was now a successful author. But he knew he had tuberculosis and his mood was blacker than ever. After they left, Scott went over his manuscript once more before sending it to Perkins October 27. He was pleased with it ("I think that at last I've done something really my own"[23]) and could turn now to practical details of publication: the book was to have the same format and binding as his previous books, but there were to be no critical blurbs, not even from Mencken or Lewis, on the jacket. Fitzgerald wanted to change his image. "I'm tired of being the author of *This Side of Paradise*," he informed Perkins, "and I want to start over."

The five-month lease he had signed on the Villa Marie expired and the family moved into the Lardners' hotel, the Continental, on November 3. There Scott finished his short story "Love in the Night"; he hoped that if it and two others he wrote sold well, they would bring him enough money to pay for a winter in Rome.

"Love in the Night" recreates the charms of the Riviera after dark, its lights and its orchestras, as seen through the eyes of a young Russian exile fallen from his princely rank but proud of his ancestry; he announces, "I am Russian" as though he were saying, "I am an archangel." This allowed Fitzgerald to trace a parallel between the opulence of Russian tourists in czarist days and of Americans in the twenties. The Russians, he observed, were the ones who lived high before the war. Of the three peoples that made France their fairground, they were by far the most gifted for making grand gestures; the English were too matter-of-fact, the Americans, although they spent lavishly, had no romantic tradition. But the Russians, he thought, had a sense of magnificence, like the Latins, and they were rich to boot.

Of all the Americans he met in Europe, only the Murphys, perhaps, had style and could be compared, in a less ostentatious way, with the grand dukes of the past. In this story Fitzgerald said a sad farewell to this corner of the earth where he had once thought he could live happily. Some descriptive material would resurface in *Tender Is the Night,* when Rosemary, like Fitzgerald when he arrived in Saint-Raphaël, took a taxi driven by "a Russian czar of the period of Ivan the Terrible" and was over-whelmed with nostalgia for a bygone era: "Ten years ago, when the season ended in April, the doors of the Orthodox church were locked, and the sweet champagnes they favored were put away until their return. 'We'll be back next season,' they said, but this was premature, for they were never coming back any more."[24]

The image foreshadows another fate, that of Dick Diver, who will also leave the Riviera at the end of the book, a dispossessed king condemned to exile.

Around the middle of November 1924 the Fitzgeralds drove their Renault in easy stages to Rome. They checked into the Quirinal Hotel, which was as infested with Britons and fleas as the Grimm's Park Hotel in Hyères. A few days later they found a smaller hotel on the Piazza di Spagna, at the foot of the Spanish Steps. Full board for three, including wine and service, was $525 a month. But money flowed out faster than Scott expected and he telegraphed a request to Perkins for a $750 advance, which brought his debt to Scribner's to $5,000. Because Scott found writing difficult in a hotel room, he and Zelda looked for an apartment, but in vain:

Pope Pius XI had just proclaimed 1925 a Holy Year and all Italy was caught up in a fever of preparation for the ceremonies; visitors poured in from everywhere, making housing scarce. All the talk was about the coming canonization of Sister Thérèse of the Christ Child and the beatification of Bernadette Soubirous.[25]

This Catholic ferment reminded Scott of his distaste for the piety and bigotry of the St. Paul Irish. In Italy Mussolini had been in power for two years, and the Fitzgeralds were offended by the haughtiness of officers, government officials and the Roman aristocracy. This was the period when Scott wrote "The Adjuster," a short story reflecting his marital troubles. The story was also a screen in which to examine his xenophobia, which he ascribed to a peculiarly American cultural lag. "They were of that enormous American class who wander over Europe every summer, sneering rather pathetically and wistfully at the customs and traditions and pastimes of other countries, because they have no customs or traditions or pastimes of their own," he wrote. "It is a class sprung yesterday from fathers and mothers who might just as well have lived two hundred years ago."[26]

Except for walks in the Pincio and sporadic visits to bars patronized by Americans, Scott took no part in Roman life. When he knocked off work, he began drinking, another way to reject the outside world. And he thought about his next novel, which he estimated would take a year of work. Meanwhile, he was waiting for the proofs of *Gatsby*, due in late December, and planning extensive changes in them. Through Ober he tried to sell the serial rights to his book to *Liberty* magazine for $15,000. The offer was turned down on the grounds of the novel's immorality; "We could not publish this story," the magazine said, "with as many mistresses and as much adultery as there is in it."[27] Early in January *College Humor* offered $10,000, but Fitzgerald refused it because the magazine was a monthly and serialization in it would have pushed publication of the book back to the autumn. Besides, he feared that the general silliness of *College Humor* would damage his reputation and reduce sales of the book. Most of all he dreaded "the gaudy and ill-advised advertising"[28] the magazine's editor, H. N. Swanson, would use, exploiting Fitzgerald's name to promote readership.

The winter was cold and wet. Scott caught the grippe and Zelda suffered from persistent abdominal pain, which a local doctor diagnosed as colitis. Fitzgerald had planned to write a follow-up to his two articles on their financial problems; the *Post* had run "How to Live on Practically Nothing" in September and had asked for a third installment on Italy. But his animosity toward the country and its people spoiled the poetic and humorous tone in which he had told of his first contact with France. "I hate Italy and the Italians so violently that I can't bring myself to write about them for the *Post*—unless they'd like an article called 'Pope Siphilis the Sixth and His Morons' or something like that. But we're resolutely trying to economize, so we wouldn't move back to France till March even if we could afford it."[29] He was not to turn out "The High Cost of Macaroni" until the end of his stay, and it was so poor that the *Post* refused it.

The article, nevertheless, is biographically interesting. In it Fitzgerald recounted his troubles with Roman taxi drivers who tried to cheat him one drunken evening on the fare for taking him and Zelda to their hotel; the row became a brawl and Scott unfortunately slugged a plainclothes policeman who tried to intervene. He was arrested, roughed up and tossed into a cell from which Zelda and a friend managed only with great difficulty to extract him the next morning. The incident figures in a first draft of *Tender Is the Night*, written shortly after, which opens with a chapter on it. Ten years later he would mention it in a letter as "just about the rottenest thing that ever happened in my life."[30] Was he subconsciously seeking humiliation, making a scandal in the unavowed hope of punishing himself? Did he feel guilty about Zelda, whose colitis seemed to indicate how much trouble she was having in recovering from the summer's "big crisis"?

He also devoted a few pages of his new novel to the Roman studios on the Appian Way, where Fred Niblo was filming *Ben Hur* for M-G-M, the first of the historical superproductions—250 extras, a $6 million budget, three years in the making. The Fitzgeralds became friendly with Carmel Myers, who costarred in the film with Ramon Novarro, and they celebrated Christmas together. Writing about their meeting and the Viennese shawl the actress gave her, Zelda noted that the film's action was set "in bigger and grander papier-maché arenas than the real ones."[31]

In January the Fitzgeralds took a few excursions, to Tivoli, Frascati and, later, Naples. Sunny Capri seemed the ideal place in which to wait out the winter. They soon went back there and took a room in the Tiberio Hotel, on a hill overlooking the sea. But their two months there were spoiled by Zelda's fragile health and Scott's constant drinking. They quarreled frequently, but this does not seem to have diminished their love for each other. "The cheerfulest things in my life," Scott wrote to John Peale Bishop, "are first Zelda and second the hope that my book has something extraordinary about it. I want to be extravagantly admired again. Zelda and I sometimes indulge in terrible four-day rows that always start with a drinking party but we're still enormously in love and about the only truly happily married people I know."[32]

With Scott absorbed in correcting the proofs of *Gatsby*, Zelda took up painting. And they met a few people who broke their solitude. Aunt Annabel, who maintained the Fitzgerald family tradition of travel in Italy, had come to Rome for the Holy Year observances and spent several days with Zelda and Scott in Capri. Chance brought Fitzgerald in touch with one of his former idols, Compton Mackenzie, who had been living on the island for the past seven years. Despite his excitement, Scott judged the writer lucidly and considered him completely out of date. But it was Mackenzie who introduced him into the British colony the Fitzgeralds had never known existed.

At the end of the nineteenth century, after Oscar Wilde's imprisonment, Capri had become a haven for British homosexuals who, following Tiberius, had made it a pagan paradise sheltered from Victorian hypocrisy. Norman Douglas, Somerset Maugham and his friend John Ellingham Brooks, novelist Edward Frederick Benson, son of the Archbishop of Canterbury, had made the island famous. After the war two more British novelists arrived to nurse their war-shattered health: Francis Brett Young and Mackenzie. The latter, suffering from chronic dysentery he contracted in the Middle East, lived with his wife, Faith, in the Villa Solitaria, perched on a cliff above the sea. There, around a table that had once belonged to Maxim Gorki, Fitzgerald met some of the island's rare fauna and was fascinated by some of the expatriate folklore Mackenzie would record in his *Memoirs* and in his roman à clef *Extraordinary Women.* There Scott saw Romaine Brooks, the immensely wealthy heiress and talented painter who had just broken off her affair with pianist Renata Borgatti; John Brooks, whom she had married a quarter of a century earlier and left after a year of marriage; Benson and Mary Roberts Rinehart, who, like Mackenzie, had been heroes of Scott's youth; and even Axel Munthe, a youthful sixty-seven-year-old who would publish his best-selling *The Story of San Michele* four years later.

Mackenzie, whom Fitzgerald considered finished, was only forty-two and would produce his best books in the forty-seven years of life remaining to him. But Scott saw him only as a survivor of a fabulous era and thought of how far he himself had come since the days when he considered *Sinister Street* the summit of romantic literature. "I found him cordial, attractive and pleasantly mundane," Fitzgerald said in his letter to Bishop. "You get no sense from him that [he] feels his work has gone to pieces. He's not pompous about his present output. I think he's just tired. The war wrecked him as it did Wells and many of that generation."[33]

Now sure of himself, Fitzgerald also included Mencken in his repudiation of the men who had most influenced him. He reiterated to Perkins that he wanted to owe nothing to his elders' approval: "Please have *no blurbs of any kind on the jacket!!!* No Mencken or Lewis or Sid Howard or anything. I don't believe in them *one bit* any more."[34]

He received the final batch of proofs in the second week of January and worked on them uninterruptedly for six weeks, then returned them with extensive changes after giving strict instructions to Perkins: "*The conditions are two.* a) That someone reads it *very carefully twice* to see that every one of my inserts are put in correctly. There are so many of them that I'm in terror of a mistake. b) That no changes *whatsoever* are made in it except in the case of a misprint so glaring as to be certain, and that only by you."[35]

Perkins reacted to the manuscript with an enthusiasm he had never shown before. "I think you have every right to be proud of the book," he wrote to Fitzgerald. "It is an extraordinary book, suggestive of all sorts of thoughts and moods. You adopted exactly the right method of telling it, that of employing a narrator who is more of a spectator than an actor: this puts the reader upon a point of observation on a higher level than that on which the characters stand and at a distance that gives perspective. In no other way could your irony have been so immensely effective. . . . In the eyes of Dr. Eckleburg various readers will see different significances; but their presence gives a superb touch to the whole thing: great, unblinking eyes, expressionless, looking down upon the human scene. It's magnificent!"[36]

Aside from his aesthetic pleasure, Perkins had other reasons, moral ones, for admiring Fitzgerald. Knowing the writer's constant need of money, the editor was amazed that Scott had been strong enough to refuse *College Humor*'s offer: "I congratulate you on resisting the $10,000. I don't see how you managed it. But it delighted us. . . ."[37]

In reading Fitzgerald's frequent letters to Perkins that winter, one is struck by their lack of complaints about money that had spattered the period preceding the publication of *The Beautiful and Damned* three years earlier. He suggested no advertising for floating the new book. He even refused a renewal of the favorable contract he had imposed on Scribner's for his previous novel (17.5 percent royalties after the first 20,000 sales and 20 percent after 40,000) and settled for 15 percent after 40,000 to show his gratitude, he explained, for the big advances the publisher had granted him.

Fitzgerald lingered on Capri for several more weeks, sending letters and telegrams to change details even though the novel was already being printed. He could have gone to Paris or London to be available when the book came out, but he did not leave the island until a week after its appearance on April 10. To avoid the long drive, the Fitzgeralds put their car aboard a ship in Naples; the roof was damaged while it was being onloaded. In Marseilles they stayed at the Hotel Regina, where they found a telegram from Perkins, sent ten days after the book's release and prefiguring its subsequent fate: "Sales situation doubtful. Excellent reviews."[38]

Scott immediately fired off a letter expressing his disappointment and trying to anticipate why it might not sell well. The title was bad, he thought. More serious was the novel's lack of a major female character; it was women readers who determined a book's popularity. He was already resigned to having to write a clutch of stories to wipe out his debts and live in France until he completed his next book. And if that one did not end his financial problems, he was ready to abandon literature and head for Hollywood.

Thus unburdened, he felt free to roam with Zelda through the streets of Marseilles, savoring again the familiar scenes and voices of southern France. On Zelda's recommendation—she preferred convertible cars—a mechanic removed the Renault's roof instead of trying to fix it. Then the Fitzgeralds started off for Paris. They got as far as Lyons, where torrential rains prevented them from driving any farther in their now irrevocably open car. Too impatient to wait around before learning what reception his book was getting, Scott abandoned the Renault in a Lyons garage and the family continued north by train. As soon as they reached Paris, Scott rushed to his bank, the Guaranty Trust, and found a second telegram modifying the earlier message's pessimism about the book's sales; with it was a letter containing the first favorable reviews. Perkins had prudently omitted the New York *World* critic's verdict, offered under the headline "F. Scott Fitzgerald's Latest a Dud," as well as the Brooklyn *Eagle*'s opinion that there was not "one chemical trace of magic, life, irony, romance or mysticism in all of 'The Great Gatsby.' "[39]

While waiting to move into the apartment they had rented as soon as they arrived, the Fitzgeralds established headquarters in the Hotel Florida, on the Boulevard Malesherbes. Scott immediately cabled Scribner's with a request for $1,000. The next day, May 1, he wrote to Perkins, seemingly resigned to the relative failure of *Gatsby*. His only hope now was that it would sell well enough to cover his advances, and he calculated the break-even point at 23,000 copies. He thought that, with one exception, the critics had not understood his book at all. But he seemed to have overcome his earlier bitterness; he dealt at length in the letter with other new books out, the critical success of Lardner's work and Scribner's lack of initiative, which allowed rival publishers to filch its promising young writers. Why, he wanted to know, hadn't they followed his advice about Hemingway? Meanwhile, he was readying his next collection of stories, *All the Sad Young Men*.

On May 12 he moved into a new apartment at 14, Rue de Tilsitt, near the Arc de Triomphe. Certain that he would rapidly finish his next novel, he signed a lease for eight months, approximately the time he had spent on *Gatsby*. The apartment, a sixth-floor walk-up with windows that gave on a courtyard, was furnished with fake, mass-produced Louis XV furniture. It was all rather dreary. What mattered, though, was that they were in Paris, close to the sun-warmed café terraces and chestnut trees on the Champs-Élysées. The Fitzgeralds were at home in Paris now and highly critical of unenterprising American tourists—the kind they themselves had been four years earlier. Scott may have thought back on the letters he had exchanged with Wilson in those early days. In any case, the one he wrote two weeks after reaching the French capital this time contrasted sharply with them: "This city is full of Americans—most of them former friends—whom we spend most of our time dodging, not because we don't want to see them but because Zelda's only just well and I've got to work; and they seem incapable of any sort of conversation not composed of semi-malicious gossip about New York courtesy celebrities. I've gotten to like France. . . . I'm filled with disgust for Americans in general after two weeks' sight of the ones in Paris—these preposterous, pushing women and girls who assume that you have any personal interest in them, who have all (so they say) read James Joyce and who simply adore Mencken. I suppose we're no worse than anyone, only contact with other races brings out all our worst qualities."[40]

Fitzgerald was mistaken, for he still knew little about Paris and even less about the Americans who had more or less entered its artistic life. Not the moneyed Americans who, like him, patronized the big Right Bank hotels from the Opéra to the Étoile, but those on the Left Bank who followed in the wake of Joyce and Gertrude Stein, trying to find forms of expression appropriate to the twentieth century. In his letter to Wilson Fitzgerald mentioned two names: "I have met Hemingway. He is taking me to see Gertrude Stein tomorrow." These were the two keys that would open to him a world whose existence he scarcely suspected. Even on the Right Bank his education continued despite the time wasted at the Ritz in "1,000 parties and no work," as he twice noted in his *Ledger*.[41] Esther Murphy was there; her brother Gerald had rented Gounod's house for her on the heights of suburban Saint-Cloud. Gerald and his wife, Sara, were opening other perspectives to the Fitzgeralds in music, ballet and painting. Through these contacts Scott was at least sensitized to the spirit of freedom and innovation that had developed in all the arts since the war, even if he did not participate directly in it.

Paris then was the capital of imagination, the promised land of artists from all over the world. How timid and backward the rebellious New York intelligentsia seemed amid Paris's fecund and stimulating upheavals. This was the high place where all the world's scattered and repressed aspirations converged and flowered. And 1925 was a year of intellectual euphoria, the peak of a decade that ironist Maurice Sachs called "the decade of illusion" and "a perpetual Fourteenth of July."[42]

Except for jazz, the arts were stagnating in the United States. The whole country had eyes only for Wall Street, where financial speculation had reached fever pitch. The dollar was god and Babbitt was his prophet. This unprecedented wave of prosperity was matched by the profound disaffection of America's intellectual elite. Even in the last third of the nineteenth century, writers unhappy with the country's triumphant materialism had sought refuge in Europe, Henry James permanently and Henry Adams in a way that, for all his coming and going between Europe and the United States, was no less a rejection of an America in which he no longer felt he had a place. When good Americans die, he said in effect, they go to Paris. In the postwar years their example was followed by a handful of pioneers in search of a new cultural context. Gertrude Stein and her brothers settled in Paris in 1903, Edith Wharton in 1907; Ezra Pound and T. S. Eliot were established in London in 1912. When the United States entered the war in 1917, volunteers flooded into France to serve as ambulance drivers and stretcher-bearers with the Norton-Harjes organization and the American Ambulance Service under French Army command. Many of these volunteers were young writers who had just been graduated from Harvard and Yale and for whom the theaters of military operation would be—in the words of one of them, Malcolm Cowley, who was to become their historian —"college-extension courses for a generation of writers."[43] Among the best-known: Dos Passos, Hemingway, e. e. cummings, Julian Green, Harry Crosby, Louis Bromfield, Dashiell Hammett, Edmund Wilson.

What lessons did they learn on the roads of France? Cowley summarized them very well: "[These courses] carried us to a foreign country, the first that most of us had seen; they taught us to make love, stammer love, in a foreign language. . . . They made us more irresponsible than ever. Livelihood was not a problem; we had a minimum of choices to make; we could let the future take care of itself, feeling that it would bear us into new adventures. They taught us courage, extravagance, fatalism, these being the virtues of men at war; they taught us to regard as vices the civilian virtues of thrift, caution and sobriety; they made us fear boredom more than death. [And] ambulance service had a lesson of its own: it instilled into us what might be called a *spectatorial* attitude."[44]

After brief efforts to readapt to American values, these young men, spectators of exotica, lovers of change, collectors of the unusual, returned to Europe. Europe's capitals, especially Paris, offered them freedom, stimulation, infinite possibilities for contacts that made Main Street henceforth uninhabitable for them. A favorable dollar exchange rate bought them the right to idleness and reverie, to the leisure that fosters creation, at a price low enough to perpetuate all this, to make it a life-style. Climbing exchange rates released a flow of American intellectuals to France: one dollar bought eight francs in September 1919, fifteen a year later; in July 1925 it hit twenty-two francs, and after a brief halt during the 1926 financial crisis, the rate settled at around twenty-five francs until 1932. By the time it dropped back to fifteen francs to the dollar in 1934, the great American invasion had long since ended.

In his autobiography poet William Carlos Williams recalled how surprised he was that he and his wife could live comfortably in a pension in Villefranche-sur-Mer, not far from Monte Carlo, for twenty dollars a week. Although he did not have much money, he and his American friends could afford to lunch in the best restaurants in Paris. And prices in France were high compared with those in Italy, Germany and Austria. Hemingway spent his winters in the Tyrol and his summers in Spain; even Fitzgerald went to Italy in the fall and winter of 1924 "to economize."

Montparnasse became the artistic and intellectual capital where a new, gilded bohemia could live at ease on an income that would have qualified them as poor in the United States. In place of the gloomy solitude of America's shady and clandestine speakeasies, they found the welcoming terraces of the Dôme, the Rotonde, the Sélect, where everybody eventually knew everybody. There were the old-timers, like Man Ray, who knew the painters, the models, the surrealists. Some of these, including writers Tristan Tzara, René Crevel, Philippe Soupault and Louis Aragon, would sometimes turn up at soirées given by Nancy Cunard and Etienne de Beaumont. Joyce could be seen dining at the Trianon; the laughter of the surrealist brotherhood soared above the shrubbery at the Closerie des Lilas. Angry young men spit on the corpse of Anatole France and acclaimed the Surrealist Revolution. Oh, yes, Paris in 1925 was a ball for American expatriates.

The wealthiest among them assumed the roles of patrons, founding publishing houses, presiding over salons. Little avant-garde magazines proliferated: in Vienna 500 copies of *Secession* could be printed for twenty dollars. The low cost of publishing fertilized such growths as Harold Loeb's *Broom*, Ford Madox Ford's *Transatlantic Review*, Ernest Walsh's *This Quarter* and, later on, Eugene Jolas's *Transition* and Samuel Putnam's *The New Review*. Robert McAlmon set up Contacts Editions, William Bird the Three Mountain Press, Harry and Caress Crosby the Black Sun Press, which published the works of such innovators as Joyce, Stein, Pound, Djuna Barnes, McAlmon, Hemingway.

Literary life was concentrated on the Left Bank under the aegis of three women living in three different places: 27, Rue de Fleurus, 12, Rue de l'Odéon, and 20, Rue Jacob. Since the war Gertrude Stein's studio on the Rue de Fleurus had become a rallying point and filter for new arrivals. Paintings on the walls by Cézanne, Matisse, Picasso, Gris and Braque warned these young writers fresh from the Middle West that, as Miss Stein announced, "Paris was where the twentieth century was." Refugees from the American desert passed along the address, scribbled the passwords; Sylvia Beach recommended Sherwood Anderson, who in turn wrote a letter of introduction for Hemingway, who introduced Fitzgerald to the Steins; a whole network stretched out from the Pythian recess on the Rue de Fleurus. There a sculptural, massive, enigmatic Gertrude, ensconced in a huge armchair, held court under the portrait Picasso painted of her in 1905 (other artists were also fascinated by her impenetrable expression, Félix Vallotton in 1907, Jacques Lipchitz in 1921, Francis Picabia in 1928), and conducted her interrogations. On the other side of the fireplace her companion, Alice B. Toklas, dark and dry as a prune under Joan of Arc bangs, knitted quietly, listening and sharpening her comments, which would bubble up after their visitor had left.

The second contact point, more easily accessible, was Shakespeare and Company, the English-language bookstore Sylvia Beach founded on the Rue Dupuytren in 1919 and moved two years later to 12, Rue de l'Odéon, where she officiated until 1941. She was a different Egeria. Gertrude was fifty-one years old in 1925, Sylvia thirty-eight. Gertrude's silences contrasted with Sylvia's exuberance. Enthusiastic, generous, this quicksilver woman helped writers get started, comforted, encouraged, advised, enlightened them. It was she who published Joyce's *Ulysses* in 1922 with money from her own pocket that she never recovered. Shakespeare and Company was a book-store, a lending library, a place where the penniless could float a loan and where checks were cashed after the banks closed. Most of all, it was a place where ideas were exchanged, a literary club.

There had been a falling-out with Gertrude when Sylvia consented to share an apartment with Adrienne Monnier, who ran another bookstore, the Maison des Amis des Livres, across the street from Shakespeare and Com-pany. In compensation Sylvia made new friends, for the Friends of Books included some of the period's leading literary figures: André Gide, Paul Valéry, Léon-Paul Fargue, Valéry Larbaud, Jules Romains, and a few young novelists like André Chamson. The Rue de l'Odéon became a tiny cultural Atlantic bringing Sylvia's friends and Adrienne's into a common current. There were musicians as well as writers; Eric Satie, Darius Milhaud, Francis Poulenc liked to linger at the American's shop, where they could meet the new generation's young lions, cummings, Dos Passos, Hem-ingway, Glenway Wescott, Bromfield, as well as such visiting veterans as Conrad, Eliot and, of course, the man they all respected, Joyce.

At 20, Rue Jacob a third woman without a man, Natalie Barney—writer Rémy de Gourmont's "Amazon"—received on Fridays from 5 P.M. to 8. She was forty-nine years old then; for thirty years more she would remain the tireless seductress, the "Popess of Lesbos," whose tumultuous career began early in the century with Liane de Pougy and Renée Vivien. Here the Franco-American exchanges were on the highest level, bringing together everyone who was anyone in cosmopolitan, social and political Paris: diplo-mat Philippe Berthelot and fashion designer Paul Poiret rubbed elbows there with Colette and Gide, Gabriele d'Annunzio, Rilke, poet Oscar Milosz, Jean Cocteau, Pierre Louÿs and Robert de Montesquieu. Among the Americans deemed suitable to mix with such an assemblage were Eliot, Pound, Edna St. Vincent Millay, Carl Van Vechten, Wescott, Bromfield, Hemingway, Fitzgerald. As a gauge to the tone of these gatherings, note that Valéry read his then unpublished and difficult novel *La Jeune Parque* there in 1917.

The more elaborate receptions might draw as many as two hundred guests to the Barney garden, where stood a Temple of Friendship secretly dedicated to Sappho. Among Miss Barney's ambitions was to bring to 20, Rue Jacob the models who inspired certain passages of Proust's *Remem-brance of Things Past*. Fitzgerald would have all this in mind when he drew his portraits of lesbians for *Tender Is the Night*. Natalie's salon, however, was a world away from Gertrude's studio: here the cubist angularities of Art Deco never deposed the vaporous softness of the Belle Epoque. Only paintings by Raoul Dufy and Marie Laurencin were allowed to interject a modern note.

In the background, eclipsed by these three vigorous women, was Edith Wharton, then sixty-three; she owned a château near the Forest of Montmorency, where she received a small circle of more solemn celebrities, notably Paul Claudel and novelist Paul Bourget. Margaret Winthrop Chanler, Sigourney Fay's friend, and her son, composer Theodore Chanler, as well as Esther Murphy, were regulars there. Fitzgerald, as we shall see, would attend one such gathering, to his great mortification.

Rich American women allied to princely European houses liked to patronize the arts. Princesse Marguerite de Bassiano, née Chapin, founded the quarterly review *Commerce*, which was edited by Valéry, Fargue and Larbaud from the summer of 1924 until the winter of 1932. Another American, Princesse Edmond de Polignac, the Singer sewing machine heiress, preferred musicians: she commissioned ballets by Igor Stravinsky and helped Sergei Diaghilev's Ballet Russe, which had been appearing in Paris since 1909.

American entertainers were all the rage. Bricktop opened her Montmartre nightclub in 1924. In October 1925 Josephine Baker, just turned nineteen, was a smash hit at the Champs-Élysées Theater. She had come to Paris with the Negro Revue, a troupe of twenty-five black performers (the saxophonist's name was Sydney Bechet) put together by Caroline Dudley, the future wife of surrealist Joseph Delteil, with the express aim of conquering Europe. It was Fernand Léger, then the set designer for the Swedish Ballet Company in Paris, who persuaded the company's director, Rolf de Maré, to stage an all-black American show.

Paris audiences went wild over it; soon everyone was doing the Charleston in the dance halls that had mushroomed since the war. The troupe won more notoriety than popularity in Germany, where Josephine was viewed as the incarnation of expressionism. Max Reinhardt wanted to be Josephine's impresario, but Paul Derval, who ran the Folies-Bergère, brought her back to Paris on an irresistible contract to be the pivot of his new show. Surrounded by 500 performers, she was to dance to music by Spencer William and Irving Berlin. A follow-up show confirmed her success; she was now a star in her own right. In December 1926 she opened her own nightclub, Chez Josephine; movie producer Rex Ingram dreamed up a lavish spectacle for her, Maurice Dekobra wrote "The Siren of the Tropics" for her—it was all glory. Five years later, in a story called "Babylon Revisited," Fitzgerald's hero would watch "Josephine Baker go through her chocolate arabesques" at the Casino de Paris.[45]

A center of more general attention in that early summer of 1925 was the Decorative Arts Exposition, inaugurated July 18 by President Gaston Doumergue even before the rubble of preparation had been cleared away. Sprawling on both banks of the Seine between the Hôtel des Invalides and the Grand Palais, it formalized every aspect of the cultural revolution that had radically changed the way people saw and felt things since the 1900 Universal Exposition. The lines and volumes of cubism had triumphed; of the fin-de-siècle spirit, only the floral motifs in ornamentation survived. Architecture, furniture, accessories all proclaimed the victory of the new spirit. Furniture by Emile Ruhlmann and René Lalique's crystal fountains testified to both the innovations and survivals of the period. Robert Delaunay made the Eiffel Tower dance on his canvases, while Léger glorified cogwheels and piping. Poiret, who had dethroned fashion designers Jacques Doucet and Philippe Worth, was in turn being threatened by the new wave; he had virtually given up dress designing for interior decoration. Moored near the Invalides bridge, his three houseboats, *Amours*, *Délices* and *Orgues*, blazed with light like an Oriental vision, but the elegant Europe of the Belle Epoque was gone: Sarah Bernhardt died in 1923 and Eleanora Duse the following year. There were new fashion czars now, Lanvin and Callot and Jenny; Coco Chanel, who had opened her house in 1922, the year of the Victor Margueritte book *La Garçonne*,[46] simplified the line popularized by Mistinguett: bobbed hair, shaved armpits, exposed knees, flat bust and boyish hips. African rhythms replaced the vaguely genteel measures aboard the Orient Express, not only in painting but in music too, from Stravinsky to Milhaud.

In this electrified atmosphere the Fitzgeralds felt they were alive again after their months in a bigoted, reactionary Italy. Scott found that the misty yearnings that had made the young men of his generation rebels without a cause in New York in 1922-23, squandering their energies in futile gestures, were systematized in Paris, incandescent, crystallized in action and creation. In self-abnegation and solitude, he had finally succeeded in channeling into his book this hitherto unfocused energy that rejected a social system only to succumb to the system's mercenary values. Fitzgerald also recognized the new spirit in the integrity, the total lack of concessions in the few things he had read by the still unknown Hemingway. All the people he had admired until now had been influential elders, tradition bearers, and even in Scott's most exaggerated praise of them there had lurked a kind of reserve and a touch of opportunism. There was a symbolic value in the impetus that swept him toward Hemingway: it bespoke a complete break with the way the older generation had expressed itself. When he went looking for Hemingway one day in May 1925, he was turning to the future, to the beginner he would have liked to be, whose career he would encourage as ardently as he could.

Fitzgerald's interest in Hemingway had been stimulated by an article by Edmund Wilson in the October issue of *The Dial*, hailing the newcomer's entrance into American literature under the guidance of Gertrude Stein and Sherwood Anderson. Fitzgerald, in an essay published in *The Bookman* in

May 1926, would tell of his pleasure in reading the vignettes interspersed between the tales in *In Our Time:* "these interpolated sketches . . . fascinated me, as they did when Edmund Wilson first showed them to me in an earlier pamphlet, over two years ago."[47] On October 18, 1924, although he was feverishly busy revising the *Gatsby* manuscript that he was to send to Perkins ten days later, he nonetheless found time to write "a hurried scrawl as I am working like a dog," calling Perkins's, and Scribner's, attention to this clearly promising young writer whose genuine artistry was praised in the Jamesian expression, "He's the real thing."[48] (Zelda would always disagree; to her Hemingway was always "bogus.")

Thanks to Wilson's endorsement, then, Fitzgerald took an active interest in his junior's career after the publication of *Gatsby*. Most of what we know about their relationship derives from Hemingway's account in three chapters of *A Moveable Feast*, written over thirty years later. But the letters the two men exchanged reveal a very different Fitzgerald from the one caricatured in Hemingway's memoirs as a sort of wan, broken puppet who seemed a fugitive from a silent film that was—what? A tragic farce, or a grotesque tragedy? Scott's contemporaries thought he was subjugated by Hemingway in his humble and enthusiastic pursuit of the promotional campaign begun in his letter to Perkins.

In his reminiscences on the period, Glenway Wescott, whose first novel, *The Apple of the Eye*, was published in 1924, depicted Fitzgerald in Antibes, impatient to win recognition for Hemingway's talent, which he considered superior to his own and to Wescott's: "Obviously, Ernest was the one true genius of our decade, he said; and yet he was neglected and misunderstood and, above all, insufficiently remunerated. He thought I would agree that *The Apple of the Eye* and *The Great Gatsby* were rather inflated market values just then. What could I do to help launch Hemingway? Why didn't I write a laudatory essay on him? With this questioning, Fitzgerald now and then impatiently grasped and shook my elbow."[49]

Nevertheless, encouraged by the favorable critical reception given Gatsby and, especially, by his new friends' approval ("Ernest Hemingway and Gertrude Stein are quite enthusiastic"),[50] Fitzgerald placed great hopes in the novel he was preparing to write. He saw it as something entirely new in conception, form and structure. Before he had gotten very far into it, he was convinced that the writing experience he had assimilated during the previous year would make him "much better than any of the young Americans, *without exception*."[51] Yet, at that point his thoughts immediately turned to Hemingway: the paragraph directly following his boast in his letter to Perkins begins, "Hemingway is a fine, charming fellow."

Hemingway was beginning to be talked about. In Spain during the summer of 1925 he wrote a first version of *The Sun Also Rises;* a second draft of *In Our Time*, much better fleshed out than the first, was published in New York by Boni and Liveright. He was dissatisfied with his publisher, however. Only 1,300 copies of his book had been printed and it was selling badly. He now regretted having been unable to accept Perkins's offer, which arrived too late, especially since Scribner's ran a literary magazine, which could have published his stories. *The Transatlantic Review*, which ran his stories in Paris, was defunct, and he had not stayed long with Walsh's *This Quarter*; it ran only one of his stories, "The Undefeated," the first to bring him a little money. "He's anxious to get a foot-hold in your magazine," Fitzgerald wrote to Perkins; "One story I've sent you, the other, to my horror, he'd given for about $40 to an 'arty' publication called *This Quarter*, over here."[52] About a month later Scott mentioned Hemingway's feelings toward Liveright: "To hear him talk you'd think Liveright had broken up his home and robbed him of millions—but that's because he knows nothing of publishing, except in the cuckoo magazines, is very young and feels helpless so far away. You won't be able to help liking him—he's one of the nicest fellows I ever knew."[53]

At the end of 1925 Hemingway wrote *The Torrents of Spring*, a parody of Sherwood Anderson's novels. Liveright refused it: Anderson was one of its authors, a more important one than Hemingway then. This broke their contract with Hemingway, and he asked Fitzgerald to intercede for him at Scribner's, even though Bromfield had promised him that Harcourt was willing to take him on. He went to New York a month later to complete his separation from Liveright and find a new publisher who would publish both the parody and his novel, by then almost completely rewritten. Fitzgerald was busy in the background, advising Perkins on how best to snare Hemingway and dissuade him from accepting the attractive offers put forth by both Harcourt and Knopf. Hemingway finally followed Fitzgerald's counsel and signed a satisfactory contract with Scribner's. After rereading it early in March, on returning to Paris, Fitzgerald implied that the deal was his work: "I'm glad that you got Hemingway . . . ," he wrote Perkins. "I've brought you two successes (Ring and Tom Boyd) and two failures. . . . Ernest will decide whether my opinions are more of a hindrance or a help."[54]

Nor did Scott limit himself to acting as his friend's volunteer literary agent. Through his criticism of Hemingway's work, he labored actively to make him recognize precisely where his talent lay. He recommended cutting passages in which the author's comments weighed down his terse narrative and descriptive language. This persuaded Hemingway to eliminate long introductory passages to "Fifty Grand" and "The Killers," which had slowed their pace and diluted their dramatic impact. And the advice was soon confirmed: Hemingway's earlier version of "Fifty Grand" had been refused by *Scribner's Magazine*, but "The Killers" was accepted in the version corrected by Fitzgerald.

Equal vigilance was brought to bear on the manuscript of *The Sun Also Rises*. Out of pride or modesty, Hemingway could not bring himself to show Scott a carbon until he had sent the original to Perkins in June 1926. Fitzgerald was immediately struck by the long biographical backgrounds Hemingway had used to introduce his characters. Aside from the heaviness caused by mistakes in tone, the sections clearly violated the aesthetic implicitly developed in Hemingway's short stories: confining action to the present and showing it exclusively through the characters' words and gestures at a specific moment and in a specific place. The characters' historical, cultural or biographical contexts were merely suggested by their behavior. Introductions trying to establish a time perspective were, therefore, artistic errors.

Fitzgerald was applying here the criteria he had adopted to explain why Hemingway's stories were so good. The dominant principle in Hemingway's literary world is not time. Its fundamental unit is the moment, and the overall effect is not procured by accumulation of these units but by their juxtaposition, their constant recurrence, their uninterrupted, closely meshed sequence. This is an aesthetic diametrically opposed to Fitzgerald's, which was based on a keen sense of the past's survival in the present. In Fitzgerald's work the present moment is always charged with nostalgia or hope, is necessarily defined by the past or the future whether of a character, a group or a civilization. The time perspective that dictates action and the fate of the heroes in Fitzgerald's work justifies long backward glances and precise historical patterning; in Hemingway's work these would violate his aesthetic laws. Jake Barnes cannot allow himself the rumination and commentary natural to Nick Carraway or to the narrator of "The Rich Boy," who are observers fed on history, have a sense of social distinctions and whose world has not been radically fragmented by a traumatic war.

Fitzgerald put his criticism in writing with sometimes brutal firmness: "careless and ineffectual," "flat as hell," "O. Henry stuff," "from p. 30 I began to like the novel, but Ernest, I can't tell you the sense of disappointment that beginning with its elephantine facetiousness gave me. Please do what you can about it in proofs."[55] Most of his criticism concerned those opening pages, especially the long historical and social analyses of the aristocratic circles in which Brett Ashley moved during the war. "It hasn't even your rhythm and the fact that it may be 'true' is utterly immaterial. . . ."[56] He knew that the originality of Hemingway's work lay precisely in his use of language in translating his personal experience undidactically, and that his first duty was to eliminate all time elements not implicit in the dialogue and action. Fitzgerald took his mentorship seriously, and he took the implacable tone Wilson had used in commenting on his own work. Hemingway recognized the soundness of his remarks and eliminated the first fifteen pages of his novel, including the biographies of Mike Campbell and Brett as well as the autobiography of narrator Barnes.

This relationship of influential master to ambitious disciple characterized the first phase of their friendship. In fact, the professional gap separating them was soon closed. *The Sun Also Rises* was published in October, two years after Fitzgerald's letter to Perkins recommending the unknown young author. By the time Fitzgerald left Europe at the end of the year, 7,000 copies of the book had been sold; a year later the figure stood at 23,000, or 3,000 more than *Gatsby* had sold. In the farewell letter he wrote Hemingway from the ship en route to New York, Fitzgerald summarized his feelings about his friend: "I can't tell you how much your friendship has meant to me during this year and a half—it is the brightest thing in our trip to Europe for me. I will try to look out for your interests with Scribners in America, but I gather that the need of that is past now and that soon you'll be financially more than on your feet."[57]

Fitzgerald's natural generosity informed his interest in Hemingway's career, the same sort of generosity he had already shown toward Boyd and Lardner and would show in future for others. Probably, too, he felt the urge of a more or less successful writer to use his influence on behalf of a younger author who was less experienced in the ways of publishing.

But the attachment he felt for Hemingway for the rest of his life, despite serious strains on their relationship, exceeded mere professional respect or the impulse to grease a career he thought was off to a sticky start. Real as these motives were, deeper ones are discernible. Personality counts for more than talent here, or, rather, Hemingway's talent was simply an aspect of his personality, the means by which it was expressed in literary terms, a happy conjunction of temperament, experience and style.

We have seen Fitzgerald defend the purity and integrity of that style against Hemingway himself. It was a metaphor for Hemingway's life and, in the final analysis, the key to the man. It was probably the fact of this metaphoric key to Hemingway's temperament and experience that most attracted Fitzgerald when he came to know the man after having discovered the stylist. The next chapter will show the ambiguity of this friendship, spontaneous on one side, reticent on the other. An attraction of opposites, fascination with a complementary personality worked strongly in Fitzgerald's enthusiasm, which, while not unprecedented in his experience, was nevertheless the most important and revealing such impulse in his adult life. For Hemingway represented everything Fitzgerald was not and could never be. Christian Gauss, who was in Paris in 1925 and to whom Fitzgerald eagerly introduced Hemingway, clearly saw how antithetical these men and their talents were. Nine years later, writing to his former student to congratulate him on the publication of *Tender Is the Night*, Gauss rejoiced at seeing the two friends' names combined in the blurb from T. S. Eliot printed on the jacket: "I have been waiting impatiently for another book by Mr. Scott Fitzgerald with more eagerness and curiosity than I should feel towards the work of any of his contemporaries except that of Mr. Ernest Hemingway." This gave Gauss a pretext to draw a parallel between the man he had described in 1925 as "naive" and "Balzacian" and the Princetonian whose sensibility was closer to his own. "You two take your places at the opposite ends of the modern spectrum," he wrote. "Without disrespect to him I put Hemingway down at the infrared side and you on the ultra-violet. His rhythm is like the beating of an African tom-tom—primitive, simple, but it gets you in the end. You are on the other end. You have a feeling for musical intervals and the tone-color of words which makes your prose the finest instrument for rendering all the varied shades of our complex emotional states."[58]

13. PARIS–LYONS–THE MEDITERRANEAN

(June 1925–December 1926)

Fitzgerald had met Hemingway in Le Dingo, a bar on the Rue Delambre 300 yards from the corner on which the Café du Dôme stands. He knew nothing about him except what the Murphys had told him; all he had read of Hemingway's were the few poems and stories McAlmon had published and Wilson's article about him. When Fitzgerald walked into Le Dingo with a Princeton baseball star who was functioning as his guide, he saw Hemingway seated at the bar. He was a husky, casually dressed fellow, over six feet tall, with a weathered face, bright, laughing eyes and brown, brushed-back hair. With him were a couple of British expatriates slightly older than he: a long, straight, boyish woman with gray eyes and very short blond hair, whose name was Duff Twysden, and her escort, Pat Guthrie, slim and bent, with the battered-looking face of a heavy drinker. Both were Montparnasse regulars who were to have pivotal places in *The Sun Also Rises*, of which Hemingway would write the first draft that summer.

Scott Fitzgerald, as Hemingway first saw him, frail and elegant in his impeccably cut Brooks Brothers suit and white shirt with button-down collar, also seemed a character in search of an author, a little incongruous among the ragtag bohemians of Montparnasse. In *A Moveable Feast*, a settling of accounts published by Scribner's in 1964, three years after its author's death and twenty-four after Fitzgerald's, Hemingway told about that meeting, suggesting in his preface that the reader read it as he would a piece of fiction. His portrait of Scott is as much his own as it is the model's. The close attention paid to Fitzgerald's features, especially his mouth, is singularly revealing: "Scott was a man who looked like a boy with a face between handsome and pretty. He had very fair wavy hair, a high forehead, excited and friendly eyes and a delicate long-lipped Irish mouth that, on a girl, would have been the mouth of beauty." Hemingway's scrutiny lingered on that mouth, that "worried you until you knew him and then it worried you more." Then the author's eye, sharp as a fashionable woman's vivisecting a rival's outfit, inspected his subject's figure, searching for a flaw that would confirm his sense of his own superiority. He found it at once. This handsome, slightly effeminate young man was ill-proportioned. "When he sat down on one of the bar stools," Hemingway wrote, "I saw that he had very short legs. With normal legs he would have been perhaps two inches taller."[1]

Scott ordered a bottle of champagne and launched on a dithyrambic speech in praise of Hemingway while Ernest watched him coldly. He asked some overly personal questions that the other man avoided with joking answers. Suddenly, Fitzgerald's face was covered with sweat; it puckered, took on a deathly look. Then he passed out. He was taken home in a taxi.

He saw Hemingway again a few days later at the Closerie des Lilas. All his affectation was gone; he behaved simply, spoke of his books with detachment, aware of their weaknesses. Of *Gatsby* he spoke with modesty and humility, "puzzled and hurt that the book was not selling well,"[2] but comforted by the praise it had received from the critics. The two Scotch highballs he drank did not appear to bother him, and Hemingway seemed amazed to be dealing with a rather appealing human being. Scott "asked no shameless questions, did nothing embarrassing, made no speeches, and acted as a normal, intelligent and charming person."[3] When Fitzgerald told him about the Renault he had abandoned in a Lyons garage, Ernest agreed to accompany him on the train ride down to retrieve it.

The trip is described in detail in *A Moveable Feast:* how Fitzgerald failed to show up at the station and did not meet Hemingway until the next morning in Lyons, how incessant rain forced them to spend a night on the way back at Chalon-sur-Saône, where Scott, rain-soaked in his roofless car, thought he was getting pneumonia. Fitzgerald is allowed a great deal of charm and some virtues, but the account stresses his irresponsibility and childishness. We feel that Hemingway was prodigiously annoyed by his spoiled-brat behavior. Yet when he read *The Great Gatsby* a few days later, it showed him an unexpected side of Fitzgerald and he decided to cultivate Scott's friendship. "When I had finished the book," he wrote, "I knew that no matter what Scott did, nor how he behaved, I must know it was like a sickness and be of any help I could to him and try to be a good friend. He had many good, good friends, more than anyone I knew. But I enlisted as one more, whether I could be of any use to him or not. If he could write a book as fine as *The Great Gatsby*, I was sure that he could write an even better one."[4]

Before the trip Hemingway had brought Fitzgerald to the Rue de Fleurus to introduce him to Gertrude Stein, whom Ernest had known for three years. They came across her in the street while she was looking for a place to park her car. The meeting was probably cordial, Fitzgerald charmingly modest, Stein kindness itself. At least this is how the roles were assigned in the few letters they later exchanged. The one she wrote to him from her summer home in Belley on May 22 after reading *Gatsby* clearly suggests the teacher-master relationship Fitzgerald allowed to grow up between them. "Here we are and have read your book and it is a good book. I like the melody of your dedication and it shows that you have a background of beauty and tenderness and that is a comfort. The next good thing is that you write naturally in sentences and that too is a comfort."[5]

In his reply he adopted a tone of humility and deference, leaving it, he said, to superior people like her to think for him. This the better to express his surprise that a mind such as hers could place *This Side of Paradise* and *The Great Gatsby* on the same level. Yet she insisted on the parallel in her autobiography, just as she recalled that "Fitzgerald was the only one of the younger writers who wrote naturally in sentences." Her tone seven years after their meeting was less doctoral, less pontifical than it was in her letter: "Gertrude Stein and Fitzgerald are very peculiar in their relation to each other. . . . She thinks Fitzgerald will be read when many of his well-known contemporaries are forgotten. Fitzgerald says that he thinks Gertrude Stein says these things just to annoy him by making him think she means them, and he adds in his favorite way, and her doing it is the cruellest thing I ever heard. They always, however, have a very good time when they meet. And the last time they met they had a good time with themselves and Hemingway."[6]

Fitzgerald also had sent his book to Edith Wharton, at whose feet he had once thrown himself in Charles Scribner's office. She and Conrad, both inspired by Henry James's theory of the novel, had replaced Mackenzie et al. in his pantheon of great novelists. He maintained his respect for *Ethan Frome;* its construction in scenes and tableaux, inherited from James, perhaps had something in common with the structure of *The Great Gatsby.* And he had always been drawn to the sacred cows of literature.

The letter she wrote him early in June differed in every particular from Stein's. Instead of appearing oracular, Wharton, then in her sixties, modestly stressed her kinship with a bygone world. "To your generation," she wrote, "which has taken such a flying leap into the future, I must represent the literary equivalent of tufted furniture and gas chandeliers. So you will understand that it is in a spirit of sincere deprecation that I shall venture, in a few days, to offer you in return the last product of my manufactory."[7] The reference was probably to "The Writing of Fiction," an essay in which she paid tribute to the methods of Henry James, who had been her friend and confidant.

Instead of putting *Gatsby* on the same plane as Fitzgerald's previous books, she stressed its novelty, not in vague terms, but in detailed analysis of its strong points and explanation of her judgment. The letter ended with an invitation to the Fitzgeralds to lunch or tea at her château de Saint-Brice.

Versions vary concerning this expedition, too; several people have claimed the privilege of having accompanied Fitzgerald on his pilgrimage to the distinguished New York aristocrat's home. Biographer Andrew Turnbull reports the assertion by Theodore Chanler that he served as guide on the short trip. But Esther Murphy told me that she was the one who rode in the Renault with Fitzgerald to show him the way. Whoever the passenger may have been, all the accounts agree on the essentials regarding the visit.

Zelda, not very interested in being judged by a woman of the world known for her caustic wit, refused to go along, and Fitzgerald, full of apprehension, went without her. He stopped frequently in cafés along the road for quick drinks to calm his nerves. According to Miss Murphy, this took so much time that she had to phone Saint-Brice to warn that they would be late for lunch. She said this was an important affair, to which the Bourgets and the Claudels had also been invited.

Fitzgerald's reception was distinctly cool. Mrs. Wharton was more spontaneous in her letters than in her encounters with people she did not know. After a protracted series of opening compliments and niceties, the conversation lagged and Fitzgerald, already a little tight, decided to shock his hostess. He remarked that her isolation in her country palace cut her off from the realities of life. One had to live to know the world. By way of illustration, he asked permission to tell a "rough story." This was graciously granted and he sailed into an account of something that, he said, had happened to a couple of friends of his. They had taken a quiet hotel room and it was not until three days later that, puzzled by the furtive air of the baggageless guests they encountered on the stairs, they realized they were in a brothel.

His story ended, Scott noticed that his companions were not at all shocked, as he expected, but were waiting with interest to know what had happened next. Instead of coming to his rescue, Mrs. Wharton remarked after a long silence that his story had ended rather abruptly and that his experience of Paris fancy houses had not produced anything very new. Who were these furtive couples, why were they there, how did they act? A novelist should know such things. Unable to go on in the same vein, embarrassed by the questioning looks converging on him and thrown off stride by his indignant hostess's direct questions, Fitzgerald stammered, lost countenance and said nothing more until lunch was over. Back in Paris, he at first tried to present the day to Zelda as a success, but he suddenly slumped against a table and pounded it with his fist. "They beat me!" he shouted. "They beat me!"

Mrs. Wharton wrote a single word opposite Fitzgerald's name in her diary that evening: "Horrible."

Fitzgerald's mortification was soon swept away, however, on the flood of letters as flattering as Mrs. Wharton's he received from everywhere. One was from another, lesser imitator of James, Willa Cather, whose technique and nostalgic grace in her best book, *A Lost Lady*, anticipated those in *Gatsby;* the letter was so complimentary that Fitzgerald got the Gausses out of bed at one o'clock in the morning to celebrate. Similar missives came from Gilbert Seldes, Nathan, Alexander Woollcott, Van Wyck Brooks and Paul Rosenfeld, all of them difficult readers to please. T. S. Eliot, who was away from London, did not read the book until later, but it was of his letter that Fitzgerald was proudest. "*The Great Gatsby*," Eliot said, ". . . has interested and excited me more than any new novel I have seen, either English or American, for a number of years. . . . In fact, it seems to me the first step that American fiction has taken since Henry James. . . ."[8] This was enough to cancel out the haughty irony of a Jamesian disciple.

Moreover, his humiliation was softened by the presence of friends who accepted him with all his faults and virtues. He celebrated the Fourth of July with two Princetonians, Sap Donahoe and Ludlow Fowler, who were among the many friends in Paris that year. Scott was probably most eager for the company of Gauss, who had just been appointed Dean of the College at Princeton. They discussed *Gatsby* at length. Gauss considered it a masterpiece; nine years later, after the appearance of *Tender Is the Night*, Fitzgerald still remembered word for word some of his former teacher's remarks, which, he wrote, "had a large and valuable influence in some of my problems."[9] He lost no time in introducing Gauss to Hemingway, whose stories he gave him to read. Gauss was unimpressed by both the writing and the man, whom, we recall, he saw as a "naive, earnest, Balzacian-type boy."[10] The three men dined together several times and Fitzgerald, knowing that Hemingway had always regretted not having gone to college, tried to get him to profit from his mentor's knowledge. Every time they scheduled a meeting, they chose a subject for discussion for which each prepared.

On June 25, 1925, Ernest and Hadley Hemingway left Paris by train for the *feria* of San Fermin in Pamplona, where they were to join Don Stewart, Harold Loeb, Bill Smith and the Dingo couple, Duff Twysden and Pat Guthrie. Loeb's unhappy love affair with Duff would give Hemingway the main vehicle for his first novel, which he was to begin in Madrid, continue in Hendaye and complete in Paris on September 21, after six weeks of work.

The Fitzgeralds, in turn, set off by car on August 4 for Antibes after putting Scottie and her nurse on a southbound train. Scott had worked very little in Paris, merely revising and completing "The Rich Boy," which he had begun in Italy. At the end of August he gave Perkins a few details about the novel he was planning. Its working title was *Our Type,* and it was about the murder of a possessive mother by her unstable son. "Incidentally, it is about Zelda and me and the hysteria of last May and June in Paris (confidential)."[11] The idea sprang generally from the Fitzgeralds' meeting with the Murphys, from their way of living and its setting in their Cap d'Antibes villa. Initially, the plan revolved around the central character of the son, Francis Melarky; this idea would be dropped and revived several times in the next five years. Violent and disobedient, Francis receives the same treatment from Rome's police that Fitzgerald did. Arriving on the Riviera with his mother, he is taken up by a rich American couple, Seth and

Dinah Roreback, who are obviously drawn from the Murphys. Having been trained as a Hollywood technician, Francis wants to find a job in the movie studios in Nice, but his mother, fearful that film people might be a harmful influence on him, opposes the idea. He then returns to Paris with the Rorebacks and falls in love with Dinah, who does not flatly discourage his attentions. A friend of Seth, a composer of genius ruined by alcohol, goes with them. All these elements were to appear in the novel's final draft after the matricide theme was abandoned. Melarky would change sex, become Rosemary and fall for Seth-Dick in Paris.

Melarky's excesses of violence and moral disintegration are attributed in *Tender Is the Night* to Dick Diver, who is demoralized by his idleness and the corruptive power of Nicole's wealth. Francis is the first sketch of a theme that was to develop over the years, that of the degradation of a rootless creator who succumbs to facility and becomes an alcoholic. The musician—Abe North in the final version of the novel—gives the theme at the beginning. This was obviously a subject that closely concerned Fitzgerald and became more important as time went by with no novel being produced.

That summer at Cap d'Antibes Scott met the young composer Theodore Chanler at the Murphys' villa; Chanler told him that he felt his talent dissolve in that atmosphere of permanent carnival, that he was becoming dissipated, he was drinking and disgusted with himself. Finally, he decided to break with the Murphys and their circle and try to pull himself together. This is the real subject of Fitzgerald's novel, as Matthew Bruccoli, who tells of the incident, underlines. The matricidal theme, which would block progress on the book until 1930, was a dead end, a decoy that, instead of revealing some secret impulsion, simply postponed solution of Fitzgerald's greatest problem; it masked the dilemma that had already arisen in the past. He could live with Zelda in a festival tumult, or live as he would have preferred and as he did live while writing *The Great Gatsby*. He could accept the pleasure of existing with no responsibility except writing for *The Saturday Evening Post,* or heed the call of a higher vocation that could be answered only through self-abnegation. The basic alternative appeared in almost allegorical terms after he came to know the Murphys and Hemingway: to expend his talent in living or in writing. Until 1930 the exemplary fates of the dandy and the writer would tug dialectically at his imagination.

Murphy is still the unknown quantity in the equation; it is time to train our spotlight on him. Gerald Murphy, eight years older than Fitzgerald, incarnated a life-style, became the model to which the writer aspired in a muddled way. They had enough in common to cement a quick friendship. Both were of Irish ancestry and both had been subjected to a strict Catholic education. Like Fitzgerald, Murphy had tried to shine at college by cornering as many campus honors as he could. He had been elected to Yale's most exclusive club, the Skull and Bones, and directed the Glee Club—Yale's equivalent to Princeton's Triangle; there he had introduced a young sophomore named Cole Porter, who was as fascinated as he by Gilbert and Sullivan and whose music made hits of the club's annual revues. But Murphy had been as deeply disappointed in his university career as Fitzgerald had; he felt that he had gained nothing from his four years at Yale. The two men's common disappointment also extended to the war. After months spent in learning to fly a plane, Murphy too was about to sail for Europe when the armistice was signed.

The two shared a love of elegance, of the social whirl. But whereas Fitzgerald remained on its outer edges, with a chronic feeling of being shut out, his elder was deeply immersed in high society, not merely accepted but liked and sought after. Murphy's father headed the exclusive New York leather-goods firm of Mark Cross; his older brother ran the firm's factory in England, and after Gerald came out of Yale in 1912, he worked with his father until the war. Retail trade, even the carriage trade, did not interest him, however, and the upholstered existence of moneyed New York bored him. A sort of centrifugal movement carried him toward the out-of-doors, toward botany and garden architecture. Where Fitzgerald had failed to land Ginevra King, the more fortunate Murphy had realized a boyhood dream in 1915 by marrying Sara Wiborg, whom he had met ten years earlier, when he was sixteen. The father of Sara and her two sisters, Olga and Mary, was an extremely rich Cincinnati manufacturer; all the girls had been presented at court in England and, under Lady Diana Cooper's sponsorship, were the rage of London in 1914.

Different reasons persuaded Fitzgerald and Murphy to leave the United States and live in Europe, and they were distinguished once they got there by the way they lived; the Murphys were well supplied with funds, and their culture, infinitely broader than the Fitzgeralds', naturally involved them in France's intellectual and artistic life.

Murphy arrived in Paris in the fall of 1921 and was at once impressed by the painting of Braque, Gris and Picasso, whose work he saw at the Rosenberg Gallery. He decided that he too would paint. He had studied under Natalia Goncharova, the set designer for the Ballets Russes, and when the troupe's sets were damaged by fire, he volunteered to help repaint them in their Paris warehouse. This brought Murphy in touch with Diaghilev and his scene designers, among them Picasso, Braque and André Derain, who were in charge of restoring the sets. In 1923 Murphy had his first showing at the Salon des Indépendants with a painting called "Razor," a precursor of pop art that showed a blown-up matchbox, fountain pen and mechanical razor; it was original enough to elicit from Léger the comment that Murphy was the only real painter among the Americans in Paris, that is, the only one who had shaken off the influence of the School of Paris. He showed again in 1925 and 1926 and, until 1929, turned out ten canvases, most of which were exhibited at the Bernheim Jeune Gallery in 1936.

Soon the Murphys were friendly with Diaghilev, Stravinsky and the painters who gravitated around the Ballets Russes. They attended all the rehearsals of Stravinsky's *The Wedding* and, on June 17, 1923, gave a memorable opening-night party aboard a houseboat anchored in the Seine near the Concorde bridge; it drew Paris's artistic elite, including Ernest Ansermet, Francis Poulenc, Georges Auric, Vittorio Rieti and Marcelle Meyer, as well as painters and such writers as Tzara, Blaise Cendrars and Cocteau.

Also present was Darius Milhaud, whose *La Création du Monde* was to be given that fall by the Swedish Ballet with costumes and a curtain designed by Léger. The company's director, Rolf de Maré, asked Murphy if he knew a young American musician who could compose a curtain raiser for the occasion. Gerald immediately thought of Porter, who had invited the Murphys the previous summer to the château d'Antibes, which he had rented for the season. The deal went through, and Murphy was to do the backdrop and costumes for it as well as supply the scenario. The story line of *Within the Quota*, devised five years before George Gershwin's *An American in Paris*, could have been called *A European in New York*, the story of a Swedish immigrant's first impressions of Manhattan. The ballet opened in October at the Champs-Élysées Theater. Picasso congratulated Murphy on his original curtain for it, a parody of a Hearst front page bearing such huge headlines as "UNKNOWN BANKER BUYS ATLANTIC."

Remember the miserable failure of *The Vegetable* that same autumn in Atlantic City; Murphy, the rich and brilliant amateur, had scored again while Fitzgerald, after two years of work, had seen his hopes of fortune collapse.

It was far from Paris's scandals and social jockeying, however, that the Murphys crafted their true masterpiece: a subtle art of living. Their apartment at 23, Quai des Grands-Augustins was soon no more than a pied-à-terre, for they had found the ideal place in which to display their talents. In 1922, after a cold, wet winter in Houlgate, on the Channel coast, they had been introduced by Porter to the charms of the Riviera, then deserted in favor of the Norman beaches. They returned there after *The Wedding* and moved into the Hôtel du Cap, at Cap d'Antibes, near the beach of La Garoupe. The owner, who had closed his hotel for the summer to spend a season in the Italian Alps, leased part of the establishment to them during his absence, leaving them the chef, a waiter and a chambermaid, all of whom they shared with a Chinese family.

A few friends came to visit: Gertrude Stein, with the inescapable Alice B. Toklas; Picasso, his mother, his son Paolo and his wife Olga, a ballerina with the Diaghilev company. The place pleased the Picassos, who rented a villa in Antibes and spent part of almost every day at La Garoupe, where the Murphys had cleaned a patch of beach of the seaweed and pebbles covering the sand. Picasso, curious about Americans and a great admirer of Lincoln, whose photographs he collected, liked to be with the Murphys, enjoyed their sense of carnival and their gift for improvising on the most humdrum circumstances. And his clowning and disguises amused them. There he is in Murphy's photos with a big fig leaf pinned to his bathing suit, or posing in the same suit with a hat in his hand, extending his arm to Sara with a conquering air; in another he is wearing a huge white hat faced with feathers, garlands crossed on his chest and a long necklace of white balls. He was struck by the way Sara wore her pearl necklace on the beach, dangling down her back to expose them, she said, to the sun. In Picasso's neoclassical paintings from this period—he was just back from a trip to Rome with Olga and the Diaghilev company—his gigantic women all wear pearl necklaces crossed between their shoulders. Nicole, "the young woman with the string of pearls," is pictured in the opening pages of *Tender Is the Night* with "her brown back hanging from her pearls."[12]

Picasso was also a born storyteller who delighted his hosts with his curious tales—the one about the owner of his villa who was so indignant because Picasso painted a fresco on his wall that he demanded payment to have it removed. And about Gertrude Stein, who wrote to him to ask that he trade the portrait he had done of her in 1905 for a painting she had seen at Rosenberg's. When Gertrude arrived, the meeting of these titans enchanted the Murphys. "She and Picasso were phenomenal together. Each stimulated the other to such an extent that everyone felt recharged witnessing it."[13]

The place, peaceful and isolated, pleased the Murphys so that they decided to settle there. They bought a villa from an officer in France's colonial army. It stood on the heights overlooking the La Garoupe lighthouse and was surrounded by a big garden full of exotic plants that trailed down the hill. The Murphys spent most of the summer of 1924 at the Hôtel du Cap overseeing the remodeling of the house. There they received their friends, the Picassos again, the Count and Countess de Beaumont, the Seldeses on their honeymoon. Rudolph Valentino came, too, on his way back from an Italian tour. He drove down to the beach in an open Voisin automobile with his wife, Natasha Rambova, who owned a splendid château at nearby Juan-les-Pins. Her real name was Winifred Hudnut and she was the adopted daughter of an American millionaire, but she had been so influenced by her romantic Russian friend Alla Nazimova, who had performed for the Imperial Court before the war and was now a star in Hollywood, that she chose a Russian name that chimed more sweetly with the name Rudolph—which was also an invention.

Quickly, then, a nucleus of celebrities formed around the Americans on the beach of La Garoupe, composed of a Spanish painter, a Russian ballerina, an Italian actor, a French patron of the arts, and Natasha, whose phantom name raised echoes of another age, other splendors. This was the period when the Fitzgeralds formed the habit of crossing the Esterel, the range of cliffs bordering the coast, to visit their friends. "4th trip to Monte-Carlo again and often to Antibes," we read in the August 1924 section of the *Ledger*. "Good work on novel. Zelda and I close together."[14] Yet it was at the end of that month, when they were staying overnight at the Hôtel du Cap, that Zelda took her overdose of sleeping pills. In the middle of the night Scott, holding a candle in one trembling hand, knocked at the Murphys' door. Zelda's sick, he told them. He thought it was an accident. To keep her awake, they walked her up and down the corridors of the hotel until dawn. No explanation was asked or given. After Zelda was examined by a doctor the next day, no one said any more about the incident.

Other events showed the suicidal impulse that moved not only Zelda but Scott as well. A year later, during a dinner on the terrace of the Colombe d'Or at Saint-Paul-de-Vence, the Murphys and the Fitzgeralds saw Isadora Duncan, her dyed red hair blending with her flame-colored dress, seated at a nearby table dining by candlelight with three men. While the others stared at them, Zelda filched the salt and pepper shakers, which were shaped like toy cars. "Nobody was looking because Isadora Duncan was giving one of her last parties at the next table. She had got too old and fat to care whether people accepted her theories of life and art, and she gallantly toasted the world's obliviousness in lukewarm champagne."[15]

The dancer was forty-seven years old then, still two years away from the day when her trailing scarf caught in the wheel of a roadster and broke her neck. Murphy had just been remarking that Saint-Paul had been one of the relay stations at which Roman soldiers lighted fires to signal their victories against the Gauls. When Scott was told who the woman at the next table was, he bounded up and knelt at Isadora's feet. He repeated what Murphy had said while she stroked his hair and called him her centurion. Zelda watched silently. Later, when she heard Isadora give Scott the name of her hotel as she left, Zelda got up, scaled the low wall bordering the terrace and leaped into the stairwell below, tumbling down the stone steps. She was on her feet and climbing back up before her friends could reach her. At the edge of the parapet she stopped briefly, then, still wordless, headed for the lavatory to clean her skinned knees.

When she returned—calmly, as though nothing had happened—she and Scott agreed that it would be fun to put every chicken in the restaurant's coop on the spit and roast them in the huge, wood-burning fireplace. They were dissuaded from this by the Murphys, and the two couples left the Colombe d'Or. The Fitzgeralds' car followed their friends' for a moment, then Scott turned off at a grade crossing and began driving along the rails. The Renault bounced over the ties for a few yards, then stalled. There, heedless of the danger, they fell asleep. A farmer going to market found them there at dawn. He hitched his team to the car and hauled it off the tracks moments before the day's first train went by.

Seldes was also struck by the deliberate risks the Fitzgeralds took. There was a particularly nasty blind curve on the narrow, twisting road that led down from Valescure to the beach at Saint-Raphaël. Every time they approached it, with Scott hunched over the wheel (he was always a bad driver), Zelda invariably said, "Give me a cigarette, Goofo." Without slowing down, Scott would fumble in his pockets with one hand, fish out a package of Chesterfields, then a lighter, steering desperately with one hand while Seldes and his bride huddled in their seats, expecting the worst.

On another occasion Zelda lay down in front of their car just as it was about to start rolling. "Scott," she called, "run me over." He coldly grasped the wheel, stepped on the accelerator and was about to shift into first gear when someone reached over and put on the hand brake.

Yet again, when she was driving her car along the cliff road, Zelda turned to her passenger and, glancing at the drop alongside them, said, "I think I'll turn here." Her companion had to grab the wheel to keep them from going over. Another time, driving up to Paris through the Cévennes mountains of central France, it was she who tried to grab the wheel from Scott to send the Renault off the road. "When the car swerved to the crest of a hill," she later recounted, "it seemed to me it was going into oblivion beyond and I had to hold the sides of the car."[16] The incident was picked up in *Tender Is the Night*, placed first on the Riviera, then shifted to Switzerland, during the visit of Nicole and Dick to the festival at Agiri.

When the Fitzgeralds stayed with the Murphys at Cap d'Antibes, Zelda liked to dive into the sea from the high rocks, especially at night; as she had in Montgomery, she insisted that Scott follow her. There were narrow ledges cut into the rock at regular intervals to a height of around ten yards. Watching the Fitzgeralds climb to the top frightened Sara. "One had to be a superb diver in order to make it during the day . . . especially at night, one had to have a perfect sense of timing or one would have been smashed on the rocks below. Zelda would strip to her slip and very quietly ask Scott if he cared for a swim." Everyone recognized this as the prelude to the usual challenge. "I remember one evening when I was with them that he was absolutely trembling when she challenged him, but he followed her. It was breathtaking. They took each dive, returning from the sea all shivering and white, until the last, the one at thirty feet. Scott hesitated and watched Zelda until she surfaced; I didn't think he could go through with it, but he did." When Sara scolded them, Zelda replied calmly, "But Sayra—didn't you know, we don't believe in conservation."[17]

In contrast with this restlessness, this morbid fascination with self-destruction, the Murphys offered a model of serenity and balance; they embodied a standard inaccessible to the Fitzgeralds. But Scott saw too much of himself in Gerald to be completely fooled by the role he was playing. Scott watched him, studied him, trying to pry out the secret that enabled Murphy to overcome the weaknesses one guessed he had. Fitzgerald sensed that if that secret was to be found anywhere, it was with Sara. As a novelist, Scott was fascinated by this man so like him in his vulnerability, but who had created a role to play, who protected his deepest self by erecting an imposing series of obstacles and tricks between himself and whatever might threaten him.

Gerald was posing. His look was untroubled, distant, his chin was up just a little, showing his better profile; he never let himself be surprised by a camera. He was the one who wanted to do the surprising. Tall, slender, slim-wristed and relaxed, his head erect, he would have been a perfect model for a Roman sculptor seeking to capture imperiousness. His jaw was imperious, his neatly trimmed, reddish-blond hair flamboyant. He dressed with casual care. As the corsair of La Garoupe in his fisherman's striped jersey and plasterer's peaked cap, leaning nonchalantly on his bamboo cane, he was the very picture of elegance. It was in street clothes that he really triumphed, however. In these he was the unapproachable fashion plate, with his trilby hat pulled dreamily low, his straight-cut, belted jackets, his leather carrying case designed to save his pockets from bulging and spoiling his line, his felt spats over polished pumps and, always, the cane that lent the figure distinction and poise.

Under the hint of haughtiness, a trace of uneasiness: there was a naked soul beneath the frosting of poses and it was subject to fits of deep sadness. A photo shows Murphy, shadowy under his hat, in a hall of mirrors, looking at himself look at himself from the back, in profile, in a three-quarters view, fragmented into five planes. He was too purposefully balanced to have a strong point, and his many skills left no room for a single strong talent. He admired rugged people who obeyed their genius and left the rest of their garden unweeded, those who were wholly commandeered by their life-force, the Légers and Picassos and Hemingways. He let himself be consumed by aestheticism, a frivolousness he pretended was serious and that he knew was vulnerable. This sense of decorum and ceremony pervaded his private life; he would be the high priest of the private festival, prophet of the unusual and the exclusive, deprecating what was shopworn, a fount of fashions and discoverer of talent. There was something in him of the impresario and of the great clothes designer.

It was Sara, however, who was the planet Murphy's center of gravity. She was the wind and Gerald the sail, their friends said, she the source of imagination and inventiveness; through her husband she steered the ship, maintained its course and looked out for squalls. To uneasy Gerald she represented permanence, the nest, the center, moral security. Feminine, sensual, worldly, in perfect harmony with things and people, blending with her flower garden, her Provençal crockery, the ritual of baths and meals, she was the image of the kind of tranquillity and well-being that is satisfied by the simplest pleasures. All her other qualities, it seemed, were extras. Hating the affectation of conventional, boring society, she avoided her sisters, who had married into the English nobility. But she was at ease with people who contributed to the festival of wit, such friends as the Princesse de Polignac and the Count and Countess de Beaumont. This discernment comforted those she accepted into her small circle of friends; they were aware of their privileges and duties, stimulated by the tacit contract that made them members of a community of people whose company they chose.

With her clear profile, her long blond hair worn in a knot on her neck and her figure molded in dresses of brightly colored floral patterns, she impressed people by her easy grace and natural generosity, charmed them effortlessly. Nor was this seductiveness limited to her person; it was diffuse; it seemed to arise also from the beauty of her three children, the pleasant-ness of her home, from Gerald's conversation. She melted happily into the background, refusing to be distinguishable from everything she had created around her, refusing personal compliments that would have separated her from her setting. Fitzgerald understood her unwillingness to provide a ground for the disjunctive power that scrutiny generated. "You hate any-one to examine any single part of your person, no matter how appreci-atively," he wrote to her. "That's why you wore bright clothes."[18]

Ever present but inaccessible, she inspired in the men around her the longing that is aroused by the contemplation of utter fulfillment. By just being herself, she captivated Picasso, charmed Léger, overwhelmed Fitz-gerald. In Gerald, Scott recognized his own ambitions and weaknesses; he admired the impeccable surface his friend showed the world, his unques-tioned assurance, the natural grace that Scott lacked. And, sensing Sara's part in creating the character of Gerald, he compared it with Zelda's corro-siveness. The united front the Murphys turned to the world contrasted with the widening crack between the Fitzgeralds, between Scott's self-image and the person he was becoming. Sara and Zelda were so close in their awareness of what escaped him, in their fundamental sense of the present, of the earth and the elements. In Sara he thought he recognized what he knew of Zelda. But Sara was generous, self-effacing. Gerald-Scott, Sara-Zelda, Scott-Sara in juxtaposition, permutation, fascination with themselves and each other. The identification would be complete in the various phases of *Tender Is the Night;* the novel's subject would be the degradation of the Murphys in Fitzgerald, the insensible passage from pole to pole. Seen through the worshiping eyes of Rosemary against a background of sea and sun, Dick Diver in the opening chapters is Gerald, serene and magnanimous, ready to dare anything and do anything. And Nicole resembles Sara.

Harassing them with questions, importuning them intolerably, rejected, recalled, Scott was passionate in his relationship with the Murphys. It was an impossible romance in which the beloved's face was sometimes Gerald's, sometimes Sara's, seen in shifting moods of admiration and despite and defiance. Jealous of their interest in others, Fitzgerald, like an aggrieved child, tried to force them to pay attention to him.

Not that this was a one-way attachment. The Murphys were sincerely fond of the Fitzgeralds, and the transferences we have just analyzed were not merely fantasies secreted in Scott by feelings of anxiety and insecurity. Gerald wrote a kind of love letter to the Fitzgeralds on September 19, 1925, shortly after their return to Paris. After stressing "the hush and the emptiness" left by their departure, he described exactly that process of symbiosis that would form the composite character of the Divers in *Tender Is the Night.* "We four communicate by our presence," he wrote, "rather than any means; so that where we meet and when will never count. Currents run between us regardless: Scott will uncover for me values in Sara, just as Sara has known them in Zelda through her affection for Scott."

He included the Fitzgeralds among the elect: "Most people are dull, without distinction and without value, even *humanly,* I believe (even in the depths of my expansive Irish heart). For Sara most people are guilty of the above until they are proved innocent. All this one can believe without presumption or personal vanity—and the proof that it's true is found in the fact that you two belong so irrevocably to that rare race of people who are *valuable.* As yet in this world we have found four."

There is a recollection of shared happiness: "whenever you were coming to dinner in the garden we were happy, and showed it to each other. We were happy whenever we were with you. My God how *rare* it is. How rare." The letter ends on an unquestionably sincere note of anxious affection: "Take care of yourselves, please. Thank God for you both."[19]

Scott, meanwhile, was reunited with Hemingway, who had just finished the first draft of *The Sun Also Rises,* but who refused to show him the seven copybooks he had filled with his writing during the summer. Proudly he showed the Fitzgeralds a painting by Miro, "The Farm," which he had bought for five thousand francs for Hadley's thirty-fourth birthday. Used to a regular schedule, Hemingway did not always look kindly on Fitzgerald's habit of dropping in at any hour of the day or night at Ernest's apartment at 118, Rue Notre-Dame-des-Champs, a few steps away from the Closerie des Lilas. Especially since Scott was sometimes so drunk that he had to be taken home to the Rue de Tilsitt in a taxi.

Scott wrote to a friend that he had written the first chapter of his own novel and thought it was "marvelous," adding that "you may recognize certain things and people in it."[20] In the context the allusion is doubtless to the Murphys and their circle. But the end of the year came and the work had gone no further. Scott made two trips to the World War I battlefields in the Lorraine region, paid brief visits to Brussels and London, where he seems to have been guilty of the same mistakes he made at Mrs. Wharton's: "Saw Leslie also, and went on some very high-tone parties with Mountbattens and all that sort of thing. Very impressed, but not very, as I furnished most of the amusement myself."[21] Zelda fell ill again, and they left in January 1926 for Salies-de-Béarn, in the foothills of the Pyrenees, to take the waters. Her fragile health forced them to refuse an invitation to visit Gertrude Stein at the end of December, but they did spend Christmas Eve with the Archibald MacLeishes and the Bromfields.

In his December 27 letter to Perkins, Fitzgerald sounded a mournful note. "I write to you from the depth of one of my unholy depressions," he confessed. "The book is wonderful—I honestly think that when it's published I shall be the best American novelist (which isn't saying a lot) but the end seems far away. . . . You remember I used to say I wanted to die at thirty—well, I'm now twenty-nine and the prospect is still welcome. My work is the only thing that makes me happy—except to be a little tight—and for those two indulgences I pay a big price in mental and physical hangovers."[22]

His eight-month lease on the apartment on the Rue de Tilsitt ran out two weeks later. He had barely begun the novel he had hoped to write there. All his plans for his stay in Paris, all his hopes were dashed. He had let Hemingway steal a march on him, and he had not been able to match the Murphys in harmonious living.

Despite his warm relationship with the Murphys, Fitzgerald's attitude toward them was ambivalent. He admired them as elders with easy entrée into the fabulous world of music and painting. Not that these interested him: Picasso, Stravinsky and Diaghilev had only symbolic value for him, but that the Murphys were intimate with them was a gauge of their position at the top of the social ladder. They were among the most discerning of the American expatriates, friends of Dos Passos, whom they had met while working on *The Wedding*, and of MacLeish, a fellow Yale man who had quit the law for poetry and moved to Paris in 1923. In confirmation of their sure taste, they shared Fitzgerald's enthusiasm for Hemingway's early stories. They would be his guides, therefore, his initiators, the people who would fill the role Edmund Wilson would have liked to play during Scott's first visit to Paris four years earlier. Scott refused to be annoyed that the Murphys had read nothing he had written, or that they had shown no enthusiasm when *The Great Gatsby* appeared. After all, he did not care about Gerald's paintings; it was enough to know that they had created a sensation at the Salon des Indépendants.

So much for the late summer of 1924, when the Fitzgeralds' frequent visits to Antibes had brought them from their trouble at Saint-Raphaël into the shelter of an idyll. The two couples met again in Paris in June 1925. And in August in Antibes their friendship deepened; it was then that the Fitzgeralds came to appreciate fully the Murphys' magic. In a letter to a young woman he had met at the Murphys' still unfinished house, Villa America, Fitzgerald contrasted the uneasiness and disappointment of American life ("America is the story of a moon that never rose") with the fullness of life with the Murphys. America, he remarked, did not fulfill its promise, it was not even capable of living in the present. "Nor does the 'minute itself' ever come to life either," he wrote, "the minute not of unrest and hope but of a glowing peace—such as when the moon rose that night on Gerald and Sara's garden and you said you were happy to be there. No one ever makes things in America with that vast, magnificent, cynical disillusion with which Gerald and Sara make things like their parties."[23]

In 1926 the friendship went a little flat. The Murphys visibly favored Hemingway over Fitzgerald. They had spotted big game, the rare kind of personality that conforms to no known model, a writer whose work was going to open a new way of seeing things, of living. As they did when they repainted Diaghilev's stage sets, they now became apprentices; in Ernest's wake Gerald learned about skiing and bullfighting, more or less getting the hang of christies and veronicas. In March, with Dos Passos, they joined Hemingway in Schruns, in the Vorarlberg, where he had spent several previous winters. And they joined him again in early July at the *feria* in Pamplona, where he went every year; they were eager to sample the atmosphere of *The Sun Also Rises*, which Hemingway had read to them in manuscript in Austria. Gerald even agreed to go down into the ring, acquitting himself honorably when a bull charged him. "Next year I'll do it well, Papa," he told Hemingway. "To want to do a thing well . . . is still one of my complications."[24]

Although he was flattered by their attention, Hemingway never quite believed that the Murphys had no personal stake in their friendship. With time he came to feel that he had been made a fool of, had been exploited by idle celebrity hunters who had bet on him as they had on Picasso and Léger. Some thirty years later, although he did not mention them by name, he concluded *A Moveable Feast* with a bitter reference to their negative influence when their interest in him was aroused by the "pilot fish" (a reference to Dos Passos, or to Donald Stewart, who brought Hemingway into the Murphys' circle?): "The rich came led by the pilot fish. A year before they would never have come. There was no certainty then. . . . When they said, 'It's great, Ernest. Truly it's great. You cannot know the thing it has,' I wagged my tail . . . instead of thinking, 'If these bastards like it what is wrong with it?' "[25]

Unwittingly, he attributed to the "rich," to the Murphys, the corrosive power that another rich person, Pauline Pfeiffer, had loosed on his marriage. In fact, the serpent in this Eden was his own weakness, which led him into a divorce he did not want.

1926. The Fitzgeralds went into reclusion in the small spa town of Salies-de-Béarn while Zelda treated the colitis she had contracted in Rome. The Hôtel Bellevue was the only one open, and its clientele consisted entirely of seven people there to take the waters. It was all mortally boring. Fitzgerald sported a beret, a cane and knickers. He and Zelda made weekly excursions to Biarritz, Pau, Lourdes, but the days were long. He wrote an article about the contemporary American novel in which he blamed Mencken and Anderson for having led young novelists into blind alleys. In a second installment he enthusiastically reviewed the fourteen stories in the American edition of *In Our Time*, praising the sobriety and effectiveness of their style; Hemingway, he said, had taken a new turn in American literature.

Good news came that helped him bear his gloom patiently. His third collection of stories, *All the Sad Young Men*, was to appear February 26. More important, Ober had sold the stage rights to *Gatsby*, and on February 2 the adaptation, directed by George Cukor, opened at the Ambassador Theater on Broadway; it was a hit in New York and a hit on tour later. Ober then sold film rights to Paramount. All this brought Fitzgerald some $20,000, which allowed him to live well without having to bother to write magazine stories for ready cash. It paid his debts and carried him until June 1927; for the first time in four years he owed not a penny to Scribner's.

Early in March, stopping in Paris on their way to the Riviera, the Fitzgeralds met Hemingway, who was just back from New York and about to join Hadley and his son at Schruns. He had finally managed to break his contract with Liveright and had moved to Scribner's. Hemingway was also beginning the affair with Pauline Pfeiffer that would lead to his break with Hadley at the end of the summer. An unsuspecting Scott pressed him to spend the summer with them in Juan-les-Pins, where the Murphys had already rented a house for them, Villa Paquita, for three months.

It was when he reached there that Fitzgerald sent Perkins one of the few optimistic letters he wrote in that period. "I'm happier than I've been for years," he exulted. "It's one of those strange, precious and all too transitory moments when everything in one's life seems to be going well." He gave a number of reasons for this euphoria: the continuing success of *Gatsby* on the stage, the new novel in which he was absorbed, his return to "a nice villa on my beloved Riviera."[26] There was also the feeling of liberation after leaving the wintry, empty Béarn region and, most of all, the unaccustomed sensation of having plenty of money in the coming months. He seemed to have taken hold of himself; he was convinced he would finish his novel by the end of the year. "The novel is about one-fourth done and will be delivered for possible serialization about January 1st," he told Ober in late April. "It will be about 75,000 words long, divided into 12 chapters."[27] On the strength of this assurance, Ober sold the serial rights to *Liberty* for $35,000.

That spring of 1926, then, was full of promise. In a few months Fitzgerald would reach the fateful and much-dreaded age of thirty, but when he looked back, he had every cause for satisfaction: seven of his books had been published since 1920, and he was again imbued with an almost mystical conception of destiny that he thought was peculiar to people who succeed early in life.

"The compensation of a very early success is a conviction that life is a romantic matter," he later wrote. "In the best sense one stays young. When the primary objects of love and money could be taken for granted and a shaky eminence had lost its fascination, I had fair years to waste, years that I can't honestly regret, in seeking the eternal Carnival by the Sea."[28] In the essay "Early Success," written when he was broke a decade later, Fitzgerald sadly recalled these moments of happiness when the past and future blended in an ecstatic whole, when the present really existed and the moon finally rose:

> Once in the middle twenties I was driving along the High Corniche Road through the twilight with the whole French Riviera twinkling on the sea below. As far ahead as I could see was Monte Carlo, and though it was out of season and there were no Grand Dukes left to gamble . . . the very name was so incorrigibly enchanting that I could only stop the car and like the Chinese whisper: "Ah me! Ah me!" It was not Monte Carlo I was looking at. It was back into the mind of the young man with cardboard soles who had walked the streets of New York. I was with him again—for an instant I had the good fortune to share his dreams, I who had no more dreams of my own. . . . But never again as during that all too short period when he and I were one person, when the fulfilled future and the wistful past were mingled in a single gorgeous moment—when life was literally a dream.[29]

People flocked back to the Riviera after the Fitzgeralds got there. First the Murphys, bronzed by the Austrian sun, then the MacLeishes, back from a tour of Persia. Gerald had also invited the Hemingways to their fortress, but Ernest left for Spain early in May and Hadley and Bumby Hemingway went to Cap d'Antibes without him. Both had returned from Schruns with a persistent cough, and the Murphys' doctor said Bumby had whooping cough. When Sara, always worried about her children's health, asked the Hemingways to leave Villa America and stay in quarantine, Fitzgerald offered them Villa Paquita, which was free until June 15. He had found a bigger house, Villa Saint-Louis, located on the coast with a private beach about three hundred yards from the Juan-les-Pins casino. France was deep in a recession then and the dollar's value had climbed to thirty-six francs. A month later Raymond Poincaré succeeded Edouard Herriot as the country's Premier and stabilized the franc, but Fitzgerald nevertheless felt rich and munificent: he had scored a point on the Murphys.

The Hôtel du Cap was now open, and full, all summer; cabanas covered La Garoupe beach. Fitzgerald wrote to Bishop that there "was no one at Antibes this summer except me, Zelda, the Valentinos, the Murphys, Mistinguet, Rex Ingram, Dos Passos, Alice Terry, the MacLeishes, Charlie Brackett, Maude Kahn, Esther Murphy, Marguerite Namara, E. Phillips Oppenheim, Mannes the violinist, Floyd Dell, Max and Crystal Eastman, ex-Premier Orlando, Etienne de Beaumont—just a real place to rough it, an escape from all the world."[30]

Among the new arrivals was a Fitzgerald friend from their Long Island days, Charles MacArthur, who in the following months was to become his evil genius, a sort of anti-Murphy. MacArthur had been a Hearst reporter for ten years and had just written a play called *Lulu Belle* with a black Carmen as a heroine. He was one of the wits at the Round Table in the Hotel Algonquin in New York; his was the cynical, nihilistic wit of the newsman with no illusions who, two years later, would be the protagonist in *The Front Page*, the play he wrote with Ben Hecht. Scott felt at home with MacArthur's brand of imagination, so much so that he was sorely tempted to live fiction instead of writing it. To them the Riviera was a kind of Dadaist enclave where, in a booze-induced dream, everything seemed possible and easy money provided a shield against hard knocks. The two men were united in the same subversive, destructive attitude that constantly pushed them to outdo themselves in shocking and pointless games. They gravely debated whether a man could really be sawed in half. The only way to find out was to try it. So Charlie produced a long saw and went in search of a volunteer. Seduced by a fat tip, a bartender used to Americans' extravagances lay down across two chairs placed side by side and let himself be tied up. But when he saw MacArthur and Fitzgerald grab the saw with what seemed every intention of carrying out their experiment, he woke up the whole neighborhood with his howls.

The incident was picked up in *Tender Is the Night*, when Dick Diver and the composer Abe North wonder what café waiters are made of—tips, bits of broken cups, pencil stubs? "The thing was to prove it scientifically"[31] by cutting their waiter in half, being careful to relieve the experiment of any squalor by using a musical saw.

Fitzgerald and MacArthur were not the only writers gravitating around the Murphys that summer. Donald Ogden Stewart and his bride, Beatrice, spent part of their honeymoon at Villa America. There was also Alexander Woollcott, a member of Gerald's generation and the most eminent among the wits at the Algonquin's Round Table; the previous year he had published his study of Irving Berlin, Fitzgerald's favorite composer, but Woollcott owed his fame chiefly to the caustic tongue that made him one of the best paid and most feared critics of the New York *World* and *The New Yorker* magazine. He had built his reputation on insults even more cruel than Mencken's; his presence in Antibes may have aroused some verbal aggressiveness in Fitzgerald that had been tempered until then by the Murphys' urbanity.

Charles and Elizabeth Brackett and Philip and Ellen Barry brought a judiciousness that contrasted with the unchecked and aggressive impulsiveness of MacArthur and Woollcott. Like the Murphys, the Bracketts and the Barrys loved music and painting, good manners and refined conversation. Brackett did have a keen talent for derision, however, which quickly saw through fakery; this was the quality that would make his association with Billy Wilder in Hollywood a success in the thirties. Among the films the team would work on was *Lost Weekend*, with its haunting similarities to Fitzgerald's life.

Barry was a favorite of the Murphys and the two couples were close friends. Both satiric and mystical, Barry would use Villa America as the setting for one of his best plays, *Hotel Universe* (1930).

Perhaps because he now felt stripped of the privileged status he had enjoyed with the Murphys in 1925, Fitzgerald became more critical of them, made increasingly direct remarks that cast doubt on the unconditional admiration in which he had held them. To stress the gap that had opened between him and Gerald, Scott would arrive at the beach with the ironic question, "I suppose you have some special plans for us today?"[32] and this was usually so, because the Murphys liked to organize their days around some new discovery to surprise their friends. But Scott's frustration was to take more direct forms.

It surfaced for the first time when the Murphys gave a party at the casino to celebrate Hemingway's arrival in early June. Ernest, who had just spent three weeks in Madrid, had reread the carbon of the manuscript he had sent to Perkins in April. He had been putting off showing *The Sun Also Rises* to Scott. But now, sure of himself, he gave him the manuscript as soon as he arrived at Villa Paquita and asked his opinion. Fitzgerald took his task seriously, spent part of the night reading the book and noting the commentaries we have already read.

When the Fitzgeralds showed up at the casino party on June 4, Zelda was suffering from a relapse and Scott was already drunk. Had reading Ernest's novel recalled their meeting at Le Dingo a year earlier, when Scott's hopes had been disappointed, when his own book was stalled despite what he said in his letters? Or was he miserable that evening because Hemingway was getting all the attention? His friends were already deep in conversation on the casino terrace; no one seemed to notice him. When Gerald finally rose to welcome the Fitzgeralds, Scott made a few sour remarks about the idea of inviting his friends to feast on champagne and caviar, which he called the height of affectation. He turned ironically to Vladimir Orloff, a designer for the Ballets Russes: did Gerald think he was an exiled grand duke perpetuating the grandeur of the imperial court? When nobody rose to the bait, Scott turned his chair around, straddled it with his chin resting on its back and gave his full attention to a young woman who had just sat down with a man much older than she. So insistently did he stare that they summoned the headwaiter and changed their table. He then snatched up a stack of ashtrays and, roaring with laughter, tossed them onto a nearby table, again bringing the headwaiter down upon him. Irritated by such horseplay, Murphy rose and swept out, followed by Sara, leaving a surprised and angry Fitzgerald behind him. "He [Fitzgerald] really had the most appalling sense of humor," Murphy commented in recalling the incident, "sophomoric and—well, trashy."[33] Yet, he admitted, Scott could be the most charming of companions: "What we loved about Scott was the region in him where his gift came from, and which was never completely buried. There were moments when he wasn't harassed or trying to shock you, moments when he'd be gentle and quiet, and he'd tell you his real thoughts about people, and lose himself in defining what he felt about them. Those were the moments when you saw the beauty of his mind and nature, and they compelled you to love and value him."[34]

The Fitzgeralds left a few days later for Paris. Zelda's health had deteriorated: now the diagnosis was appendicitis; she would have to be operated on. She went into the American Hospital in Paris and Scott rented a room nearby. For two weeks he cruised the city's night spots, sometimes with actor James Rennie, who had played Gatsby on Broadway, or with novelist Michael Arlen, who introduced him into Nancy Cunard's circle. Sara Mayfield, a childhood friend of Zelda's who was then attending the Sorbonne, was amazed by the way he squandered money.

By the time the Fitzgeralds returned to Juan-les-Pins in early July, the Hemingways had left Villa Paquita and were staying in the Hôtel de la Pinède, where Pauline joined them. They were preparing to leave for Pamplona with the Murphys. When he returned two weeks later, Gerald sent Hemingway a letter of the kind once reserved for Fitzgerald: "You're so right because you're so close to what's elemental. Your values are hitched up to the universe. We're proud to know you. Yours are the things that count."[35]

Ernest was now in Madrid with Hadley, the casino incident seemed forgotten, but the Murphys nevertheless kept their distance from the Fitzgeralds. Scott's spirit of provocation became obsessive; his need to shock took forms that went beyond a mere need to affirm his independence of the decorum insisted on by the Murphys. He seemed compelled to wound people in their most deeply held beliefs. For example, he alienated the waiters at the casino by saying that the Germans should have won the war and that someday they would return and brush away the French Army. Yet he left lavish tips, as though to emphasize his inviolable status as a rich foreigner and the mercenary instincts of those he considered his inferiors.

When the mood was on him, he lost the most elementary sense of decency. Dos Passos tells of "the horrible time" when, entering a restaurant with the Murphys and the Fitzgeralds, Scott kicked the tray of cigarettes held by the elderly woman selling them. Stunned and embarrassed, his reproachfully silent friends retrieved the packages scattered under chairs and tables while Fitzgerald hastily tugged a wad of bills from his pocket and slipped it into his victim's hand. "It was hard to laugh that off,"[36] Dos Passos wrote with his usual restraint. No clowning was too gross for Scott. Not dropping on all fours, wriggling under the big straw mat in front of the casino entrance and stalking forward under his "shell," growling. Nor, when he encountered an obstacle, pretending to faint and falling in a heap at his antagonist's feet; once when the guard on the door of the gambling room in Monte Carlo refused to let him in until he showed his passport, Scott insulted the man, then collapsed. After watching the stunt several times, Murphy finally lost patience. "Scott," he admonished, "this is *not* Princeton and I am *not* your roommate. Get up!"[37] Sheepishly, Fitzgerald obeyed the order.

Understandably, he preferred to be with MacArthur, who, instead of reproaching him, encouraged him to act on his impulses. They were joined by a third cutup, Ben Finney. Together the three men set about making a movie, an amateur phantasmagoria set in the Hôtel du Cap. Its protagonist was to be "the wickedest woman of Europe," a composite of Duff Twysden and Nancy Cunard. They may have been inspired by Picasso, who in 1925 had put together a collection of back-view snapshots of his models: he tricked them into bending over and, without their knowing it, photographed their upraised posteriors. Similarly, the three pocket Griffiths tried to surprise hotel guests in comic attitudes, at one point chasing singer Grace Moore with their camera. Their faintly obscene subtitles were painted in large letters on the wall of her house. She had them whitewashed over several times, but, seeing that this only stimulated their inventiveness, she finally gave up, preferring, she explained, "to do with the four-letter words one knew than those one knew not of."[38]

Zelda took no part in this merriment. She liked to be with the Murphys and spent her days with them on the corner of the beach they had sectioned off with their umbrellas and deck chairs. She never earned their irony or reproach; even her most surprising stunts were imbued with a dignity and gravity that commanded respect. No one in the casino smiled, for example, when she left the Murphys' table and began to dance, with her skirt pulled up to her waist. "She was dancing for herself," Gerald later commented; "she didn't look left or right, or catch anyone's eyes. She looked at no one, not once, not even at Scott. I saw a mass of lace ruffles as she whirled—I'll never forget it. We were frozen. She had this tremendous natural dignity. . . . Somehow she was incapable of doing anything unladylike."[39]

Woollcott and "Chato" Elizaga, Miss Moore's fiancé, gave a farewell dinner one evening on the terrace at the Eden Roc Hotel. When all the toasts had been made, Zelda decided that all this chat was pointless and proposed a more concrete gesture of friendship: she stripped off her black lace panties and tossed them to her hosts. Elizaga caught them and, vowing that he would show himself worthy of the favor, dived off the rocks fronting the terrace, followed by several of the guests. Woollcott, meanwhile, took off *all* his clothes, saluted the remaining guests, straightened his straw hat, lit a cigarette and, his great belly preceding him like an escort vessel, waddled nonchalantly toward the lobby.

The Murphys had planned to go to the United States at the end of the summer, and they gave a lavish dinner at Villa America that may have inspired the Divers' farewell evening in *Tender Is the Night.* As usual, Fitzgerald played the clown. As soon as he arrived, he walked over to an effeminate-looking young man and, loudly enough to be heard by everyone in the room, asked if he was a homosexual. When the man calmly agreed that he was, Fitzgerald beat a disconcerted retreat and tried to look inconspicuous. But when the dessert came, he was circulating among the tables and spied the bare back of the Princesse de Caraman-Chimay, who had been spending the summer with a neighbor of the Murphys, Princesse de Poix. He grabbed a piece of fruit from a table and tossed it, hitting her between the shoulder blades. Her poise was too much for him: she could not help straightening in surprise, but she went right on with her conversation as though nothing had happened. MacLeish saw it all, took Scott aside and bawled him out. Scott punched him in the jaw. Moments later, Fitzgerald grabbed a Venetian glass from the table and threw it over the garden wall, then another, shouting with laughter when he heard them smash. He destroyed a third glass before Gerald curtly told him to stop. Nothing was said about it then, but as the Fitzgeralds were leaving, Gerald took Scott aside and told him he did not want to see him at Villa America for the next three weeks.

Twenty-one days later Scott rang the Murphys' doorbell, and their friendship picked up from where it had been interrupted—on the surface. In any case, three weeks of ostracism did not have the desired chastening effect on Fitzgerald. On the evening before the Murphys left, he made another scene, which was followed by another "mawkish reconciliation," as he put it in a letter to Hemingway on his thirtieth birthday. He added that the Murphys had "grown dim" in his mind; "I don't like them much any more," he asserted.[40] Was he falling in behind Ernest, who liked Sara but never lost his feeling of rivalry with Gerald? Whatever the motive, the fact was that in that autumn of 1926 Fitzgerald became estranged from the Murphys and could no longer count on Ernest's friendship. Just how did Hemingway feel toward him?

14. HOME AND BACK AGAIN

(Winter 1927–Spring 1930)

The two men had nothing in common except that each thought of the other as a kind of man or writer he would more or less have liked to be. Even this was less perceptible in Hemingway, who mainly envied the privileges Fitzgerald enjoyed when he first met him. If we accept the portrait he left of Fitzgerald in *A Moveable Feast*, he probably had little reason to admire anything about Fitzgerald but his talent. And he was even lukewarm about that. "You are twice as good now as you were at the time you think you were so marvellous," Hemingway declared in a letter to Fitzgerald on May 28, 1934. "You know, I never thought so much of *Gatsby* at the time."[1] Besides, Hemingway was too sure of himself and of his own genius to admit any kind of superiority in another writer, except a dead one. Yet he could not help envying Fitzgerald's healthy earnings when he, Hemingway, was living very simply indeed on his wife's income. It was symptomatic that when he and Hadley separated and he gave her all the cash he had, he classed Fitzgerald with MacLeish and Murphy as "rich" people who were in a position to help him financially. Even after the success of *A Farewell to Arms*, he went on living on the resources his second wife, Pauline, received from her wealthy family; this included the house on Key West, a gift from one of her uncles, in which they lived beginning in 1931.

Another of Hemingway's regrets was that he had never gone to college. He so envied Fitzgerald his years at Princeton that in one drunken, revealing moment in 1931 he bragged that he, too, had studied there, a lie he later retracted. In his 1933 "Homage to Switzerland," he alluded to Fitzgerald and Princeton with leaden irony in a conversation between an American and a Swiss waitress with a diploma from Berlitz.

No wonder, then, that ten years after the two men met, Hemingway even remembered the name of Newman School. That was at the end of 1935, one of the lowest points in Fitzgerald's life, when Hemingway tried in his fashion to console him by proposing to hire a killer to put him out of his misery; he even imagined a funeral for which "we will get MacLeish to write a mystic poem to be read at that Catholic school (Newman?) you went to."[2] Their only meeting between July 1926 and the spring of 1929 was at a Princeton-Yale football game.

It seems certain that Hemingway was impressed by Princeton's prestige even while judging critically, even ironically, one of its most famous though least typical alumni. He knew such authentic Princeton intellectuals as Wilson and Gauss, of course, but in Fitzgerald he saw a combination of culture and cash. This allowed him to develop a comfortably ambiguous attitude in which irony counterbalanced his regret at having had no share in the cultural rituals common to his new friends. Dos Passos had gone to Harvard, MacLeish, Stewart and Murphy to Yale. Hemingway's feeling of inferiority in this showed in his aggressiveness. The pitiless view of Robert Cohn taken, despite his protestations of friendship, by the narrator in *The Sun Also Rises* is that of Hemingway judging Cohn's model, Harold Loeb, and the privileges a rich family gave him: a Princeton education, a college wrestling championship, editorship of a magazine in Europe, the recent publication of a novel. That Loeb trusted and befriended him, that, along with Anderson, he helped persuade Boni and Liveright to publish *In Our Time*, only nourished Hemingway's secret resentment. Hemingway's relations with Loeb in 1924–26 prefigured in an almost exemplary and allegorical way the more subtle connection he would develop with Fitzgerald in later years.

To Fitzgerald, on the other hand, Hemingway was the very image of the man he would have wished to be. There was no trace of ambiguity or irony in the enthusiastic approval expressed in his letters. He seemed to feel that Hemingway had succeeded where he, Fitzgerald, had failed in combining the man of letters with the man of action. While he had wasted his time at Princeton, his friend had been living the great adventure of war on the Italian front, had intensely experienced the big, basic emotions one feels in the face of danger and death, had known the virile comradeship that unites men who share combat and danger. In a letter written in 1925, Hemingway insisted on war as an ideal subject for a novelist. "The reason you are so sore you missed the war," he informed Fitzgerald, "is because war is the best subject of all. It groups the maximum of material and speeds up the action and brings out all sorts of stuff that normally you have to wait a lifetime to get. . . ."[3]

Fitzgerald was only too aware of the limits of his experience; his regret at having missed the war, intensified by Hemingway's example, sometimes took morbid form, as in his interest in photos of horribly mutilated victims of shellfire. Hemingway also had a suitably heroic physique; Fitzgerald envied him his height, his athletic build and, generally speaking, what he called his "magnetism," an attribute that Scott felt was lacking in himself. Most of all, a Fitzgerald discouraged at the time of their meeting by the disappointing showing of *Gatsby*, even though he considered himself the "best" writer of his generation, saw in Hemingway an artist who had chosen the strait gate. Hemingway, after all, devoted himself entirely to literature, living in poverty, supported by Hadley, who consented to share the privation imposed by his stern calling. Scott compared this wise asceticism with his own prodigality and with Zelda's extravagance, but he knew that he could not live in any other way.

Fitzgerald was thirty, which meant to him that his youth was gone, and he seems to have subconsciously made his choice in the dilemma facing him. Murphy and Hemingway, the two friends he had made in France, seemed perfect, one might say ideal, examples of the only possible alternatives: Gerald and Sara incarnated the grace, the optimum fulfillment of a civilized state based on culture, leisure and money, but also on elegance and generosity. To Fitzgerald, who knew little of the America of the rich except the vulgar and ostentatious parties he attended in New York and Long Island, the Murphys clearly represented the sole justification of a society based on money. Between them and the Americans he had previously known, the difference was as great as that between Gatsby's flashy parties and the refined evenings with the Divers in *Tender Is the Night*.

It was the Fitzgeralds' imaginativeness and spontaneity that won the Murphys' friendship, not the novelist's fame; they were accepted because of their personal qualities, and they were temporarily excluded on several occasions when those qualities deteriorated. To the Murphys the writer who was full of promise, the really modern innovator, apparently was Hemingway. He was the artist of the group, the one who was respected and encouraged and whose company was sought. Fitzgerald was sorely tempted, because he considered the Murphys archetypes of an admirable life-style, to view his writer's trade as a means rather than as the end it had been up to then. "Living well is the best revenge"[4] for life's hard knocks, the Murphys believed. If a man can invest all his talent in living, why bother building up a body of work in which those he most admires and whose esteem he most values do not believe?

Hemingway, celebrated and accepted as a true creator, privileged with the immunity of the genuine artist of whom all is forgiven, played the gruff and boorish brute. He did not, as Fitzgerald did, try to keep up with the Murphys on their own ground; instead, he loudly claimed the right to be himself, sustained by his almost mystical conviction—confirmed by the unanimous approbation he received—that he was a Great Writer. He was sure enough of himself and his talent to refuse to rush, to take his time, dividing his life between writing, loafing and sports.

Faced with this serene determination, so different from his own anxieties and his inner turbulence, Fitzgerald made an obscure and predictable decision: without admitting it to himself or those close to him, he opted for the easy way, for the life of a gentleman, a prince, rather, a life of aristocratic leisure negligently financed by a few shallow, effortless stories written to amuse the *Post*'s three million readers. To Hemingway, younger, tougher, sure of himself, more naive, too, was left the ungrateful, never satisfying daily chore of writing for his peers, with no other reward but their approval—or their spite. Glenway Wescott was surely right in an essay written after Scott's death in which he suggested that Hemingway may have relieved Fitzgerald of the responsibility of writing for glory: "He not only said but, I believe, honestly felt that Hemingway was inimitably, essentially superior. From the moment Hemingway began to appear in print, perhaps it did not matter what he himself produced or failed to produce. He felt free to write just for profit, and to live for fun, if possible. Hemingway could be entrusted with the graver responsibilities and higher rewards such as glory, immortality. This extreme of admiration—this excuse for a morbid belittlement and abandonment of himself was bad for Fitzgerald, I imagine."[5] This was true in part, at least in the few years preceding *Tender Is the Night,* years of real demoralization in Fitzgerald, of the disintegration of his creative faculties while the novelist abdicated in favor of the "gentleman."

The year 1926 was certainly a determinant in this process. Money flowed in from the stage and screen adaptations of *Gatsby,* freeing Fitzgerald of debt for the first time in four years; this may have made him feel that he had reached a professional equilibrium from which he could now view writing novels as a luxury. The constantly fatter fees he was receiving for his stories allowed him to live the life of the idle rich. Obviously, he lacked any keen sense of urgency in completing the novel he had started immediately after finishing *Gatsby.*

Hemingway understood this very well. "I wish there was some way that your economic existence would depend on this novel or on novels rather than the damned stories," he told him, "because that is one thing that drives you and gives you an outlet and an excuse too—the damned stories."[6] It was a theme he harped on: a week earlier he had accused Scott of "using the juice to write for the *Post* and trying to write masterpieces with the dregs."[7] By 1926 a Fitzgerald who had been convinced only the previous year that he was going to write his generation's novel, the book that neither Joyce nor Stein could write, may now have decided that Hemingway had already staked out the territory he had wanted to explore, had already discovered the formula that nullified all Fitzgerald's searching and rendered obsolete the complex architecture in *Gatsby.*

On December 10, 1926, the Fitzgeralds embarked in Genoa aboard the *Conte Biancamano.* Also aboard was Ludlow Fowler, who, with his young wife, had spent the summer in Europe. Six years earlier he had been the best man at the Fitzgeralds' wedding and now he was witness to the disillusionment in their marriage. Zelda warned him about it: "Now Ludlow, take it from an old souse like me—don't let drinking get you in the position it's gotten Scott if you want your marriage to be any good."[8] And Scott was returning home empty-handed: the euphoria generated by his new wealth had borne no fruit. A letter written in early August announced what he represented as a triumphant homecoming: "I'll be home with the finished manuscript of my book about mid-December. We'll be a week in New York, then south to Washington and Montgomery to see our respective parents and spend Christmas—and back in New York in mid-January to spend the rest of the winter." His stay in Europe was summed up this way: "God, how much I've learned in these two and a half years in Europe. It seems like a decade and I feel pretty old but I wouldn't have missed it, even its most unpleasant and painful aspects."[9]

After sending a telegram to Ober asking him to extend by six months the deadline for submitting his manuscript to *Liberty*, he and Zelda went to California in early January, leaving Scottie with Mrs. Fitzgerald. He had been hired by United Artists producer John Considine to write the script for *Lipstick*, a film in which Constance Talmadge had grabbed the leading role. Scott was to be paid $3,500 for writing the script and $12,000 if it was accepted. The Fitzgeralds were warmly received by the movie colony, and the newspapers devoted columns of space to them. At the palatial Ambassador Hotel in Los Angeles they occupied a suite in a huge bungalow set in a palm grove, where their neighbors were John Barrymore, Carl Van Vechten and their old friend from Rome, Carmel Myers. The swirl of parties that followed brought them in touch with other stars: Richard Barthelmess, Pola Negri, Lillian Gish and a seventeen-year-old newcomer, Lois Moran. With the Charleston now out of style, Zelda applied herself to learning the intricacies of the Black Bottom.

The unending round of festivities did not eclipse their memories of France. Zelda's letters to Scottie were full of nostalgia for Paris, "for the pink lights and the trees and the gay streets."[10] She would give all of Hollywood, she said, for the thrill of driving from Paris to the Riviera. And in an interview with a Los Angeles newspaper, Scott expressed with Mencken-esque violence his disappointment in the America he saw. "I was shocked," he asserted, "when I returned to America. . . . I had been, you know, three years in Paris. I saw shows on the New York stage which would have shocked the French. Everything in New York seems mouldy, rotten. We went to night clubs. It was like going to a big mining camp in the boom days. . . . I got a sensation of horror. . . . There was nothing fine about it all. It was vulgarity without the faintest trace of redeeming wit. Coming from Paris to New York was like plunging from a moral world to a state of anarchy."[11]

He pursued his philippic in an interview given to the New York *World* two months later, in which he justified expatriation in terms recalling those employed by Henry Adams thirty years earlier: "The best of America drifts to Paris. The American in Paris is the best American. It is more fun for an intelligent person to live in an intelligent country. France has the only two things toward which we drift as we grow older—intelligence and good manners."[12]

Intelligence and good manners, however, seem to have been the qualities he too often forgot in his public life. In the unreal atmosphere of Hollywood, he and Zelda strained to compete with the actors in eccentricity and cheekiness. When they failed to receive an invitation to a costume party given by Samuel Goldwyn for the Talmadge sisters, they appeared at the door on all fours, pleading between howls to be admitted as puppies. Zelda then went upstairs, had a bath and, doubtless feeling more presentable, went back down to the party. On another occasion, aping the actors' habit of leaving their costumes on in town, they went to a party with Zelda in a nightgown and Scott in pajamas. At a tea party given by Lois Moran's mother, they went the rounds of the guests asking like magicians for their jewelry and watches; they then vanished into the kitchen, where they were found cooking their loot in a pot of tomato sauce.

Among the performers—who, like Scott, were always acting—Lois Moran impressed him by her freshness and naturalness. She was just back from four years in Europe with her mother, she was cultivated and spoke French fluently. Their affinity led them to meet whenever they had a chance. Lois asked Scott to take a screen test, to which he agreed with delight. But he resisted her pleas that he take a part in one of her films. Blond and pink, with innocent blue eyes, she took her work seriously. She was the model for a type of honest and independent young actress, courted by an older man, who would soon appear in some of Scott's stories and, as Rosemary, would take the lead in *Tender Is the Night*. If we are to believe George Jean Nathan, the affair did not go very far. "She was a lovely kid of such tender years that it was rumored she still wore the kind of flannel nightie that was bound around her ankles with ribbons," he recalled, "and Scott never visited her save when her mother was present."[13]

It enraged Zelda to hear Scott speak admiringly of Lois, saying she owed her success entirely to her talent and perseverance, an accomplishment that made her a woman after his own heart. Zelda feigned indifference, but she showed in her special way how she suffered from Scott's attentions to a girl she thought of as a rival. Once while he was having dinner with Lois, Zelda burned in the bathtub all the dresses she had just made. In the train taking them back to New York some weeks later, she reproached him for inviting Lois to visit them; feeling herself betrayed, she climaxed their violent quarrel by opening the window and throwing out the platinum wristwatch Scott had given her as an engagement present.

Fitzgerald spent most of his time in Hollywood, however, working alone in a United Artists office, keeping strict hours like all the other scriptwriters. In eight weeks he concocted a contemporary Cinderella story set in a fairy-tale Princeton. Hollywood was less given to such sparkling trifles than *The Saturday Evening Post*, and the script was rejected. In a letter to his daughter written ten years later, Fitzgerald summed up the lesson Hollywood had taught him: "I honestly believed that with *no effort on my part* I was a sort of a mgaician with words. . . . Total result—a great time and no work."[14]

He had wasted money as well as time, having spent far more in Hollywood than he earned. Perkins, meanwhile, was trying to summon him back to duty: in January he asked Fitzgerald to approve the novel's new title, *The World Fair*, so that he could announce it, thus keeping it exclusive and calling the public's attention to the serialization soon to appear in *Liberty*. He renewed his efforts in April, asking for details from the book that could help the jacket designer. But Fitzgerald had run through his cash reserves and had to go back to writing bread-and-butter stories.

Returning to the East Coast, he looked for a house to rent. After a few days in Washington, he reached New York around the end of March and paid a visit to Lardner in Great Neck. Living near a big city was out of the question now for the Fitzgeralds. Perkins suggested that they try Delaware. Scott's college roommate, John Biggs, a Washington lawyer now, found him a huge old colonial-style house on a bank of the Delaware River. Charmed by the dignity of the house and the lovely landscape, Fitzgerald on April 1 signed a lease that, for the absurdly low rent of $150 a month, made him the tenant of Ellerslie for eighteen months. It was a pastoral paradise of oaks and chestnut trees surrounding a house with a four-columned portico. There were nearly thirty rooms in Ellerslie, all so big that Zelda had outsized furniture made to scale for them. The result was surprising: people looked like pygmies amid all that giant furniture, like figures out of *Gulliver* or *Alice*. She restored a kind of balance a few months later by building a doll's house for Scottie that she furnished and upholstered and garnished with mirrors and windows as though it were a real home.

In May 1927, six weeks after they moved into the house, their first guests arrived—Lois and her mother, critic Ernest Boyd and Carl Van Vechten—and they all picnicked under the flowering chestnut trees at the river's edge. That was the weekend when Lindbergh landed at the Paris airport of Le Bourget. So everyone talked of Paris and Scottie chattered in French to Lois. Zelda hid her feelings about Lois, but when Van Vechten returned alone the following week, she seems to have gotten drunk and poured out her resentment of the girl, as we learn from a half-serious, half-joking note she later sent him. "From the depths of my polluted soul," she wrote, "I am sorry the week-end was such a mess. Do forgive my iniquities and my putrid drunkenness. This was such a nice place, and it should have been a good party if I had not explored my abyss in public."[15] From then on Van Vechten became her confidant and she sent him streams of letters about everything and nothing.

Perhaps stung by Scott's criticism, she began to write again, too, after a three-years interval; three of her articles were published the following year in *Harper's Bazaar* and *College Humor*. The second of these, "Looking

Back Eight Years," is interesting for its analysis of the feeling of frustration she thought beset the men and women of her generation. Keen insight took her straight to the heart of a problem that specially affected her and Scott: how to survive their youth, how to accede to maturity? "It is not altogether the prosperity of the country and the consequent softness of life which has made them unstable, for almost invariably they are tremendously energetic . . . ," she wrote. "It is a great emotional disappointment resulting from the fact that life moved in poetic gestures when they were younger and has now settled back into buffoonery. And with the current insistence upon youth as the finest and richest time in the life of man it is small wonder that sensitive young people are haunted and harassed by a sense of unfilled destiny and grope about between the ages of twenty-five and forty with a baffled feeling of frustration."[16]

Not only was she writing, but she also returned to the paintbrushes she had not touched since her stay in Capri. An oil painting of the facade of Ellerslie bathed in amber light against a pale green sky shows a real sense of atmosphere and tonal values. But her nostalgia took her imagination to the happy days of the past. Around a lampshade she painted a merry-go-round; in the background is a brightly colored montage of the Fitzgeralds' former homes, the Yacht Club on White Bear Lake, the Plaza Hotel in New York, the house in Westport, Villa Marie, the Piazza di Spagna in Rome, the terrace in Capri, Villa Saint-Louis and Ellerslie, shown from the same angle as in the painting. In the foreground fairgoers ride the carousel horses amid gardeners and governesses; Zelda herself is pictured riding a rooster, Scottie a horse, Scott an elephant and Nathan a lion.

People from the past surged back into the Fitzgeralds' lives, too. During a stay at Virginia Beach in July, they met cousin Ceci, whose daughters were now grown up. In August they went back to Long Island, where they were reunited with Tommy Hitchcock, the polo star on whom Tom Buchanan was modeled. Then they visited the now elderly Margaret Chanler at her Hudson Valley home, where Sigourney Fay had first introduced Scott to her; she had probably heard of Fitzgerald's encounter with her friend Edith Wharton, and she strictly rationed the liquor. Scott had to exert all his charm on Venturino, the butler, to wheedle an extra whiskey: "Mrs. Chanler is so brilliant," he pleaded, "that I simply have to have another drink to keep up with her."[17]

In September Ludlow Fowler and Townsend Martin stayed at Ellerslie, taking part in a polo tournament for which Fitzgerald, his love of parody jogged by his contact with Hitchcock, hired some workhorses from neighboring farmers. A dance band was brought in for the evening, as though the place were Gatsby's, and so were a great many other guests. Bootleg whiskey flowed like water. Everything had been provided—except food. Dos Passos was so starved that he rounded up some of the other guests and went to Wilmington in search of a sandwich.

This was also the period when Fitzgerald, at Gauss's urging, renewed his ties with Princeton. *College Humor*, which published a series of articles on American colleges, asked him to write the piece on Princeton. In it Fitzgerald extolled the school he had not seen since the day in May 1920 when he was literally thrown out of the Cottage Club. Now he was readmitted to Cottage and, some months later, was invited to a discussion on his problems as a writer. Anxious to make a good impression, he quit drinking, but he was too nervous to speak; after several tries, he gave up and everyone sat around and swapped dirty stories. Disgusted, Fitzgerald got drunk during the reception given afterward by Edgar Palmer, one of the university's most generous patrons, to whom it owed its new stadium. "You know, I've been studying you," Fitzgerald informed him, "and thank God I don't look like that. It must be because you have so much money."[18]

Some of the students had read his article when it appeared in December. Aboard the train to Trenton the next day, one of them, an idealistic freshman, told him that the honor code vaunted in the article was frequently violated during exams. It says much about his own idealism that Fitzgerald sent a telegram to Dean Gauss expressing his dismay, and this was followed by a long letter on the subject. His passion for football also revived, and he attended a number of scrimmages. Among the five stories he turned out beginning in June 1927, one of the best is "The Bowl," written in November in the middle of the college football season. Two others, "Jacob's Ladder" and "Magnetism," reveal how persistent were the feelings triggered in him by Lois Moran. An image of an actress struggling with a difficult profession finally replaced the carefree flapper in his fiction.

Zelda plunged into ballet lessons, which, she thought, would provide a means of self-expression in an area all her own, would make her the kind of professional Scott so insistently praised. She was just turned twenty-seven, but she was convinced she could make a career as a ballerina. Hadn't she danced well, after all, as a girl in the shows in Montgomery? She enrolled in the dancing class taught by Catherine Littlefield, who directed the Philadelphia Opera Ballet Corps and who had studied in Paris with Madame Lubow Egorova, director of the Ballets Russes school. Zelda was determined to be "a Pavlova, nothing less." Three times a week she went up to Philadelphia with Scottie, whom she had enrolled in the same school. In an antique shop she found a huge gilt mirror with a lavishly carved Victorian frame; this she hung in the front room, installed a ballet bar in front of it and, playing the same record over and over, practiced the movements learned at Miss Littlefield's. Practiced, in fact, to the point of exhaustion, even if there were guests, even during meals, dripping perspiration, breaking off only to gulp a glass of water or a cup of tea while Scott watched in exasperation.

Zelda was living in her own world now, entirely cut off from the real world around her. In one of her letters to Van Vechten she told him how determined she was to preserve her integrity amid the decay: "I joined the Philadelphia Opera Ballet . . . and everybody has been so drunk in this country lately that I am just finding enough chaos to pursue my own ends in, undisturbed, again . . . I hope that I will never again feel attractive."[19]

With Scott absorbed in writing short stories, his novel was at a standstill. To Hemingway, who had just come out with a new collection of stories, he reported in November that the manuscript would be ready December 1. He also lied to Perkins, who in October had told Lardner in a letter that the book was within five thousand words—a dozen pages or so—of the end. But Scott did admit to Hemingway that his health was shaky. "Have got nervous as hell lately," he said, "purely physical, but scared me somewhat—to the point of putting me on the wagon and smoking denicotinized cigarettes."[20]

At the end of January 1928, Zelda and Scott spent a few days in Quebec as guests of the Canadian tourist office, but the break did nothing to ease their tenseness (it was after this hasty trip that Scott went mute at the Cottage Club). Then Zelda's sister Rosalind and her husband, Newman Smith, came to visit them at Ellerslie.

Tired, humiliated by his breakdown at Princeton, disturbed by what he had learned about cheating on the honor code, Scott picked a quarrel with Zelda in front of their guests and smashed one of her favorite vases against a mantelpiece. The row grew increasingly nasty, and when Zelda insulted Scott's parents, calling his father an Irish cop, he saw red and slapped her hard across the face. Shouts, chairs overturned, a bloody nose, tears. Smith intervened, Rosalind was indignant. But the beaten wife claimed her right to be beaten if she chose. The two sisters turned on each other, and it was the men who then tried to calm them.

As soon as the outraged Smiths left the following morning, Zelda wound up her Victrola and returned to her work at the ballet bar. Scott shut himself in his study, reviewing his past as he leafed through his *Ledger*. His next novel would have no heroine, no flappers or actresses or dancers. Just a thirteen-year-old boy and his imaginary world and his first contact with life, when anything seemed possible. This would be his own childhood and adolescence reenacted by Basil Duke Lee. To this enchanted world he exiled himself in 1928: seven stories, written between March and October, would temporarily serve him as home and homeland.

He missed his friends and their advice. So he gathered some of them together for a weekend made memorable by his pressing Bunny Wilson to describe him in detail. Scott had seen Bunny only fleetingly since his return from France, and he wanted his opinion on the part of the novel he had already written. He had shown a few pages of it to Dos Passos and been told that they were not very good. Two judges being better than one, he also invited Seldes for the weekend, remembering the useful advice he had offered on *The Great Gatsby* in August 1924 at Villa Marie, during the crisis in the Fitzgeralds' marriage. Because Wilson and Seldes had been the first to send him enthusiastic letters when *Gatsby* appeared and had written particularly penetrating reviews of it in the newspapers, Scott felt he could trust them. Also invited were neighbors John and Ann Biggs, Esther Murphy and Thornton Wilder, then a young novelist teaching at Lawrenceville, near Princeton; Fitzgerald had been impressed by his first novels, *The Cabala* and *The Bridge of San Luis Rey*.

We can skip over the usual hijinks, the drunkenness and chaos. The important moment came when Scott, in pajamas and dressing gown and finally alone with Bunny and Gilbert, read them his introductory chapter, the one in which Melarky and his mother arrive at the Murphys' beach. Wilson admired the prose, which he found polished, supple and glittering in the best Fitzgerald manner, and was surprised later to find that the details that had struck him were not in the final version of *Tender Is the Night*. The subject, an "intellectual murder" combined with the deterioration of a young man exposed to the refined existence of expatriates of the Riviera, was, he thought, too complicated. "He had now gone on to tackle a subject that might well have taxed Dostoevsky, and he was eventually to find it beyond him," Wilson wrote. "It must have been a psychological 'block' as well as the invincible compulsion to live like a millionaire that led him even more than usual to interrupt his serious work and turn out stories for the commercial magazines."[21]

After this confrontation with his peers, Fitzgerald wrote two stories in the Basil cycle. Then, with spring back, he and Zelda thought that perhaps Paris, which haunted their memories, might once more open a new way for them as it did in the time of *The Great Gatsby*. But, as Zelda said in *Save Me the Waltz*, "they hadn't much faith in travel nor a great belief in a change of scene as a panacea for spiritual ills; they were simply glad to be going."[22]

They reached France aboard the *Paris* on April 27, 1928. This time they settled on the Left Bank because that was where the Murphys were living at the time. They rented an apartment at 58, Rue de Vaugirard, on the corner of the Rue Bonaparte; the rooms facing the inner court were gloomy, but the place did face on the Luxembourg Gardens and was only a two-minute walk from the apartment the Murphys were renting in a new building at 14, Rue Guynemer. This meant that Scottie could play with Honoria, Patrick and Baoth. Gerald was a good friend of Madame Egorova's (Princess Troubetskoy), the ballet mistress, who had been giving lessons to Honoria for years; Zelda was extremely eager to meet her and Gerald introduced them. Madame's studio was at 8, Rue Caumartin, over the Olympia Music Hall. And there Zelda went regularly for five months, carrying on the work begun by Catherine Littlefield the previous September.

Hemingway had remarried that spring and had left Paris in March, but the Fitzgeralds saw Hadley, who stayed on in the French capital with Bumby. They also saw Gertrude Stein, who was somewhat estranged from Ernest and who amused them with stories about him. The irresistible athlete, it seems, had been in a series of mishaps: most recently he had cracked his skull in his apartment bathroom when the chain he yanked turned out to control a transom and not the cistern.

The Murphys introduced them to Léger and Sylvia Beach; they met Cole Porter at the Murphy home several times, and Natalie Barney invited them to her Fridays. Fitzgerald's sharp eye took in the details of Miss Barney's circus, along with that of her protégée of the moment, Dorothy Wilde, Oscar's niece. Following in the footsteps of Proust, whose books both Wilder and Wilson insisted that he read, he wrote twenty remarkable pages on lesbians in Paris, in which the two women appear under the names of Miss Retchmore and Vivian Taube. Nothing remains of these pages but a few lines in *Tender Is the Night,* in a scene in which one of them propositions Rosemary.

Zelda, exhausted by her dancing, had little appetite left for social life. Scott became friendly with King Vidor, who had just finished filming *Peg o' My Heart* with Laurette Taylor. He and his wife, Eleanor, lived in a big house in Neuilly and gave parties at the Ritz, from which the drunken Fitzgeralds sometimes had to be poured into taxis to get them home.

Seldes had given Scott two letters of recommendation, one to Tristan Tzara and the other to Cocteau, but he did not use them. He did, however, follow Miss Beach's advice to look up a young French novelist named André Chamson, who had just missed winning the important Goncourt literary prize the previous autumn. Chamson was then living on the meager pay of a reporter covering the Chamber of Deputies; he and his wife, Lucie, like him a graduate of the prestigious École des Chartes, lived in a small seventh-floor apartment at 17, Rue Thouin, near the Pantheon. It was there that Fitzgerald came to introduce himself one May morning, standing in a wash of light in the hallway that Chamson remembered thirty years later: "He came into my life with that smile and, probably because of the sunlight coming through the stairway window . . . , as though in a halo of light."[23] Although the Frenchman's English was as rudimentary as the American's French, and though they seemed to have nothing in common, not origins, culture or life-style, they liked each other from the start. "It took no more to bring us together than the time to exchange a few smiles and to say the essential things while making small talk. He became my friend in a matter of minutes. That sort of lightning stroke has never happened to me since." Instinctively, Chamson chose the same terms to describe this friendship—which briefly blended with his admiration for the United States as a whole—that Fitzgerald would later use to express the essence of America: "My friendship with Scott was truly the last of my youthful friendships—inspired mind, vulnerable soul and generous heart—and in it I encountered the freshness of all that country's people."[24] And in a short story entitled "The Swimmers," Fitzgerald would declare that "France was a land, England was a people, but America, having about it still that quality of the idea, was harder to utter. . . . It was a willingness of the heart."[25]

It was precisely this willingness of the heart, this outgoing receptivity, a mutual attraction and respect, that united the two men. Chamson, like Hemingway, was a writer who was wholly devoted to his work, admitting no distraction, indifferent to wealth, self-contained. It was a sign of confidence that Fitzgerald asked him to read the French translation of *The Great Gatsby*, which appeared in October 1926; in turn, he struggled through Chamson's *Les Hommes de la route* and, enthusiastic about it, alerted Perkins. "He's head over heels the best young man here," he announced. "Like Ernest and Thornton Wilder rolled into one."[26] And he got results: Scribner's found a noted writer, Van Wyck Brooks, to translate it.* Scott did not let it go at that; knowing that Vidor was looking for a subject for a film, he showed him his new friend's book. Vidor liked it and agreed to adapt it for film. But first the book had to be simplified, boiled down to its essence.

For weeks Chamson, Vidor and Fitzgerald walked and talked together, spent hours in small cafés discussing the script. They went to the movies together, invited each other to dinner; the Americans took the Chamsons to the most expensive restaurants and they, in turn, skirted financial disaster by feeding their friends in their garret apartment.

When the Chamsons visited the Fitzgeralds, their hosts, like Gatsby, naively displayed their riches, "drawers full of lingerie, embroidered hand-kerchiefs and ties, gold cigarette lighters, silver cigarette cases."[27] Scott pressed his guest to choose a tie or a handkerchief given him by Zelda, dismissing her objections with irrefutable logic ("if I didn't like them, I wouldn't give them to anyone") and overcoming Chamson's reluctance by the childish innocence that prompted him to share his treasures. Chamson was tactful enough not to hurt him by refusing, so he gracefully accepted what he called "this small precursor of the Marshall Plan, this generous aid to underdeveloped friends." He recognized that Scott was not patronizing him, but was displaying a deep goodness, a more profound generosity: "He would have liked it if everyone could have what he dreamed of, glory and love, fortune and peace of heart."[28]

Of course, Chamson went through some embarrassing, even terrifying moments, for "Fitzgerald was one of those who would tempt the Devil, but the Devil tempted him in return." He was embarrassed, for example, when Scott, climbing the stairs with him at the Rue Thouin clutching bottles of champagne and an ice bucket, stopped at a landing and asked him if he could swim. He set down the bucket full of ice cubes and pointed to it. "Could you swim in that?"

---

* *The Road*, New York, 1929.

"In that? Impossible."

"You'll see."

Whereupon Fitzgerald whipped off his jacket and shirt, unbuckled his belt and was about to slip off his trousers under the eyes of scandalized neighbors in the stairway when Chamson persuaded him that the swimming was better in his apartment. Scott's imagination grasped the logic of this proposition: indeed, it would be easier to dive from a chair.

On another occasion, while admiring the view of the Pantheon from the Chamsons' balcony, he climbed up on the railing and, waving his arms and struggling to keep his balance, took to yelling "I'm Voltaire, I'm Rousseau," while the Chamsons, afraid to make a move, waited in horror for him to drop to the street seven stories below.

Sometimes the incidents were merely alarming. One Sunday at a fair in Neuilly, Scott spied two policemen on bicycles. He stopped them and asked how much they wanted to sell their bikes. The "swallows," as the French call their bicycle police, didn't understand at first. Scott, gesticulating, pointing from his wallet to the bicycles and himself, finally made himself understood. Furious, the police were ready to haul him off to the station. The Chamsons intervened, there were confused explanations, a crowd gathered, the police scolded, the Chamsons pleaded, Fitzgerald was contrite and was let off. Crazy, these Americans! Scott had been through it all before. It was an extra sideshow at the fair.

The time came for Vidor to return to the United States. He wanted Chamson to go to Hollywood with him as a scriptwriter. Why, he would make a fortune; he would earn more in a week there than he did in a year in his Paris job. Fitzgerald admired the obstinacy with which the Frenchman refused these tantalizing offers. Instead, a gentlemen's agreement was reached: Vidor would adapt *The Road* and Chamson would collect royalties when the script was accepted. The Frenchman heard no more about it until years later, when an indignant Sylvia Beach told him that Vidor's film *Our Daily Bread* was based on the book's plot. She urged him to sue, but he wisely refused.

Fitzgerald, aware of Vidor's intention to make a movie about the black roots of jazz, also put the director in touch with Murphy, an expert on the subject. This time his effort paid off: Murphy agreed to go to the United States the following autumn as technical adviser for Vidor's first talking film, *Hallelujah!*

Adrienne Monnier and Miss Beach, who had brought Scott and André together, decided to celebrate the new friendship. They invited the two men and their wives to dinner in their apartment at 18, Rue de l'Odéon and, knowing Fitzgerald's admiration for Joyce, arranged for the Great Man to be there too. For Scott it was an unforgettable evening. Always prone to grandiose gestures, he offered to jump from the fifth floor to show his enthusiasm. The meeting was commemorated by a drawing on the flyleaf of a copy of *Gatsby* originally intended for Nancy Cunard, whose name was crossed out and replaced by that of Sylvia Beach. It shows a table with the hostesses as sirens at the ends; from left to right are Lucie and André Chamson, Zelda, and Scott, kneeling with arms outstretched toward the Master in eyeglasses and mustache and crowned with a halo. The caption reads, "The festival of Saint James."

"That young man must be mad," James later told Sylvia. "I'm afraid he'll do himself some injury."[29] Some days later Fitzgerald sent him a copy of *Portrait of the Artist as a Young Man* with a request for a dedication. In the note Joyce sent when he returned the book, he referred to the fright Scott had caused during their first meeting. "Herewith is the book you gave me, signed," he said, "and I am adding a portrait of the artist as a once young man with the thought of your much obliged but most pusillanimous guest."[30]

Fitzgerald drew some comfort from his brief contact with Joyce. The man, who was then forty-six years old, had published *Ulysses* only six years before and had told him he would probably spend three or four years more on his next book. Scott felt justified in taking so much time with his own book, and he promised Perkins he would bring a finished manuscript home with him in September.

There was also some contact with Bromfield, who lived in Senlis, some thirty miles north of Paris, in a big house set among rose gardens. They agreed on the benefits of expatriation. Living abroad, they thought, was not a denial of America, but a way of looking at it that gave a clear view of its finest qualities; on the terrace of a Paris café, an American felt more American than he did in the United States.

Fitzgerald, however, was no longer sure that the Americans in Paris were the best of the breed. On the contrary, he now thought it was the dregs of his country that were dumped on Europe every summer. "And by 1928," he later wrote, "Paris had grown suffocating. With each new shipment of Americans spewed up by the boom the quality fell off, until toward the end there was something sinister about the crazy boatloads. They were no longer the simple pa and ma and son and daughter, infinitely superior in their qualities of kindness and curiosity to the corresponding class in Europe, but fantastic neanderthals who believed something, something vague, that you remembered from a very cheap novel. . . . It was evident that money and power were falling into the hands of people in comparison with whom the leader of a village Soviet would be a gold-mine of judgment and culture."[31]

John Bishop, living with his family in the château of Orgeval in Tressancourt, near Versailles, saw Fitzgerald occasionally. Scott read him sections of his novel and Bishop, whose standards were as demanding as Wilson's, said he liked them. In Tressancourt the two friends resumed their old literary discussions, interminably exploring the merits of *Madame Bovary*.

Murphy, Vidor, Chamson, Joyce, Bishop, Bromfield—names that represent moments of peace and serenity in an otherwise calamitous summer. Zelda danced obsessively and seldom went out, except to a performance by the Ballets Russes. Egorova had become her Joyce, a prophetess whose goddess was Pavlova—a goddess Zelda was allowed to approach one May evening, but whose perfection gave her acolyte the measure of how far she still had to go. Scott, meanwhile, went to seed. In July he made a "first trip to jail," in August a second: the facts were noted soberly in his *Ledger;* no explanations are given, but none are really needed when you read of "drinking and general unpleasantness" in July, "general aimlessness and boredom" in August.[32] His financial situation was alarming, but he continued to squander his money. In August he owed Ober around $4,000 and Scribner's $2,000 more, for he was now living entirely on advances against his stories and his novel.

When the Fitzgeralds returned to New York October 7, after a rough crossing in the *Carmania,* they had two servants in tow: Mademoiselle, Scottie's new nurse, and Philippe, a Paris taxi driver and ex-boxer whom Scott had hired as his valet. Perkins met them at the pier and Fitzgerald assured him that the first draft of the novel was in his suitcase. A little more time was needed for revision, however. In November Scott offered to send his editor two revised chapters a month until February. And he did shortly send the first two chapters: 18,000 words, a quarter of the book, he said. Then he would write a story before working over chapters 3 and 4, and so on until February. Perkins approved of what he saw; he told Fitzgerald it contained "some of the best writing you have ever done . . . a wonderfully promising start off."[33] These may have been the same parts Fitzgerald had already read to Wilson and Bishop, for Perkins received nothing else from him that winter.

Two brief visits interrupted his work. The Murphys, on their way to Hollywood, stopped in New York before joining the Hemingways at their western hunting lodge. Then, the hunting over, Hemingway himself came with Pauline to watch a Princeton-Yale football game. Fitzgerald invited him to the Cottage Club to celebrate Princeton's victory and got so drunk that Philippe had to carry him out to the family Buick; he slept all the way to Ellerslie while Hemingway, once again, watched and judged. The story had been included in *A Moveable Feast,* but was withdrawn just before publication.

Zelda was more distant than ever, dividing her time between dancing and writing a series of portraits of women for *College Humor* so that, she said, she could pay for her own ballet lessons without having to take the money from Scott. Perhaps she was also trying to prove that she could carry out her projects even if he could not. Aside from the five stories he wrote after reaching the United States, he was dry, unable to do anything but saloon-crawl with Philippe, quarrel with everyone around him and become the talk of Wilmington. His friend John Biggs was called on several times to get him out of jail in the middle of the night. Mademoiselle had fallen for Philippe, who left her to pine while he chased after other women. She spent her days weeping so bitterly that the valet was shipped back to France. Scott's quarrels with Zelda were as venomous as those they had had in Rosalind's presence. He struck her symbolically, if not physically, by smashing a statuette on the floor one evening when Zelda bawled him out for coming home drunk.

When the winter ended, they trekked back to Europe aboard the *Conte Biancamano*. They planned only to spend the summer in France, but, partly stuck there by circumstances, this stay would last two and a half years, about as long as their first extended visit. "I'm sneaking away like a thief without leaving the chapters," he wrote Perkins before sailing. ". . . I haven't been able to do it. I'll do it on the boat and send it from Genoa. A thousand thanks for your patience—just trust me a few months longer, Max —it's been a discouraging time for me too, but I will never forget your kindness and the fact that you've never reproached me."[34]

From Genoa, where they arrived on March 12, 1929, after a stormy crossing, they went to Nice, staying in the Beau Rivage Hotel until the end of the month—time enough for Scott to write "The Rough Crossing," inspired by the Atlantic gales he had just been through. He gambled at the casino, kicked up a row and wound up, again, in a station-house cell. On April 1 the Fitzgeralds were in Paris, in a large apartment in the Rue Palatine, near the church of Saint-Sulpice. Hemingway arrived three weeks later with Pauline and their one-year-old son, Patrick, taking an apartment at 6, Rue Férou; the place was two minutes' walk from the Fitzgeralds', but Ernest did not give them the address.

They did pick up their friendship with the Chamsons, and they made new friends: poet Allen Tate and his novelist wife, Caroline Gordon, who were living in the Odéon Hotel, near the theater. Tate was a Southerner and championed an agrarian society, and his conversations with them confirmed Scott's antipathy toward the industrial and mercantile society he had already criticized in his interviews. On his return to the United States two years later, Scott would choose Maryland, his ancestral land, as his refuge.

The Fitzgeralds also saw the Amazon, Natalie Barney, again, along with Esther Murphy, an assiduous visitor to the Fridays at the house on the Rue Jacob. Divorced from John Strachey, Esther was married again in May to Chester Arthur, descendant of the twenty-first President, and the Fitzgeralds were invited to the wedding. Once she took them to the Passy studio of Romaine Brooks, Miss Barney's intimate for some four decades. On the top floor of the building at 74, Rue Raynouard, they entered what Zelda described as "a glass-enclosed square of heaven swung high above Paris."[35] Miss Brooks's paintings stood on easels around the walls of the vast studio,

each hidden by a rolling blind. As they were unveiled, the studio became a
sort of temple to sexual inversion, a museum of the leading citizens of
Sodom and Gomorrah. A few of the portraits were of men—Robert de
Montesquieu, Reynaldo Hahn, Jean Cocteau—but most were of women
sporting monocles, cravats, hats: Renée Vivien, Lily de Clermont-Tonnerre,
Lady Una Troubridge, Radclyffe Hall, Ida Rubenstein, Romaine herself in
redingote and top hat, and the Amazon, one hand on her hip, the other
holding a whip. In 1928 a series of memoirs had appeared that revolved
around these famous lesbians, such books as *The Ladies' Almanac* by Djuna
Barnes, Radclyffe Hall's *The Well of Loneliness*, and *Extraordinary
Women* by Compton Mackenzie, who had made of Capri a new Lesbos
where Romaine Brooks was the tutelary goddess.

A disturbing experience, this, that certainly stirred echoes in the psyches
of both Scott and Zelda. Since she took up dancing, sexual intercourse between them had become less and less frequent, less and less satisfactory.
Zelda's imagination was dominated by Egorova, a figure of Olympian authority before whom, for the first time, she could humble herself, become
simply a docile object. "My attitude towards Egorova," she would later
write, "has always been one of an intense love: I wanted to help her some
way because she is a good woman who has worked hard and has nothing, or
lost everything. I wanted to dance well so that she would be proud of me
and have another instrument for the symbols of beauty that passed in her
head that I understood, though apparently could not execute . . . and of
course I wanted to be near her because she was cool and white and
beautiful."[36]

Scott, meanwhile, was worried about his own virility. Psychologically,
Zelda had always been the strong partner in this couple. "In the last analysis," he told Zelda's doctor years later, "she is a stronger person than I am. I
have creative fire, but I am a weak individual. She knows this and really
looks upon me as a woman."[37] Hemingway reported that she even criticized
certain physical inadequacies in Scott, "a matter of measurement" that
prevented him from satisfying her sexually. In 1929 the astonishing incident
took place that Hemingway described in *A Moveable Feast* under just that
title, "A Matter of Measurement"; he told of going to the men's lavatory
with Scott at Michaud's, a restaurant at the corner of the Rue Jacob and the
Rue des Saints-Pères, where Scott exhibited his penis for an informed opinion on his sexual aptitude. Hemingway reassured him by taking him to the
Louvre and showing him how moderate the male organs were in repose on
the statues there. An opinion from an obliging woman who could have
brought the organ in question out of repose might have been more conclusive. But Fitzgerald, although he was not a virgin when he met Zelda, apparently had slept with no one else in the previous ten years.

What did happen in 1929? A congenital failure in Scott, or partial impotence caused by Zelda's increasing frigidity? Some light is shed on the question by Sheilah Graham, who shared the last three years of Fitzgerald's life. "Zelda had tried to emasculate Scott," she frankly declared, "by telling him that he was too small in the vital area to give a woman satisfaction." Sheilah said he possessed "a healthy sexual appetite. As a lover, in terms of giving physical pleasure, he was very satisfactory." No gross sensuality, but a kind of permanent modesty. She could not remember ever having seen him entirely naked, and even she, who complained that her breasts were too large, wore her brassiere in bed. "However, this modesty did not prevent us from having a good time sexually. We satisfied each other and could lie in each other's arms for a long time afterwards, delighting in our proximity. It was not exhausting, frenzied love-making, but gentle and tender, an absolutely happy state. . . . Our love, I have thought, was like being in a warm bath, totally suffusing and relaxing."38 But this happiness would not come until ten years later. For the moment, what Scott felt was loneliness, sexual distress, anxiety about homosexuality.

One evening a twenty-six-year-old Canadian novelist named Morley Callaghan showed up at the Fitzgeralds' door with his wife, Loretta, on an assurance from Perkins that Scott thought highly of his work. He had already seen Hemingway, whom he had met six years earlier at the Toronto *Star;* Callaghan had boxed in college and he was a fine sparring partner for Hemingway, with whom he frequently went a few rounds at the American Club. Joan Miró, whose friend Ernest had become, once functioned as referee.

Fitzgerald listened to the young man with great interest, questioned him about his taste in books and read him a chapter from the manuscript of *A Farewell to Arms*, which Hemingway had lent him for criticism. When Callaghan failed to react with the enthusiasm expected of him, Fitzgerald's humor darkened. He put aside the manuscript and observed sarcastically, "Who does impress you, Morley? Would this impress you?"39 And he got down on all fours on the rug and tried to stand on his head. But he had been drinking and fell over on his back. Scarlet with humiliation, Callaghan helped him up. Annoyed with himself and with Fitzgerald, who had been his idol at college, the Canadian sent him a cold letter the next day. He was determined not to see Scott again.

On the following night the Callaghans returned to their apartment on the Rue de la Santé, in a Left Bank workers' district, to find three express messages under the door. Their landlady, a Russian émigrée, told them a couple had been there asking for them. At that moment a taxi stopped at the door and the Fitzgeralds appeared; they were on their way to dinner, but they had to see the Callaghans again. Afraid that the great man had been offended by his note, Morley expected the worst. Instead, it was Fitzgerald who excused himself, insisting that the incident be forgotten. "You see, Morley," he said, "there are too few of us."⁴⁰ They agreed to meet the following evening.

The Fitzgeralds took them to dinner at Joyce's favorite restaurant, the Trianon, near the Montparnasse station, promising that they would sit at Joyce's regular table. Scott seemed so happy to act as his new friends' literary guide that Morley could not bring himself to confess that he was quite familiar with the table on the right-hand side of the room because he had spent an evening at it with McAlmon and the Joyces themselves. So he let Scott lead them to a table—on the left. From the first, the conversation was relaxed and lively. Fitzgerald asked what the Callaghans thought of Pauline, who had received them coldly at the Rue Férou apartment. They hid their true feelings, but Morley did hint that his affection for her was something less than boundless. Then Scott launched into a theory about Ernest's relationships with his wives. Every time Hemingway finished a book, Scott said, he felt a need for a change. He had to have a new wife for each book. Wait until he starts on his next one and you'll see Pauline disappear. . . .

A little later, at the Dôme, Fitzgerald asked if Callaghan couldn't suggest to Ernest that the three couples dine together some evening. Morley was surprised: Perkins had told him that Fitzgerald and Hemingway were the best of friends, that they saw each other often. In fact, Ernest had answered evasively whenever Callaghan mentioned Fitzgerald to him, and he had never volunteered an opinion of him or of *Gatsby*. Fitzgerald, conversely, had been unstinting at their first meeting in his praise of Hemingway and his books. By asking him to serve as intermediary, Fitzgerald seemed to imply that he was not as close to Hemingway as Morley was.

The Callaghans saw Scott frequently, usually alone. One day at the Closerie des Lilas, where he joined them with Mary Blair, Wilson's ex-wife, Morley admired his superb pearl-gray fedora. Fitzgerald at once plunked it on Callaghan's head and insisted that he keep it; Morley put it back on its owner's head. The business continued like a scene from a slapstick movie, each man growing more irritated and more stubborn with every switch. Loretta saw that Scott was becoming angry, and she declared firmly that "I simply won't have Morley take that lovely hat from you, Scott. Give it back to him, Morley."⁴¹ This put Fitzgerald in the position of having to avert a row between the Callaghans. Magnanimously, he accepted his hat. His steaming generosity found other outlets, however. The conversation that day turned on Proust, whose work Morley refused to read. The next day a messenger from Brentano's brought him the first two volumes of the English translation of *Remembrance of Things Past*, with a note from Fitzgerald.

There was nevertheless an equivocal side to this friendship. Scott knew that Callaghan was a friend of McAlmon, who had been the first to publish his work. On arriving in Paris, Callaghan had gone to see him in his house on the Rue de Vaugirard, and McAlmon had insinuated that Hemingway was a homosexual who had made advances to him some years earlier. Aware of McAlmon's malicious side, Callaghan paid no attention to this. He had not felt obliged to break off his relationship with the man, as Fitzgerald had in 1925 when McAlmon made the same remarks, or as Hemingway had when he in turn was assured that Fitzgerald was inverted. Now the publisher renewed his suggestions about Fitzgerald, and word of it got back to Scott. Zelda, jealous of his affection toward his friends, learned of the rumors, and she too accused him of having homosexual tendencies. Perhaps she was projecting temptations or propositions she had experienced in the closed world of ballet. Or her attachment to Egorova may have grown so passionate that the teacher avoided being alone with her.

Three years later Zelda would declare: "I adored her. She lived in poverty and seemed very poignant. Once we took her to a Russian cabaret and I filled her champagne glass with daisies. . . . She seemed to me like a gardenia, so I gave her gardenias and found some Oriental gardenia perfume for her. She was reticent and I don't know what she thought."[42]

Nancy Milford reports that one night, when Zelda heard Scott talk in his sleep after coming home drunk from an evening with the Hemingways, she was convinced the two men were having a sexual relationship. Her accusations touched off a violent quarrel. A year later he recalled the incident to her in a letter: "The nearest I ever came to leaving you was when you told me you [thought] that I was a fairy in the Rue Palatine but now whatever you said aroused a sort of detached pity for you."[43]

The rumors were so persistent that Fitzgerald mentioned them to Perkins. "McAlmon," he wrote, "is a bitter rat and I'm not surprised at anything he does or says. He's failed as a writer and tries to fortify himself by tieing up to the big boys like Joyce and Stein and despising everything else. Part of his quarrel with Ernest some years ago was because he assured Ernest I was a fairy—God knows he shows more creative imagination in his malice than in his work. Next he told Callaghan that Ernest was a fairy. He's a pretty good person to avoid."[44]

All this made Fitzgerald somewhat less outgoing with the Callaghans. Once, as they left his apartment building to go to the Café des Deux Magots at Saint-Germain-de-Près, they crossed the square in front of Saint-Sulpice, Scott's parish church, where Scottie attended catechism classes and where the Hemingways went to mass on Sundays. The Callaghans were also Catholic, but they derided the Saint-Sulpice style of architecture stamped on the neighborhood and thought the church itself was ugly. Scott told them its piers were the most massive in Paris. Curious, they wanted to go inside with him and see them. He stubbornly refused, and when they pressed him for an explanation, he replied, "Don't ask me about it. It's personal. The Irish Catholic background and all that. You go ahead."[45]

When they came out, he rejoined them, walking alongside Morley. He said quietly, "I was going to take your arm, Morley."

"Well, so . . ."

"Remember the night I was in bad shape? I took your arm. Well, I dropped it. It was like holding on to a cold fish. You thought I was a fairy, didn't you?"[46]

The incident in question had happened late one evening some time earlier when Callaghan had come by the Fitzgeralds' apartment to give Scott one of his manuscripts. He had found Fitzgerald exhausted after hours spent in a police station because he had falsely accused a black man of stealing his wallet; it had indeed been stolen, but he had accused the wrong man of the theft. Interrogation and confrontation had used up the rest of the night and part of the next day. Tranquilized by Callaghan's visit, Scott had insisted on going to the Deux Magots with him and Loretta, who was waiting for her husband in the hallway. "Getting between us," Callaghan recalled, "he linked his arm in mine. For about fifty paces he held on to my arm affectionately. I didn't notice him suddenly withdrawing his arm."[47]

When Fitzgerald reminded him of this, all Callaghan could find to say was, "You're crazy, Scott," but he later admitted in *That Summer in Paris* that "I wished I had been more consoling, more demonstrative with him that night."[48]

Fitzgerald had always wanted to watch one of the sparring matches between Callaghan and Hemingway. He couldn't believe that Morley, who was of average height and already paunchy, could stand up against the man he thought of as "the champ," the man who excelled in every solo sport. Morley never dared pass along Scott's repeated requests, any more than he had mentioned the suggestion that the three couples have dinner together. He was surprised, then, when his two friends rang at his door. It was the first time he had seen them together. They had just lunched lavishly at Prunier's, but Ernest insisted on boxing as usual. All three went to the American Club and, as Miró had some weeks before, Scott was assigned to watch the clock; there were to be one-minute intervals between three-minute rounds.

Ernest immediately took the offensive in the first round, but warily; he had learned to respect Morley's left hook. Then, probably to impress Scott, he forgot his caution—and wound up early in the second round with a split lip. At that he charged even more wildly, but Callaghan's legwork was impeccable and he danced around Ernest, jabbing with his left at that cracked lip. Hemingway seemed exasperated that he could not reach him; he threw looping punches that certainly would have floored Callaghan had they connected. Morley knew that his partner could lose all control of himself if he thought he was losing; the first time he had split Ernest's lip, when they had first started sparring, Hemingway had spit blood in Morley's face.

Ernest attacked, Morley backed off and Scott watched, mesmerized. The only sounds were the whisper of soles against canvas, the fighters' panting, the click of billiard balls from next door. Hemingway suddenly charged, but Callaghan got in first with a left to the jaw that sent his partner toppling over backward. Sprawled on the canvas, Hemingway shook his head to clear it. As he got up, Fitzgerald was heard to gasp, "Oh, my God. . . . I let the round go for four minutes." And he continued to stare incredulously at the time clock.

"Christ!" Hemingway exploded as he reached his feet. Glaring at Fitzgerald, he roared, "All right, Scott. If you wanted to see me getting the shit knocked out of me, just say so. Only don't say you made a mistake."[49] Wiping his lip, he trudged off to the showers.

Pale, consternated, Scott tried to convince Morley that he hadn't done it on purpose, that he had been so fascinated by the fight that he had forgotten the time. Callaghan reassured him: Ernest would quickly realize that his accusation had been unfair, insulting. "But Scott didn't answer. He looked as lonely and as desperate as he had looked that night when he had insisted on coming to the Deux-Magots with Loretta and me. The anguish on his face was the anguish of a man who felt that everything he had stood for when he had been at his best, had been belittled."[50]

Hemingway had calmed down by the time he returned, but he offered no apology. To clear the air, Callaghan suggested that they resume the match as though nothing had happened. While they squared off, Scott temporarily forgot his humiliation and busied himself with the clock.

The evening ended at the Falstaff, a bar-restaurant in Montparnasse, in a peaceful literary discussion. Callaghan, however, was not fooled by Scott's manner; he thought the man "had some class, some real style there at the bar." Morley knew that Scott had been deeply hurt. "I knew how Scott felt. . . . He felt bitter, insulted, disillusioned in the sense that he had been made aware of an antagonism in Ernest. Only one thing would have saved him for Ernest. An apology. A restoration of respect, a lifting of the accusation. But Ernest had no intention of apologizing. He obviously saw no reason why he should. So we all behaved splendidly. We struck up a forceful camaraderie. Ernest was jovial with Scott. We were all jovial."[51]

VI. SALVAGE AND SALVATION

(1930-37)

15. THE BEGINNING OF THE END

(1930–31)

The summer of 1929 the Fitzgeralds did not go to Cap d'Antibes. On July 1 they moved into Villa Fleur des Bois at 12, Boulevard Cazagnaire in Cannes, which they rented for three months. Fitzgerald bought his second French car, a blue Renault open touring car. Egorova had recommended Zelda to Nevalskaya, ballet master at the Nice Opera, with whom she continued to study. She was hired to dance a few times during the season in Nice and Cannes; in September she was even asked to dance a solo in the Naples Opera production of *Aida*, under the direction of Julia Sedova.

Scott had written three stories since he reached France (the last, like most of those to follow, was bought by the *Post* for $4,000) and finished a fourth, "The Swimmers," in July. As soon as he arrived in Cannes, he informed Perkins that "I am working night and day on novel from new angle that I think will solve previous difficulties."[1] The new angle involved an Atlantic crossing that introduced a new character, a first-rank film director named Lew Kelly, apparently modeled on Rex Ingram. Kelly deserts Hollywood to settle on the Riviera with his wife, who drinks more than she should and has a jealous nature. They make friends with Rosemary, a young actress traveling with her mother and a young man fresh out of Yale who, for some unknown reason, leaps overboard in mid-Atlantic. Francis Melarky is out of—or, at least, not yet in—this new, 11,000-word opening chapter. Fitzgerald worked on it all summer, apparently without a very firm idea of where it was taking him. Not until November, when he was back in Paris, did he see it clearly. "For the first time since August," he wrote Perkins, "I see my way clear to a long stretch on the novel."[2]

The only thing that seemed obvious was that Seth and Dinah, the wealthy expatriates, were to become the book's focal characters. The beach at La Garoupe as Fitzgerald had known it in 1925 was only a memory now; even the Murphys had become mysterious to him, a subject for psychological and sociological examination. Their world had been denatured by hordes of tourists. "From 1926 to 1929, the great years of the Cap d'Antibes," he later wrote, "this corner of France was dominated by a group quite distinct from that American society which is dominated by Europeans. Pretty much of anything went at Antibes—by 1929, at the most gorgeous paradise for swimmers on the Mediterranean, no one swam any more, save for a short hang-over dip at noon. . . . The Americans were content to discuss each other in the bar."[3]

Every time he went to Villa America, he observed the Murphys, questioning them until they lost patience. After one of these visits an exasperated Sara wrote him a caustic letter: "You can't expect anyone to like or stand a continual feeling of analysis and subanalysis and criticism—on the whole unfriendly—such as we have felt for quite a while. It is definitely in the air—and quite unpleasant. . . . If you don't know what people are like it's your loss." The theme was developed in another letter: "I feel obliged in honesty as a friend to write you: that the ability to know what another person feels in a given situation will make—or ruin—lives. Your infuriating but devoted and rather nice old friend, Sara."[4]

By now Fitzgerald's health was shaky. Not only did he drink too much in company, but he had formed the habit at Ellerslie of using alcohol as a stimulant when he wrote. He knew how much damage liquor does, but he joked about it. In the spring of 1930 he sent Chamson a postcard printed by the Temperance League showing a normal liver and a drinker's; under the first he wrote "yours" and under the second "mine." The effect of the alcohol was magnified by the fatigue of writing a score of stories in two years in the worst of conditions. His efforts that summer to get ahead with his novel had him spitting blood, wakening his old terror of tuberculosis. He went to see a doctor named Villot in Cannes on September 24; X-rays revealed a slight film at the top of his left lung and ganglions on the porta of the liver. Everything else seemed to be more or less in order.

The findings were a shock: he had thought his health was sound. Just before leaving in February, he had taken out a policy with the Canadian Sun Life Insurance Company that guaranteed him $65,000 at age fifty-eight; the letter accompanying his contract said that "you are to be congratulated on your splendid physical condition."[5]

In October the Fitzgeralds returned to Paris, making a wide swing north through Arles, the Pont du Gard aqueduct, the mountain roads of the Cévennes, Vichy, Tours and the Loire Valley châteaux. After a few days in a hotel on the Rue du Bac, they deserted the Left Bank for an apartment west of the Bois de Boulogne, at 10, Rue Pergolèse, within walking distance of the Bois. Zelda, who had turned down the offer to dance in Naples, resumed her work with Egorova, more feverishly intent than ever on being "Pavlova, nothing less." As she had the previous spring, she worked out in class in the mornings and took private lessons in the afternoons. Diaghilev's death that year in Venice upset her, because she had hoped to win a minor spot with the Ballets Russes. To her dismay the only offer she did get was to dance the shimmy at the Folies-Bergère.

Then, on October 24, 1929, came the crash on Wall Street, the start of the Great Depression. Fitzgerald's worst fears, the intimations of disaster that had haunted even his first stories, were now realized. The depression that would ruin his country became confused in his mind with his own physical, moral and emotional ruin.

He saw Bishop again, then Hemingway. The story of Ernest's sparring match with Callaghan appeared in the New York *Herald Tribune* on November 24 in a version that made Hemingway look ridiculous. Furious, convinced that Callaghan had given out the story on his return to the United States, Hemingway pestered Fitzgerald to wire a demand that Morley deny the story. By that time the young Canadian had already written to the *Tribune;* his letter correcting the account was run a few days later. He also wrote an indignant letter to Fitzgerald accusing him of being influenced by Ernest's suspicion and resentment instead of letting him shoulder his own responsibilities. The answer came from Hemingway, who expressed his regret over the whole incident and confessed that it was he who had insisted, over Scott's reluctance, that the telegram be sent; he would take Morley's reproaches on himself, he said, and was ready to settle the business with his fists on his next trip to the States.

This was followed by a letter from Fitzgerald apologizing for his "stupid and hasty" telegram.[6] "The dignified, half-formal tone of the apology shamed me," Callaghan admitted. "Poor Scott. Once again he was caught in the middle . . . he was always the one who managed to get caught in a bad light. . . . Having been insulted by Ernest that day in the American Club, [Scott] was now insulted by me because he had acted to please Ernest."[7]

The confusion had not yet been dispelled when Fitzgerald dined with the Hemingways at the Rue Férou apartment on December 9. They talked about the way Americans in Paris gossiped nastily about each other. Hemingway had overlooked his ill feelings toward McAlmon and had recommended him to Perkins, but a conversation with McAlmon persuaded the editor not to publish his work. Perkins explained why to Fitzgerald, who relayed the information to Hemingway that evening: McAlmon had outraged him by asserting that Ernest was a fairy and Pauline a lesbian, and that Bumby had been born prematurely because Hemingway had beaten Hadley during her pregnancy. This was the atmosphere of calumny and defamation surrounding Hemingway's insistence that Fitzgerald demand a rectification from Callaghan.

Two days later they learned of the suicide of Harry Crosby, a rich and brilliant young expatriate who had founded the Black Sun Press. Saddened, Hemingway wrote to Fitzgerald the following day absolving him, for the first time, of blame for the incident at the American Club. Such mistakes were common in boxing, he explained; Scott had taken too seriously a remark made in anger. It was all because Scott had a chivalric view of sports, whereas in fact the rules were often broken. Why, Ernest affirmed, he had cheated in a bout with Frenchman Jean Prévost in 1925: feeling off his form, he had asked his friend Bill Smith, who was acting as timekeeper, to shorten a round if he saw that Hemingway was in trouble and to lengthen it if he had the upper hand. This was done all the time, Ernest said, and he did not want a misunderstanding to spoil their friendship.

The arrival of Dos Passos, who had just married Smith's sister, Katharine, lightened the atmosphere. These piddling expatriates' wranglings were reduced to their proper proportion when the friends discussed the really serious troubles besetting the Murphys: their youngest son, nine-year-old Patrick, was showing all the symptoms of tuberculosis, and they had left Villa America to place him in a sanatorium at Montana-Vermala, in the Bernese Alps; they would live there until the boy recovered eighteen months later. The Hemingways, with John and Katharine Dos Passos, went to Switzerland for the last two weeks in December; Dorothy Parker was already there, living near the Murphys.

When he returned to Paris, Dos Passos, who had finished reading the proofs of *The 42nd Parallel*, looked up some of his old friends, including Blaise Cendrars, who invited the couple to lunch in the garden of his suburban home, and Léger, who had them home for one of Jeanne's succulent blanquettes of veal. There were no such reunions with the Fitzgeralds, whom Dos Passos found in a stew of unhappiness. The opinion he had formed of Zelda on a Ferris wheel seven years earlier was now confirmed, along with his fears about Scott's alcoholism: "Scott was drinking and Zelda was far from being in her right mind. . . . For anyone who was fond of the Fitzgeralds it was heartbreaking to be with them," he later recalled.[8] They kept to themselves. Early in January the Hemingways sailed for Florida, where the Dos Passoses were to join them.

Fitzgerald, who had produced no stories since the previous October, finally wrote "First Blood," based on his adolescent romances, as the Basil cycle had been. This time he used Ginevra King as the model for Josephine, a sixteen-year-old flirt very like the girls in *This Side of Paradise*. Josephine was to take the lead in four stories written in 1930; four others were rooted in that year's events.

In February both Scott and Zelda felt exhausted and in need of a vacation. They signed up for a Compagnie Transatlantique tour of Algeria, at 2,700 francs each, sailing from Port-Vendres on February 7 to Bou Saâda, Biskra, Batna, Tingad, Constantine and Algiers. Throughout the trip Zelda remained tense and impatient to get back to Paris, unable to brush Egorova and dancing from her mind. "Algiers," she would report, "will always remain colored for me by my impatience and drive to get back, my jealousy of Scott's ability to amuse himself, and an implacable sense of desperation." A single sentence sums it up: "It was an awful trip, though there was a pleasant half-hour with Scott in Biskra."[9] And even Biskra remained in her memory as a suffocating place of loneliness and horror: "The world crumbled to pieces in Biskra; the streets crept through the town like streams of hot white lava. Arabs sold nougat and cakes of poisonous pink under the flare of open gas jets. Since *The Garden of Allah* and *The Sheik*, the town has been filled with frustrated women. In the steep cobbled alleys we flinched at the brightness of mutton carcasses swung from the butchers' booths."[10] Away from the ballet studio, from Egorova's iron discipline and the search for an impossible perfection, Zelda felt exiled, threatened, unable to express herself or to communicate. Her obsession with dancing devoured everything else.

She was no sooner back in Paris than she rushed to the studio on the Rue Caumartin like a junkie to her fix, her arms loaded with blossoms bought in the flower market on the Place de la Madeleine. Thin and haggard, she thought she was being watched, spied on, whispered about. When Bishop lunched with the Fitzgeralds one day, she was sure that he and Scott were talking about her. Her few contacts with old friends depressed her. Xandra and Oscar Kalman, the Fitzgeralds' only close friends in St. Paul, were invited to the Rue Pergolèse. In the middle of lunch Zelda jumped up and dashed off, hastily explaining that she had to leave, that she would be late for her dancing lesson. In the taxi in which Kalman took her to the studio, she changed into her ballet clothes, indifferent to his vehement objections, anxious only to be on time, fuming at the taxi's slow progress. When it got stuck in a traffic jam, she threw open the door and disappeared at a run in her tights and tutu.

A few days later, on April 23, 1930, ten years after her marriage, Zelda's mental condition became so alarming that a doctor advised treatment at the Malmaison clinic, just west of Paris. She arrived in a state of extreme nervousness and anxiety, wanting to leave there at once. "It's dreadful, it's horrible," she complained, "what's to become of me, I must work and I won't be able to, I should die but I must work . . . let me leave, I must go to see 'Madame' [Egorova], she has given me the greatest possible joy."[11]

She was slightly drunk when she was admitted; for some time, she explained, she had needed the stimulation of alcohol for her work. A report by Professor Claude, whom she tried to seduce, ended with the notation: "In sum, it is a question of a *petite anxieuse* worn out by her work in a milieu of professional dancers. Violent reactions, several suicidal attempts never pushed to the limit. Leaves the hospital May 2 against the doctor's advice."[12]

While she plunged frenziedly back into her ballet work, Scott was being dragged into a series of dinners and receptions in celebration of the marriage of Ludlow Fowler's brother, Powell. These were distilled at the end of May into a short story, "The Bridal Party." Zelda was more alone than ever, and more deranged. She suffered from hallucinations, heard threatening, frightening voices, attempted suicide again. On May 22 she entered a clinic in Valmont, near Montreux, in Switzerland, but only physical ailments were treated there, and Zelda needed a psychiatrist. A noted specialist, Dr. Oscar Forel, was called in; he diagnosed her case as schizophrenia and recommended temporary isolation and extended treatment. Two weeks later she was taken to Les Rives de Prangins, the luxurious clinic Forel had opened at the beginning of that year near Rolle, on the shore of Lake Geneva, between Geneva and Lausanne. By 1930 standards it was a horrendously expensive place—one thousand dollars a month—and she would remain there until September 1931.

Forel had banned visits by Scott, but Zelda was allowed to see Scottie ten days after her admittance. Her face, neck and shoulders were covered with a rash that remained with her for the next three months. When it became increasingly inflamed, Dr. Forel resorted to hypnotism, with spectacular results: by the time she awoke from a long sleep, the rash had almost entirely disappeared.

But as soon as she regained some lucidity, as soon as awareness returned of the failure of her relations with Scott, the symptoms reappeared like an alarm signal. His first visit to her, planned for August, had to be postponed until September, and it produced the worsening of her condition that Dr. Forel had feared. The revulsion she felt for her husband was accompanied by fits of affection for a number of women patients and nurses. In November, after another relapse, Dr. Forel called in an authority on psychoses, Dr. Eugen Bleuler, the man who had coined the term "schizophrenia."

Fitzgerald's voluminous correspondence with Zelda and Forel are revealing. His letters show his eagerness to understand the situation, to assess his professional and conjugal life, to bring out his and Zelda's mistakes and, also, to justify himself, to disown total responsibility for Zelda's collapse. Dr. Forel became the moral tribunal to whom he submitted the evidence in his case, often in the form of a plea in his own defense. These documents, which Nancy Milford procured despite Dr. Forel's initial reluctance, are essential to an understanding of Fitzgerald's feelings during the crisis that marked the turning point in his life.

Fitzgerald attributed the couple's growing mutual antagonism, the increasing rarity of their lovemaking, not to any coldness on his part, "as she would have it understood," he wrote to Dr. Forel, but to the fact that Zelda became more and more absorbed in her dancing and could no longer participate in family life, even neglecting Scottie. She was too tired to go out in the evening, he said, while he needed relaxation after working all day. Another bone of contention: he had been drinking more since Zelda took up ballet. "The ballet idea was something I inaugurated in 1927 to stop her idle drinking after she had already so lost herself in it as to make suicidal attempts," Fitzgerald explained. "Since then I have drunk more, from unhappiness, and she has less, because of her physical work."[13]

When Forel insisted, as a precondition to treating Zelda, that Scott drink no alcohol at all, not so much as a glass of wine at meals, Fitzgerald rebelled. He had needed wine ever since he came to France; it was the only thing that made life bearable. "I cannot consider one pint of wine at the day's end as anything but one of the rights of man," he protested. Besides, it was Zelda who had got him into this habit. "The regular use of wine . . . was something that I dreaded but she encouraged," he wrote, "because she found I was more cheerful then and allowed her to drink more." The habit had become a need; when he stopped drinking, he grew apathetic, felt tired and uninterested in work. "I found that a moderate amount of wine, a pint at each meal, made all the difference in how I felt," he told Forel. "I looked forward to my dinner instead of staring at it, and life didn't seem a hopeless grind to support a woman whose tastes were daily diverging from mine. . . . Wine was almost a necessity for me to be able to stand her long monologues about ballet steps, alternating with a glazed eye toward any civilized conversation whatsoever."[14]

So Scott agreed to avoid hard liquor for the time being, but he refused to give up wine. He made a question of principle of it, a matter of dignity. Wasn't this an unconscious, insidious trick of Zelda's? He had already given up other women for her, "and it wasn't easy in the position my success gave me—what pleasure I got from comradeship she has pretty well mined." Giving up drinking would be tantamount to admitting that this was the only reason for his misfortune, admitting that he alone was responsible for his troubles and Zelda's. "Any human value I might have would disappear if I condemned myself to a lifelong asceticism to which I am not adapted either by habit, temperament or the circumstances of my metier."[15]

His intuition that Zelda was vaguely trying to manipulate him, especially by blackmailing him about drinking, was confirmed by a remark she made in a moment of lucid candor. "I can't make head or tails out of all this dreary experience," she said in a letter to Scott, "since I do not know how much was accidental and how much deliberate—how big a role circumstance played and what proportion was voluntary—but if such a thing as expiation exists it is taking place and I hope you will forgive me the rest of my part—"[16]

There had, of course, been no dissimulation when she discovered ballet in 1927. She had openly claimed her independence, had seceded from their union, had plunged with all her being into dancing as if she had found a faith. Sharing this was impossible. She had abandoned all the functions she had filled until then—wife, mother, hostess, muse. Possessed by the self-image she yearned to create, she dispossessed the others. A stubborn ardor fed the flame that raised her and set her spinning, a burning intoxication that charred anything that came near it. Beside this consuming spiritual passion, this stunning asceticism that lifted her high off the earth, how absurd were daily life and its bonds—sex, alcohol, friends, home: just so many obstacles, so many cross fires to halt her incendiary surge.

Now, struck down as she soared, a fallen angel, prisoner of common sense, she tried to find her way back to lucidity, to speak the language of her jailers. Deep in her eczema-scorched body, shrouded in bandages like a mummy, she struggled to rearticulate her illusion through voices from outside, others' voices. She repeated what Scott and Dr. Forel wanted to hear: "This story is the fault of nobody but me. I believed I was a salamander and it seems that I am nothing but an impediment."[17]

At other times she tried to knit her experience into the texture of a short story and so hold off her obsession with burning and with spiritual death. In "Miss Ella" her heroine is a stern, Victorian Southern spinster whose dress catches fire during a Christmas celebration. She falls in love with the man who beat out the flames with his bare hands, and she jilts another with whom she had contracted a marriage of convenience. But on the day she is to be married to her savior, her former fiancé shoots himself. Henceforth she will live as a solitary recluse behind her high garden walls, away from warmth and fire, with only the memory of a sudden, brief blaze.

Zelda's effort at detachment is sometimes visible in her heartrending letters to Scott. "The panic seems to have settled into a persistent gloom punctuated by moments of bombastic hysteria," she wrote at one point, "which is, I suppose, a relatively wholesome state."[18] Or she would dream of a normal future when "there will be Sundays and Mondays again which are different from each other and there will be Christmas and winter fires . . . and my life won't lie up the back-stairs of music-halls and yours won't keep trailing down the gutters of Paris—if it will only work, and I can keep sane and not a bitter maniac."[19]

He wrote her a long letter in which he tried to analyze the disorder in their lives since their arrival in France six years earlier. The sadness and loneliness that followed him from Rome to Paris, despite his celebrity, was blamed on Zelda's illness. "You were endlessly sick and at home everything was unhappy," he wrote. This was where liquor came in, the liquor of conviviality and of remorse. The former—"I got drunk with [Ernest] on the Left Bank in careless cafés"—merely prolonged the masculine rites inaugurated at Princeton, showing that he belonged to a community of friends and peers, and this explained the meaning of the interminable parties that punctuated the Fitzgeralds' married life. His solitary drinking, especially when he was drowning his sorrows, was something else, the sign of how difficult life was: "I was alone all the time and I had to get drunk before I could leave you so sick and not care and I was only happy a little while before I got too drunk. Afterwards there were all the usual penalties for being drunk."

He recalled the year 1926, when Zelda had recovered her health, there was plenty of money and he thought his novel would write itself effortlessly: "I forgot how I'd dragged *The Great Gatsby* out of the pit of my stomach in a time of misery." He thought he could forget his own nature, could gather to himself his friends' most enviable qualities, "a mixture of Ernest in fine clothes and Gerald with a career—and Charlie MacArthur with a past. Anybody that could make me believe that, like Lois Moran did, was precious to me."[20] The luxury at Ellerslie, the entertaining, were "all attempts to make up from without for being undernourished now from within."[21] He wanted to be loved, Fitzgerald went on, wanted confirmation not that he had a measure of genius but that he was "a great man of the world." At the same time he was aware of how nonsensical this was. "Somewhere in there I had a sense of being exploited, not by you but by something I resented terribly: no happiness. . . . I remember wondering why I kept working to pay the bills of this desolate menage I had evolved." Then came Cannes and loneliness after he had been humiliated, first by Hemingway and then by the Murphys. A feeling of inferiority that made it impossible for him to face anyone unless he was tight. "You were going crazy and calling it genius—I was going to ruin and calling it anything that came to hand. And I think everyone far enough away to see us outside of our glib presentations of ourselves guessed at your almost meglomaniac [sic] selfishness and my insane indulgence in drink."[22]

Scott's letter aroused a violent reaction in Zelda, who rebelled against his notion of their behavior, "your working to preserve the family and my working to get away from it." She accused him of "giving your absolute minimum of effort both to your work and to our mutual welfare with no hope or plans for the future save the vague capricices [sic] which drive you from one place to another." She felt that their attitudes were completely at odds and saw nothing in him on which to base a new relationship except his good looks, which she said he shared with the headwaiter at the Plaza and her hairdresser in Paris. And "since we have never found either help or satisfaction in each other the best thing is to seek it separately. You might as well start whatever you start for a divorce immediately."[23]

The letter's acerbity contrasted with the tenderness of others that recalled Zelda's letters to Scott before they were married. When he phoned one evening to compliment her on a piece of writing she had sent him, she gushed in gratitude. But her reactions were unpredictable. She could reply to affection with recrimination, even violence. Yet an attention could also make her euphoric, fill her with airy well-being that she expressed gracefully in the image of an acrobat: "I don't believe I've ever been so heavy with happiness. . . . I love you most and you 'phoned me just because you 'phoned me to-night—I walked on those telephone wires for two hours after holding your love like a parasol to balance me. My dear—"[24]

Tired, confused, worried about his health ("my lungs sprang a leak," he wrote Ober[25]), Fitzgerald withdrew to the heights of Caux, above Montreux, for the month of June and managed to write a story. His time was divided between the frothy adventures of Josephine, his letters to Zelda and the long reports he sent Forel on his patient's background. During the summer he turned out forty thousand words for the psychiatrist, tried to reassure the Sayres and to behave toward Scottie, who was still in Paris with her nurse, like a sweet, thoughtful and feminine mother. At one point he had to grab a night flight to rush his daughter to a hospital in response to a telegram announcing that she had appendicitis.

It was in this woebegone frame of mind that he saw Gerald, who was passing through Lausanne and who was just as worried about his son's illness as Scott was about Zelda's. At the end of June Fitzgerald spent a few days in Paris to watch Scottie receive first prize in school at the end of second grade. While there he met Thomas Wolfe, then a young novelist whose first book had been published the year before by Scribner's. The ungainly, expansive, voluble, exuberantly gesticulating giant charmed the downcast dandy. They lunched together and wound up late that evening at the Ritz. Despite their different notions of what constitutes a novel, they liked each other. Wolfe, lyric and prolific, thought of a novel as a natural vehicle through which to discharge his moods, his multitudinous observations, his Whitmanesque sense of the multiplicity of things. He was incapable of reining himself in, of constructing a book; it was Perkins who had to winnow a novel from the thousands of pages Wolfe delivered. Fitzgerald saw him again in Montreux in July and, having read his novel in the meanwhile, wrote to Perkins: "All the world seems to end up in this flat and antiseptic smelling land—with an overlay of flowers. Tom Wolfe is the only man I've met here who isn't sick or hasn't sickness to deal with. You have a great find in him—what he'll do is incalculable. He has a deeper culture than Ernest and more vitality, if he is slightly less of a poet that goes with the immense surface he wants to cover. Also he lacks Ernest's quality of a stick hardened in the fire—he is more susceptible to the world."[26]

Fitzgerald saw common ground on which all three writers stood: "What family resemblance there is between we three as writers is the attempt that crops up in our fiction from time to time to recapture the exact feel of a moment in time and space, exemplified by people rather than by things— that is, an attempt at what Wordsworth was trying to do rather than what Keats did with such magnificent ease, an attempt at a mature memory of a deep experience."[27] He was so struck by his meeting with Wolfe that, a few years later, he was already uncertain how much was truth and how much legend in the stories about the man. "Some of our experiences have become legendary to me," he wrote Wolfe, "and I am not sure even if they happened at all. One story (a lie or a truth) which I am in the habit of telling is how you put out the lights of Lake Geneva with a Gargantuan gesture. . . . I don't know any more whether I was with you when it happened, or whether it ever happened at all!"[28]

In July Fitzgerald was again in Paris briefly, seeing the Bishops, Townsend Martin, Michael Arlen and other friends. Scottie returned to Switzerland with him, along with her Alsatian nurse Berthe. She paid a quick visit to her mother in which Zelda tried so hard to act normal that she suffered a nervous collapse after the child left. Fitzgerald then went to Vevey, where he worked on a story, and then to Caux, spending most of

August there working on still another. The last week of the month was spent with the Murphys in Montana, in the company of Dorothy Parker.

The subjects of the two stories Fitzgerald wrote that summer are symptomatic of his confusion and distress. The first, "A Woman with a Past," which he did not like, is part of the Josephine cycle; it is set in the years before the war when his heroine, a combination of Ginevra and Zelda, begins to feel herself adrift. The second, "One Trip Abroad," deals with the disintegration of a young American couple in Europe, the same couple Fitzgerald had introduced into his novel the previous year after his Atlantic crossing. Nelson and Nicole Kelly begin their European trip in Algeria. Four years later, hurt, disappointed, demoralized, they are on the shore of Lake Geneva, "the dreary one of sanatoriums and rest hotels. . . . Switzerland is a country where very few things begin, but many end."[29] Throughout their travels, in Algeria, in Italy, in Paris, on the Riviera, they encounter the same couple, a schizoid projection of themselves, which, like the portrait of Dorian Gray, follows the stages of their own degradation. The story, picking up the theme of Fitzgerald's neglected novel, is *Tender Is the Night* in miniature, with the difference that in the story it is a couple —not an unsuccessful artist—who are the victims of expatriate Europe's decadent influence. Nicole Kelly prefigures Nicole Diver, and both recall Zelda, their common model.

To be closer to his wife, even though he still was not allowed to see her, Fitzgerald moved to Lausanne in September, staying first in the Beau Rivage Hotel in Ouchy, then in the Grand Hôtel de la Paix, observing the predatory fauna that haunted the luxury hotels: women on the prowl, diplomats, penniless noblemen who cheated at cards and chased after dowries, Europeanized Americans who no longer had a homeland.

He met Bijou O'Connor, a titled Englishwoman who maintained, on a small scale, the traditions of the Nancy Cunards and Duff Twysdens. The thirty-six-year-old daughter of diplomat Sir Francis Elliot, she was aristocratic-looking, wealthy, hard-drinking; she snubbed the rich and showy Americans, terrified staff and servants, smoked cigarettes in a long holder, carried a Pekingese under her arm and was always imperturbable. She knew Gertrude Stein well, and detested her, and Picasso, whom she admired. This was enough to bring her into contact with Fitzgerald, who was attracted by her poise and her acid, insolent grace. She thought him charming and let him pay court to her, became his confidante, then his mistress. He proposed marriage; she refused. Since he was always short of material, none of this prevented him from drawing unflattering portraits of her and her friend Napier Allington as Lady Capps-Karr and "Bopes," the Marquess of Kinkallow, in a story he wrote in November called "The Hotel Child." "Practically the whole damn thing" was true, he wrote Ober, "bizarre as it may seem. Lord Allington and the famous Bijou O'Connor were furious at me putting them in."[30]

After Dr. Bleuler examined Zelda on November 22, Scott took a few days off to spend Thanksgiving with the Murphys in Montana. From there he accompanied Gerald to Munich, where Baoth was in school. Honoria was then in school in Paris; both had been separated from Patrick for fear of contagion.

A month later, at Zelda's request, Fitzgerald fetched Scottie to Switzerland to spend the Christmas holidays with her parents. A mistake: it was too soon for Zelda, who lost control of herself when the child appeared, breaking the ornaments on a Christmas tree. So Scott took his daughter to Gstaad, where they both went skiing for the first time. This was also the first time Fitzgerald devoted more than a few days to Scottie; he had been reminded of his paternal duties by both Zelda and her sister Rosalind, who was then living in Brussels and who wanted Scottie to come and live with her.

In December he wrote "Babylon Revisited," investing the story with his own problems. Like him, its hero, Charlie Wales, is profoundly lonely, and his financial prosperity contrasts ironically with his moral poverty; like his creator, he is torn by remorse and anxiety. Fitzgerald named Charlie's daughter Honoria (pointing it out specially in a letter to the Murphys), but, he later told Scottie, he really had his own daughter and his feelings about her in mind. In the story he movingly depicts a typical day spent with her during one of his brief trips to Paris: dinner at the Grand Vatel, a visit to the Nain Bleu toy store, a vaudeville show at the Empire—moments of intense joy and anxious affection. He sent a copy of the manuscript to Rosalind to counter her criticism of him.

The story also marks the end of an era, the foreclosure of the almost divine privileges Americans had enjoyed before the Depression. Charlie Wales feels like a king stripped of his kingdom, his past, his illusions. Ten years later Fitzgerald would say that "Babylon Revisited" was his farewell to youth. "I not only announced the birth of my young illusions in *This Side of Paradise*," he wrote, "but pretty much the death of them in some of my last *Post* stories like 'Babylon Revisited.'"[31] Fearing that his wife's and his own irresponsibility—"the traits of both that had brought them to disaster" —would be passed on to Honoria, Charlie wants to wipe out the shameful past, revive an earlier virtue: "A great wave of protectiveness went over him. He thought he knew what to do for her. He believed in character; he wanted to jump back a whole generation and trust in character again as the eternally valuable element."[32]

This was Fitzgerald's frame of mind when he learned of his father's sudden death in Washington at the age of seventy-seven. To his son, Edward Fitzgerald, despite his failures, personified the traditional virtues. In similar circumstances Dick Diver would feel this sudden loss cruelly. "How will it affect me," he wonders, "now that this earliest and strongest of protections is gone?"[33] In a manuscript written at this period, which would later be used in his novel, Fitzgerald paid tribute to his father: "I loved my father—always deep in my subconscious I have referred judgment back to him, what he would have thought, or done. He loved me—and felt a deep responsibility for me. . . ."[34] Scott saw his erratic father in his own relationship with Scottie. He decided to return to the United States for the funeral. Before leaving, he visited Zelda, who was as upset by the news as he. The meeting went the way most of them had. After expressing her sorrow, she behaved hatefully during lunch. "After lunch she returned to the affectionate tender mood, utterly normal, so that with pressure I could have maneuvered her into intercourse but the eczema was almost visibly increasing so I left early. Toward the very end she was back in schizophrenia."[35]

Fitzgerald left Switzerland January 27 and sailed from Cherbourg three days later aboard the *New York*. He forgot his cares during the crossing in the company of an American girl named Bert Barr; she was a funny, witty girl and she delighted him, amazed him with card tricks and told him she was a professional bridge sharp who was using the voyage to fleece the Texas millionaire with whom she was traveling. She and her protector enjoyed Fitzgerald's indignation; when they finally told him they were in cahoots, he could only admire the natural way they had played their parts. He saw Bert again at the Hotel New Yorker before heading South; by that time he was on familiar enough terms with her to call her Mickey Mouse. They met again the following spring in Paris and on several occasions in the years that followed.

Fitzgerald's stories fed on such chance meetings. "Indecision," written in January 1931, was based on his stay in Gstaad. A letter to Ober showed that he planned to use the new setting even before seeing it: "I'm going to write a story about Gstaad, a Swiss winter sport place where I'm taking my daughter for the holidays," he announced.[36] Later he would use a crack that Mickey Mouse had made on deck on the *New York* as they watched the liner *Bremen*, all lights blazing, cruise nearby. "Oh, Daddy," she exclaimed, "buy me that!"[37] Short of ideas, Scott offered her a percentage of his fees if she could supply him with more such material.

Similar offers would be made to other people who he thought might be able to stimulate his imagination as Zelda had done until 1924. He was having more and more trouble satisfying his readers, and his output reflected this. For the time being, he made do with watching the idlers around him in the familiar setting of a Swiss village, manipulating plots to justify the presence of a character in a place he knew. In "Flight and Pursuit," for example, his heroine's nervous breakdown gave him an opportunity to evoke the troubled atmosphere he found in Montana-Vermala, an isolated town, a sort of ghost town, in fact, like the western gold camps where, as in Thomas Mann's *The Magic Mountain*, there was "an air of secret ribaldry."[38]

Fitzgerald's subjects reflect his state of mind, his preoccupations; all deal with the deterioration of an exceptional character to whom life seems to have granted every favor. "A New Leaf," written in April 1931, the same month that produced "Flight and Pursuit," is built around a friend of Fitzgerald's who was also ruined by alcoholism and whose effort to break the habit breaks him instead.

There is not much dramatic interest in these stories, nor much appeal to Depression-stricken *Post* readers with little patience for the problems of rich, suicidal expatriates. Ober told him the *Post* was reluctant to take the first three stories written in 1931: their quality was down, their plots nonexistent and they were not set in the United States. And the agent added some criticism of his own: " 'F[light] and P[ursuit],' 'a N[ew] L[eaf]' and 'I[ndecision]' have been interesting to me because they were very vivid bits of life, but I do feel that in these three stories you have failed to make the reader care about any one of the characters. . . . I do not think it is necessary for a story to have a plot but I think a story must either move the reader or amuse him."[39] A fourth story written in the same period, the one in which Mickey Mouse appears, was rejected by seven magazines. A warning: the *Post* let a year go by before publishing "Flight and Pursuit"; its author's name was no longer on the magazine's cover, and the story was dropped to fourth position in the table of contents.

Fitzgerald attended his father's funeral in the small cemetery in Rockville where the rest of his paternal ancestors lay. There was a reunion with his sister, Annabel, now married and a mother, with cousin Ceci and her daughters, and his uncles and aunts. Scott felt a strong attachment to this corner of Maryland earth, which his years of wandering had made emblematic of the stability and permanence to which he would aspire for the rest of his life. Regretfully, he tore himself away and went to Montgomery to reassure the Sayres about Zelda's condition. Warned against him by Rosalind, alarmed by the incoherent letters they received from Zelda, they received him coolly; a little distractedly, too, because the judge was ill and confined to his bed. Mrs. Sayre was nevertheless grateful that her son-in-law had taken the trouble to visit them.

Zelda, meanwhile, was making surprising progress. Soon she was skiing regularly at Saint-Cergues, in the Jura above Nyon. With Scott away there were no letters from him to stir conflicts in her mind; physical exercise, the feeling of independence and responsibility her mountain forays gave her also aided her recovery. When her husband returned early in March, he was amazed at her lack of acrimony, at her coherence. Now he could see her more often without causing her to break out in a rash; she could spend days with him in Geneva and Lausanne, shop, lunch in a restaurant without fearing the explosions of nerves such outings once provoked. One evening he took her to Montreux to see Serge Lifar dance. Her letters to him grew more tender: "And theres always my infinite love—You are a sweet person —the sweetest and dearest of all and I love you as I love my vanished youth —which is as much as a human heart can hold."[40]

In April he went alone for a few days to Lake Como, made a quick visit to Paris (in both cases he seems to have gone to see a married woman designated only by an initial in his *Ledger*) and, at the end of the month, spent a few days with Zelda at Annecy, on the French side of the border. In May his mother passed through Paris, and he flew there to see her, returning by car with Scottie and Mademoiselle. They were back in Paris at the end of June for Scottie's grade-school graduation ceremonies, in which she received a medal of honor. The trip coincided with Mrs. Fitzgerald's departure for the United States. The Murphys, with Sara's sister, Hoyty, were also in the French capital to visit the Colonial Exposition. Before introducing his mother to these sophisticates, Fitzgerald went through all kinds of oratorical contortions, warning them about her eccentricities and her whimsical personality. Prepared to find a shrew, they were surprised to meet an elderly, small-town woman, a little intimidated, dignified and placid in her mourning clothes.

Scottie went back to Switzerland with her father. By this time Zelda's health was judged to be so satisfactory that her doctor suggested she leave the clinic for an extended trial period. Because she had liked Annecy during her short visit there in April, they went there. All three set out in the little Renault and spent two weeks on the shore of Lake Annecy, first amid the climbing roses at the Beau Rivage Hotel in Annecy, then in Menthon, across the lake. "The water was greener there and the shadows long and cool and the scraggly gardens staggered up the shelved precipice to the Hôtel Palace."[41] Swimming, Vienna waltzes, boating—the happy days were back. Photos show Zelda smiling and relaxed, in contrast with those taken in Algeria, in which she looks hunted, haggard and drawn. These July 1931 pictures give no hint of the crisis the Fitzgeralds had just been through; "[we] said at the end that we'd never go there again because those weeks had been perfect and no other time could match them."[42]

Even the occasional alarms heightened their newfound delight, as Scott felt, for example, when through a lavatory window he watched Zelda wander off to shop alone in the village. His apprehension turned to relief and then to inexpressible joy when he saw that, for the first time, she was simply a woman like any other, that she no longer behaved oddly. "It was," he would record, "like the good gone times when we still believed in summer hotels and the philosophies of popular songs."[43]

Back in Switzerland Zelda celebrated her return to stability in a teasing letter to Scott:

My dearest and most precious Monsieur,

We have here a kind of maniac who seems to have been inspired with erotic aberrations on your behalf. Apart from that she is a person of excellent character, willing to work, would accept a nominal salary while learning, fair complexion, green eyes would like correspondence with refined young man of your description with intent to marry. Previous experience unnecessary. Very fond of family life and a wonderful pet to have in the home. Marked behind the left ear with a slight tendency to schitzophrenie.

Sending Scottie off to Brittany, Scott and Zelda then spent a few days in Caux. "At the Caux Palace, a thousand yards in the air, we tea-danced on the uneven boards of a pavillion and sopped our toast in mountain honey."[44] The setting, already used dramatically in "One Trip Abroad," would provide the background for the beginning of the love affair between Dick and Nicole in *Tender Is the Night*.

When Zelda reentered the clinic, Scott settled in to work in Les Rives de Prangins. Despite his constant travels the previous month, he had written two stories, including the last of the Josephine series, which bore a revealing title, "Emotional Bankruptcy." At peace again, he now wrote two others.

Dr. Forel was pleased with the good her first outing had done Zelda, and he now advised Scott to repeat the experiment so as to ease her back into normal life. An opportunity came in the form of an invitation from the Murphys to spend a few days with them. Patrick's health had improved and he could spend more and more time out of the sanatorium. Gerald had rented a farm at Bad Aussee, in the Austrian Tyrol, for part of the summer. The Fitzgeralds joined them there, reuniting Scottie with her playmates from La Garoupe, Honoria, Baoth and Patrick. Among the other guests were their Aunt Hoyty and Léger. Thornton Wilder came and carried the Fitzgeralds off to Vienna. In Munich, when they went through, the hotels were empty, and they were given the royal suite at the Regina-Palast. For the first time Scott understood the seriousness of what was happening in Europe. "The young Germans stalking the ill-lit streets wore a sinister air," he would note, "and the talk that underscored the beer-garden waltzes was of war and hard times."[45]

They found the same gloom in Vienna. The windows of the best hotel, the Bristol, looked out on the dilapidated baroque opera house, and behind it "the city was poor already, or still, and the faces about us were harassed and defensive."[46] Gerald had already taken Baoth out of school in Munich when he learned that the boy was expected to take the same military training as his classmates and, with them, to shout "Heil Hitler!" Fitzgerald had won Gerald's gratitude by offering to accompany him to the Bavarian capital. As they traveled, the two men compared their experiences, noting the strange coincidence of their private disasters with the onset of the Depression that had stricken their country: Patrick and Zelda hospitalized, the death of Scott's father followed by that of Sara's father (Murphy's father and Judge Sayre would also die that year); Gerald had stopped painting and Scott had abandoned work on his novel. When Fitzgerald remarked how stoically his friend seemed to face his misfortunes, Gerald outlined his philosophy of life: "I replied that of course I accepted them, but that I didn't feel they were the important things really. It's not what we do but what we do with our minds that counts, and for me only the *invented* part of our life has any real meaning."[47]

Fitzgerald would use these ideas in the final version of his novel, and Murphy, experiencing another run of bad luck, would write: "I know now that what you said in *Tender Is the Night* is true. Only the invented part of our life—the unreal part—has any scheme, any beauty. Life itself has stepped in now and blundered, scarred and destroyed."[48] This was the period when Baoth, the sturdiest of the Murphy children, died of meningitis at school before his parents could reach him. Patrick was to die two years later.

For the moment, however, it was a time of hope. The Murphys, thinking Patrick had recovered from his tuberculosis, returned to Villa America in the autumn; they were not to leave France for good until 1933, when he suffered a relapse. The Fitzgeralds, cheered by their successful trip through central Europe, could hope for a return of harmony, could look forward to loving again as they had seven years before. Toward the end of her stay at the clinic, however, it was Zelda who comforted Scott when his notes betrayed his pessimism: "nothing is sad about you except your sadness. . . . You are the only person who's ever done all they had to do, damn well, and had enough left over to be dissatisfied. . . . Can't you possibly be just a little bit glad that we are alive and that all the year that's coming we can be to-gether and work and love and get some peace for all the things we've paid so much for learning. Stop looking for solace: there isn't any, and if there were life would be a baby affair. . . ."[49]

On September 15, 1931, fifteen months after she entered it, Zelda left the clinic in Les Rives de Prangins. Dr. Forel thought the outlook was favorable, on condition that both the Fitzgeralds give up liquor forever and that they could avoid their old conflicts. Loading Scottie and a mountain of luggage into the Renault, they drove to France, getting as far as Dijon before a breakdown forced them to abandon the car. They went on to Paris by train, took rooms at the Hôtel Majestic long enough to visit the multitude of pavillions at the Colonial Exposition. In 1925 the Decorative Arts Exposition had crystallized all their ideas about the dynamic movement of the Jazz Age. Now, six years later, their final impressions of Europe matched the new zeitgeist: the exoticism of the Colonial Exposition "told us an immutable story of work and death. The juxtaposition of so many replicas of so many civilizations was confusing, and depressing."[50] This was to be Paris's last word to them. On September 19 they sailed on the *Aquitania*, the same liner that had carried them to Europe for the first time in May 1921. Their European parenthesis was closed forever.

16. ILLUSIONS AND DEPRESSIONS

(1931–32)

They lingered ten days in New York seeing old friends, Alex, Townsend, Ludlow, John and Margaret Bishop, Hemingway, Perkins and Ober. They found a new city, bereft of its once feverish activity and now an "echoing tomb."[1] The tallest skyscraper, a symbol of prosperity, had been completed during the Depression. "From the ruins," Fitzgerald remarked, "lonely and inexplicable as the sphinx, rose the Empire State Building."[2] What it now symbolized was disillusionment. If one rode to the top of it, as Fitzgerald did, one could see the boundaries of New York—and of the dream of unending expansion of which it was the image: "From the tallest structure he saw for the first time that it faded out into the country on all sides, into an expanse of green and blue that alone was limitless. And with the awful realization that New York was a city after all and not a universe, the whole shining edifice that he had reared in his imagination came crashing to the ground."[3]

He found continuity in Montgomery, which had not profited from the years of wild speculation and expansion and so was not suffering from the Depression. "Nothing had happened there," he reflected, "since the Civil War."[4] It was in this changeless, somnolent land that Zelda and Scott decided to put down new roots. Judge Sayre still had not recovered from the grippe he caught the previous winter, and the household was gloomy. So Zelda and Scott stayed at a hotel until they could find a suitable house.

They found it in the suburb of Cloverdale, a vast building lost among trees. Fitzgerald signed a six-month lease, hired a couple of black servants and bought a used Stutz automobile. While Zelda renovated and decorated the place, Scott returned to his writing. Although the life-style at 819 Felder Avenue was far less lavish than it had been in Europe and they no longer had to pay Dr. Forel $1,000 a month, the Fitzgeralds were still heavily in debt. Scott had never worked so hard to earn his living as he had since Zelda fell ill: eight stories in 1930, as many more in Switzerland until September 1931. He was polishing off a ninth at the end of October when he received an offer from Hollywood, just as he had the last time he returned to the United States in 1927. But that first expedition to California had made him wary. Metro-Goldwyn-Mayer was now proposing a five-week contract at $750 a week; he insisted on $1,200 and got it.

There was no question of Zelda's going with him. Besides, she wanted to be near her father, whose health was still frail. Scott, knowing his father-in-law's low opinion of him, lingered at his bedside before leaving Montgomery, trying to win absolution from the judge. "Tell me you believe in me," he asked Sayre. With keen insight the old man granted him the sole moral virtue he thought Scott had: "I think you will always pay your bills." Wise words, for Fitzgerald would always have debts to square. His moral conscience would be stronger than his artistic conscience. He would prostitute his talent and kill himself doing it to pay the bills for Zelda, Scottie and himself.

Having given up ballet after trying to work with a local teacher, who thought she was overambitious, Zelda kept busy writing. Pavlova died in 1931. In Scott's absence Zelda outlined a novel and wrote seven short stories. She sent them to Ober as she turned them out, but he could sell only one, which she had called "A Couple of Nuts" but which was published in *Scribner's Magazine* as "Miss Ella."

Then, on November 19, her father died. She felt the loss keenly even though he had never been very affectionate toward her. She began to suffer from asthma and recognized with horror the beginnings of a rash. Worn out by the funeral services and the influx of relatives trooping through the house, she decided to go to Florida for a few days. She pleaded her case in a letter to Scott, who finally agreed on condition that she have a nurse with her. Zelda mourned, but she was also saddened by her isolation in a society of women whose talk irritated her. "I miss my Daddy horribly," she wrote Scott. "I am losing my identity here without men." She compared the house to a cracked phonograph record on which the needle always sticks at the same spot. But the appearance of "Miss Ella" in the December *Scribner's* made something of a stir in Montgomery and her self-confidence perked up. She even sent a copy of the magazine to Dr. Forel.

Scott, meanwhile, was coming to grips with the script of *The Redheaded Woman*, in which Jean Harlow was to star as a social-climbing nymphomaniac. It was to be adapted from a 1931 best-seller, the second successful novel by Katherine Brush, an imitator of Fitzgerald's who had made big money where he had not. Not only had he to work with a disciple's book, but he was given a cowriter whom he considered incompetent. The script soon became a battleground. Producer Irving Thalberg, whom Fitzgerald admired and would take as his model for Monroe Stahr in *The Last Tycoon*, did not like the result. His writers had made the heroine antipathetic and had spoiled a subject that was difficult to handle but new to the screen. Far from Zelda, disappointed in his work, Scott began drinking again, although he made himself stay sober during working hours. Only the friendship of a young scriptwriter named Dwight Taylor, the son of actress Laurette Taylor, brought him a measure of comfort; Taylor would become the protagonist of Fitzgerald's story "Crazy Sunday."

At a party given by Thalberg's wife, actress Norma Shearer, Scott had one whiskey too many and made a fool of himself before Hollywood society by insisting on singing a silly ballad he had once written with Edmund Wilson. The next day a sympathetic Miss Shearer sent him a telegram assuring him that he had been "one of the most agreeable persons at our tea."[5] But Thalberg, who had watched the performance from across the room and who despised alcoholics, fired him at the end of the week. On December 15 Fitzgerald left Hollywood, swearing he would never return.

Although he had again been humiliated and disappointed (he had written Zelda that if his script was accepted, he would be paid $75,000), his trip had not been entirely wasted. "I'm not sorry I went," he conceded, "because I've got a fine story about Hollywood which will be along in several days."[6] The story was "Crazy Sunday," built around his exhibition before the Thalbergs and their guests. It is a remarkable piece of work, the best since "Babylon Revisited" and a sharp departure from his previous stories; it was too adult for the editors at the *Post* and the other mass-circulation magazines, who were shocked by the heroine's behavior. After they had all refused it, the story was sold to *The American Mercury* for a trifling $200.

The Christmas holidays spent with her family had upset Zelda and brought on a serious attack of asthma. Florida had healed her once before, so she and Scott went there now. Hollywood had put $6,000 in his bank account, which he hoped would see him through the five months he thought he needed to complete his novel. Zelda wanted to get ahead with hers, too. The beach at St. Petersburg was warm and welcoming; they swam and sunbathed; Zelda's asthma receded. Then, for no apparent reason, her eczema reappeared, disappeared, then broke out again two days later. The vacation was over. Zelda had to be gotten home at once. On the first night of the trip she could not sleep. She found a flask of whiskey in Scott's luggage and drained it. The next day she was hysterical.

Despairing, Scott wrote to Dr. Forel to ask his advice. "It seems terrible," he said, "because we have both been so utterly happy, happier almost than we have ever been."[7] He was to repeat this the following year to Zelda's American doctor, averring that "the nine months before her second breakdown were the happiest of my life and I think, save for the agonies of her father's death, the happiest of hers."[8] Once more he saw his novel threatened, his financial reserves imperiled if Zelda went back into a hospital, as she requested. "What the moral effect on me would be I do not know," he wrote Forel, "and I hardly dare to think what it would be on her."[9] But a second onset of hysteria two days later forced them to the decision they both dreaded: on February 10 they left for Baltimore; on the twelfth she entered the Henry Phipps Psychiatric Clinic of the Johns Hopkins University Hospital.

The effects of this second internment turned out, however, to be less calamitous than those of the first, possibly because the attack was less critical.

Freed of all pressure and responsibility, Zelda went feverishly to work on her book. "I am proud of my novel," she wrote Scott, "but I can hardly restrain myself to get it written. You will like it—It is distinctly Ecole Fitzgerald, though more ecstatic than yours. Perhaps too much so."[10]

Less than a month after she went into the hospital, the book's four chapters were written and typed. It is clearly, even naively, autobiographical. Its heroine's name is Alabama and her husband's is Amory Blaine, filched from the protagonist of *This Side of Paradise*. It chronicles the Fitzgeralds' quarrels, adventures, travels. Rightly fearing that Scott would accuse her of plagiarizing his work—she was familiar with the drafts of his current novel and did base some of her scenes on it—she sent the manuscript directly to Perkins without telling her husband.

When Scott received a copy, he was furious. Only the first chapter dealing with Alabama's childhood and adolescence, and the last, in which surgery ends her career as a ballerina in Naples, contained original material. This was especially true of chapter 4, the best of the book, entirely the work of Zelda's imagination except for the end, which describes Judge Sayre's death. But chapters 2 and 3 were almost straight transcriptions of the couple's experiences. Scott could not complain too much about her account of her affair with Jozan or her details about the first years of their married life, which recall parts of *The Beautiful and Damned*. Hadn't he used Zelda's writing in his own book then? But the sections on the Blaines' stays in Paris and on the Riviera consisted of incidents and situations he had used in his own manuscripts.

Scott immediately wired Perkins to wait for a revised version before deciding about the book. On March 14 he sent a letter of protest to Dr. Mildred Squires, whose patient Zelda was. He said that "literally one whole section of her novel is an imitation of [his own], of its rhythm, materials. . . . This mixture of fact and fiction is calculated to ruin us both, or what is left of us, and I can't let it stand. Using the name of a character I invented to put intimate facts in the hands of the friends and enemies we have accumulated en route—my God, my books make her a legend and her single intention in this somewhat thin portrait is to make me a nonentity."[11]

Informed by Dr. Squires of Scott's reaction, Zelda wrote him a contrite letter: "Scott, I love you more than anything on earth and if you were offended I am miserable." She explained that she had sent her novel directly to Perkins for fear of the sort of "scathing criticism" Scott had already turned on her short stories. "I have had enough discouragement, generally, and could scream with that sense of inertia that hovers over my life and everything I do." But she could not hide her real motive: "I was also afraid we might have touched the same material."[12] In another letter a renewed attempt at self-justification took a firmer tone: her revision, she told him, would be aesthetic; the material she used belonged as much to her as to him and she planned to exploit it fully in her next novel. "The other material which I will elect is nevertheless legitimate stuff which has cost me a pretty emotional penny to amass and which I intend to use when I can get the tranquility of spirit necessary to write the story of myself versus myself. That is the book I really want to write."[13]

Scribner's accepted the manuscript. The novel was published in October 1932 under the title *Save Me the Waltz*, which Zelda said she had taken from a record catalog. A flop! Only 1,392 copies were sold, and all Zelda earned from it, once the high cost of her revisions in the proofs was deducted, was $120.73. Fitzgerald, despite Zelda's remorse, was still angry as well as humiliated that an amateur like Zelda could write a novel, flawed as it was, in three months while he was still fiddling with his own book. A newspaper review that Zelda pasted in her scrapbook was headlined in big type, "Mrs. Fitzgerald's First Novel Places Her on Scott's Level."[14] Scott's reaction can be imagined.

A breach had reopened between them, and it was widened by the feeling of rivalry that Zelda now nursed. But when Dr. Squires, surprised by the violence of Fitzgerald's resentment, suggested to him that a separation might be logical, he rejected the idea harshly: "My whole stomach hurts when I contemplate such an eventuality—it would be throwing her [Zelda] broken upon a world which she despises; I would be a ruined man for years . . . ," he wrote. Yet, he continued, he knew that half his friends thought his drinking drove Zelda insane and that all of them thought that "each of us would be well rid of the other—in full face of the irony that we have never been so desperately in love with each other in our lives. Liquor on my mouth is sweet to her; I cherish her most extravagant hallucinations."[15]

Back in Montgomery, Fitzgerald had to put up with Rosalind, his bête noire, and look after Scottie, who was also laid up. "Rosalind still there," he recorded in his *Ledger* for March 1932. ". . . Scotty sick, me sick, Mrs. Sayre playing the fool. . . . Everything worser and worser. Zelda's novel arrives, neurosis, strained relations."[16] When his lease expired, he left Alabama by car and moved alone into the Hotel Rennert in Baltimore, near the clinic.

Scott was determined not to go back to Montgomery, and he began looking for a new home. Satisfied with Zelda's progress, but anxious that she always be near a psychiatrist, he confirmed his attachment to Maryland by settling on Baltimore. In May he rented La Paix, a big, austere-looking Victorian house hung with gables, balconies and porches, in the middle of Towson Park, just north of the city. The land it stood on was owned by architect Bayard Turnbull, whose son Andrew, born the same year as Scottie, would become Fitzgerald's biographer. The whole property covered some twenty acres of isolated, rolling country covered with rare trees and shrubs and punctuated with rose gardens; there was a tennis court and a small lake for swimming.

This was where Zelda gradually learned to live again in the world outside the hospital. In early June she was dividing her time between La Paix and the clinic; on June 26 she was discharged from the hospital, although her condition was still uncertain. Scott sent for Scottie and hired a secretary, Isabel Owens, and a staff of black servants. He had never had a full-time secretary before, and he expected a lot of her; the first thing was that she not be the kind of woman to romance her boss. She was also to function for the moment as Scottie's governess and, in her spare time, as Zelda's companion, to ride, swim and play tennis with her, and so forth. Compared with Fitzgerald's other expenses, her salary was a drop in the bucket—twelve dollars a week—but jobs were scarce and applicants plentiful.

Her main job, of course, was to type Fitzgerald's manuscripts and, if necessary, his wife's. Zelda and her doctors had agreed on a program designed to keep her busy throughout the day while Scott worked. In the morning she wrote, first on sketches for her second novel, then, when she had finished revising the proofs of *Save Me the Waltz*, on a play. She played tennis before lunch and spent the afternoon painting.

As the months passed, Scott's need for Mrs. Owens's services grew. After writing two short stories in April and another in May, he seemed set to carry out the plans he had made in Montgomery concerning his novel. That spring he worked out a new scheme for it and a new title, *A Drunkard's Holiday*. In August he noted in his *Ledger* that the novel was "now plotted and planned, never more to be permanently interrupted."[17]

This was its seventh version since the 1925 outline of *Our Type*, and it would take final form in *Tender Is the Night*. The initial idea had not changed, as attest the notes Fitzgerald wrote in the spring of 1932, but now the accent was placed on the degeneration of a couple. The subject, prefigured in "One Trip Abroad," drew on the author's experience since Zelda's collapse: the woman's mental illness would cause and hasten the man's decline. The hero, Dick Diver, is a brilliant psychologist who makes the mistake of falling in love with and marrying Nicole, a rich patient. As in earlier versions, Nicole's circle of cosmopolitan wastrels is still blamed for debauching a poor young man seduced by their way of life. But now Fitzgerald managed to objectify that class through one of its members, Nicole. Diver remains the victim, as in the earlier versions. "The novel should do this: show a man who is a natural idealist, a spoiled priest, giving in for various reasons to the ideas of the haute Burgeoise [*sic*]," Fitzgerald explained, "and in his rise to the top of the social world losing his idealism, his talent, and turning to drink and dissipation. Background one in which the leisure class is at their truly most brilliant and glamorous such as Murphys."[18]

This was Fitzgerald's notion of his own fate; the autobiographical element is confirmed in his notes defining the hero: "A man like myself brought up in a family sunk from haute burgeoisie to petit burgeoisie, yet expensively educated."[19] Similar gleanings from reality, with the chronology slightly altered, are found in his note on Nicole: "Portrait of Zelda— that is, a part of Zelda," mentioning her meeting with a "Frenchman (or what have you in summer of 1923 after almost 4 years of marriage)."[20] The couple's children are identified with the Fitzgeralds' child: "One child almost 5 (Scotty in Juan-les-Pins). One child 3 (Scotty in Pincio)."[21]

His new plot was centered on his vital concern, the ambiguity of his love for Zelda, who was both agent and victim of his own collapse. Instead of being a mere statement of the failure of a civilization based on fascination with wealth, the story could now develop dialectically. There was to be a transfer of Dick's vitality to Nicole; her cure is inseparably linked to his degradation.

Bolstered by this new concept, which fed on his personal conflicts, Fitzgerald worked steadily on his manuscript. He would send it to Perkins in October 1933. By that time Mrs. Owens had typed the book more than three times and, as she remarked, knew it almost by heart. An inscription over the front door to the house said *Pax Vobiscum*, but it was in anguish, even despair, in La Paix that Fitzgerald finally struggled through a book begun eight years earlier in a spirit of confidence and euphoria.

In "One Hundred False Starts," an essay written in February 1933, he explained that "whether it's something that happened twenty years ago or only yesterday, I must start out with an emotion—one that's close to me and that I can understand." However promising it may have seemed, any subject foreign to his preoccupations, whether it was suggested to him by people or found in newspapers or books, was useless to him unless it touched some secret chord. His drawers were full of unfinished manuscripts, for he was forever condemned to rework the same story: "Mostly, we authors must repeat ourselves—that's the truth. We have two or three great moving experiences in our lives—experiences so great and moving that it doesn't seem at the time that anyone else has been so caught up and pounded and dazzled and astonished—beaten and broken and rescued and illuminated and rewarded and humbled in just that way before." This is the line that mobilizes his creative powers. A writer's trade consists in exploiting these two or three experiences, "each time in a new disguise—maybe ten times, maybe a hundred, as long as people will listen."[22] The dilemma, then, can be expressed as "plot without emotion or emotion without plot," the plot being the new, unexpected, convincing form that will turn the emotion into a narrative.

Fitzgerald gave an example of the unpredictability of inspiration: the previous summer, he said, he had been hospitalized with a fever that was wrongly diagnosed as typhoid; he described his dismay at having to interrupt work on a short story that was to pay his most pressing debts, his rage at being condemned to two weeks of inactivity and at having to put up with the nurses' chatter. Three days after his discharge he wrote a story called "One Interne," built around his observation of hospital life—or, rather, it wrote itself, providing a new mold for what he had been trying in vain to say for weeks before his illness.

This was a kind of parable to sum up the history of his efforts to finish a novel that had gotten off to a false start with a plot that, for being too removed from his vital experience, had failed to mobilize the deepest resources of his imagination. Only a fortuitous and painful event, Zelda's hospitalization, precipitated and crystallized the subject. Had he then to scrap all the work he had already done on it, throw away passages that had cost him months of effort? "There are often occasions," he noted, "when such a decision is doubly difficult. In the last stages of a novel, for instance, where there is no question of junking the whole, but when an entire favorite character has to be hauled out by the heels, screeching, and dragging half a dozen good scenes with him."[23]

The professional in him rebelled at sacrificing these well-built scenes, the artist hated to unravel a texture in which all the threads were inextricably woven together. The problem at this point is less to eliminate elements alien to the theme as to recycle them to function in the book's new structure. Fitzgerald's solution, at which we have already peeked, was both simple and elegant. Melarky's fascination with his lavish hosts was transferred to Rosemary; it is through her eyes that they are henceforth seen, with the difference that because she is protected by her mother rather than oppressed by her, she can maintain a certain detachment. The couple modeled on the Murphys retain their earlier charm, but disorder peers from behind their dazzling front, madness and alcoholism, and their behavior takes new forms, those that led the Fitzgeralds to their ruin. In Dick Diver's fall, Fitzgerald found a correlative with which to measure the distance between the Gerald with whom he would have wished to identify himself and the man he had become since 1927. This distance was clearly seen in the attitude Rosemary (Lois Moran) took toward him at first (adoration) and at the end of the book (compassion).

At the same time, however, the distance was bridged by the real fact that Fitzgerald was once again able to dominate the situation, to halt what had seemed an irreversible slide, to confirm the strength of the writer in him by recounting the failure of the man.

There is irony here: in 1926, when money was plentiful, his health flourishing, his leisure unlimited, he had failed to grasp his opportunity; when his luck turned bad, when he was in debt, in conflict with Zelda and exhausted by work on stories he mostly dragged his feet in writing, he triumphed. The man receded before the storm of responsibilities he faced, toward Zelda, Scottie, the *Post*, his creditors; five years, he complained, had estranged him from himself to the point that he no longer knew exactly who he was or even if he was still anyone at all.

In this amorphous condition his political conscience grew firmer. By 1932 the Depression had reached catastrophic proportions. America had lost confidence in its future. Thousands of banks failed, ruining and bankrupting millions of people; a third of the nation's factories were shut down and fifteen million men were out of work. Farmers were in open rebellion, fifteen thousand war veterans marched on Washington and ran into a barrage of troops. Endless lines stretched before the soup kitchens. When Franklin D. Roosevelt took office on March 12, 1933, he declared a bank moratorium and announced a series of measures to take effect within the next one hundred days. The United States temporarily abandoned the unbridled free enterprise that had brought it low and, with the New Deal, accepted a planned economy.

Fitzgerald was not seriously affected by the crisis itself. If his income was down, it was because he no longer had the energy he had poured into storywriting in previous years and because he was now spending more and more time on his novel. Despite his debts, he maintained his living standard; when the banks closed, it was he who came to the Turnbulls' rescue by coming up with $1,800 in gold from a secret fund. He nevertheless felt morally united with those of his fellow citizens who were suffering because of the Depression.

After the war his attitude had been one of anarchic cynicism, of pessimism reinforced by his reading of Spengler; now he came to an awareness he shared with most other writers in the thirties. After Roosevelt's election Fitzgerald came in contact with leftist organizations, even lectured at Johns Hopkins in November to an association of antifascist students. He read *Capital* instead of *The Decline of the West* and spent evenings arguing so earnestly with a communist that in his *Ledger* we find the notation "Political worries, almost neuroses."[24] In the notes for his novel he has Diver sending his children to school in Russia to receive an education adapted to the times, and years later he would cast Brimmer, a communist labor-union leader, as the prime opponent of Monroe Stahr, the last tycoon.

Fitzgerald's new convictions remained theoretical, however, fitting into the logic of his criticism of the American system and the power of money; they did not encroach on his hedonistic notion of life. When he learned that Wilson had espoused communism, he detailed his reaction in a letter to Perkins that remarked on how gloomy he had found Bunny: "The decision to adopt Communism definitely, no matter how good for the soul, must of necessity be a saddening process for anyone who has ever tasted the intellectual pleasures of the world we live in."[25] To Wilson, whose long study on symbolism, *Axel's Castle*, had been published in 1932, he wrote at about the same time, expressing his surprise at his friend's deep involvement in politics. Although the stamp on Wilson's last letter to him had borne a picture of Lenin, Bunny had not mentioned his activities. Fitzgerald learned of his conversion from Dos Passos, whom he saw in Baltimore, and from Alex McKaig, who amazed him by reporting that Wilson had spent a whole evening trying to indoctrinate him in the principles of Marxism-Leninism. "Back to Mallarmé," Fitzgerald exhorted his friend.[26]

Fitzgerald told Wilson of T. S. Eliot's recent visit to Johns Hopkins to lecture in a chair endowed by Bayard Turnbull's father. Eliot had stayed with the Turnbulls, and they, knowing Fitzgerald's admiration for him, invited him to dinner with the poet. Andrew Turnbull was there and he recalled the moment when Scott read *The Wasteland* aloud. "In the intimacy of the fire-lit room Fitzgerald was asked to read some of Eliot's verse, which he did without hesitation in that moving voice of his that could bring out all the beauty and hint at all the mystery of words."[27]

He was more at ease in *The Wasteland*, which is in the spirit of *The Decline of the West*, than in analyzing *Capital*, despite his conviction that Marxism was moving with history. Kremlinologist Maurice Hindus had great difficulty persuading him that there was no chance at all for a revolution that would bring the communists to power in the United States.

Zelda took the problem much less seriously, as we gather from one of her letters in which she remarked: "Scott reads Marx—I read the Cosmological philosophers. The brightest moments of our day are when we get them mixed up."[28] And to Perkins she wrote: "The Community Communist comes and tells us about a kind of Luna Park Utopia. . . . I have taken, somewhat eccetricly [*sic*] at my age, to horseback riding which I do as non-comittally as possible so as not to annoy the horse. Also very apologeticly since we've had so much of communism lately that I'm not sure it's not the horse who should be riding me."[29] Oddly, the ideas of communism and horses had also come together in a letter written to Scott in Hollywood: "Scottie and I have had a long bed-time talk about the Soviets and the Russian idea. . . . You will be absolutely ravished by her riding trousers and yellow shirt and Scottie rearing back in her saddle like a messenger of victory. Each time she goes she conquers herself and the pony, the sky, the fields. . . ."[30] We note the bright, graceful writing here, the evocative skill found in many of Zelda's letters, which contrast with the labored, overly ornate prose that spoiled her published work.

Now she wove and rewove her material with the same stubborn patience she once applied to learning ballet positions. Summer was a fertile time for her. She wrote a long and highly confused play, *Scandalabra,* which she sent to Ober just when *Save Me the Waltz* was being released. It is a slightly zany comedy in the spirit of Scott's early stories, but it is weighed down by digressions and nonsense scenes written in a vein of labored fantasy.

Ober could not interest a producer in it, but Zelda met a young actor the following spring who belonged to a local university troupe, the Vagabonds. She had him to dinner at La Paix and gave him the manuscript to read. He was delighted with it. Rehearsals began in June and Zelda painted the curtain. Fitzgerald invited a crowd of friends, critics and impresarios to the opening-night performance. The heat was ferocious and the play went on for over four hours, ending at one o'clock in the morning. It was *The Vegetable* repeated: the play was a resounding dud; by the time the final curtain fell, there was only a handful of people in the audience.

Disappointed, Zelda now placed her hopes in painting while secretly maintaining her rivalry with Scott as a novelist. For whole days she locked herself in her room to work on a subject that coincided with that of *The Drunkard's Holiday:* her own experience with psychiatric hospitals. Her idea was to describe the lives of a man and a woman driven mad by the wickedness of their daughter, writing it in such a way that not until the end of the book would a reader realize that the characters lived in a mental home. Knowing how furious Scott would be if he found the manuscript, she kept it locked away, too. She was probing for a mode of expression, a language like that of ballet, which had given her a taste, she said, for flights of the human soul that were outside individual psychology. One had only to translate the inexpressible into choreographic terms for everything to become clear.

Of painting, too, she asked the immediate and total expression of feelings for which words were inadequate. Van Gogh's work spoke her language: "Those crawling flowers and venomous vindictive blossoms are the hallucinations of a mad-man—without organization or rhythm but with the power to sting and strangle. . . . I loved them at Prangins. They reassured me. . . ."[31] From now on, her paintings would also have this obsessive quality, the bursting dynamism of a universe in flux, forms that are twisted and dislocated and astoundingly expressive. We shall come back to them.

Conceding that painting could enable her to exteriorize her impulses, Scott warned her against her literary illusions; stories and novels are not instruments of self-expression, he told her. This was an amateur's notion. "There has never been any question as to your 'value' as a personality," he insisted; "there is however a question as to your ability to use your values to any practical purpose. To repeat a phrase that became anathema in my ears during the last months of our trying to make a go of it, '*expressing oneself,*' I can only say there isn't any such thing. It simply doesn't exist. What one expresses in a work of art is the dark tragic destiny of being an instrument of something uncomprehended, incomprehensible, unknown—you came to the threshold of that discovery and then decided that in the face of all logic you would crash the gate. You succeeded merely in crashing yourself, almost me, and Scotty, if I hadn't interposed."[32]

Scott, meanwhile, was drinking to forget their constant quarreling, drinking to bolster his courage, drinking to be able to work. In January 1933 he went to New York and fell out with Wilson and Hemingway, whom he had not seen for some time. He immediately sent an apologetic letter to Bunny: "I came to New York to get drunk and swinish and I shouldn't have looked up you and Ernest in such a humor of impotent desperation. I assume full responsibility for all unpleasantness . . . with Ernest I seemed to have reached a state where when we drink together I half bait, half truckle to him."[33]

He was arrested for drunk driving and his license was suspended. A New York doctor told him that his life was in danger if he went on drinking too much; the doctor gave him a small, measured glass that represented his daily limit. On the way home Fitzgerald stopped in Wilmington to visit John Biggs and told him the story, showed him the glass, carefully filled it to the line with gin and gulped it down. A little later he poured another dose, measuring it just as scrupulously before tossing it down. By the time he left, the gin bottle was empty. There was no reasoning with him at such times. His mother, who sometimes traveled to Baltimore from Washington to see him, brought him packages of candy, hoping the sweets would curb his appetite for liquor. An endearing little strategem, and it made Fitzgerald furious, especially when Zelda took his mother's side.

He nevertheless got on with his novel. Insomniac, he prowled the circular room in which he spent his days and nights dressed in an old bathrobe, battling himself and his demons, alone with a sick cat in his faded blue room, watching the bare February branches sway in the wind, and on his desk a paperweight asserting that "Business Is Good." From behind the leaded windows he called "my iron grille"[34] he watched winter, spring and summer move across the paths, watched children playing on the lawn, a gardener pushing a wheelbarrow—a faraway world with which he had only the most tenuous contact. His real life was being spent in an imaginary world populated by Dick, Nicole, Tom and Rosemary. "I have lived so long within the circle of this book," he wrote Perkins, "and with these characters that often it seems to me that the real world does not exist but that only these characters exist and, however pretentious that remark may sound . . . it is an absolute fact—so much so that their glees and woes are just exactly as important to me as what happens in life."[35] Mrs. Owens recalls that in that study reeking of gin and tobacco, with diagrams and work schedules tacked to the walls, he "just wasn't a stationary man—even when he wrote he kept moving around, walking back and forth. . . . I'll never forget him wandering around that spooky house, talking all the time to himself."[36] Zelda's memory was better than his, and he would sometimes go up to her room to ask her for details of an anecdote, or what a friend had said in such and such a situation; "that seemed at the heart of the matter," his secretary said; "they talked and talked and talked. One of them would remember something that had happened and off they'd go laughing and chatting."[37] These were doubtless the good moments: it was only in reviewing the past that they could come together.

In February 1933 Dos Passos went into the hospital at Johns Hopkins. With Dreiser he had been agitating on behalf of the miners in Harlan County, Kentucky, and had become active in politics until he was stopped by an attack of rheumatoid arthritis. Fitzgerald went to see him, but it was Dos Passos who had to buck *him* up. "Scott was meeting adversity with a consistency of purpose that I found admirable," he reported. "He was trying to raise Scottie, to do the best thing possible for Zelda, to handle his drinking and to keep a flow of stories into the magazines to raise the enormous sums Zelda's illness cost. At the same time he was determined to continue writing first-rate novels. . . . I never admired a man more. He was so much worse off than I was that I felt I ought to be sitting at his bedside instead of his sitting at mine."[38]

When Malcolm Cowley visited the Fitzgeralds in May, Scott showed him the hundreds of manuscript pages piled on his desk. When he met Zelda, Cowley understood the obstacles Scott was facing; he said she frightened him: "Her face was emaciated and twitched as she talked. Her mouth, with deep lines above it, fell into unhappy shapes." The monsters writhing in the paintings he was shown were like the ones Fitzgerald wanted to exorcise. He took Cowley aside. "That girl had everything," he told his visitor. ". . . She had beauty, talent, family, she could do anything she wanted to, and she's thrown it all away." When Cowley remarked that she seemed a character in one of his novels, Fitzgerald replied, "Sometimes I don't know whether Zelda isn't a character that I created myself. And you know, she's cuckoo, she's crazy as a loon. I'm madly in love with her."[39]

Increasingly, that love was showing itself as hate. Scott and Zelda had violent quarrels, and their visits to the Phipps Clinic were the occasions for endless confrontations before her psychiatrist, Dr. Thomas Rennie. He believed that Scott was as sick as Zelda was. At the end of one of these long sessions, which Mrs. Owens took down in shorthand, he turned wearily to the secretary and asked, "Now who do you think ought to be in a sanitorium?"

"All three of you," came the icy reply.[40]

That was in May, and after this particularly trying session, Fitzgerald seriously thought of divorcing his wife; but a brief talk with his lawyer convinced him of how disgraceful a divorce suit would be. Besides, his relationship with Zelda was not all dark shadows and tragedy. During the May row at the hospital in which each aired his griefs, Scott mentioned Zelda's bizarre seat when she rode a horse. She vehemently denied this. Well, he said, "maybe it was a schizophrenic horse." Zelda got the giggles: "Oh, Scott, that's really good; that's priceless."[41] Then Scott started laughing and the doctor, who couldn't help joining in, allowed as how it was a good line, a very good line.

In June, a year after they moved into La Paix, Zelda set fire to the house; the blaze ruined the second-floor rooms and destroyed several of her paintings, along with part of Scott's collection of books on World War I. Manuscripts, books, paintings, souvenirs piled up on the lawn while firemen sprayed the building. Fitzgerald kept cool, directing operations and offering drinks to all hands when the fire was put out. The newspapers blamed the fire on defective wiring; Zelda confessed that she had been burning old clothes in an abandoned fireplace. Fitzgerald asked Turnbull not to make repairs at once because he did not want to interrupt his work. So, in a smoke-blackened house with a partly caved-in roof, he went stoically about his writing.

The atmosphere was sinister. It was at the end of June that the *Scandalabra* fiasco occurred. In August Zelda learned that her brother, Anthony, had committed suicide. In September, after spending four days in the hospital, Scott was informed that Lardner had died. Scott had just finished the first draft of his book. Another month to polish the early chapters; the manuscript went to Perkins at the end of October. La Paix, a little like Villa Marie in Valescure, where *Gatsby* had been written nine years before, like Ellerslie and so many other homes, had become uninhabitable. It was haunted by their bitter quarrels. The Fitzgeralds moved into a smaller house in Baltimore, at 1307 Park Avenue, near the Fine Art School where Zelda went to improve her painting technique.

Fitzgerald had written only two stories since the summer, and his income for 1933 was around $12,000—his worst year since the start of his career—to which was added a then generous $4,000 advance on *Tender Is the Night* from Scribner's. In 1932 and 1933 his earnings were half what they had been in 1931, a record year in which he had sold nine stories to the *Post*. Now he was staking everything on his novel.

Scribner's Magazine bought the serial rights to it for $10,000 (*Liberty* had changed owners and dropped its option); the first of four installments was to run in January 1934. He was to begin sending a section of the final version of his manuscript each month from October to January. Six thousand dollars was withheld in payment of some of his debts to his publisher; the rest was turned over to Ober, who doled cash out to Fitzgerald as needed. Various titles were announced in advertisements for the book—*The Drunkard's Holiday* was replaced by *Dr. Diver's Holiday*, then by *Richard Diver*. At the last moment agreement was reached on *Tender Is the Night*, taken from Keats's *Ode to a Nightingale*. Hardcover publication was scheduled for April, when the final magazine installment was to appear.

Fitzgerald was not satisfied with his work; he had rushed the final version through too fast and, drawing optimism from gin, hoped he could make the needed changes in the *Scribner's Magazine* proofs. For the time being he was exhausted from eighteen months' unceasing effort, and at the end of November, after correcting the proofs of the first two installments, he took Zelda off to Bermuda. But his health was shaky, the weather was rainy and he caught pleurisy. He spent much of December in bed working on the last two installments of the book while Zelda, her zest for life revived, bicycled along the beaches. She would conclude an autobiographical essay written some months later with a premonitory reflection: "We had travelled a lot, we thought. Maybe this would be the last trip for a long while. We thought Bermuda was a nice place to be the last one of so many many years of travelling."[42]

Fitzgerald returned to Baltimore behind in his work schedule and, in early January, faced with a number of chores: completing work on the final installment of *Tender Is the Night*, correcting the proofs of the second and third parts and beginning on a final version of the book rooted in the already published first installment. Suggestions from Perkins further confused an already complicated situation. "I know that you are having a hell of a time jumping from iron to iron to keep them all at the right temperature," Perkins wrote on January 15, 1934, "but I think you might consider (I say it with much hesitation and doubt) the possibility of reducing in length what was in the first installment and the first part of the second. It is probably impossible, and perhaps unwise anyhow. . . . I merely suggest the idea in order that your subconscious mind may work upon it a little without distracting you at all from anything else."[43]

Fitzgerald saw Wilson and quarreled with him again and with the Murphys; he was drunk when he saw Lois Moran. He was also preparing for a show of Zelda's painting to be held in New York at the end of March. Then, in February, she suffered a second relapse, deeper than the first, and went back into Phipps exactly two years after she had first entered it. After a month there during which her condition showed no improvement, Scott, on Dr. Forel's advice, took her to Craig House, a private hospital in Beacon, New York, which was as elegant and expensive as Les Rives de Prangins.

Grim conditions in which to work, against time, against his book, against his problems. He completed the novel on a wave of gin and repented afterward. "It has become increasingly plain to me that the very excellent organization of a long book or the finest perceptions and judgement in time of revision do not go well with liquor," he told Perkins. "A short story can be written on a bottle, but for a novel you need the mental speed that enables you to keep the whole pattern in your head and ruthlessly sacrifice the sideshows as Ernest did in *A Farewell to Arms*. . . . I would give anything if I hadn't had to write Part III of *Tender Is the Night* entirely on stimulant. If I had one more crack at it cold sober I believe it might have made a great difference."[44]

By the time he sent the final pages to his editor, a month before the book's publication, *Tender Is the Night* had gone through seventeen versions, twelve of them done before the proofs were revised. All the material, carefully stored by Fitzgerald, who kept everything he wrote, filled seven big cartons, which are now in the Princeton University library. It includes the three major concepts of the book worked out over the years. First there is *Our Type*, composed of three chapters set in Rome and on the Riviera; the same version reworked, beginning in 1926, as a first-person narrative under a variety of titles, *The Boy Who Killed His Mother*, *The Melarky*

Case, The World Fair, which lengthened it to four chapters and located the characters in Paris. A third refashioning of the same theme was developed in 1930, with the narrator eliminated.

The 1929 Kelly version, untitled, consisted of two long chapters introducing Rosemary and her mother and Nicole and Lew Kelly, who would reappear, thinly disguised, in "One Trip Abroad."

Finally, the Diver version begun in 1932 introduced the theme of insanity combined with the alcoholism already used in the earlier attempts. This early material, polished and repolished, was used in the first part of the novel; parts two and three were entirely written in the eighteen months Fitzgerald lived in La Paix, although they were studded with lines and paragraphs taken from at least twenty-four short stories and essays published in magazines since 1925. When, in mid-March, he completed his revision of *Tender Is the Night,* he was, as he later told Ober, "in the black hole of Calcutta, mentally exhausted, physically exhausted, emotionally exhausted, and perhaps, morally exhausted."[45]

Fitzgerald was still hoping against hope that his new novel would restore his standing as a first-rank writer. His reputation had faded since *Gatsby;* except to a few faithful followers he was now considered merely a hack, a mercenary who exploited and wasted his talent. The first letters he received were enthusiastic: he had recovered his genius, exceeded the promise shown in *Gatsby.* Messages of admiration and encouragement flowed in. His peers and friends were unanimous: *Tender Is the Night* was his best book. Only two sour notes were heard in the chorus of praise, but they came from people who were dearest to his heart. The Murphys, to whom the book was dedicated ("To Gerald and Sara—Many Fêtes"), did not like the book, for obvious personal reasons, although they recognized its fine literary qualities. And Ernest remained stubbornly silent. Perkins reassured him on this score, however, by forwarding a letter he had received from Hemingway: "It's amazing how *excellent* much of it is. Much of it is better than anything else he ever wrote. How I wish he would have kept on writing. Is it really all over or will he write again?"[46]

A strange question from someone who had pronounced the book "excellent."

17. TENDER IS THE NIGHT

(1933-35)

Although it lingered two or three weeks on the best-seller list (at the tail end, to be sure), the novel did not sell well—fewer than 12,000 copies during the season; its career ended before the year did. The blow shook Fitzgerald; he had counted on more than mere critical success. His royalties did not begin to cover his advances from Scribner's. He was $12,000 in debt and Zelda's costs at Craig House were running at least $750 a month. Despite the certain commercial failure of his book, however, he reacted with amazing energy given the state of physical and moral decrepitude to which he had been reduced by the trials and ceaseless effort of the previous two years.

He went to work immediately, and from April to December 1934, he wrote a short story a month, except in June, when a nervous collapse complicated by delirium tremens put him in a New York hospital for a week. In May he suggested a series of possibilities to Perkins for the collection of stories Scribner's traditionally published after the appearance of each of his novels; one was to intersperse stories already included in previous volumes with a few new pieces; or to assemble everything he had written on Basil and Josephine in a single book; or a collection of some fifteen stories chosen from among the forty or so he had written since 1926. Fitzgerald also considered a fourth possibility: pulling together all his autobiographical writings of the past several years, a total of around 60,000 words. He finally settled for the usual formula after Perkins rejected the idea of an anthology.

He could not simply send stories from the *Post* and other magazines directly to the printer, however; he had to rework them carefully because he had used many bits from them in his novel, and some of the best of them had to be junked or, at least, partly rewritten to avoid repeating identical passages. Despite his vigilance, a careless printer allowed a description of the Parisian Place de la Concorde used in *Tender Is the Night* to appear in "Babylon Revisited" along with the description of the Avenue de l'Opéra that Fitzgerald had written to substitute for it. Work on *Taps at Reveille* dragged on because Fitzgerald was writing new stories at the same time. "My plan," he explained, "was to do my regular work in the daytime and do one story every night, but as it works out, after a good day's work I am so exhausted that I drag out the work on a story to two hours when it should be done in one and go to bed so tired and wrought up, toss around sleepless, and am good for nothing next morning. . . ."[1]

That year's three best-sellers were all historical novels, led by *Anthony Adverse*, by one Hervey Allen. In April 1934, stung by critics who remarked that he had written only about the rich, and convinced that he had to renew his manner and his material, Fitzgerald considered writing a historical novel, *The Castle*, to be set in the Middle Ages. This he saw as an ideal way to end the conflict between novels and short stories that had scarred his whole career. He would design the chapters of his new novel as short stories that he could sell as they were written, a little like the way he had turned out *Tender Is the Night*.

Disappointment came quickly: the first story, "In the Darkest Hour," conceived as the first link in a chain of eleven chapters, was refused by every magazine but *Redbook*, which bought it at half the price the *Post* usually paid. Discouraged, Fitzgerald laid the project aside until the autumn, when he wrote three further episodes. He knew that he was wasting his time and money, however, and he spent only ten hours on each of them, including the time for the historical research they required; the results were predictable: botched work that *Redbook* accepted reluctantly. The last of the three, in fact, was bought but never printed. Nine months after its inception, the shining idea flickered out.

In general, the quality of Fitzgerald's stories continued to decline, and he knew it. Of the nine he wrote that year, only three were accepted by the *Post*, which now dropped its price to $3,000. His by-line would soon cease to be a talisman that drew bids from rival editors. Only *Esquire*, founded in 1933, was still wide open to him; its editor, Arnold Gingrich, was an old admirer of his and bought everything Fitzgerald sent him. Unfortunately, *Esquire* did not pay well—$2,000 to $3,000 for stories that, true enough, were much shorter than those required by the big magazines and were not subject to the dictates of convention and editorial intrigue. Despite its giddy makeup and the pictures of scantily clad women it featured, the magazine was aimed at a more eclectic and cultivated readership than the *Post*'s, for example, which flattered the tastes and prejudices of the average American. Any subject, any treatment went in *Esquire*. In 1934 Fitzgerald sold it two of Zelda's autobiographical sketches, "Show Mr. and Mrs. F. to Number—" and "Auction—Model 1934," which ran under their double by-line; they dealt with the hallucinations caused by her insomnia and anticipated the big introspective essays of 1936. They were short, easily written, and allowed Zelda to express herself as an adult and an artist, as in her novels.

Three weeks after Zelda entered Craig House, an exhibit of thirteen of her paintings and fifteen drawings opened in a gallery on Eighty-sixth Street in New York owned by their friend Cary Ross. She was allowed to leave Beacon for a day, accompanied by a nurse, to attend the opening on

March 29. Most of the guests were friends—the Murphys, Dorothy Parker and Max Perkins, among others—and the few paintings sold went to intimates. Sara Murphy paid $200 for a *Chinese Theater*, which *Time* described as "a gnarled mass of acrobats"[2] and which Gerald spoke of as "monstrous, hideous men, all red with swollen intertwining legs. They were obscene . . . figures out of a nightmare, monstrous and morbid."[3] Mrs. Parker chose *Arabesque*, a self-portrait of Zelda as a ballerina, and *The Cornet Player*, one of the two portraits shown of Scott; the other portrayed him wearing a crown of thorns.

Fitzgerald remained in New York to await the release of his novel, scheduled for April 12, staying at the Hotel Algonquin, where a few of Zelda's paintings were being shown in the lobby. One evening he ran into James Thurber in a bar. Thurber had seen the show in the Ross gallery and had been struck by Zelda's portrait of Scott, "a sharp, warm, ironic study of her husband's handsome and sensitive profile which she had called 'Scott in Thorns.'" He had not met Fitzgerald until then and found him "witty, forlorn, pathetic, romantic, worried, hopeful and despondent. . . . He thought of his talent as something that could be lost, like his watch, or mislaid like his hat, or slowly depleted, like his bank account, but in his last year there it still was, perhaps surer and more mature than it had been before."[4]

Around 3 A.M. Scott asked Thurber if he knew "a *good* girl" they could call on. Thurber got an actress he knew out of bed and the two men went to her apartment. Scott spent the rest of the night talking to the call girl and passing her countless catalogs of Zelda's exhibit. He was moved by his hostess's human qualities and, according to Thurber, made her the narrator of "The Night at Chancellorsville," a story about a gentle prostitute who is dragged uncomprehendingly through the Civil War battle. Perplexed, Thurber accompanied Fitzgerald to his hotel at dawn. "This was the year," he recalled, "that Fitzgerald made several pathetically futile attempts to interest himself in other women, in an effort to survive the mental and emotional strain of Zelda's recurring psychotic states."[5]

It was the period of Scott's brief affair with Dorothy Parker, a fleeting encounter between two wounded souls. He probably went into it more out of despair and she out of compassion than because of love or desire. "Dotty," who had attempted suicide when her unhappy love affair with Charles MacArthur broke up, was just the person to understand Scott's loneliness and confusion.

While correcting his proofs, he found time to comfort and encourage a penniless, twenty-nine-year-old newspaperman who showed him the beginning of his first novel; thanks to Fitzgerald, John O'Hara was launched on his career that year with a resounding success, *Appointment in Samara*. After receiving a copy of *Tender Is the Night*, O'Hara wrote him an admiring letter. "You helped me finish my novel," he said. "I finished it yesterday. The little we talked when you were in New York did it."⁶ When he could, the young man took over from Thurber in the weeks that followed, keeping Fitzgerald company when he came to New York, bucking him up, going out on the town with him. In the *Ledger* is a remark for June 1934: "O'Hara—a wild night with him."⁷ But O'Hara was married and not always available. June ended in an alcoholic haze at the Plaza with "the four Yale acrobats" and a "crazy week" with one of the women in the troupe.⁸

When he returned to Baltimore, he collapsed and had to go into a hospital. Before he did, though, he sent Ober the manuscript of "New Types," in which he used the confidences of his acrobat friend, drawing a deeply appealing portrait of her. She recognized herself in the story and signed one of her letters to Scott with the name of its heroine, Paula Jorgensen. A few days later, dried out and worried about his awesome collection of debts, he was staggered by the amount of the bill sent him by the Plaza.

Perkins watched these doings from a distance. When Fitzgerald was back on his feet, the editor intervened tactfully, introducing him to a distant cousin, Elizabeth Lemmon, whose reserve, grace and culture immediately attracted him. She lived in an old house in Welbourne, Virginia, near Middleburg, of Civil War fame. Fitzgerald formed the habit of spending weekends there, and an intimacy born of respect and tenderness grew up between them. The circle in which she moved was both progressive and backward-looking. Among her friends was Mary Rumsey, the daughter of railroad magnate Edward Harriman, a rival of J. J. Hill; she was a generous patron of the arts and a militant defender of the poor. There were also novelist James Boyd, who specialized in brushing historical frescoes, and Victor Calverton, the Marxist editor of *The Modern Monthly* magazine, which opposed Stalinism and viewed American history and culture from a sociological perspective. Perkins sometimes joined in these brief weekends; Thomas Wolfe, whose second novel they were carving out of a monumental mass of manuscript, accompanied Perkins on one occasion and spent a night at Welbourne. There Fitzgerald found all-too-brief interludes of peace. His interest in Southern history fed on the learned conversation there and on contact with the countless vestiges of the Old South he discovered in and around Welbourne. It was a sad day for him when, in November 1934, Elizabeth closed the house she could no longer afford to run and went to spend the winter with her family.

On May 19 Zelda left Craig House in critical condition. After the remission in which she was able to write her two autobiographical essays, she again relapsed into alternate states of hysteria and apathy. She was interned in the Enoch Pratt psychiatric hospital, near La Paix, where she was to spend the next two years. Those last two essays—no others would ever be published—were a farewell to her life with Scott. In "Show Mr. and Mrs. F. to Number——" she drew up a nostalgic catalog of the hotel rooms they occupied from their marriage in 1920 until their final trip to Bermuda in 1933. "Auction—Model 1934" was an inventory of the few possessions the couple had accumulated over the years, most of which were to be sold at a mock auction; everything was broken, flawed, useless; the objects' only value was in the memories, both intact and eroded, that they stirred, like the "many impressive photographs of old and very dear friends whose names we have forgotten." After sorting out these relics of the past, she finds that, really, nothing can be auctioned: "We shall keep it all—the tangible remnant of the four hundred thousand we made from hard words and spent with easy ones these fifteen years. And the collection, after all, is just as valuable now as the Polish and Peruvian bonds of our thriftier friends."[9]

One summer day, during one of the rare visits Scott was allowed with Zelda, they strolled along a local railroad track separating their former home from the hospital grounds. She had wanted to go there. "It seems rather Proustian to be rambling these deep shades again so close to La Paix," she wrote in a letter to him. "It makes me sad."[10] She heard a train approaching, broke away from Scott and darted toward the track. He dragged her back moments before the train sped by. This was not her only suicide attempt. She had given up hope of recovering and was burrowing into her illness, refusing to communicate with anyone but Scott, to whom she wrote to reiterate her love for him: "There is no way to ask you to forgive me for the missery and pain which I have caused you. I can only ask you to believe that I have done the best I could and that since we first met I have loved you with whatever I had to love you with."[11] Heartrending little entries in Fitzgerald's notes testify to his anguish and his impotence, such lines as "I left my capacity for hoping on the little roads that led to Zelda's sanitorium."[12]

A slight improvement did occur, however, raising the hope that she could spend Christmas at home. Gertrude Stein was making a triumphal tour out of her first trip to the United States in thirty years. In *The Autobiography of Alice B. Toklas*, published the previous year, she had spoken warmly of Fitzgerald. When she went through Baltimore, he sent her a facetious invitation: "I have a small but efficient establishment here and would be more than delighted to give you lunch alone, dinner alone, lunch alone and a group of your choosing, dinner alone and a group of your choosing, lunch alone and a group of my choosing. . . ."[13] She had tea with Zelda and Scott on the day before Christmas. He asked Zelda to show her paintings and, without consulting her, told Miss Stein to take the ones she liked. Zelda refused to let her take the two she chose because she had promised them to her doctor. Scott tried to persuade her that once the paintings were hung in Miss Stein's Rue de Fleurus apartment, Zelda would be famous, but she refused to budge and the Pythia of letters had to make do with two other paintings.

A few days later he wrote to her thanking her for her visit. "It meant so much to Zelda," he said, "giving her a tangible sense of her own existence, for you to have liked two of her pictures enough to want to own them . . . everyone felt their Christmas Eve was well spent in the company of your handsome face . . . and sentences 'that never leak.' "[14]

The year 1935 began badly. In January Fitzgerald noted in his *Ledger:* "Scotty sick. . . . Work and worry. Sickness and debt. Zelda seems less well." Then, in February, "Very sick. Debts terrible." In March, "Zelda very bad on return."[15] Elizabeth joined him in Baltimore, but her presence irritated him. He had not had a vacation since the unfortunate trip to Bermuda a year earlier, and now he needed a rest. "I have honestly tried to stick it out to the end," he explained to Ober in a letter on February 1, ". . . but even that hasn't any point any more, because I am half crazy with illness and worry, and in a state where each aggravation only adds to the accumulation of anxiety, strain, self-pity, or what have you."[16] Two days later he left for Tryon, in the North Carolina hills, where he moved into Oak Hall, a comfortable hotel on a height overlooking the town's main street.

There he met a distinguished group of residents, including historian Charles Beard and novelist Margaret Culkin Banning, a fellow Minnesotan. He was immediately attracted to Nora and Maurice Flynn, a couple who reminded him a bit of the Murphys. Like Sara, Nora had been brought up to wealth and social prominence. Born a Langhorne, in a Virginia family noted for the number and beauty of its women, she had two internationally famous older sisters. One was Irene Gibson, the model for the Gibson Girl whom her husband, painter Charles Gibson, imposed on America in 1896 as the prototype of feminine grace; the other was the socially and politically active Nancy, Lady Astor, the first woman ever to occupy a seat in Britain's House of Commons, to which her husband arranged her election in 1919 when he entered the House of Lords. Two years Fitzgerald's senior, Nora Flynn had lived an adventurous life before settling down to reign over Tryon. She was a radiant forty, dressed elegantly, brimmed with vitality and wit.

Maurice Flynn, like Murphy a Yale alumnus, had been the kind of person Fitzgerald most admired, an athletic hero at college. He had acted in silent movies and had been a flying ace in the war. Like the Murphys, the Flynns were a cosmopolitan couple who entertained famous actors and musicians; like them, too, but with more vivacity and less constraint, they gaily adopted impromptu roles at the slightest provocation. No liquor was served in the Flynn home; Maurice—his nickname was Lefty—had been a dipsomaniac and Nora, a Christian Scientist, had cured him after their marriage in 1931. She took a liking to Fitzgerald and tried, quietly and without scolding, to help him swear off drinking. His *Ledger* records a resolution to go "on the wagon for all liquor and alcohol on Thursday 7th (or Wed. 6th at

8:30 p.m.)."[17] He soon had the run of Little Orchard, the Flynns' home, where he enjoyed the happiest and most relaxed hours he had spent in years.

Fitzgerald was short of ideas for stories, and in the Flynns' lives he found a ready-made subject for a story. The one that resulted from his conversations with Nora, "The Intimate Stranger," in which he called her Sara, shows how much his talent had lost of power and persuasiveness when it was forced into the conventional mold of mass-media fiction. His material could have been used for a novel, but it was not purified, simplified, linked within a thematic line that kept the dramatic interest rising until the end, as the rules of the art required. Instead, he merely accumulated details and incidents in a kind of monotonous review.

When he returned to Baltimore in March, he learned of Lois Moran's marriage to a high official in Washington. He met Sara Murphy, despondent over the sudden death of her son Baoth. Thomas Boyd, Fitzgerald's old friend from St. Paul, was also dead, of a brain tumor. In April Scott broke with Elizabeth, who left Baltimore. Zelda's condition had worsened. Scott began drinking again, which reactivated the lesion on his lung. His doctor examined his X-ray plates, warned him that the drinking would kill him if he kept it up and recommended a specialist in Asheville, North Carolina, near Tryon. Fitzgerald began commuting between the two cities, making occasional trips to New York, where, at the end of June, he spent a weekend with Mickey Mouse.

Back in Asheville on July 3, he encountered two women who were to be important to him in the weeks that followed. He had met them early in June while living at the Grove Park Inn, a luxury hotel on a wooded hill overlooking the city. The first, Laura Guthrie Hearne, would succeed Isabel Owens as secretary, governess and confidante. When he met her, she was swathed in oriental finery, wore a turban and earned her living by telling the fortunes of rich hotel clients. The pseudo-Gypsy was in fact a graduate of the Columbia School of Journalism, who was in the process of divorcing her husband and who had custody of a son a little younger than Scottie. In a long account of that summer of 1935 she told of her first meetings with Fitzgerald, who tried to seduce her while she read his palm. He had just finished a story in which a fortune-teller figured, and he invited Laura to dinner to show her the manuscript. But his attempt at seduction was defeated by the amount of beer he drank at dinner; he was not used to the stuff, and it made him sleepy. When she left, he was snoring on the divan.

Mrs. Guthrie's highly detailed report is one of the few to show Fitzgerald as seducer, exerting his charm, betraying his impulsive need to be loved and admired. She had no illusions about his real feelings toward her. "He kept looking at me so lovingly with his large bluish-green eyes," she recounted. "He told me how my voice had attracted him at the first, and then he felt something queer when we met for he knew that we were going to love each other. He drank his ale and loved me with his eyes, and then with his lips, for he said, 'I love you Laura.' I told him that it was nice to see he had a sense of humor, for I had too."[18]

That first day together had lighted a fire in her that was doused the next evening when she saw him in equally intense courtship of a young married woman vacationing at the hotel with her younger sister. Fitzgerald's new flame was conquered at once, and the idyll developed under the half-bitter, half-ironic gaze of a Laura who was thrust into the background. Fitzgerald had no intention of pursuing the affair because he had already gotten what he wanted from it: testimony that he existed, that someone believed in him, that he could attract a beautiful young woman. Beatrice, a blond Southern beauty, had charm and breeding that were only accentuated by an oddly British lisp. She had been married for eleven years and had never before betrayed her husband. But she had read *Tender Is the Night* and she viewed Fitzgerald as Rosemary had Dick Diver, with fervent, loving eyes.

This carried him back five years to Lausanne, where Bijou O'Connor had succeeded Miss Moran in confirming his self-image. In his files, under the heading "descriptions of Girls," he noted a "Tremendous resemblance between Bijou and Beatrice." A little farther along he said: "I am astonished sometimes by the fearlessness of women, the recklessness—like Nora, Zelda, Beatrice—in each case it's partly they are all three spoiled babies who never felt the economic urge on their shoulders. But it's heartening when it stays this side of recklessness. In each case I've had to strike a balance and become the cautious petit bourgeoise after, in each case, throwing them off their initial balance."[19]

When he returned to Asheville on July 3, Beatrice went on the offensive, laying siege to him. The seducer was caught in his own trap; the pursuer pursued, hunted, tracked into his very suite. In June he had asked Laura to go to the movies with him to keep him away from drinking for a couple of hours. Now he shut himself up in his room with her, ostensibly to dictate his letters to her, but in fact to postpone the moment when he would be alone with Beatrice. As soon as Laura left to tell the fortunes of the hatmakers holding a convention in the hotel, Beatrice forced her way into the room of her hangdog Don Juan. Laura contemplated with detachment the ravages of love: "He says that she is terribly passionate, almost a nymphomaniac. What a curse that would be."[20]

Two days later the inevitable happened. Fitzgerald went down to the lobby, sat Laura down beside the fire roaring in the vast stone fireplace and confessed. "She did it all," he said. "I was disappointed when it happened, it was just a repetition of so many other times. I am just an old roué."[21] At such moments he felt closer to Laura than to Beatrice and regretted that his fortune-teller showed no signs of jealousy, that she was now completely inaccessible.

He played the game nevertheless, and when Beatrice's husband came to join her on July 14 and Fitzgerald had to take leave of her, he realized that he had fallen in love with her. She wanted to throw everything over and run away with him. They could live together at the end of the earth on her private fortune. Fitzgerald refused because he could not desert Zelda; he was miserable when Beatrice left Grove Park with her husband and her sister Eleanor for Highlands, seventy-five miles away, but as far as he was concerned, the affair was over.

She did not see it that way. She wrote to him several times a day. Laura, who now functioned as Fitzgerald's secretary, knew his secrets and played the Marquise de Merteuil to Fitzgerald's Valmont,[22] except that the problem here was not to seduce a woman but to get rid of one. She read the letters, filed them and listened to her employer's complaints of persecution. Eleanor fell ill and Beatrice insisted on going with her to Asheville; while her husband played golf under the windows of the Grove Park Inn, she rushed to Scott's room. A treatment lasting several days was ordered for Eleanor, and Beatrice stayed on to keep her company while the husband returned to Highlands. The whole hotel knew about the romance; the hall porter was told not to put telephone calls from Highlands through to the ladies' room, on the pretext that Eleanor was too ill to be disturbed. On one occasion, when the husband insisted on speaking to his wife, a bellboy was sent to Scott's room to warn her, and it was there that she took the call. Eleanor, with whom Beatrice shared a room, was beginning to make a fuss because of her sister's long absences and her public demonstrations of love for Scott. And what if Beatrice's husband were to appear unexpectedly?

His nerves shattered, Fitzgerald sneaked out of the hotel after explaining his plan to Laura and hid out in total solitude for three days at a mountain lake. From there he stopped in Asheville only long enough for Laura to bring his luggage to the station; then he took the first train for Baltimore. It was Zelda's birthday, but he hadn't the courage to see her, so he continued on to New York.

He was back in Asheville on August 3, and Beatrice, more passionate than ever, joined him at the Royal Hotel. He forgot all about flight. Since his presence in Asheville put Eleanor into a fit of nerves, they tried to avoid her. Asheville's hotels became the scenes of a game of hide-and-seek; registered under false names, Fitzgerald flitted from room to room, sometimes with Laura, sometimes with Beatrice. Eleanor spent one whole night trying to trace her sister and her lover; she got drunk and fell asleep on the Grove Park golf course, where she was found the next morning and taken to her room. She felt personally responsible for her elder sister's disgraceful escapade and bewildered by its passion. Her already delicate health deteriorated, and her relationship with the lovers took on a pathological edge. Certainly she was attracted to Scott, but she blamed Beatrice, not him; "Scott is a very weak person," she declared. "I have nothing against him, but he is so selfish and like a weak drowning person and he is grabbing at [Beatrice]

like a straw. . . . But if he is to be saved someone will have to go on helping him."[23] Was this a role in which she saw herself?

Laura, meanwhile, was busy inventing lies to explain Beatrice's absences
both to Eleanor and to her husband, who was forever phoning from Texas.
She felt as though she were having a great love affair by proxy and was
apparently an enthusiastic confidante. "'August,'" she noted, "has been a hot
month so far—in every way! If I ever have to live through more excitement
in a short time . . . I hope I will be able to endure it. For this has been
night and day and actions and strange experiences that do not come frequently in a lifetime. I have long wanted not to be an actor in the drama of
life but to be on the outskirts . . . seeing everything but not being the principal actor—mainly perhaps because I am afraid of being hurt. Well, that is
the way it has been. I have even had a deciding influence on the lives of
those who were the principal actors."[24]

That was indeed her role throughout the summer, a supporting player attentively ad-libbing on the star's cues, stepping between him and Beatrice
when he asked her to, or smoothing the way to a meeting, relaying an
angry husband's phone messages and mollifying him with lies, consoling
Scott, comforting Beatrice, babying Eleanor. She was the only person to
maintain good relations with all four principals, all of whom considered her
their ally. A tireless female Harlequin, she bounded from her bed like a jack
out of its box when the phone rang; she was always there in a pinch, always
available, at midnight or at dawn, always ready to fish a fresh alibi from her
bag of tricks. When the stars cracked up, one after the other, and collapsed
around her, she kept going, drunk with emotion, feeding on passion by
proxy.

The situation worsened; the tension became intolerable. Scott was not
eating, and he slept only a few hours a night. Eleanor charged that Scott
tried to seduce her. She refused to consult a psychiatrist, and a nurse was
hired to keep constant watch over her. Beatrice went to pieces and phoned
her husband in tears. He flew to Asheville with a Dr. Cole, the family doctor Eleanor insisted on seeing. Scott expected, and dreaded, a showdown; he
kept a can opener on his table as a defensive weapon if he was attacked. He
spoke to the physician, won his confidence, told him the whole story,
confessed his fears and his determination to meet violence with violence.

The crisis passed without hostilities coming into the open. A day later, on
August 8, Fitzgerald again packed his bags to leave Asheville. He called
Cole to announce his decision and was told that on the doctor's advice, Beatrice, her husband and her sister had left early that morning. Scott, Laura
reported, shouted, wept and ranted. The adventure was over, as he had so
often wished, but now he could not bear the separation.

Beatrice continued to phone him and to write heartrending letters. Both
sisters were hospitalized and the husband suffered a critical heart attack.

Even then, Scott was not out of the woods. A few days later he noticed suspicious spots on his chest and legs. He was sure it was syphilis contracted on his last trip to New York, and he was horrified at the thought that he might have infected Beatrice. He considered suicide, but changed his mind: killing himself would invalidate his life insurance. He wrote to Dr. Cole, warning him of this new horror and asking his advice. Then he worked up the courage to see a doctor—under a false name—in a city some distance from Asheville. When he phoned two days later to learn the results of the tests and was told that he did not have syphilis after all, he was too weak even to rejoice. "I would like a blank period in my life," he told Laura. "I have suffered too much and too long. I'd like not to feel for a while, and I'm tired of life."[25]

Fitzgerald now bitterly regretted the six weeks he had wasted; he saw the disorder in his life as symptomatic of a more general crisis. "Everyone is turning to sex," he informed Laura. "It is in the air, as is the case always before great catastrophes."[26] He tried to cut down on his beer intake—he had been swilling as many as thirty-seven bottles a day—which kept him from eating properly and made him logy. In a letter to James Boyd, he cynically summed up his idyll: "I have just emerged not totally unscathed, I'm afraid, from a short violent love affair. . . . I had done much better to let it alone because this was scarcely a time in my life for one more emotion. Still it's done now and tied up in cellophane and—and maybe someday I'll get a chapter out of it. God, what a hell of a profession to be a writer."[27] He was, in any event, vigorous enough to write a radio skit that brought him $700 and to finish a short story, but when he left Asheville for Baltimore on September 29, his physical condition, under the stress of the summer's excitement, was worse than it had been when he arrived there. Back he went into the hospital.

There he found the "blank period" he sought, a holiday from care, temporary abdication of his responsibilities. Before he left Asheville, he had written to Ober of his weariness of life: "If I would only die, at best she [Scotty] and Zelda would have the Life Insurance and it would be a general good riddance, but it seems as if life had been playing some long joke with me for the last eight months and can't decide when to leave off."[28] Now what had been a purgatory haunted by nurses and doctors became a sanctuary where he could stop struggling—though not long enough to forget his troubles completely, to forget that even this fleeting blankness had to be paid for. Hospitals, on which *Tender Is the Night* had already focused, became just another subject, to be milked as quickly as possible. The only story he sold to the *Post* that year, "Zone of Accident," picked up the setting and characters from "One Interne," which had opened the series in 1932. Here again is the huge, livid statue looming in the hospital lobby, "a gigantic Christ [gesturing] in marble pity over the entrance hall."[29] It would appear again in "Trouble," the last of his stories the *Post* would buy, looking more like the statue of the Commander in *Don Juan* than it did like the Redeemer.

The respite for Fitzgerald was brief. Scottie returned from the vacation she had spent with the Obers and he had to take charge of her again. He left the hospital after a five-day stay, left his daughter with Mrs. Owens while he looked for a new home, a cheaper and less spacious place, since Zelda seemed condemned to internment for life. He sent news of himself to Laura: Scottie had appeared "like a sun goddess . . . all radiant and glowing"; Zelda was a little better, needed only one nurse now and was no longer obsessed with suicide. "It was wonderful to sit with her head on my shoulder for hours and feel as I always have even now, closer to her than to any other human being. This is not a denial of other emotions—Oh, you understand."[30]

He rented an apartment in the Cambridge Arms, an apartment building facing Johns Hopkins University with windows giving on the campus. Living with Scottie was not always easy. She was fourteen now, with a fully formed personality and an independent spirit that was beginning to give her father new cause for alarm. Even these cares were recycled, packaged and offered for sale. Exploiting his situation, he offered CBS a ten-minute serial, to be aired once a week for thirteen weeks, about a father's trials with his rebellious daughter. When this was turned down, he tried to work the idea into material for the *Post*, hoping to write a series of stories about Gwen, his young heroine, comparable with the Josephine series.

But Fitzgerald's luck remained stubbornly bad, and writing came hard. The manuscripts he sent Ober were incoherent, even illegible; the agent wept one day when he showed a visitor beer-stained pages covered with undecipherable corrections. Fitzgerald wore himself down trying to reconquer the magazine market. Even the stuff he sent Gingrich for *Esquire* was unusable. To top it all off, his neighbor at the Cambridge Arms was a pianist whose arpeggios were all too audible through the thin walls. One morning in November he gave Scottie a ten-dollar bill, told Mrs. Owens he was placing his daughter in her care and, with no luggage, drove out of Baltimore.

He headed South, pulling up six hundred miles later in Hendersonville, a small town near Asheville, where he took a two-dollar-a-day room in a third-rate hotel called the Skyland. "I arrived here weak as hell, got the grippe and spat blood again (1st time in 9 months) and took to bed for six days," he reported to Ober.[31] Broke, absolutely alone, he completed his first story about Gwen Bowers, the thirteen-year-old girl "too cute for words," through whom he hoped to revive the propositions he had made to the *Post*.

Fitzgerald still had the courage to view his situation with irony. "Money again rears its ugly head," he commented in his letter to Ober. "I am getting accustomed to poverty and bankruptcy (in fact for myself I rather enjoy washing my own clothes and eating 20 cent meals twice a day, after so many years in the flesh pots)—don't worry, this is only half true though I did it for the 1st week here to penalize myself for the expense of the journey. *But* I do object to the jails and I have almost $200 due on income tax the 15th (what a typically modern joke this is—me, with $11 in the bank at the moment)."

This might have been an oblique way to tap Ober for a loan, but the same details and the same detachment recur in a note in his files: "It was fun to be poor—especially when you haven't enough liver power for an appetite. But the air is fine here and I liked what I had—and there was nothing to do about it anyhow because I was afraid to cash any checks and I had to save enough for postage for the story. But it was funny coming into the hotel and the very deferential clerk not knowing that I was not only thousands, nay tens of thousands in debt, but had less than 40 cents cash in the world and probably a $13 deficit at my bank. . . . Nevertheless I haven't told you the half of it, i.e., my underwear, I started with a pair of pajama pants—*just that.* . . . I washed my two handkerchiefs and my shirt every night, but the pajama trousers I had to wear all the time and I am presenting it to the Hendersonville Museum."[32]

He lived on the proceeds from an essay he wrote soon after reaching Hendersonville and sold directly to *Esquire* on November 18 for $200. Gingrich, who had published three short short stories at the beginning of the year, had met with Fitzgerald in Baltimore and asked him for more contributions. Scott had confessed that, at the moment, he could not write a word. Knowing he was broke, Gingrich had urged him to submit anything at all—anything that would justify the sending of a check. Even a dozen pages covered with "I can't write" five hundred times could go down in the records as a manuscript from Fitzgerald. Scott then agreed to write everything he could about the fact that he couldn't write.

And this is precisely what he did in Hendersonville. What he sent was "The Crack-Up."

This was the first of a series of three articles he wrote in the late autumn of 1935 in the confessional tone of the 1933 "One Hundred False Starts" and of "Sleeping and Waking," published in 1934. Others were to follow in 1936—"Afternoon of an Author," "Author's House," "An Author's Mother," also based on his recent experience, written in a minor tone of disabused lucidity and assumed despair. The end of "Sleeping and Waking," about his insomnia while he was writing *Tender Is the Night*, anticipated the tone of "The Crack-Up," his middle-of-the-night anguish when memory and remorse overwhelmed him. "Waste and horror—what I might have been and done that is lost, spent, gone, dissipated, unrecapturable. I could have acted thus, refrained from this, been bold where I was timid, cautious where I was rash." This was the soul's night, metaphysical solitude, the moment of truth. "What if this night prefigured the night after death—what if all thereafter was an eternal quivering on the edge of an abyss, with everything base and vicious in oneself urging one forward and the baseness and viciousness of the world just ahead. No choice, no road, no hope—only the endless repetition of the sordid and the semi-tragic. Or to stand forever, perhaps, on the threshold of life unable to pass it and return to it. I am a ghost now as the clock strikes four."[33]

This afterlife foretasted, this nether world that coexisted with everyday life—this was the pale purgatory in which Fitzgerald gyrated during those years of grief. In "Afternoon of an Author" he described himself as a cautious old man, a sick man living on borrowed time. Before getting up from his desk ("I'm just stale—I shouldn't have touched a pencil for two days"), he stares at his reflection in a mirror: "The perfect neurotic. . . . By-product of an idea, slag of a dream." He makes a celebration out of a bus ride on a sunny April day, as though he were leaving on vacation, just a spectator of the world who is suddenly, fleetingly reincarnated, revived by the sight of beauty: "There were suddenly brightly dressed girls, all very beautiful—he thought he had never seen such beautiful girls . . . dressed in real colors all the way from six to thirty, no plans or struggles in their faces, only a state of sweet suspension, provocative and serene. He loved life terribly for a minute, not wanting to give it up at all."[34] But this puff of vitality worries him, and the next line—"He thought perhaps he had made a mistake in coming out so soon"—brings him back to his feeling of precariousness, of being a visitor from the beyond.

The brief, shattering understanding that the world still existed and that living in it was good lends poignancy to the fragments published in *Esquire*. "The Lost Decade," run in the magazine four years later, may be the one that most intensely conveys the particularity of what might be called the Lazarus look. It's the story of an architect who resurfaces after a ten-year drunk. When he returns among the living, he is asked what he wants to see in New York and he replies: "Well—the back of people's heads . . . Their necks—how their heads are joined to their bodies. I'd like to hear what those two little girls are saying to their father. Not exactly what they're saying but whether the words float or submerge, how their mouths shut when they've finished speaking. Just a matter of rhythm . . . The weight of spoons, so light." When his guide suggests they visit a skyscraper he designed ten years earlier, he refuses and insists, with the obstinacy of a man who by a miracle has rediscovered the world of men, on concentrating his attention on the lowly but fundamental details of daily life: "I wouldn't ever be able to see it now. I simply want to see how people walk and what their clothes and shoes and hats are made of. And their eyes and hands. Would you mind shaking hands with me?"[35] The lyricism of the days of *The Great Gatsby* is gone, but there is the sense of wonder that a visitor from another planet would feel.

When the reader emerges from this rediscovery of naked reality perceived in its original freshness, he, like the architect's guide, begins to doubt his own existence. He too feels a need to finger the cloth he is wearing, to heft a glove in his hand, to run his hand over the grain of the stone in a skyscraper that, until then, had been as abstract as a symbol. Such is the power of Fitzgerald's imagination—never so alive as during those dead years —to make people see and feel the world with senses sharpened by the nearness of the void. "The sense of things, the feel of things, the hint of rain in the wind on the cheek,"[36] these are what subsist of the great debacle: a sense of, and a fierce love of, life really lived.

Everything Fitzgerald did, privately and publicly, was a step in his search for this intense feeling of the newness of life. All his follies, his excesses were aimed at breaking through appearances to the heart of the mystery, at feeling himself live as though the world had just been created—or was about to disappear. And all his nostalgia centered on those wondrous times of childhood and youth when this feeling of strangeness gave every minute its specific value. Love, money, liquor were all ways for him to alter his field of vision, to make way for the unpredictable, to regain that lost innocence, even if this meant he had to concede the erosion of his senses, even if the unheard-of grew commonplace, even if he had to cheat in his search for reality—the unprecedented event, its strangeness fully recognized and felt.

His inability to survive this acceleration of his mission is reflected in his writing. Each novel, every story was meant as a trap in which to capture something unprecedented. He recognized their futility: "The conjuror's hat was empty. To draw things out of it had long been a sort of sleight of hand, and now, to change the metaphor, I was off the dispensing end of the relief roll forever."[37]

18. THE CRACK-UP

(1936–37)

It was when he thought he had nothing else to say that he found the subject destined for him, and when he was convinced he could no longer write that he developed a new style, sober and effective. For he no longer wrote to please. He stopped worrying about his readers. No more entertainments; he went for what was essential—and it came to him: what he was, what he had become, what his illusions had made of him, the breach, the crack-up that estranged him from himself and others.

"The Crack-Up": the title suggests the dismemberment of an empire, the failure of an enterprise, the Wall Street crash, as well as a nervous breakdown. This in turn evokes the personal moral bankruptcy that follows from a mass depression. Joy in life was, after all, merely a passing, exceptional state. "It was not the natural thing but the unnatural—unnatural as the Boom; and my recent experience parallels the wave of despair that swept the nation when the Boom was over."[1] Depression, breakdown, crack-up: a single moral reality. Word and concept are so compelling that Fitzgerald had to coin a word for a macabre title given to one of the countless lists of the vanquished scattered through his papers: "Necrology and Breakdownology." These lists resound like an obsessive appeal to the dead, the suicides, the mentally ill who haunted his memory. On one page, for example, he drew a circle and around it wrote the names of the vanished, like so many ghosts invited to a funeral feast, Boyd, Lardner, Emily Vanderbilt, Mary Rumsey, Julian (the hero of "A New Leaf") and others; presiding at this symbolic table is Zelda, the archfigure of the dispossessed.

It was not just his friends, the ones he listed, who filled the ranks of history's victims. The wreckage of a boom based on illusion and euphoria was matched by an inner ruin that showed itself in lost vitality, an exhaustion of nervous energy, universal pessimism and a morbid attraction to nothingness. Harry Crosby's suicide, the nervous breakdown of Edmund Wilson and many others had been preludes to a kind of general pathological crisis, as one of them, Carl Van Doren, noted in an essay called "Private Depression" when he remarked that "in the midst of the general depression each man had a depression of his own." His experience resembled Fitzgerald's in many particulars. "The collapse of Wall Street," he wrote, "did not at once affect me, and my income in 1930 was larger than in 1929, and in 1931 larger still. My own depression was far more than simple economics. It was surfeit and lethargy, soreness and inertness together."[2]

In the triptych of Fitzgerald essays called "The Crack-Up," "Pasting It Together" and "Handle with Care,"[3] each "panel" is a stage in the descent into hell by which he strove stubbornly to exorcise his despair.

This journey into darkness begins with a statement of the evidence that set the tone for what follows, as much by the sobriety and the effortlessly lapidary restraint of its style as by the categorical, irrefutable nature of what it says. "Of course all life is a process of breaking down": its essence is contained in its opening line. Then, after a few observations on how this comes about, a second postulate is advanced: "the test of a first-rate intelligence is the ability to hold two opposed ideas in the mind at the same time, and still retain the ability to function. One should, for example, be able to see that things are hopeless and yet be determined to make them otherwise." It was on this conviction that he built his career as a writer, in full knowledge that "the improbable, the implausible, often the 'impossible,' come true." And the astounding conclusion, in the straight line of America's ideology: "Life was something you dominated if you were any good."[4]

This royal certainty seemed self-evident until the moment, which Fitzgerald placed in 1933, when a short circuit burned out the terminals. Suddenly, the power no longer flowed. He found himself the victim of a deep depression that, he says, affected his nervous system rather than his mind or body. This statement of his physical condition is to be taken cautiously. A letter he wrote in May 1935 to Gingrich puts it in focus: "As to health, the body has been gradually sliding toward annihilation for two years but the process didn't get acute until about six months ago, and when it did, it went fast. I was doing my stuff on gin, cigarettes, bromides, and hope."[5] He was careful to distinguish his case from that of journalist William Seabrook, whose book *Asylum,* an account of a seven-month cure for alcoholism in a New York psychiatric hospital, had just been published: "What led to his alcoholism or was bound up with it, was a collapse of his nervous system."[6] Fitzgerald denied that he was himself an alcoholic, "having at the time not tasted so much as a glass of beer for six months." We know what that statement is worth too, but we remember the extreme tension of his life at La Paix while he was writing *Tender Is the Night.* "I began to realize," he records, "that for two years my life had been drawing on resources that I did not possess, that I had been mortgaging myself physically and spiritually up to the hilt."

He perceived that he was cut off from the things he loved, that he had to strain to perform the simplest acts, that he no longer liked to be with people, "but only followed the rickety old pretense of liking." What was more, the categories of people he actively could not tolerate became legion, from blacks to British, politicians, even writers, "all the classes as classes and most of them as members of their class. . . ." He was comfortable only with doctors, children and the elderly. "All rather inhuman and undernourished, isn't it? Well, that, children, is the true sign of cracking-up."[7]

In summing up, he alludes, without naming her, to Nora Flynn as "a person whose life makes other people's lives seem like death—even this time when she was cast in the usually unappealing role of Job's comforter. . . . 'Instead of being so sorry for yourself, listen—' she said. . . . 'Suppose this wasn't a crack in you—suppose it was a crack in the Grand Canyon. . . . The world only exists in your eyes—your conception of it. You can make it as big or as small as you want to. And you're trying to be a little puny individual. By God, if I ever cracked, I'd try to make the world crack with me.' "[8]

But he could not do that, and this is the final indication of how great his crisis is. His vitality has deserted him and not even all of Nora's can help him, for vitality can neither be transmitted nor shared. In *Gatsby*, Nick remarks about the colorless Wilson, "it occurred to me that there was no difference between men, in intelligence or race, so profound as the difference between the sick and the well. Wilson was so sick that he looked guilty, unforgivably guilty—as if he just got some poor girl with child."[9]

Fitzgerald, whose vitality was once as potent as Nora's and who had tried to bestow it on others, knew now that "vitality never 'takes.' You have it or you haven't it, like health or brown eyes or honor or a baritone voice." He was cut off from the living: "I could walk from her door, holding myself very carefully like cracked crockery, and go away into the world of bitterness, where I was making a home with such materials as are found there—and quote to myself after I left her door:

" *'Ye are the salt of the earth. But if the salt hath lost its savour, wherewith shall it be salted?' Matthew 5:13.*"[10]

The rest of the verse is implicit: "it is thenceforth good for nothing, but to be cast out, and to be trodden under foot of men."

These references to Job and Matthew, along with Nora's advice to view the crack outside himself, to see it in its ideological origins, in the system, point two possible ways to broaden the importance of his personal crisis. But Fitzgerald rejects mysticism and heroism, an encounter with God, political struggle; he concludes the second essay, "Pasting It Together," this way: "I have the feeling that someone, I'm not sure who, is sound asleep—someone who could have helped me to keep my shop open. It wasn't Lenin, and it wasn't God."[11] No new illusions will be admitted; the grandeur in his experience lies in his refusal to follow Kierkegaard or Nietzsche, in facing his crisis without the help of metaphysics.

In a sensitive essay on "The Crack-Up," E. M. Cioran criticized Fitzgerald precisely for not being "loyal enough to his failure," for not having "delved deeply enough into it or exploited it. His crisis did not lead him to mysticism or to final despair or to suicide, but to disabusement"; hence he could not maintain himself "at the level of his tragedy [and so] cannot be counted as quality among the anxiety-ridden." For Fitzgerald, "tottering among irreparable truths," denied himself the luxury of a halo, saint's or martyr's. In the ridiculous crown of thorns Zelda planted on his head, it was as a man, with human means, humble and stubborn, that he tried to see himself clearly. Cioran had to admit that he did after all come to know the darkness and the void that his soul stubbornly rejected. "And instead of blessing that darkness as a source of revelation," Cioran said, "Fitzgerald damned it, assimilated it into his degradation and emptied it of its weight of knowledge. He went through a Pascalian experience without a Pascalian mind. Like all frivolous people, he dreaded going farther into himself. Yet destiny pushed him to it. He hated to extend his being to its limits, and he reached them despite himself."

Cioran also criticized Fitzgerald for trying to write after recognizing the truth about himself. "It's a second-rate mind that cannot choose between literature and the 'true night of the soul.'" But did Fitzgerald know that the "literature" he was still trying to produce was a miserable absurdity, a vain effort to sell the only thing he had left to offer, but that nobody wanted—the lowest degree of shame and self-denigration?[12]

Our perspective is righted by a comment from French writer Michel Déon, who views the situation from a point of view of literary creation: ". . . no one has ever read a more appalling confession than Scott Fitzgerald's *The Crack-Up.* . . . This short, lucid and absurd essay is an admission of failure such as no other writer has ever dared to make. No one who has ever tried to write . . . can fail to feel concerned by such a confession. . . . Fitzgerald thought he could not write anymore, except for these few pages finally analyzing—he supposed—his own impotence. But this very type of confession circuits back into literary creation. Carefully detailing everything that turned him away from magazine stories, and having given up novels, Fitzgerald raised his paralysis to the level of a work of art."[13]

In "Pasting It Together," written after Fitzgerald's return to Baltimore—while, ironically, he was slaving to complete a second story in the Gwen series—he follows up the cracked-crockery episode. Picking up the thread of "Sleeping and Waking," he lists his nighttime obsessions, gorges himself on his failures and humiliations, dropping out of Princeton, Zelda's refusal to marry him when he was poor, his relationships with the idle rich: "the man with the jingle of money in his pocket who married the girl a year later would always cherish an abiding distrust, an animosity, toward the leisure class—not the conviction of a revolutionist but the smouldering hatred of a peasant."[14]

He nursed this rancor toward the rich, who might, while he was still disqualified, have exercised "a sort of *droit de seigneur* . . . to give one of them my girl," but he also worked as hard as he could "to share their mobility and the grace that some of them brought into their lives."[15] Now, however, he recognized the symptoms of inadequacy he had felt in 1916 and again in 1919, but this time they were incurable: "Only gradually did a certain family resemblance come through—an over-extension of the flank, a burning of the candle at both ends; a call upon physical resources that I did not command, like a man over-drawing at his bank. In its impact this blow was more violent than the other two but it was the same in kind—a feeling that I was standing at twilight on a deserted range, with an empty rifle in my hands and the targets down. No problem set — simply a silence with only the sound of my own breathing."[16]

This loneliness and anxiety crowded in upon him at night: "at three o'clock in the morning, a forgotten package has the same tragic importance as a death sentence . . . and in a real dark night of the soul it is always three o'clock in the morning. . . . One is not waiting for the fade-out of a single sorrow, but rather being an unwilling witness of an execution, the disintegration of one's own personality. . . ."[17]

This was the terminus of his journey, the evaporation of his identity, the realization that his illusions about the man he had been were all vanished. He was no more than the sum of the influences to which he had been subjected, the men to whom he had entrusted the chore of thinking and acting for him: Wilson, whom he recognized as his intellectual conscience; Hemingway, his artistic conscience; a friend whose name he preferred to withhold (Sap Donahoe?), his moral conscience; Murphy, his aesthetic conscience in his relations with other people; and a young communist who was his political conscience. "So there was not an 'I' any more—not a basis on which I could organize my self-respect—save my limitless capacity for toil that it seemed I possessed no more."[18]

In the triptych's third panel, "Handle with Care," he accepts his fundamental emptiness. He describes his flight to Hendersonville in a search for "absolute quiet to think out why I had developed a sad attitude toward sadness, a melancholy attitude toward melancholy and a tragic attitude toward tragedy—*why I had become identified with the objects of my horror or compassion.*"[19] In other words, why he was now unable to accept his initial postulate, holding two opposed ideas in the mind at the same time and continuing to function. His only out was to accept the schism between his self-image and what he had become. And, because he could not "slay the empty shell who had been posturing at it [fulfilling life's obligations] for four years,"[20] he opted to identify with it, to disown the man inside it, to be wholly a writer, since that was the only way he could survive, to ignore everything but his work. As we shall see, he was anticipating the rule of life that Hemingway would recommend at the same period. And he concluded on a note that not even Ernest could have surpassed in cynicism and harshness: "the sign *Cave Canem* is hung permanently just above my door. I will try to be a correct animal though, and if you throw me a bone with enough meat on it I may even lick your hand."[21]

Fitzgerald thought he had successfully lopped off a part of himself: "I have now at last become a writer only. The man I had persistently tried to be became such a burden that I have 'cut him loose' with as little compunction as a Negro lady cuts loose a rival on Saturday night."[22] For he really did have to get rid of a rival, a pest, the whole sensitive, vulnerable, feminine side of him that he blamed for his illusions and his defeats. He had already begun his withdrawal four months earlier in a farewell letter to Beatrice and in his remarks to James Boyd concerning his love affair "wrapped in cellophane" to feed the writer's need of material.

He disposed of Beatrice, the living image of his own passionate nature, by loosing masculine hypocrisy on feminine impetuousness, applying the timorous and petit-bourgeois attitude he prescribed in his notes as his antidote to passion. It had made him "lose his head" and now it had to restore his equilibrium. The writer "cut loose" his love, his rival, by enclosing a heartrending letter from Zelda with his note to Beatrice. And he lectured her by citing Hemingway, the masculine exemplar of the hardness to which Fitzgerald aspired: "Your charm and the heightened womanliness that makes you attractive to men depends on what Ernest Hemingway once called . . . 'grace under pressure.' . . . when you let that balance become disturbed, don't you become just another victim of self-indulgence?— breaking down the solid things around you and, moreover, making *yourself* terribly vulnerable?" He was sending Zelda's letter, he said, so that Beatrice might understand that "You have an existence outside of me. I don't belittle your fine intelligence by supposing that anything written here *need* be said, but I thought maybe the manner of saying it might emphasize those old dull truths by which we live. We can't just let our worlds crash around us like a lot of dropped trays."[23]

These trays shattered on the ground prefigured his "cracked crockery" just as his farewell to Beatrice prefigured the farewell to himself contained in the three essays. Beatrice and Ernest, the sensitive man in him and the pitiless writer—the poles of the dilemma that he resolved by eliminating the first. It is useful now to return for a moment to Hemingway, to Fitzgerald's artistic conscience, because contrasts in their work supply the key to the period that opened with "The Crack-Up."

When the three essays appeared, in February–April 1936, Hemingway was annoyed by their confessional nature and said as much to Dos Passos and Perkins. As early as May 1934, in a letter to Fitzgerald about *Tender Is the Night*, he had urged him to be stoical. "Forget your personal tragedy," he had advised. "We are all bitched up from the start and you especially have to be hurt like hell before you can write seriously. But when you get the damned hurt use it—don't cheat with it. . . . You see, Bo, you're not a tragic character. Neither am I. All we are is writers and what we should do is write. . . . All you need to do is write truly and not care about what the fate of it is."[24]

Hemingway thought Fitzgerald had cheated in *Tender Is the Night*, especially in taking the Murphys as his starting point for the composite portrait of the Divers. This was his only comment on the novel. He had said nothing at all when the book came out, and after a month of this silence Fitzgerald had written to him, insisting on his opinion: "Did you like the book? For God's sake drop me a line and tell me one way or another. You can't hurt my feelings."[25] The answer, as we have seen, was not at all comforting. But Hemingway seemed to have changed his mind a year later and indicated this through Perkins, who he knew would relay the message. "A strange thing," he wrote, "is that in retrospect his *Tender Is the Night* gets better and better."[26] By this time Fitzgerald considered their friendship finished, however. "Thanks for the message from Ernest," he wrote Perkins. "I'd like to see him too and I always think of my friendship with him as being one of the high spots of life. But I still believe that such things have a mortality, perhaps in reaction to their very excessive life, and that we will never again see much of each other. I appreciate what he said about *Tender Is the Night*."[27] He had in fact refused an invitation the previous year to join Dos Passos on a deep-sea fishing party off Key West because he did not think the reunion with Hemingway would be opportune. In a note written at the end of his life, he recapitulated his last meetings with Hemingway: "Four times in eleven years (1929–1940). No real friendship since 1926,"[28] noting that at least two years had elapsed between each meeting. He saw Hemingway only three or four times in the closing months of 1929, once in October 1931 before leaving for Montgomery with Zelda, again in January 1933, with Wilson, and twice in the early summer of 1937. On the last two occasions Hemingway was just back from Spain and was being hailed as a hero, and the meetings were casual.

In each of these reunions Fitzgerald felt inferior, off balance, and he took refuge in aggressiveness, flattery or silence, unable to talk to Hemingway as an equal. His admission to Wilson after the time when he had failed to connect with Hemingway is symptomatic: when dealing with Ernest, he said, he had no alternatives but sarcasm or obsequiousness. Gone were the mutual respect, the criticism accepted in a spirit of manly comradeship, the dirty jokes and burlesque remarks on the possible influence of one work on another, which had figured in their letters.

After 1929 the tone sharpened, the idea of rivalry lurked behind their discussion and the labored justifications provoked, for example, by a remark by Gertrude Stein about the nature of their different "flames," in which

Fitzgerald thought he was slighted.* Impatience and condescension are evident from then on in Hemingway's stream of assurances. His comments to Perkins after the unfortunate 1933 meeting tell us a lot about his real feelings: his impatience had turned to genuine disdain for Fitzgerald's "damned bloody romanticism" and the "cheap Irish love of defeat" in his work.[29] Hemingway's irritation was expressed in a series of brutal ad hominem comments that gained wide currency.

We recall how he had shown his gratitude to Sherwood Anderson for opening the doors of literary Paris to him in 1922, to Harold Loeb for helping Anderson persuade Liveright to publish his *In Our Time: The Torrents of Spring* had burlesqued Anderson's style, and *The Sun Also Rises* had exposed Loeb's private life, in the book's thinly veiled character of Cohn, to the ridicule of the American colony in Paris. At least Ernest had not mentioned them by name; however acid and cruel his mockery was, it remained allusive. But once Hemingway was established, Fitzgerald seemed to become his whipping boy. Even in *The Torrents of Spring*, Scott had been shown squatting drunkenly in his chimney fire, but the scene had not been vicious and other contemporary writers, including Dos Passos, had been named in the satire. In 1933 "Homage to Switzerland" appeared with sarcastic remarks about Fitzgerald and his university career. Two years later a passage in the manuscript of *The Green Hills of Africa*, dealing with the various forms of courage and their relationships with charm, referred to Fitzgerald as "a coward of great charm"; the remark was deleted before publication. It was an odd judgment and in bad taste; what gives it its spice is that Hemingway did not have the brass to include it in the printed version, but did leave in a passage that was equally offensive to Gertrude Stein. In the first chapter of Part Two he ponders an accusation of cowardice made against him by a woman whom he had once helped, he said, to find a publisher for her books and who had plagiarized his dialogue. The allusion was to *The Autobiography of Alice B. Toklas*, in which Stein made clear her low opinion of him: "Gertrude Stein and Sherwood Anderson are very funny on the subject of H. . . . They admitted that he was yellow, he is, Gertrude Stein insisted, just like the flat-boat men on the Mississippi River as described by Mark Twain."[30]

Yet this was the year when Hemingway tried to renew his friendship with Fitzgerald, despite his indifference to *Tender Is the Night* the previous year. In a December 16, 1935, letter to Perkins he reiterated his remark

---

* During a visit to the Rue de Fleurus in 1929, Fitzgerald challenged Hemingway to explain how he "achieves his great moments." Ernest replied, "When I have an idea, I turn down the flame, as if it were a little alcohol stove, as low as it will go. Then it explodes and that is my idea." Apparently sensing Fitzgerald's irritation, Miss Stein remarked that his "flame" and Hemingway's were different, but Scott misinterpreted this to mean that she thought Hemingway's flame was superior. The incident is reported in James R. Mellow's biography of Miss Stein, *Charmed Circle* (New York: Avon, 1975), p. 332. (Translator's note.)

about Fitzgerald's novel, and when he learned that Scott was going through a low period, he tried, in a letter to him a few days later, to revive the old joking tone. "If you really feel blue enough," he said, "get yourself heavily insured and I'll see you can get killed . . . and I'll write you a fine obituary . . . and we can take your liver out and give it to the Princeton Museum, your heart to the Plaza Hotel, one lung to Max Perkins and the other to George Horace Lorimer."[31]

The funeral oration he did write for Fitzgerald appeared in the August issue of *Esquire*, four months after the magazine had run "Handle with Care." This was Hemingway's long short story "The Snows of Kilimanjaro." It picks up the idea discussed in *The Green Hills* about the inability of American writers to develop harmoniously. Behind the narrative mask, the subject connects with "The Crack-Up": a writer's degeneration. With the difference that Hemingway is more specific than Fitzgerald about the motivations that lead his spokesman, Harry, to destroy his talent: consorting with the rich, especially his marriage to Helen, whose fortune distracted him from his mission. Here are both the subject of *Tender Is the Night* and the introspective tone of the Fitzgerald essays: "Why should he blame this woman because she kept him well? He had destroyed his talent by not using it, by betrayals of himself and what he believed in, by drinking so much that he blunted the edge of his perceptions, by laziness, by sloth, and by snobbery, by pride and prejudice, by hook and by crook."[32]

But the confessional thread snaps abruptly. Harry reconsiders; he certainly is not going to collapse like Fitzgerald. "He had been contemptuous of those who wrecked. You did not have to like it because you understood it. He could beat anything, he thought, because nothing could hurt him if he didn't care."[33] "Poor Scott Fitzgerald" is cited as the prime example of a talent destroyed by a love of wealth and admiration of the rich. Hemingway mocked the fascination he said the wealthy held for Fitzgerald. The criticism is unfair coming from a man who associated as much as Fitzgerald did with the "rich" (weren't the Murphys, who denied they were rich but who were considered so by both men, their mutual friends?) and who had certainly profited more from their friendship than Scott had.

In the firm and dignified letter Fitzgerald sent him after reading the story, in which he asked that his name be removed when "The Snows" appeared in book form ("Julian" would replace the name Fitzgerald), he made his position clear: "Riches have *never* fascinated me, unless combined with the greatest charm or distinction."[34] When he wrote to Perkins about the incident his language was less restrained. He admitted he had always liked Ernest, but he seemed determined to react forthrightly if the attack was repeated. "One more crack," he said, "and I think I would have to throw my weight with the gang and lay him [out]. No one could ever hurt him in his first books but he has completely lost his head and the duller he gets about it, the more he is like a punch-drunk pug fighting himself in the movies."[35] And in a letter to Beatrice Dance four days earlier he had given as his personal opinion (and not what he wanted Perkins to relay to Hemingway) that "he is quite as nervously broken down as I am but it manifests itself in different ways. His inclination is toward megalomania and mine toward melancholy."[36]

As Fitzgerald stressed in his letter to Perkins, however, the incident did not diminish his affection for Hemingway; he still accepted him as he was, with his virtues and his flaws. Until the end he would admire Hemingway's energy, dynamism and courage. A month after the "Snows of Kilimanjaro" episode, on September 24—his fortieth birthday—Fitzgerald gave an interview to New York *Post* reporter Michael Mok. He was in a weakened state that allowed Mok to milk him for confidences that were then turned into a sensational article portraying the subject as a lush sunk in his degradation. Mok pictured Fitzgerald in his room at the Grove Park Inn, under a nurse's care, still recovering from a shoulder fracture suffered two months earlier. "The poet-prophet of the post-war neurotics observed his fortieth birthday yesterday," he wrote. "He spent the day as he spends all his days—trying to come back from the other side of Paradise, the hell of despondency in which he has agonized for the last couple of years. . . . With his visitor he chatted bravely, as an actor, consumed with fear that his name will never be in lights again, might discuss his next starring role."[37]

The story, run under the headline "The Other Side of Paradise," was picked up by *Time* Magazine on October 5. The first person to whom Fitzgerald instinctively turned in his humiliation was Hemingway. Ernest was on a ranch in Wyoming, but Scott thought he was in New York and sent him two rapid-fire telegrams asking him to intervene. "If ever you wanted to help me your chance is now," he pleaded on September 28, 1935.[88] By the time the appeal reached Hemingway, in any case, it was too late for him to step in. This was the kind of irrational reaction that pushes a weak person to ask the help of someone he thinks is morally stronger; Hemingway at that time was the figure of authority from whom Fitzgerald could request justice. It is to be noted, however, that between the time the interview appeared and the time the telegrams were sent, Fitzgerald tried to commit suicide by swallowing a bottle of morphine.

Professionally, his attitude was very different. He had not lost his critical faculty, and while he pardoned Hemingway the man his "megalomania," he found it hard to maintain the admiration and respect for Hemingway the artist from which he had not budged through the appearance of *A Farewell to Arms*. He was probably aware of the irony of his noting that Ernest in 1936 was in the same fix Fitzgerald had been in when his friend criticized him as lazy. For Hemingway had not published a novel in six years, had published nothing, in fact, but a volume of short stories that had disappointed his readers, his *Death in the Afternoon*, about bullfighting, and *The Green Hills of Africa*. At the end of 1935 Edmund Wilson, who had been the first critic to hail the appearance of a new talent with the publication of *In Our Time,* disapproved sternly of *The Green Hills.* "The literary personality of Hemingway here appears in a slightly absurd light," he wrote. "He delivers a self-confident lecture on the huge possibilities of prose-writing, with the implication that he himself, Ernest Hemingway, has realized or hopes to realize these possibilities; and then produces what are certainly, from the point of view of prose, the very worst pages of his life."[39]

A few days later Hemingway sent the two letters he hoped would renew his friendship with Fitzgerald, the man who thought of him as the literary star of their generation, who a decade earlier had reinforced the effect of Wilson's first article about him with a flattering appraisal in *The Bookman.* Was he also seeking reassurance and a friend's approval, as Fitzgerald would after the Mok interview appeared? Scott's opinion did not seem to satisfy the need, to judge from his reply, in which he likened Fitzgerald to a brilliant mathematician who came up with nothing but wrong answers. Was Hemingway aware that his friend was beginning to share Wilson's opinion? Perhaps he suspected that Fitzgerald thought the Hemingway talent was running as dry as his own, only in a different way—because of a paranoia that prevented Ernest from seeing the truth squarely, whereas "poor Scott" the melancholic had the courage to examine himself, to tell the whole truth about himself in his essays about his failure.

One very shrewd witness gives us an insight into Fitzgerald's real feelings about his friend in 1936: an affection for the man that was tinted with irony based on his perception of the difference between reality and illusion, between the mediocrity of Hemingway's latest work and the promise of his early writings. The observation comes from Marjorie Kinnan Rawlings, then a young novelist who, at Perkins's urging, visited Fitzgerald when the Mok interview had plunged him into his deepest depression. "He was also more forgiving and reasonable than I think I should have been, about Hemingway's crack at him in *The Snows of Kilimanjaro,*" she recalled. "We agreed that it was part of Hemingway's own sadistic maladjustment, which makes him go around knocking people down. . . ."[40] She said she remembered "being impressed by the affection with which he spoke of Hemingway. . . . He also spoke of [him] with a quality that puzzled me. It was not envy of the work or the man, it was not malice. I identified it as irony."[41] Contrasting Hemingway's sadism with Fitzgerald's masochism, she concluded that Scott was sturdier than one supposed: "as a writer, except for the times such as this one has been, when his misery holds him up too long, his masochism will not interfere with his work. . . . He has thrown himself on the floor and shrieked himself black in the face and pounded his heels—as lots of us do in one way or another—but when it's over he'll go back to his building blocks again."[42]

Not until his creative energy revived and he began writing *For Whom the Bell Tolls* did Hemingway reveal to Perkins the mild remorse he felt for his past attitude toward Fitzgerald. He confessed that he had always felt the childish and stupid superiority toward him that a tough, belligerent kid would feel toward a weaker, more gifted boy. After Fitzgerald's death, however, when some of his friends tried to break the silence surrounding his memory with articles in *The New Republic* and, later, with Wilson's edition of *The Crack-Up*, Hemingway contributed nothing. Most of the famous names of the twenties figure in this commemorative campaign—John Peale Bishop, Glenway Wescott, Dos Passos, Malcolm Cowley, Wilson and many others. The only name missing was that of the man for whom Fitzgerald had done the most and loved most. And when Hemingway did speak up—posthumously, it's true—it was to leave us his pitiless portrait of Fitzgerald in *A Moveable Feast.*

Scott, on the other hand, even in his last letter to Hemingway, written after reading *For Whom the Bell Tolls* in 1940, always volunteered congratulations on his success, even comparing him with Dostoevsky in the intensity of some of his scenes. "I envy you like hell," he said, "and there is no irony in this."[43] That he even mentioned the possibility of irony in his compliments is proof that Fitzgerald perceived it even if he did not intend it. We get a glimpse of where irony does obtrude. First, in the contrast between each man's situation then and what it had been fifteen years earlier. Fitzgerald was in the position of a beginner who had to make, or remake, a name for himself; partly by force of circumstances, he had given up the movies as Hemingway had given up journalism in 1924, and for the same reason: to devote himself to literature. But he had just turned forty-four, was in poor health and burdened by his obligations to his wife and daughter. So he could honestly envy Hemingway's prosperity, the hundreds of thousands of dollars in royalties earned from the 190,000 copies of *For Whom the Bell Tolls* sold in 1940. The last line in Fitzgerald's letter emphasizes his notion of this prosperity as more a means than an end: "I envy you the time it will give you to do what you want." It was a little as though he were thinking of the stories he had written for the *Post* and of the money they brought him, which should have allowed him to accomplish serious work.

Despite the praise with which he nourished Hemingway's vanity, he considered *The Bell* skillful, intelligent, but second-rate, not to be compared, for example, with *A Farewell to Arms*. This is the second level his irony reached. Hemingway had become enormously successful at just the time when he had given up what it was that made his work original and become a writer for the mass book-club public. The undisguised personal opinion Fitzgerald expressed in a letter to Zelda written two weeks before the one sent to Hemingway can be summed up this way: Ernest's new novel did not have the freshness and intensity of *A Farewell to Arms*, none of its inspired passages or its poetry. The promise contained in his early stories had fizzled out. *For Whom the Bell Tolls* was a well-made novel that un-demanding readers, the old Sinclair Lewis crowd, would enjoy.

These remarks to his wife, who had always thought of Hemingway as a "cheat"—might be seen as expressions of Fitzgerald's personal grudge, the jealousy a has-been writer feels of a more fortunate rival. Except that the same opinions are found in his notes, which were meant for no eyes but his own. The failings he found in Hemingway's recent books served as warn-ings to him when he came to write *The Last Tycoon:* he would have to keep his artistic conscience clean and not betray his genius to please the public. "I want to write scenes that are frightening and inimitable," he reminded himself. "I don't want to be as intelligible to my contemporaries as Ernest who, as Gertrude Stein said, is bound for the museums."[44]

From these documents we see that in 1935, and perhaps earlier, Fitzgerald was keenly aware that Hemingway, too, was going through a crisis that made it impossible for him to renew himself, to write anything that took him beyond what he had produced in the twenties. And, Fitzgerald thought, the precariousness of Hemingway's literary standing was made more patent by the man's thoughtlessness and arrogance. After the "Kilimanjaro" inci-dent, we recall, Fitzgerald had threatened to shed his reserve and join those critics who, like Wilson, had severely criticized what they saw as imposture and pretentiousness in Hemingway's recent work. We have seen that Hem-ingway always turned mercilessly against those to whom he thought himself somehow obliged. This was especially evident in his literary relationships. Among the novelists of his generation with whom he had been in contact, only Dos Passos and Fitzgerald escaped his iconoclastic fury for a decade or more. We may wonder why he finally pilloried both men, Fitzgerald in "The Snows of Kilimanjaro" and Dos Passos in *To Have or Have Not* (in which he appears in the guise of novelist Richard Gordon).

He had humbly accepted the sometimes stern criticism Fitzgerald proffered in the early years of their relationship, because it was aimed at cleansing his work of everything that spoiled its artistic unity. From the start, a Fitzgerald newly emerged from the creative effort that had pro-duced *Gatsby*, and that had forced him to define the essence of his own ge-nius, had clearly seen what distinguished the timber and register of *In Our Time* from other contemporary books and from his own. The temptation was strong then for Hemingway, a beginner with little knowledge of litera-ture, to try to imitate Fitzgerald's career and his work. Undeniable influences of both detail and conception are to be found in Hemingway's writing. Echoes of "The Rich Boy," which Hemingway would cite in "Kilimanjaro" as though to exorcise a regrettable influence, are heard in *The Sun Also Rises;* one also discerns in that novel the more diffuse impact of *Gatsby*. For example, the use of a dissembling narrator in the first para-graph of "The Rich Boy" and the second of *The Sun Also Rises* draws readers' attention in similar terms to the protagonist's craftiness and defines his ambiguity. (Fitzgerald: "When I hear a man proclaiming himself an 'average, honest, open fellow,' I feel pretty sure that he has some definite and perhaps terrible abnormality which he has agreed to conceal"; Hemingway: "I mistrust all frank and simple people, especially when their stories hold together.") This sort of advance warning was already implicit in *Gatsby*, in which it is turned against the narrator, Nick, whose description of himself as "normal" and a "well-rounded man" is disproved at the end of the book.

This was the kind of unconscious borrowing of method or detail, in spirit or literally, that Fitzgerald tried to purge from Hemingway's work. The jokes in the two men's letters about the hypothetical influence of *Gatsby* in Hemingway's writing clearly show that Fitzgerald's criticism had vigorously exorcised the demon. Not, we must insist, to eliminate imitation or involuntary plagiarism as such, but to flush all foreign bodies from the Hemingway corpus. Fitzgerald, who had been strongly influenced by Conrad and who shared Hemingway's admiration for *The Heart of Darkness*, had warned his friend against contaminating his style: "Like me you must beware Conrad rhythms in direct quotation from characters, especially if you're pointing a single phrase and making a man live by it."[45] The effects of this sort of contagion, unfortunate as it might have been in Fitzgerald's case—and he did not always manage to escape it—were not disastrous for him; similarity in style revealed that Conrad and Fitzgerald held very similar attitudes, nostalgic and romantic, toward the world. But the effect would have been very different in Hemingway's writing.

In the same way, and for the same reasons, Fitzgerald worked hard to resist the attraction of the obsessive cadences of Hemingway's prose, even refusing to read it to keep from surrendering to its rhythms. Here again, the problem was not to avoid any chance resemblance in details, situations or themes, but in fact to keep from falling into step behind Hemingway, from adopting methods and tone that were not his own. "I had not imitated his infectious style," he wrote, "because my own style, such as it is, was formed before he published anything, but there was an awful pull toward him when I was on a spot."[46] He even admitted in a letter to Hemingway on June 1, 1934, that he had to stop reading Ernest's writing for a year and a half, during the final reworking of *Tender Is the Night*, "because I was afraid that your particular rhythms were going to creep in on mine by process of infiltration. Perhaps you will recognize some of your remarks in *Tender*, but I did every damn thing I could to avoid that."[47]

In the first five years of the thirties a strange switch took place not only in the relative authority of the two men but also in the problems facing them as writers. After the success of *A Farewell to Arms*, Hemingway was a little in Fitzgerald's position after *Gatsby*, except that *Farewell* had scored commercially as well as critically. He was also in the paradoxical position of a writer who was immensely successful because he had insisted on his alienation, had refused to participate. The method he had patiently developed in his first stories to express this sense of dereliction and despair, the style so perfectly geared that it became the very metaphor for that secessionist spirit, reached their full potential in *A Farewell to Arms*, revealing both their scope and their limitations. As it did to Fitzgerald after the exceptional artistic triumph achieved with *Gatsby*, the problem arose for Hemingway of how to renew his technique, how to go on to greater heights. More masterpieces were expected of him as they had been of Fitzgerald. He believed that Fitzgerald's mind had been muddied by the praise of critics like Seldes. Now that was probably true of Hemingway, too.

An even more serious problem also faced him: his sincerity, the relationship of what he had to say to a method developed in totally different conditions from those he was in now. For he was now a successful author married to a rich woman, moving in social circles whose values were hard to reconcile with those the poor, unknown young man he had been in 1923 tried to defend in his stories. The problem now, therefore, was to determine if the fine instrument forged in his first stories, this understated, paratactic style could encompass the change in the man, or if he was simply imprisoned in a formula and condemned to repeat himself and reiterate truths that were no longer as compelling as they once had been.

It does seem that the method did degenerate into mere procedure and that Hemingway's attempts at renewal in *Death in the Afternoon* and *The Green Hills of Africa* produced only minor works. It does seem that Hemingway was as helpless as Fitzgerald was then, even if he did express that impotence in aggressiveness rather than self-denigration. Until then their work had been entirely antithetical, rooted in very different visions of the world. Besides, they had more or less tacitly agreed to avoid rivalry. In 1932 Fitzgerald told Perkins that he had a sort of pact with Hemingway that was designed to eliminate not only any professional friction that might arise between them but also any possibility of competing on the literary market. "Ernest," he noted, "told me once that he would 'never publish a book in the same season with me,' meaning it would lead to ill-feeling."[48]

But in 1929, because of Gertrude Stein's ambiguous compliment regarding their respective literary "flames," rivalry did grow up between them. Fitzgerald was already gauging his success or failure by Hemingway's; despite his head start, he saw himself as the tortoise outrun by the hare. We have seen how strongly Hemingway's style worked on Fitzgerald. It was as though Fitzgerald, during his long ordeal, was also seeking a new style that fit his new situation, a more pared-down style, less lyric, less nuanced too, maybe, that could serve as the stylistic equivalent of the disillusioned and desperate world he now inhabited. The backing and filling, the delays in the writing of *Tender Is the Night*, completed only by a tremendous act of will when Fitzgerald was at his lowest ebb, may be explained in part by his deep presentiment that the marvelous tool forged for *Gatsby* was no longer able to grasp the new reality struggling for expression in his new novel. Hence the constant changing of subjects. All of them, however, were centered on defeat—a defeat unrelieved by the pleasures of playing with prose, the dialectic of styles, the flights typical of *The Great Gatsby*. *Tender Is the Night* might be called the swan song for Fitzgerald's first style, baroque, sumptuous, soaring, bravura. For nine years Fitzgerald had struggled against the stream to remain faithful to what he thought was his genius, while that genius was changing form and direction.

This, we now understand, was why he was so drawn to Hemingway's system of expression, which seemed the most complete literary representation of postwar disillusionment, cynicism and indifference. What for Hemingway was simply the fruitful systematization of an attitude corresponded in Fitzgerald to a genuine mode of expression that could have given form to his all too real alienation and despair. It was in the three essays constituting "The Crack-Up" that, while writing to say he could no longer write, he found the piercing irony, the familiar language, the sober and contained tone that would stamp most of his work after 1935.

Hemingway, meanwhile, was also seeking a way to escape the iron yoke of a style whose effectiveness grew as its scope narrowed. As many critics have noted, it was a style of pure present in which past and future could find no place. It expressed present sensations that might, at best, suggest an implicit emotion of which delicacy forbade mention. Under these circumstances, it necessarily excluded nostalgia and hope, the feelings associated with the past and the future.

"The Snows of Kilimanjaro" was a funeral oration not only for Fitzgerald as a creator but for a whole era of Hemingway's own life and a whole concept of his art. Nostalgia and hope are introduced for the first time, the former explicitly, the latter implied by the liquidation of an identity that had been renounced and condemned. One of the functions of his paratactic style had been to curb the author's sentimentality, his permissiveness toward emotions he could not always control—in short, everything he detested in himself as he did in romantics such as Fitzgerald. But the shell thus constituted threatened to restrain his imagination and frustrate the expression of more legitimate emotions. And, from the point of view of his writing, it limited Hemingway's range of variations and modulations because he could offer a reader only the signs, the raw materials of these unexpressed nuances. Even for this, the reader had to be sensitive enough and interested enough to fill in the blanks.

Hemingway's early work, surprising in its novelty, had immediately conquered those creative readers who were willing and able to go more than halfway toward his work and read emotions where the author simply sketched actions. But, after *A Farewell to Arms*, the similarity of his characters' reactions, the monotony of his situations, repetition of the same effects, despite changes of setting and fauna, wearied the most sympathetic readers, such as Wilson and Fitzgerald.

With "Kilimanjaro" two components of Fitzgerald's art appeared. One was temporality. A little clumsily and obviously, but nevertheless highly effectively, the past of Harry, the dying writer, is evoked as counterpoint to his present, ineluctable agony. These passages appear in italics, a device used by Dos Passos in "The Camera Eye" sections of *The 42nd Parallel* and *1919*. But it is of Fitzgerald, more than of Dos Passos, that one is reminded by these nostalgic evocations of a past stripped of all its charms, in which acuteness of perception and imaginative power combined to make every encounter, every event an extraordinary adventure. This magical and forever vanished past, whose first freshness not even art can capture, is methodically contrasted in the story with the present, in which death prowls in the shape of a hyena. Here we recognize the dialectic crafted for *Gatsby* to contrast a sordid, murderous present with the illusions and dreams of the hero's youth. This gives Hemingway's story relief, a depth of field rarely found in his work before this.

Another, equally important element also appears. It is represented by Helen, Harry's rich wife, the product of an idle and irresponsible class, whose mere presence was enough to pervert her husband's literary talent. In the second African story, "The Short, Happy Life of Francis Macomber," published in September 1936, the theme—central in Fitzgerald's work—is handled more dramatically: Margot Macomber, another of the unscrupulous rich, as seductive and irresponsible as Daisy Buchanan and Nicole Diver, kills her husband just when he finds his manly courage in the face of danger. This, then, is an entirely new subject for Hemingway, which was borrowed from Fitzgerald's repertory and would be used again to describe the relationship of Tommy and Helen Bradley in the 1937 novel *To Have and Have Not*.

Hemingway's remarking of the rich and his citation of "The Rich Boy" announced an attitude that would develop with the years. This time he followed a path Dos Passos had long been on. The corruptive power of wealth would be one of the themes Hemingway would exploit in his new social and political direction. His third novel, awaited almost as long as *Tender Is the Night* was awaited after *Gatsby*, was a failure despite its new themes and characters and the notion of time that distinguished it from its predecessors. It was the Spanish Civil War that gave Hemingway a subject through which he could expand the innovations in "Kilimanjaro" to novel length and which would make him one of the most popular novelists in the world. At the price, however, of giving up the specificity he had brought to literature, with Fitzgerald's help, and which he had tried to preserve until 1929.

While all this was happening, Fitzgerald began work immediately after the publication of *Tender Is the Night* on a series of stories that could later be published as a novel. The subject, characters and period would be totally different from anything he had written before. This was to be a long historical narrative that would bring the hero, Philippe de Villefranche, twenty years old in the year 872, through sixty years of combat against chaos to the dawn of a new order. Originally entitled *The Castle*, it was renamed *Philippe, Count of Darkness—Philippe* for short in Fitzgerald's letters. On April 17, 1935, he wrote to Perkins to announce that he had completed a detailed outline and that the novel, some ninety thousand words, could be published in the spring or fall of 1936. He said it would be "a poignant romance of chaos and leadership." Its protagonist would be a rude young warrior who had come to reconquer his ancestral lands along the Loire River. Just as Hemingway chose distant places to give a global meaning to the conflicts he explored in his books, so Fitzgerald situated his action in Carolingian France to draw a portrait of what he called modern man. And to complete the distancing, he chose as his hero's model a resolute, implacable and invincible man: Ernest Hemingway himself. "Just as Stendhal's portrait of a Byronic man made *Le Rouge et le Noir*," he mused, "so couldn't my portrait of Ernest as Philippe make the real modern man?"[49] In Hemingway, as in the Tommy Barban of *Tender Is the Night*, he saw an heir to the romantic Byronic hero, the activist-writer and the best example among all his contemporaries of the sensibility of the new age.

Philippe, produced in 1934, is a poor piece of work, but it anticipates Hemingway's future after the publication of *To Have and Have Not*, when adventure lived became more important than adventure written about, with the first conditioned by the second and supplying material for it. Like Byron in Greece, Hemingway in Spain—even more than in the Italian hills twenty years earlier—acted on the spot in the illusion of moving effectively with history. What more convincing image of a modern hero could Fitzgerald's imagination have found? He ended one of his last letters with the remark that "I hear distant thunder about Ernest."[50] The irony is barely visible.

To some extent Fitzgerald's choice of protagonist and period conditioned his style; to write a violent adventure story, he had to forget about nice analyses and concentrate on narrative, with the speeches of his uncouth characters reduced to the primitive simplicity of the dialogue in a western comic strip. Despite the failure of the venture—as we have seen, the fourth installment, bought by *Redbook*, was not even published in the author's lifetime—Fitzgerald nourished an odd affection for his hero: "one of the best characters I've ever 'drawn,'" he assured Perkins.[51] When, at the end of 1938, he considered publishing a collection of stories that could compare with Hemingway's *First Forty-Nine Stories* and, perhaps, save his reputation from oblivion, the first story he proposed to Perkins was *Philippe*, whittled to 30,000 words, about the length bought by *Redbook*.

In January 1939 Fitzgerald was still wondering about doing the extensive research he would need to outline Philippe's life—for he recognized that the *Redbook* version as it then stood was not very unified. Then he thought he might do better to begin a modern novel in his spare time rather than resurrect a five-year-old project; this would eventually become *The Last Tycoon*. So ended Fitzgerald's only attempt to depict a man of action in action, triumphantly achieving his ends. Instead, he brought his man of action into the between-the-wars period, made him an American and so guaranteed his failure. Stahr-Fitzgerald replacing Philippe-Hemingway was a sign that after five years of more or less willful blindness concerning *Philippe*, Fitzgerald recognized that his real subject, the one that called up the deepest resources of his talent, was failure. He had failed in his only attempt to bring alive a hero who, in his way, succeeded in life, dominated events and changed the course of history. He succeeded in bringing alive, in his last book, a character whose business failed but whose life was a success because he remained faithful to the task he had set himself. We understand what Fitzgerald meant when he declared that "I talk with the authority of failure—Ernest with the authority of success. We could never sit across the same table again."[52]

VII. WRITER FOR HIRE: HOLLYWOOD

(1937-40)

19. RETURN TO HOLLYWOOD

(Summer–Autumn 1937)

In 1925, when *The Great Gatsby* appeared and Fitzgerald was worried about how much money his book would earn, he thought of scriptwriting in Hollywood as a possible alternative to writing novels. "If it will support me with no more intervals of trash I'll go on as a novelist," he had told Perkins. "If not, I'm going to quit, come home, go to Hollywood and learn the movie business. I can't reduce our scale of living and I can't stand this financial insecurity. . . . Then perhaps at 40 I can start writing again without this constant worry and interruption."[1]

He had tried Hollywood twice when he was blocked on *Tender Is the Night*, in January 1927 and again in November 1931, both times on returning from Europe. And both times he had failed. He was hesitant, therefore, about trying again, seeing it as a last resort. In January 1935, in his reply to Harold Ober's suggestion that he go to Hollywood to write the screenplay for the film version of *Tender Is the Night*, he objected: "I hate the place like poison with a sincere hatred. It will be inconvenient in every way and I should consider it only as an emergency measure."[2] Yet in August 1936 he regretted that a dislocated shoulder prevented him from accepting a four-week M-G-M contract for $1,500 a week to work on the kind of subjects that had made him famous—a love story about fifteen-year-olds—and of which he was thoroughly sick.

The emergency occurred in 1937. The stream of easy money from *The Saturday Evening Post* was drying up; the magazine published only two of his stories in 1936, and only one, "Trouble," the following year, and for that one they paid $2,000, half of what Fitzgerald commanded five years earlier. Written in June 1936, published in March 1937, "Trouble" was the last of sixty-six short stories that, in seventeen years, had brought him nearly $200,000. The other mass-circulation magazines also showed their reluctance to publish hastily written, badly constructed stories that perpetuated an obsolete formula. In 1935 three Fitzgerald stories went begging; two others were bought by *Pictorial Review* but never printed. Two stories were rejected in 1936 and three in 1937. With rare exceptions only *Esquire* henceforth accepted his work, but Gingrich insisted on very short stories and paid only $250 each for them. The days when Fitzgerald could cover his basic overhead by churning out short stories was over; the five items *Esquire* bought from him in 1937 barely paid for two and a half months of Zelda's stay at Highland. Sales of his books, which had never provided more than a small supplement to his earnings, had dwindled to almost nothing: 210 copies in 1936, only 173 in 1937. His income in 1936, just over $10,000, was the lowest since 1919, when he broke in as a writer. His debts piled up, especially to Ober, to whom he owed $12,500 when he left for California, and to Perkins and Scribner's for as much more. A $40,000 estate split between Scott and his sister six months after his mother's death in September 1936 enabled him to settle only his most urgent obligations.

This is certainly why he pressed Ober to find him a job in the movies despite the failure of H. N. Swanson, Ober's representative in Hollywood, to do so. Luckily, Edwin Knopf, who headed M-G-M's script department and with whom Swanson was in contact, refused to give up. A friend of Fitzgerald's since the twenties, he finally managed to wangle a contract for him. The two men met in New York at Ober's behest on June 24. A contract concluded after the meeting gave Fitzgerald $1,000 a week for six months and carried an option for a year's renewal at $1,250 a week.

So, on July 7, Fitzgerald went to work for Michael Balcon, who was producing *A Yank at Oxford*, starring Robert Taylor and Maureen O'Sullivan. He was in for it this time. This was no lightning raid to pick up some quick cash and a little relief from the routine strain, as his previous ventures in Hollywood had been. He was in desperate need and this was a long-term job that wrought a radical change in his life; certainly for six months, probably for eighteen and more, he hoped, he was going to be a hired writer.

In the train carrying him West—its name, the *Argonaut*, sounded like a call to adventure—Fitzgerald wrote letters to Ober and Scottie that show the position he was in. He asked his agent to manage his money: Ober would receive his whole weekly salary and would remit $400 to him to cover his own expenses plus those of Zelda and Scottie. Of the remaining $600, Ober would receive $100 to cover his commission and $150 more against the money owed him, $50 would go to Perkins and Scribner's, $200 for taxes and $100 would be set aside for vacations, which were unpaid. Fitzgerald hoped that this drastic system, plus whatever he could earn on stories that were still being hawked, would settle his debt to Ober within a year. He would keep his end of the bargain; by the time his contract with M-G-M expired in January 1939, his agent had been paid in full.

The letter to Scottie reveals other, more secret plans. It looks backward over opportunities lost and mistakes made, and forward to at least a term of financial solvency that would enable him to dream, to build a new career. "I feel a certain excitement," he said. "The third Hollywood venture. Two failures behind me though one no fault of mine. The first one was just ten years ago. At that time I had been generally acknowledged for several years as the top American writer both seriously and, as far as prices went, popularly. . . . I must be very tactful but keep my hand on the wheel from the start—find out the key man among the bosses and the most malleable among the collaborators" to reach the top of his new trade. And he called wryly on his daughter to back him up: "You can help us all best by keeping out of trouble—it will make a great difference to your important years. Take care of yourself mentally (study when you're fresh), physically (don't pluck your eyebrows), morally (don't get where you have to lie)."[3]

Fitzgerald now was turned entirely to the future, his and Scottie's: the past was no longer to be regretted, but to be learned from. The failed writer was behind him, replaced by a new man. The West, land of adventure and new starts, beckoned. He knew his creative energy was waning, and now he counted mostly on his technical skill and his ability to maneuver. The writer was silent; it was the man of action who was talking now and who was resolved to master a new trade and a new environment with whose ins and outs he was already familiar. Literature was deliberately abandoned as once the dream had been abandoned of becoming a leader of men, a college sports star, a soldier, a worldwide celebrity.

Fitzgerald adopted as fact the idea born of crisis in 1936 that the novel, "the strongest and supplest medium for conveying thought and emotion from one human being to another, was becoming subordinated to a mechanical and communal art that, whether in the hands of Hollywood merchants or Russian idealists, was capable of reflecting only the tritest thought, the most obvious emotion. . . . As long past as 1930, I had a hunch that the talkies would make even the best selling novelist as archaic as silent pictures . . . but there was a rankling indignity, that to me had become almost an obsession, in seeing the power of the written word subordinated to another power, a more glittering, a grosser power."[4] This time he had made up his mind coldly, a little cynically, aware that he was cashing in not only on his talent but also on his past celebrity.

At the same time the idea of a compensatory activity took shape in his mind that immediately transcended this artistic resignation. Action would supersede the word. The conquest of Hollywood would reactivate an ambition frayed by friction against a difficult and disappointing trade. He would no longer struggle with words, with imponderables, but with the men in Hollywood, with their ridiculous and childish system. He would work with hard facts. What he did not see, or at any rate did not say in his letters, is that where he thought he was breaking with his past, he was in fact returning, as naturally as could be, to his youthful illusions, his old dream of social conquest through action. Literature had helped him overcome his failures, but, having failed in turn in it, he was trying to heal the wound by reviving his teenage ambition.

This was not a sudden about-face dictated by circumstances, a way of conceptualizing a situation he could not alter, but a definite tendency in Fitzgerald that had hardened right after the failure of *Tender Is the Night* three years before. He had not been able to impose himself on Hollywood in 1927 or in 1931; in 1934 he had projected his dream of a life of triumphant action into fiction. Dick Diver, weak, irresolute, imaginative, had been created in Fitzgerald's image. It was Tommy Barban, the man of action, the mercenary, the barbarian, who took Dick's place with Nicole. Pygmalion's statue turned its back on its creator and gave itself to the strong, unscrupulous man who had boldly seized it. In the next novel Fitzgerald had tackled, Philippe was Diver's antithesis, a Barban resituated in a historical context in which he could exercise his brutality, his need of conquest and domination. His shadowy medieval world recalled pioneer America, where the will to win was also the sole condition of survival and success. Philippe was modeled on Hemingway, but he was also a projection of the heroes of Fitzgerald's childhood—J. J. Hill, grandfather McQuillan (whose Christian name was also Scott's)—each of whom, in his own way, had carved an empire out of a nineteenth-century America governed by the law of survival of the fittest.

So it was in the pioneer spirit that Fitzgerald headed for the city he would describe in *The Last Tycoon* as "a miners' camp in lotus land,"[5] carried on that excess energy that the novel's hero, Monroe Stahr, remarked in immigrants ("he knew that people from other places spurted a pure rill of new energy for a while"[6]). And, as at every crucial moment in his life, he projected his hopes on an image of a prestigious superman with whom he identified. This time the figure was Irving Thalberg, the brilliant and all-powerful executive producer at Metro, who had died the previous fall at the age of thirty-seven. Under the circumstances Thalberg was a more appropriate and more credible model than Philippe. We will have occasion to come back to this. Meanwhile, it is noteworthy that when Fitzgerald's contract expired and he decided to return to literature, his first thought was to resurrect *The Castle*. It was not until three months later that, with Perkins's encouragement, he embarked on a novel set in Hollywood, with Thalberg as the model for its hero.

How did Fitzgerald look in 1937, on his way to rebirth and a new career? A photograph taken by Carl Van Vechten a month before Fitzgerald left for Hollywood shows a man unsure of himself, with an uncertain look and a tight smile, uneasy, hands hesitant and awkward in close-up. He had gone to New York to attend the second American Writers' Congress June 4–5, at which his old friend from St. Paul, Donald Ogden Stewart, was presiding. There a Fitzgerald on the skids would see some old friends who were at the top of their literary careers: MacLeish, Wilson, Hemingway, who had brought back a documentary film on the Spanish Civil War and who was also due to go to California a month later. More than the photo, the interpretation of which might be influenced by what we know of the man, Van Vechten's recollection is important in understanding how physically altered Fitzgerald was. Van Vechten had known Scott well, had corresponded with

Zelda, shared a hotel bungalow with the couple in Beverly Hills and, ten years before, had spent a weekend at Ellerslie. "I was to have lunch with Edmund Wilson, I think," Van Vechten recalled. "We were to meet at the Algonquin. As I came into the room my eyes had to readjust to the darkness and I noticed a man with Wilson. I didn't recognize him and went forward to be introduced. It was a terrible moment; Scott had completely changed. He looked pale and haggard. I was awfully embarrassed. You see, I had known Scott for years. . , . ."[7]

Another portrait, by Edwin Knopf, after Fitzgerald reached Hollywood, sums up the impression of those who had known him in the old days: "Here came this completely crushed and frightened man—the features were there, the drawing, but not the face. He had almost blue paleness. Not big wrinkles, but little wrinkles all over because he was sick."[8] A contrasting picture comes from the British novelist Anthony Powell, who met Fitzgerald only once, in 1937: "It may be of interest to record that I immediately recognized [him]. In an inexplicable way he was quite different from anyone else. . . . He was smallish, neat, solidly built. Photographs—seen for the most part years later—do not do justice to him. Possibly he was a man who at once became self-conscious before a camera. Even snapshots tend to give him an air of swagger, a kind of cockiness he did not possess at all. On the contrary, one was immediately aware of an odd sort of unassuming dignity. There was no hint at all of the cantankerousness that undoubtedly lay beneath the surface. His air could be thought a trifle sad, but not in the least broken down, as he has sometimes been described at this period."[9]

On Ober's advice Fitzgerald moved into a hotel-apartment complex called the Garden of Allah at 8152 Sunset Boulevard, in Beverly Hills, which was made up of a main building and a dozen bungalows of two suites each. The name suggests oriental luxury, and, indeed, until the place was torn down a few years ago, the buildings of ocher-colored adobe set amid palm trees around a central patio and an eccentrically shaped swimming pool did resemble nothing so much as a vacation resort at a North African oasis. This simply obeyed the rule that nothing in Hollywood was what it seemed. In fact, the place owed its name to silent-film star Alla Nazimova, who built it as her home when she was at the height of her fame; the pool, designed in the shape of the Black Sea, was supposed to remind her of her native Yalta. Ruined like many other silent stars by the advent of the talkies, she auctioned off the palace and it was converted into a luxury hotel.

Most of its guests were movie people, including some who were old friends of Fitzgerald's: Dorothy Parker and her husband, Alan Campbell; Marc Connelly, the author of *Green Pastures;* John O'Hara; Robert Benchley. Here, around a miniature Black Sea, after years in the desert, after the loneliness of Baltimore and Asheville, he was reunited with friends he had known along the shore of the Mediterranean. He was in a small colony of exiles who in many ways recalled the dispossessed Russian aristocrats who had so appealed to Scott's imagination during his first stay on the Riviera. Except that these people had chosen exile, more or less permanently deserting the intellectual East and their literary careers to join, languidly, in the literary folks' new gold rush. We recall Fitzgerald's remark about "a miners' camp in lotus land"; in the same passage from *The Last Tycoon* is another observation that captures the mixture of ambition and nostalgia, of energy and depression that characterized the colony: "There was lassitude in plenty—California was filling up with weary desperadoes. And there were tense young men and women who lived back East in spirit while they carried on a losing battle against the climate. But it was everyone's secret that sustained effort was difficult here."[10]

Many accounts remain of the new power relationships of the time, with Fitzgerald's appearing to the men he had known in his great days, but who were now higher on the ladder than he, as a survivor of a bygone time, a shadow so etiolated as to be almost transparent; it seemed hard to connect the prestigious name with the man who now bore it.

Probably the most painful of all these encounters was the one with Hemingway. When they had seen each other at the writers' congress a month earlier, Fitzgerald had been struck by his old friend's prestige and authority when Ernest showed his film, *The Spanish Earth* (a few days later he functioned as narrator at a showing for President Franklin Delano Roosevelt). On July 10 Hemingway arrived in California to campaign on behalf of the Spanish Republic. Two days later actor Fredric March organized a gala evening in his honor. "Ernest came like a whirlwind," Fitzgerald reported to Perkins, "put Ernest Lubitsch the great director in his place by refusing to have his picture prettied up and remade à la Hollywood."[11]

After the film was shown in Hollywood, Scott offered to escort Lillian Hellman to a party Mrs. Parker was giving for Hemingway at the Garden of Allah. Her reaction when she saw Fitzgerald for the first time since the Paris years was by now the usual one: "I was shocked by the change in his face and manner." She was even more surprised at the way he drove his secondhand car: "We didn't talk; he was occupied with driving at ten or twelve miles an hour down Sunset Boulevard, a dangerous speed in most places, certainly in Beverly Hills. Fitzgerald crouched over the wheel when cars honked at us, we jerked to the right and then to the left, and passing drivers leaned out to shout at us."[12]

When they reached Mrs. Parker's door, Scott at first refused to enter with his passenger, admitting that he was afraid to face Hemingway without a drink to shore him up. But Miss Hellman took him by the hand and they went into the living room together just as Hemingway hurled a glass into the fireplace. Fitzgerald melted into the crowd and left a few minutes later without having spoken to the guest of honor. By way of apology, he sent Ernest a telegram the next day congratulating him on his film and his glass smashing. Miss Hellman recalls a remark he made some days later to

Ogden Nash, which showed how overpowered and inhibited he felt in Hemingway's presence. "It's no use writing so long as Ernest is around," he said.[13]

A little reluctantly, Fitzgerald plunged immediately into Hollywood life. The day after the Hemingway party he had a sort of business lunch alone with Miss O'Sullivan in Malibu. Social obligations dictated most of his partygoing: people who had known him in 1927 and 1932 wanted to see him again and the others wanted to meet him. For a while he was always seen with movie celebrities. But in his account of this social round, no mention is made of what to him was his most important encounter, the one with Sheilah Graham. She was twenty-eight years old then and writing a movie column for the North American Newspaper Alliance; although she did not compete in influence with the queen of the Hollywood columnists, Louella Parsons, her irreverent and candid items on the stars' private and public lives had given her some notoriety and a number of sworn enemies.

After a wretched childhood in an orphanage, she had begun earning her living in music-hall walk-ons; these put her in touch with newspaper people and, from one liaison to another, brought her into the outer circle of the fashionable world. She was drifting, like Dreiser's Sister Carrie and, in a way, like Gatsby on the rise. Like him, she created a persona and a glamorous past and adopted a new name to replace the common one she was born with, Lily Sheil.

Sheilah was a heroine after Fitzgerald's heart. Five years earlier she had left England and, with it, a penniless and complaisant husband twenty-five years her senior, Major John Gilham, whom she had married when she was eighteen. A month before she met Fitzgerald, she had returned to London to divorce the major and had seen her friend the Marquess of Donegall, who had already asked her to marry him. He joined her in Hollywood two weeks later and pressed an engagement ring on her; they agreed to be married on December 31, the day her British divorce was to become final. Sheilah had not rushed into the marriage, but Donegall's years of courtship finally wore down her love of independence. And how could she resist all the aristocratic titles he would bestow on her?

Robert Benchley, whom they had asked to be best man at their wedding, gave an engagement party for them at the Garden of Allah on July 14, 1937, on the eve of Donegall's return to Britain. Fitzgerald was invited to it, of course, but Miss Graham caught only a fleeting glimpse of him. They met again a few days later at a Writers' Guild dinner-dance at the Coconut Grove, at which Mrs. Parker presided. Miss Graham was in Marc Connelly's party of ten; Fitzgerald was at the next table, and she recognized him. At some point during the evening, everyone else was dancing and they were alone at their long tables. He looked at her and smiled. She smiled back, moved by a kind of melancholy grace in him. He leaned forward and, across the length of the two tables, announced with a smile, "I like you."

Flattered, conscious that her beauty was enhanced that evening by a gray evening dress with scarlet velvet trim, she replied, "I like you too."[14] Her suggestion that they dance erased the sadness from his face, lighting it with boyish excitement. No, he had promised the next dance to Mrs. Parker, but the following one. . . . But the music stopped, the speeches began and, in the confusion of leaving, she lost sight of him.

On the following Sunday both she and Fitzgerald were invited to dine with Edwin Mayer. Scott was conservatively dressed in a salt-and-pepper tweed and a bow tie. Despite the August heat, he wore a charcoal-gray topcoat and had a scarf around his neck. At the bar they met Humphrey Bogart and his wife, and to the actor's surprise, Fitzgerald turned down a drink. During the two men's brief conversation, Miss Graham detected a note of deference in Bogart's remarks. Despite his slightly stiff manner and his silences, Fitzgerald was someone who inspired respect.

He and Sheilah made a dinner date for the following Tuesday, August 10. But that afternoon she received a telegram canceling the appointment: Scottie had just arrived with Helen Hayes, a Fitzgerald family friend. Miss Graham felt oddly disappointed and, suddenly, unwilling to give up seeing him that day. She phoned him, asking him not to call off the dinner; she would be happy to meet Scottie. With some hesitation he agreed and, at the appointed hour, came for her in his car.

The dinner was a strained affair. Scott was tense, morose, touchy and constantly reprimanded his daughter. Everyone was relieved when he finally announced that it was past Scottie's bedtime; he dropped her and Miss Hayes at the Beverly Hotel, where they were staying, and drove Sheilah to her hilltop home at 1530 King Road. Better let her describe her disappointment: "He stood at the door saying good-by. . . . There had been such a magical quality about him the other night and now he was only a faded little man who was a father. He said good night. I did not want him to go. . . . In the half light as he stood there, his face was beautiful. You could not see the tiredness, the grayness, you saw only his eyes. . . . I heard myself whisper, 'Please don't go, come in,' and I drew him in and he came in and as he came in he kissed me and suddenly he was not a father any more and it was as though this was as it should be, must be, inevitable and foreordained."[15]

With the arrival of Scottie and her chaperone, the socializing took on new vigor, in the company of Miss Hayes and her husband, Charlie MacArthur, who had been writing for the screen since 1929. There were dinners in Pasadena with poet Stephen Vincent Benét and playwright Zoë Akins; in Santa Monica with Thalberg's widow, Norma Shearer; with Marion Davies, Hearst's mistress, in fabulous San Simeon, made famous soon after in the movie *Citizen Kane*. Miss Hayes knew what trouble Scott was having in adapting to his new life. "All in all," she recalled later, "I think Scott was unhappy there from the start. . . . He hated the awful discipline of the studio. Pictures took writers right back to the working climate of high school. And he was not in the best shape spiritually; he was afraid that his writing gift was going through a tunnel. His few high spots were our evenings together, especially when we went to the Benéts'. At the Benéts' he always felt like a first-class passenger again."[16]

But the critical aspect of his life was unfolding in another sector: his work at the studio. On his arrival in Hollywood he had moved into the office set aside for him in the Thalberg Building at M-G-M's Culver City Studios on Washington Boulevard. This was a fortress policed at every entrance by private security guards. Seen from Washington Boulevard, it was a sort of imperial palace with a colonnaded facade running for hundreds of yards. This was only a facade, however; behind it stood a number of administrative buildings and acres of sets, castles rising beside the streets of Western towns, a patch of English countryside, a corner of a tropical island, a railroad station. The Thalberg was a square, concrete office building that looked like a hospital.

On the top (fourth) floor were the offices of what was ironically called the College of Cardinals—the producers, most of them Jewish, who reigned over this empire. At their head was the trinity from whom all decisions flowed: Louis B. Mayer (God the father), Sam Katz and Eddie Manix. Mayer, who had started out in life as a junk dealer, was a shrewd businessman but an ignoramus in art, and until 1936 he had delegated all his duties as producer to Thalberg. The third floor, where Fitzgerald had his office, was reserved for Metro's writers.

The same pecking order prevailed in the canteen, where a long table against one wall was set aside for the writers, including Albert and Frances Hackett, Mrs. Parker, George Oppenheimer, Nash, S. J. Perelman and Benchley. In the middle of the room sat the producers, the center of attention for directors, actors and writers. One group, which Fitzgerald occasionally joined, had its own preserve and included such scriptwriters and actors as Anita Loos, Aldous Huxley, Spencer Tracy and Clark Gable. Fitzgerald did not talk much; morose, absent, wary, he made few friends. Groucho Marx remembered him as "a sick old man—not very funny stuff," and Miss Loos confirmed that "people treated him like an invalid."[17]

His first task was disappointing. No cowriter was assigned to him, as he had feared, but he was asked to alter and rewrite a half-finished script. He had been chosen for *A Yank at Oxford* because of the subject; *This Side of Paradise* seemed to qualify him automatically to handle the comic doings of a brash young American on a scholarship rebelling against the prejudices of an English university.

A second chore was more promising: to adapt Erich Maria Remarque's *Three Comrades* to the screen. The 1930 film version of *All Quiet on the Western Front* had become a classic, and *Three Comrades*, about the problems of three war veterans and the rise of Nazism, was expected to be equally successful. Was it because Fitzgerald was known as the chronicler of the postwar generation that producer Joseph Mankiewicz gave him the assignment? "I hired Scott because I admired his work," Mankiewicz said. "More than any other writer, I thought that he could recapture the European flavor and the flavor of the twenties and early thirties that *Three Comrades* required. I also thought that he would know and understand the girl."[18] Fitzgerald began work on it August 4, and for a few weeks everything went smoothly. When Miss Hayes suddenly left California in early September, he took a week's leave to accompany Scottie to Asheville before she returned to school in Connecticut. There was a family reunion with Zelda, a brief trip to Charleston. But the visit demoralized him; "Zelda is no better," he wrote to his friend Beatrice Dance. ". . . she held up well enough but there is always a gradual slipping. I've become hard there and don't feel the grief I did once—except sometimes at night or when I catch myself in some spiritual betrayal of the past."[19]

As soon as he reached Asheville, obsessed with the fear that he might be saddled with a cowriter in his absence, he sent Mankiewicz an anxious telegram; the producer wired back that he was not to worry. By September 12 Fitzgerald was back at work, hoping to complete the screenplay on his own. Two weeks later, however, Mankiewicz did give him a cowriter. The insult was complicated by the fact that the man was his old acquaintance Ted Paramore, whom he had satirized in *The Beautiful and Damned*. What the producer had hoped would be cooperation quickly became open rivalry. Three weeks later, after a stormy row, Fitzgerald sent Paramore a long, firm and dignified letter. The new man seemed to want to take charge of the script and rewrite it in language Fitzgerald thought worthy of a Western. In any case, Paramore's incursion into what Scott thought was his private preserve seems to have shaken him off the wagon. Gone were the days when he refused Bogart's offer of a drink. The relapse is corroborated by the statements of two women from whom he had sought a measure of comfort.

In an October 8 letter to Scottie he said he had just received a wire from Ginevra King, whom he had not seen for twenty-one years and who was passing through Santa Barbara. "She was the first girl I ever loved and I have faithfully avoided seeing her up to this moment to keep that illusion perfect," he said, "because she ended up by throwing me over with the most supreme boredom and indifference. I don't know whether I should go or not. It would be very, very strange."[20]

After an exchange of telegrams, it was Ginevra who went to see Scott. They lunched together. In a letter to H. D. Piper she described Fitzgerald's drinking: "He suggested we go to the bar. I settled for a lemonade but he insisted on a series of double Tom Collins. I was heartsick as he had been behaving himself for some months before that. For the next few days I was besieged with calls, but as he was in love with someone in Hollywood, I believe, he soon gave up the pursuit."[21]

His passing fling with Sheilah Graham had become a steady attachment. One September evening, after receiving the poem from which she took the title for her memoirs, *Beloved Infidel*, she wrote to Donegall, breaking off their engagement. Meanwhile, she had contracted for a series of radio talks about movies that were to be relayed to Chicago from the CBS studios in Hollywood. Her debut in October was a disaster. Her throat knotted, heart pounding, her voice reduced to a shrill piping, she stammered as she read her script. The next day a phone call from Chicago informed her that from then on a professional actress would read her material. Scott strongly urged her to refuse; her beginner's nerves would disappear, he said, and she could not let someone else impersonate her. His insistence was contagious; she opted to go to Chicago and plead her case. Scott offered to go with her to lend moral support. They would take the night plane together the following Sunday.

On Monday morning Sheilah's CBS producer went to the Drake Hotel to see her. He said he did not have the authority to promise that she would be allowed to read her script in person that evening. Scott, who had gotten drunk on the plane and continued drinking at the hotel, surged up out of the chair in which he had been listening to the conversation and demanded an immediate answer, advancing on the producer in what seemed a threatening manner. When the man insisted that the decision was out of his hands, Scott took a punch at him, which the producer ducked. Sheilah separated them and succeeded in ushering her visitor out of the room.

Then things seemed to settle down. Sheilah apologized on the phone and was told she would be given one last chance to deliver her own material. When she walked into the recording studio, Scott was sitting in the first row facing the microphone, smiling conspiratorially and signaling his encouragement. Every time she opened her mouth to speak, he called, "Now Sheilah, don't you be afraid of them. Nothing to be afraid of. Speak slowly and distinctly."[22] And he began beating time with his finger. Two studio assistants grabbed his elbows and hustled him out. Sheilah, her nerves shattered, had to make several false starts before she could get through the script; the session that was supposed to last a few minutes went on for two hours. But she won her point and it was decided that she would henceforth broadcast directly from Chicago.

Back at the hotel an even wilder spectacle awaited her. Through the connecting door between her room and Scott's she heard a babble of voices. One, which she did not recognize, was scolding, the other, Scott's, protesting. When she walked into Scott's room, he and a stranger were seated face to face and knee to knee across a tray of food, and the stranger was feeding him with a fork. Scott, wearing a coffee-stained napkin around his neck, tried to dodge the fork or bite the man's hand. When he saw Sheilah, the man rose and introduced himself as though what was happening was the most natural thing in the world. His shirtfront was spattered with the coffee Scott had spat out when the man tried to make him swallow it. The stranger was Gingrich, the editor of *Esquire*, whom Scott had phoned after being ejected from the studio. When Gingrich reached the hotel, Scott had been dead drunk and surrounded by glasses full of gin. The editor knew his man well: "He was a real Dr. Jekyll and Mr. Hyde character when he had taken on board large amounts of liquor—a vicious drunk, one of the worst I have ever known. He could hardly talk, slurring all [his] words, trying to tell me about Sheilah, this great new English girl. Scott was rather puritanical. He was the obverse of Ernest in this way. Very, very rarely would he embellish his speech with a lot of he-man obscenities. But when he was drunk he was different, and kept saying, 'I just got to have this cunt!' At this point he hadn't yet."23

Exactly a month had passed since his visit to Zelda, a crucial month in which all his fears about his status at M-G-M had been confirmed; he was thought incapable of writing an acceptable script without help. His impulse to go off to Asheville with Scottie when he knew his position was shaky, his sudden flight to Chicago without warning the men on the fourth floor of the Thalberg Building, his tendency to run away from problems, his aggressiveness, the breakdown of his resolution about drinking, all betrayed his wish to escape the tension of his growing disagreement with Mankiewicz.

On October 6, the day Ginevra King contacted him, he tried to buck himself up, or perhaps to shoo away bad luck, by writing an optimistic letter to Ober. "I finished *Three Comrades* on my own," he said. "Mankiewicz was enthusiastic about the first part and will report on the second part tomorrow. We are going over it together which means a rewriting of perhaps three weeks' duration. . . . I was two months and a week on the script, which is rather more than averagely fast time. If I do three weeks more on it, my work will still have cost them less than a fifth of what the average shooting scripts cost. So I seem to be a good investment—unless something untoward happens."

The warning that last phrase might have hidden was dodged in the next. There was a risk of outside intervention, he said, of censorship, of pressure from the German consulate because of the film's anti-Nazi theme; "The thing is rather dangerous politically."24 The fear was justified. Censor Joseph Breen went so far as to recommend that the film focus not on the rise of Nazism but on the communist threat to a defeated Germany. Scott nevertheless continued his letter on an optimistic note: "aside from that I think nothing stands in the way of its going through and of my getting the credit, which is a big thing out here. You have credits or you don't have credits, and naturally I'm eager to have one in the book." Still, a certain reservation in the following paragraph watered down the optimism: "I'm happy here, but of course the first excitement has worn off and I fret a good deal with the desire to do work on my own. Perhaps after another adaptation they will let me do an original, which will exercise the intellectual muscles in a more *amplified* manner."

Fitzgerald's professional troubles probably overflowed into and aggravated his personal woes. Three women played the key roles in that month of his life: Zelda, whom he had seen in her madness during his visit with Scottie; Ginevra, who had refreshed his memory of the casual way in which she had gotten rid of him; and Sheilah, the "beloved infidel," who he knew was a flirt and feared was fickle. During one of her stays in Chicago she mentioned in a phone conversation that she wanted to spend a few days in New York. Convinced she was going there to meet a man, he threatened to leave Hollywood, and she renounced the trip. His own eagerness to see Ginevra made him certain that Sheilah also harbored a desire to rejoin an old flame, and he interpreted her perfectly innocent travel plans as a betrayal of him. Besides, despite the tenderness he lavished on Sheilah, despite —perhaps because of—the respect, affection and docility she showed him and that confirmed how genuine their relationship was, the puritanical streak in Fitzgerald doubted her surface generosity, rebelled at a permanent attachment—especially to an adventuress, a Lily Sheil who had come out of the gutters of London. From the beginning of their affair, Miss Hayes had noticed his perhaps unconscious reticence when he and Sheilah were with other people: "Sheilah Graham was good to Scott," she remarked, "but he wasn't nice enough to her—ever."[25] She thought Sheilah reflected his inferior position, his loss of status. This was clear in the vulgar way he spoke about her to Gingrich; it came into the open some months later, during another bender, and more tragically two years later, in similar circumstances.

Emotionally and professionally, Fitzgerald was going through a crisis that cast doubt on all the fine resolutions he had adopted aboard the *Argonaut*. His letter to Paramore, written two weeks after Ginevra's visit, made public a latent conflict that he had until then tried to trick himself into ignoring. But Paramore was seen as merely a straw man for Mankiewicz, the figure of authority and oppression Fitzgerald was really attacking. Here again, the ambiguity of Fitzgerald's motives clouds the situation.

Mankiewicz had literary pretentions and he was not liked by the writers; Oppenheimer voiced the general feeling when he said the producer thought he was Shakespeare. Knopf said of him that "it is both Joe's strength and his weakness that he thought he could rewrite anyone."[26] A stylist such as Ogden Nash could spend months on a screenplay only to have Mankiewicz completely rework it in twenty-four hours. In the final analysis he was the man who could give a line its final shape with a stroke of a pencil; he considered himself a judge of language from whose decisions there was no appeal, figuring that rank gave him the right to decide how a film's dialogue should sound. And he could intelligently defend the particular nature of movie dialogue as different from the language in novels (and different from that used on the stage, we might add, since Mankiewicz lumped them together). "I didn't count on Scott for dialogue," he declared. "There could be no greater disservice done him than to have actors read his novels aloud as if they were plays. . . . After all, there is a great difference between the dialogue in a novel and in a play. In a novel, the dialogue enters through the mind. The reader endows it with a certain quality. Dialogue spoken from the stage enters through the ear rather than the mind. It has an immediate emotional impact. Scott's dialogue lacked bite, color, rhythm."[27]

Such beliefs, backed by absolute power of decision, obviously had to generate increasing misunderstanding between him and Fitzgerald, with each man asserting the sureness of his judgment and his talent. When he saw, in January, how sweeping the changes made in his script were, Fitzgerald blew up. He wrote a letter of protest to the producer, cataloging the instances of heavy-handed vulgarity disfiguring the revised script. He too claimed a kind of authority: "For nineteen years . . . I've written best-selling entertainment, and my dialogue is supposedly right up at the top. But I learn from the script that you've suddenly decided that it isn't good dialogue and you can take a few hours off and do much better."[28]

Mankiewicz may not have been altogether wrong. Perhaps Fitzgerald had erred in trying to apply to perishable, mass-consumption film scripts the criteria he had established for more durable literature. He wanted to persuade the Mankiewiczes and the Paramores to make the film he would have tried to make had he been running things. But their business was not making works of art; they were there to make money for themselves and their companies. *Three Comrades* was not a masterpiece, but it was an honorable specimen of what could be expected of M-G-M in those days. When it became a hit film, Fitzgerald felt responsible enough for its success to copy a paragraph from the New York *Daily Mirror* to send to Ober: "The screenplay of *Three Comrades* was written by F. Scott Fitzgerald and E. E. Paramore Jr. and there was grapevine news that it was one of the best scripts ever turned in at Metro."[29] And when the film was released in June, he was rewarded with his first screen credit—shared, it was true, with Paramore. This credit that had cost him so much humiliation and anger was also his last. More of his work had been used in this script than in any other he ever did, even if its rhythm and poetry had been spoiled; about a third of his scenario was used in the final version. And the hard work he put into it, even if it did not fit the notions of the men on the fourth floor about what was to be expected of a scriptwriter, nevertheless won their respect. In January 1938, a month before he completed work on *Three Comrades*, his contract was renewed for another year at the higher salary he had been promised.

20. INFIDELITY AND FIDELITY

(1938–Spring 1939)

Perhaps to relieve his conscience of the feeling that he had abandoned Zelda, Fitzgerald decided to spend the Christmas holidays of 1938 with her. Their daughter was not with them this time. The private Ethel Walker School in Connecticut, where Scottie was preparing to enter Vassar, was so expensive that Fitzgerald had to watch his pennies. So she was again sent to stay with the Obers and the Finneys, while he took the plane to Asheville, happy at having paid back the approximately one thousand dollars he still owed Perkins and pleased that he could still provide for Zelda's maintenance. He was also glad to be able to enjoy himself away from Holllywood, or so he indicated in a letter to Scottie after his return, when filming began on *Three Comrades*. "Your mother was better than ever I expected," he said, "and our trip would have been fun except that I was tired. We went to Miami and Palm Beach, flew to Montgomery, all of which sounds very gay and glamorous but wasn't particularly. I flew back to New York intending to take you out with your friends on Saturday but I discovered you were on bounds. My zero hour was Monday morning in California so there was nothing to do except fly back on Sunday afternoon."[1]

Zelda had returned to Highland January 1 to attend a New Year's Day costume party. Although he was alone in New York, Fitzgerald declined to go and see Scottie in the visitors' lounge at Ethel Walker School, perhaps as a subtle reproach for her poor conduct that he could get across without having to scold her in writing, as he did in most of his letters in 1938. He did see Perkins briefly, however, in circumstances for which he later felt a need to apologize. "My little binge lasted only three days," he said in a letter he put off writing for weeks, "and I haven't had a drop since. There was one other in September, likewise three days. Save for that, I haven't had a drop since a year ago last January. Isn't it awful that we reformed alcoholics have to preface everything by explaining exactly how we stand on that question?"[2]

His two relapses had followed his two visits to Zelda in the first six months of his stay in Hollywood. Perhaps to change the unpleasant taste these memories left, he later made a quick trip to New York with Sheilah without telling his daughter. That he wanted his mistress to meet the

Murphys, thus, in a sense, formalizing their union, tells us how strongly attached he was to her. He told Nora Flynn about his situation, and she replied in a letter that told him what he wanted to hear: "I am not sure you are doing the right thing—about Zelda—I know you have been, beyond words, wonderful to her—I also know that the time has come for you to have a life of your own—to choose your own life, not for Zelda or Scottie but just for *you*. . . . I have a strange feeling that Sheilah Graham is the right person for you—I feel she knows the real you—and that's what counts."[3]

He went back to work January 31, we learn from a letter to Ober in which Fitzgerald describes a storm that made their return flight as rough as the one depicted in the opening chapter of *The Last Tycoon*. In mid-February he entered the orbit of Hunt Stromberg, one of Metro's best producers in those days and a favorite of such writers as Dorothy Parker, Alan Campbell and the Hacketts.

Stromberg gave Fitzgerald the chance he had hoped for to do an original screenplay, specifying only two things: the title, *Infidelity* ("kick it around for a while"[4]), and the star, Joan Crawford. The title delighted Fitzgerald; the star did not. He did not think much of her as an actress. "Writing for her is difficult," he wrote to Murphy. "She can't change her emotions in the middle of a scene without going through a sort of Jeckyll and Hyde contortion of her face. . . ."[5] He nevertheless took the trouble to see all her films, carefully noting when she was at her best and the expressions that showed her off most favorably. She looked better in exteriors than interiors, for example, and laughter was more becoming to her than tears. He had to work in halftones for her, avoiding strong emotions while trying to prevent her from smiling the secret little smile that was forever twisting her face.

The real trouble was not to come from Miss Crawford, however, but from a quarter with even more stereotyped reactions: the censors. Trying to slip a film entitled *Infidelity* past the Hayes office was not easy. Louis Mayer himself, as conservative about morals as he was in politics, had appointed himself a defender of home and mother; he was touchier about films dealing with extramarital relationships than even the official censor, the Roman Catholic Joe Breen. Official prudishness had reached a stage at which all the possibilities had been codified. For example, Breen had prohibited showing two people on a bed if two of their feet were off the floor, which demonstrates both his prudishness and his lack of imagination. Adultery was taboo and, while "sometimes necessary plot material, must not be explicitly treated, or justified, or presented attractively."[6]

Compared with the unfettered cynicism of *The Redheaded Woman*, which had so shocked Thalberg, the disenchanted story of *Infidelity*, in which a businessman's love affair with his secretary costs him his wife's love, seems conventional enough to us today. Besides, the movie was more about fidelity to the man's wife than about his passing unfaithfulness, so the title was shortened to *Fidelity* to outfox the censors. They were not fooled.

Fitzgerald's ingenious streak produced another idea: since adultery, like crime, could not be allowed to pay, then so be it: after her divorce, the wife would remarry and the same secretary would seduce her second husband, after which the first one would revenge himself and his ex-wife. Stromberg was tired of all the moralizing, however, and simply canceled the film. In a letter to Scottie Fitzgerald told how he felt about it: "We have reached a censorship barrier in *Infidelity* to our infinite disappointment. . . . Pictures needed cleaning up in 1932–3 (remember I didn't like you to see them?) but because they were suggestive and salacious. Of course the moralists now want to apply that to *all* strong themes—so the crop of the last two years is feeble and false, unless it deals with children."[7]

His disappointment at not being able to do the script stemmed not so much from regret for wasting the subject matter, however, as from his enthusiasm at being authorized to deal with it freely. With Mankiewicz's criticism in mind, he felt that for the first time he had entirely conceived a scenario in cinematic terms. He had planned to eliminate almost all dialogue, moving his plot along visually, for the most part, following a general tendency to avoid the verbosity of the first talking pictures. The *Infidelity* screenplay, free of obedience to a book that obeyed rules proper to a novel, abounds in such devices. The loneliness of the businessman, Nicolas Gilbert, and his despair at the ruin of his marriage are so poignantly rendered that words are superfluous. He returns to the big house on Long Island where he had spent so many happy years, but which has been empty for months. He gives a Gatsbyish party at which he is the only guest, wandering sadly through the empty rooms while an orchestra plays cheerful music out of doors. The camera follows him through the house to the master bedroom, its furniture shrouded in dust covers. The last scene, like a blast on an organ, shows him standing motionless before the huge bed.

Fitzgerald had learned a new, truly cinematic language, simultaneously implicit, suggestive and symbolic. He had set out to be a dialogue writer and had become an accomplished screenwriter, a semiotician without knowing it. But then, hadn't he already used this elliptical artistry instinctively in *Gatsby*, in reaction against the wordiness of *The Beautiful and Damned?* Gatsby himself says only a few words in the novel. His attitudes, clothes, possessions, parties speak for him and open him to the interpretation of those around him. Fitzgerald's talent, freed from a tradition that Mankiewicz maintained of talking pictures inspired by the stage, might now have been brought to bear on a subject that interested him. But, once more, Hollywood placed other values above art.

As he had after the ruckus over *Three Comrades*, he now felt a need to get away from Hollywood, even before the threat hanging over his script was confirmed. And it was on this third visit to Zelda that hard luck again caught up with him.

Two weeks before leaving, he had written to Ober of how relieved he was that he would soon have a vacation. "I suspect that Hunt Stromberg is going to put the pressure on, but he isn't going to succeed," he wrote. "I worked myself half sick on the last picture and I am going to keep to a safe and sane schedule on this one. Also, I am not going to be kept here [for] Easter. I'm awfully glad now that I wrote the vacations into my contract."[8] Later in March he flew to meet Scottie in Baltimore; together they took a train to Norfolk, Virginia, where Zelda was to be brought by a nurse. During the trip Scott proudly showed his daughter the almost completed manuscript of *Infidelity*, 104 pages that ended abruptly with Gilbert's solitary wandering through his empty house. Another twenty pages would have completed the job, but he was never to write them: by the time he returned to Hollywood, the censors had killed the project.

The few days spent at the Cavalier Hotel in Virginia Beach were not happy ones. Fitzgerald got drunk again. Zelda was irritable, quarreling with her tennis and golf instructors, nagging at Scottie and roaming the hotel corridors spreading the rumor that Scott was a dangerous lunatic. So insistent was she, Fitzgerald said in a letter to Zelda's doctor at Highland Hospital, Dr. Robert S. Carroll, that he and Scottie were about the only people on the floor who knew he was not crazy. Before leaving Hollywood, he had expressed to Carroll his vague hope that a miracle might some day make Zelda a free agent again and that she might then be able to live without him. "With my shadow removed," he said, "perhaps she will find something in life to care for. . . . Certainly the outworn pretense that we can ever come together again is better for being shed. There is simply too much of the past between us. . . . And if the aforesaid miracle should take place, I might again find a life of my own, as opposed to this casual existence of many rooms and many doors that are not mine. So long as she is helpless, I'd never leave her or ever let her have a sense that she was deserted."[9] Against all hope he concluded his letter with the wish that there might someday be a divorce by mutual consent. Meanwhile, he was walking through the empty rooms of his life like Gilbert in *Infidelity*.

He returned to Hollywood drunk, phoned Sheilah from the airport to tell her they were going to be married, that he had requested a divorce. When she saw and spoke to him, she realized that she was once more faced with the violent and despairing alcoholic she had had to deal with in Chicago. And, again, he vanished for a few days into the purgatory of emergency medical treatment before resurfacing to deal with the daily cares awaiting him on the third floor of the Thalberg Building.

After Scott's third unfortunate visit to Zelda, Sheilah worked to cure him, keeping him away from the bars in Beverly Hills and the temptation that was constant in the party atmosphere of the Garden of Allah. He needed exercise, she told him, fresh air, relaxation after his long days at the studio. A few days after his return she rented a house at Malibu Beach, number 114, forty-five minutes' drive from the M-G-M lot, where Scott could recover his health and zest for life. It was a white house with green shutters, and a garden reached through a trellised bower. There was plenty of room inside: a big, glassed-in living room, dining room, four bedrooms. A black-skinned cleaning woman named Flora kept the place sparkling clean, and she offered to do the cooking for fifty dollars a month. The rent was a hundred dollars a month below the three hundred he paid at the Garden of Allah.

Scott liked the house. It happened to belong to a friend, Frank Case, the manager of the Algonquin Hotel in New York, who was delighted to rent it to him. A six-month lease was signed April 22. The arrangement was that Sheilah would join him there on her free evenings and at the weekends; if Scott felt like staying in the city, he could sleep in the King's Road house.

The spring and summer he spent in Malibu were not particularly productive for him. He went on working for Stromberg, first for two weeks on a quickly aborted plan (he wrote only five pages) for a film biography of Marie Antoinette, then for five months, until the beginning of October, adapting Clare Boothe Luce's play *The Women* to the screen.

Added to the irritation of Fitzgerald's ridiculous job were his worries about Scottie's peccadilloes, which his imagination blew up out of proportion to their real gravity. On his return from Virginia he had planned to enroll his daughter in a group tour to Europe, partly so that she could brush up on her French and, also, to keep her busy during the summer, for there was no question of her vacationing in Hollywood without a chaperone. She was to have only a short visit there in early June. By April he was concerned about her lackadaisical way with her schoolwork. "The marks were really so very mediocre that, if I was Vassar, I wouldn't take you unless the school swore that you were a serious character—and the school is not going to swear you are a serious character if you let a prep school dance stand even faintly in the way of your success," he warned in a letter on April 18.[10]

The growing tension feeding Fitzgerald's obsession reached the breaking point when, on the eve of Scottie's departure for Hollywood, she was expelled from school for playing hooky to hitchhike to Yale. She was then preparing for her Vassar entrance exams and, of course, her expulsion set back her plans for college. Fitzgerald treated the incident as a tragedy and wrote her a long letter, stern and wounding. "My reforming days are over," he scolded, "and if you are that way I don't want to change you. But I don't want to be upset by idlers inside my family or out. I want my energies and my earnings for people who talk my language. I have begun to fear that you don't. You don't realize that what I am doing here is the last tired effort of a man who once did something finer and better. There is not enough energy, or call it money, to carry anyone who is dead weight and I am angry and resentful in my soul when I feel that I am doing this."[11]

With this off his chest, Fitzgerald let himself be persuaded by Ober that the girl was only sixteen, after all, that the incident was not important if she was willing to work on her own to prepare for the entrance exams. So she went to Hollywood for a few days, as scheduled. Her stay must have been stormy, but on June 18, shortly after she left, Ann Ober wired Fitzgerald to tell him that Scottie had been accepted by Vassar. His delight was short-lived. A week later she ran away again. Another flurry of telegrams between New York and California, threats to cancel the European trip, finally a letter to Scottie telling her that "what I felt first, anger, then pity, then annoyance has solidified into a sort of disgust."[12]

In Malibu Fitzgerald avoided social gatherings. Even before he moved there, he and Sheilah had accepted few invitations, and when they did go out, they kept largely to themselves, sitting peacefully on a sofa, taking no part in the conversation, unnoticed, maintaining their intimacy amid the chatter and the wisecracks. Only once did he shed his reserve, when he met Thomas Mann; he spoke brilliantly of Mann's work, holding everyone under his spell. As they left, Mann took him aside and told him that Fitzgerald knew his work better than he did himself. The rest of the time, however, Scott stayed on the sidelines, saying little, observing the other guests, unable to summon any cocktail-party joviality—possibly because he refused to drink.

Even at the beach he seldom ventured out of the house, assiduously avoiding the sun, never going into the ocean. Weakened, easily chilled, sweating at night, he husbanded his strength and nursed his resentments. At the most he would walk along the beach with Sheilah at sunset.

To take his mind off his cares, she invited a few friends to Malibu one summer Sunday, including Eddie Mayer and his young son Paul, screenwriters Nunnally Johnson and Cameron Rogers and their wives, Marion and Buff. Scott had carefully organized the party, anticipating how it would develop, the games that would bring out everyone's best side; the high point was to be a Ping-Pong tournament.

Although he drank only water, Scott was the soul of gaiety; he seemed to have dismissed his troubles with Scottie and M-G-M from his mind. He was too jubilant, perhaps: was that really water he was drinking? Sheilah's fears were confirmed when she saw him suddenly hustle Johnson, who was getting ready to leave, into an adjacent room. She heard the key turn in the lock. Inside, after pocketing the key, he launched into a lecture about Johnson's having allowed Hollywood to corrupt his talent, enjoining him to leave the studios and return to New York. Johnson, who was extremely successful in Hollywood and who would later do the splendid screen adaptation of *The Grapes of Wrath*, objected that he did not consider himself a writer, that his talent was for writing movie scenarios. He finally realized that Scott was looking for a fight and was about to punch him. Luckily, the scene was interrupted by Sheilah and Marion calling and pounding on the door; on the promise that Johnson would leave Hollywood when his contract expired, Fitzgerald consented to open the door and allow him to leave.

As the Johnsons were getting into their car, Scott yelled after them, "You'll never come back here! Never!" Johnson turned toward him. "Of course I will, Scott, I want to see you and Sheilah again."

"Oh, no you won't," roared Scott. "Because I'm living with my paramour! That's why you won't!"[13] It was an unusual word to use and it immediately suggested to Johnson that Scott was a Methodist; only a Methodist, he thought, could use so strict and hurtful a word as "paramour."

In a way, Fitzgerald needed these outbursts, to blow off the steam that built up gradually in him. Once the pressure broke, once the violence ebbed and he had punished himself morally and physically, his destructive impulse gave way to guilt feelings; he felt responsible to Sheilah, whom he made the scapegoat for his frustration at work and the deep dissatisfaction that his relationships with Zelda and Scottie caused him. They were irresponsible. He had given them everything and they had done nothing in return but add to his disarray. They represented idleness, muddle, spoilage, the other side of him that he had left behind when he went to Hollywood. In Sheilah, on the other hand, he had found someone who had never received anything she had not earned by her own effort, who had escaped her sordid beginnings by dint of constant struggle and who fully deserved the standing and financial independence she had won. Yes, she was frivolous and ignorant, but she knew what her weaknesses were and tried to change them. Fitzgerald contrasted her sweet temper and willingness to please with the hangdog arrogance with which his wife and daughter resisted his attempts to educate them. Sheilah admired him as a writer, a cultivated man who enjoyed a luxury she had been denied and which she thought it disgraceful to lack: the luxury of knowledge.

She was exuberant, bright, dynamic, but she detested the idea that she was merely a good-looking woman who was courted for her charm. She felt left out of conversations about literature or history, dreamed of being admitted to the charmed circle to which the passwords were Proust and Mann. Her eagerness to learn was matched by Scott's love of teaching, training, admonishing. It was a vocation balked by Zelda, who had been too proud to owe him anything when it came to culture, and by Scottie, who seemed to be spoiling her chances for a sound education. His work frustrated it too, forcing him to drop unfinished scripts one after the other. In his common enterprise with Sheilah he found the permanence, gratitude and respect denied him elsewhere. Not to mention the profound pleasure of filling a need, of satisfying a willingness to learn. Fitzgerald's need to share what he had learned, which had so struck Mann, had also impressed Anthony Powell, who remarked that "he loved instructing. There was a schoolmasterish streak, if at the same time an attractive one; an enthusiasm, simplicity of exposition, that might have offered a career as a teacher or university don."[14]

The process that would lead, six months later, to a systematic study program got under way the day Sheilah heard Eddie Mayer mention *Swann in Love.* But she took fright when she realized that the English translation of *Remembrance of Things Past* took up seven volumes. Seeing her leaf through *Swann in Love* aroused Scott's interest, and his pedagogic instinct led him to take the matter in hand. Sheilah was not to be discouraged by the length and complexity of Proust's prose. The best way to take it, he decided, was in small doses. He carefully hid the other volumes to prevent her being intimidated by them. Reading Proust, she learned to read intelligently, to remain quietly seated with a book in her hands and lose herself completely in what she was reading. Scott spurred her interest in the book by explaining the plot's historical context, supplying biographical notes, identifying the models for Charlus and Albertine. Proust's characters became more real than the pale denizens of Beverly Hills. Sheilah caught herself imitating Madame Verdurin's mannerisms, hiding her face in her hands as though she were a prey to unspeakable emotions. Was the woman only pretending to cry and laugh? Sheilah asked Scott. And they tried to mime affliction or hilarity behind their hands.

Sheilah's education continued with the poets. Fitzgerald liked to recite verse to her during their walks. She was struck by the poignant beauty of the last stanza of *Ode on a Grecian Urn.* Scott had been seduced by Keats's poetry at Princeton; he knew the *Ode* by heart, and its forms and rhythms echo in all his work. When he and Sheilah returned to the bungalow, they found an anthology, and he gravely read the whole poem to her with the slightly theatrical manner we can still hear in the recording he made not long after. Then he leafed through other books and read her Andrew Marvell's *To His Coy Mistress,* which she found very modern; the feelings of love and lust expressed two and a half centuries ago, she thought, could easily be expressed the same way today. She asked Scott for a reading list, which he enthusiastically supplied.

As with Proust's book, he set up a precise daily program, obtained the necessary books, scribbling explanatory notes in the margins, referring the reader from one work to another for purposes of comparison. Soon Sheilah's course became a ritual; she devoted three hours a day to her reading, and every evening they discussed what she had read that day. To reward him for the infinite trouble he took to prepare her curriculum, she sometimes memorized a poem that she would recite to him during a lesson.

So the summer and early fall of 1938 passed. In September Scottie, back from Europe, came for a brief visit, which resulted in another blow to Sheilah's pride when Fitzgerald asked her to hide her personal effects at 114

Malibu Beach. On October 8 he finished work on the script for *The Women* and went on vacation. He spent a few days in Asheville, joined Sheilah in New York and went with her to Stamford, Connecticut, on the invitation of Bunny Wilson, who had just married Mary McCarthy. Still awed by his friend's immense erudition, Fitzgerald declared himself still the "ignoramus" he was at Princeton. Now, for a short while, the Malibu teacher once again became an attentive student. When he left, his reading list had been lengthened by the names of a few contemporary poets and that of a novelist, Franz Kafka, of whom he wrote to Perkins a week before his death, declaring that "he will never have a wide public but *The Trial* and *America* are two books that writers are never able to forget."[15]

By the time Fitzgerald returned to California, his Malibu lease had expired; because of the winter cold and dampness invading Malibu, he preferred not to keep the house. So Sheilah went house hunting again and found one in the sunny San Fernando Valley. This new place, at 5521 Amestoy Avenue, put Fitzgerald farther away from the M-G-M studios, but the rent was low, two hundred dollars a month, and the setting pastoral: there was a broad lawn, giant magnolia trees and a rose garden.

Fitzgerald's last assignment from Metro was an adaptation of a life of Marie Curie. His work was not accepted. In his December pay envelope was a notice from the accounting department informing him that his contract had not been renewed. Two months later, in a letter to Perkins, he tried to present his dismissal as a liberation: "I think it would be morally destructive to continue here any longer on the factory worker's basis. Conditions in the industry somehow propose the paradox: 'We brought you for your individuality but while you're here we insist that you do everything to conceal it.' "[16] Again in April he described the debilitating, Kafkaesque conditions under which scriptwriters worked: "this amazing business has a way of whizzing you along at a terrific speed and then letting you wait in a dispirited, half-cocked mood when you don't feel like undertaking anything else, while it makes up its mind. It is a strange conglomeration of a few excellent over-tired men making the pictures, and as dismal a crowd of fakes and hacks at the bottom as you can imagine."[17]

In terms of hard work and income, Fitzgerald's eighteen months with M-G-M had nevertheless been profitable. He had never before worked so steadily for so long; he had worked on six scripts totaling 2,400 pages. And he had never been so steadily and well paid: $88,457 in a year and a half. For the first time in his working life he not only did not borrow money, but was also able to pay everything he owed Perkins and Ober; in December 1938 his only creditor was Scribner's, and he was soon able to transfer to his own name the life insurance policy his publisher had been holding as security. Finally, and to him most important, he had been able to keep Zelda in her expensive hospital and send Scottie to college. Oddly, all this was earned despite his repeated failures as a screenwriter (his sole credit was given him for *Three Comrades*, a film that he deprecated); in a way, he paid a stiff price for his prosperity.

In keeping with the resolutions announced in "Handle with Care," Fitzgerald had applied himself to peeling away his illusions and literary ambition, to becoming a professional who wrote only for cash. From January 1938, when *Esquire* ran the last of his stories ("Financing Finnegan") to be published before he left for Hollywood, until November 1939, his name was missing from the magazines. "Finnegan," his farewell to literary exposition of his personal problems, is a slight and sarcastic study of his own career and his financial dealings with Perkins and Ober. Finnegan was his double: he had just broken his shoulder diving into a pool from a high board. "His was indeed a name with ingots in it. His career had started brilliantly and if it had not kept up to its first exalted level, at least it started brilliantly all over again every few years. He was the perennial man of promise in American letters."[18] Broke, improvident, he promises stories he does not deliver and is forever panhandling from his publisher and his agent. Finally they send him to the North Pole with a party of explorers, after insuring him heavily to cover his debts to them.

Even in 1937 Fitzgerald had been thought of as a survivor whose work belonged in the past. In her memoirs Sheilah told of his excitement on reading in the Los Angeles *Times* that an adaptation of "The Diamond as Big as the Ritz" was to be played at the Pasadena Playhouse, which often functioned as a tryout house for Broadway. He decided to see it on opening night and phoned to reserve two seats.

The usually crowded lobby was empty. Was this the wrong date? No, they were told, the play was indeed being given that evening, but on a stage upstairs that was used exclusively by a student company. Gamely they clumped up the stairs to a small, bare room in which a dozen empty benches were lined up. They sat down in the last row. Ten minutes before curtain time a few students arrived, looking quizzically at the two adults in evening clothes.

If anyone showed enthusiasm for this amateur production, it was the sophisticated couple in the rear who had wandered in among these blasé, snickering youngsters. Scott went on applauding after the room emptied, and then he went backstage to congratulate the actors. As he left, he tried to make light of it all. "They were all nice kids," he said to Sheilah. "They seemed a little awkward when I introduced myself. I told them they'd done a good job." But he could not hide his disappointment for long; on the way home he was silent and scowling. Sheilah thought of the youngsters in the cast: "Of course they were awkward, ran through my mind. They were embarrassed to meet a man they had long thought dead."[19]

She had never read anything he had written and she wanted to. Pleased at her interest, he offered to buy her a complete set of his books. One evening they went to Hollywood's largest bookstore where, to his surprise, he was told that there were no Scott Fitzgerald novels in stock and that hardly anyone ever asked for them. It was not until they tried two more book-stores that they found someone to whom the name seemed to mean some-thing and who offered to order the books. The polite, retiring man who es-corted Sheilah to parties and first nights must always have been faced with the same reaction when she introduced him to her friends: startled looks, "a smile of surprise as though they were astonished to find that F. Scott Fitz-gerald was still alive."[20]

Frustrated, humiliated, the writer who had prostituted himself for money now longed to be reborn. In March 1938 he had connected Thalberg's name to a remark, to Perkins, that he was making notes for a new novel. At the end of the year he sent his editor two suggestions for new editions of his work, one for a volume containing three of his novels, the other for a collection of stories, including *Philippe*. "I am desperately keen on both these schemes," he wrote. ". . . I think it is a shame to put it off. It would not sell wildly at first but unless you make some gesture of confidence I see my reputation dying on its feet from lack of nourishment."[21] Perkins coun-tered with the remark that a new novel would make reissues more attrac-tive: why not try to arrange *Philippe* in book form during the summer? It was in reply to this that Fitzgerald mentioned his plans for a new novel, which he preferred to *Philippe* because the historical novel would have required too much revision and research. "Still, if periods of three or four months are going to be possible in the next year or so I would much rather do a modern novel," he said. "One of those novels that can only be written at the moment when one is full of the idea—as *Tender* should have been written in its original conception, all laid on the Riviera."[22] In late May 1939 he was still trying to keep the subject of his new book a secret; he had not explicitly revealed it even to Perkins.

So he did feel some relief at being freed of the discipline imposed on him at M-G-M and at being able to look forward to some real writing. He hoped he could alternate profitable part-time work for the studios with work on his book. Ober was optimistic enough about his finding temporary movie work, but he was also afraid that a new novel meant new debts for Fitzgerald. The agent strongly urged him to accept other offers that would bring him enough cash to enable him to write his book without having to worry about money. And he entreated him to reduce his expenses to a mini-mum: "I know that it doesn't pay any author to work in Hollywood, unless he can keep his expenses down to where they would be somewhere else and keep a large part of what he makes for the future."[23]

In fact, the iron rule at Metro had protected Fitzgerald against himself: never had he been seen drunk on the lot. Now that he was on his own again and beset by financial problems, he could not have maintained the appear-ances he had been held to by his contract. Job offers, therefore, now grew scarce. In January he was still financially solvent; he continued to collect his salary for two weeks into the new year. Then David O. Selznick hired him to work on *Gone with the Wind*. "Working with Selznick," Fitzgerald remarked, "is like being raised from the jungle to the court. I like Eddie but I hope I may never see the Metro factory again."[24] His satisfaction did not last long: he was fired two weeks later. Luckily, Walter Wanger, who was then producing at United Artists, asked him to help a twenty-five-year-old novelist named Budd Schulberg on a scenario in which the action centered on the Dartmouth College Winter Carnival.

Wanger and Schulberg were both Dartmouth alumni. They considered *This Side of Paradise* the best novel ever written about student life, and Schulberg admired Fitzgerald's work in general. The young novelist, who would later use him as a model for Manley Halliday, the unlucky writer in *The Disenchanted*, was struck by Fitzgerald's pallor, his spectral look: "There seemed to be no colors in him. The proud, somewhat too-handsome profile of his earlier dust-jackets was crumbled. . . . The fine forehead, the leading man's nose, the matinee-idol set of the gentle, quick-to-smile eyes, the good Scotch-Irish cheekbones, the delicate, almost feminine mouth, the tasteful, Brooks Brothers attire—he had lost none of these. But there seemed to be something physically or psychologically broken in him that had pitched him forward from scintillating youth to shaken old age."[25]

The only interesting feature of the story they were working on was that it provided a pretext for delving into picturesque festivities on a snow-covered campus. Not very exciting for two talented men; it was a commercial job and they had to obey the rules, and progress on the script was barely perceptible. Worse still, Wanger, who expected to make his film at Dartmouth, suddenly realized how slowly they were going and insisted that both writers accompany him to New Hampshire.

Fitzgerald's discomfort concerning his relationship with Sheilah showed in the fact that, while she traveled in the plane with him as far as New York, he told Schulberg she was just a friend. At Hanover, where the hotels were full because of the carnival, the writers found that no rooms had been reserved for them. They were finally stuck in an icy attic furnished with nothing but a double-decker steel bunk. There they went on talking and drinking in a sort of hallucinatory atmosphere, in a panic because they were stalled on the script.

Scott was drunk all the time. He was seen stumbling through the snow, wrapped in a ragged overcoat, with a stubble of beard on his cheeks. When he was called to order by the asssistant director, he tried to phone Sheilah, declared that he was going to see Zelda and drew indignant comments from the professors at a cocktail party. Finally, after improvising some obscene songs, he staggered off through the dark streets, leaning on Schulberg's arm. He encountered Wanger on the steps of his hotel and was fired on the spot. He and Schulberg left Hanover by train. Fitzgerald had worked only one week on *Winter Carnival*, and a month went by before he found another job, working with Donald Stewart on a Paramount film called *Air Raid*. He lasted another week in this, then had to quit, possibly because his binge at Dartmouth had weakened his health.

It was five more months before he got another chance to earn money: in the second half of August he put in a week's work for Universal, in September a day for Twentieth Century-Fox and a week for Samuel Goldwyn. Then nothing more for six months.

21. THE LAST OF THE ROMANTICS

(1939–40)

In *The Disenchanted*, Schulberg's hero dies during the Dartmouth carnival. He probably had not seen under Fitzgerald's crumbling mask his tenacity, the capacity to suffer and survive like an exhausted long-distance runner. The months that followed the Dartmouth episode confirmed the defeat of the man who had set out to conquer Hollywood, the failure of his struggle against alcoholism (for he had drunk no liquor between the incident at Malibu and his arrival at Dartmouth). But they also witnessed the writer's resurrection, in doubt and pain. His difficulty in reviving his creative energy after years of inertia strained his relations with Sheilah; there were violent rows to which the humiliation she had tolerated the previous summer was merely a prelude.

At the beginning of April Fitzgerald was intent on beginning the modern novel he had mentioned to Perkins. He hired a college graduate named Frances Kroll as his secretary for $150 a month, good pay for a beginner then. But she soon found how big a job she had taken on. She was not just a secretary, but also confidante and factotum, as Isabel Owens and Laura Guthrie Hearne had been; she was called on to shop for her boss, send out his laundry, buy the books and records for Sheilah's education, pay the bills and dispose of empty liquor bottles in a number of places to avoid offending Fitzgerald's neighbors. She was routed out of bed by phone calls in the middle of the night summoning her to go and fetch the Master from wherever he had passed out. Frances performed all these chores with grace and skill; she well deserved the Proustian nickname Françoise, by which Fitzgerald addressed her in his innumerable notes to her.

Like most of the women who knew him, Miss Kroll was conquered by his charm despite his manifest weaknesses. Demanding as he was, she appreciated his wit, his generosity and, especially, the courtliness that made him seem a refugee from another era. "His attitude toward women and his courtly manners were aspects of him that were utterly removed from the twentieth century with which he is so identified," she later wrote. She noted that he was "a private drinker and rarely belligerent. . . . He was reluctant to acknowledge his alcoholism and in writing to family or friends invariably made references to being bedded, or running temperatures." And her woman's-eye view of him corrects Schulberg's more rhetorical portrait of him: "He was handsome, but faded, except for the bright blue of his eyes. His clothes had seen better days. He didn't indulge in a wardrobe until just a few months before his death when he bought a Brooks Brothers suit, and was delighted with his purchase as a child with a treat."[1]

When he hired her, he told her he was writing a novel about Hollywood and made her swear she would not tell anyone about it. And before getting the job, she had to pass another test: "I want you to put your name down, Miss Kroll," he told her. "Would you get me my notebook in that top bureau drawer?"[2] She opened the drawer and saw a dozen bottles of gin neatly lined up beside the notebook. Fitzgerald watched her ironically. She closed the drawer without betraying any curiosity or showing the slightest disapproval. She was hired at once.

It was Sheilah who reported the scene. For despite her scoldings and pleading, he now drank openly. Once, when Sheilah found a pile of empty bottles and berated him for drinking in her absence, he went to a closet, retrieved a full fifth from its cache, uncapped it and took a long drink from the bottle.

Resigned, she accepted Scott as he was, settling for a promise that he would give her his car keys and wallet when he was going to get drunk. His daily ration rose to a little over a pint of gin a day. Despite her resolution not to cause any more scenes, Sheilah raged and wept when he was tight and sometimes refused to see him for several days afterward.

After one particularly nasty quarrel, he took a plane to Asheville and, without warning, trundled Zelda off to Cuba, fulfilling a wish she had made in one of her recent letters. The trip was a disaster, with Zelda plunged in a state of religious fervor while Scott toured the bars. At one point he stumbled into a cockfighting arena and, shocked by the fight's cruelty, tried to stop it; indignant spectators beat him up.

From Havana he and Zelda flew to New York, where Zelda, convinced he was not going to sober up, turned him over to her sister Clothilde and her husband and took the train alone to North Carolina. She left him a pathetic note asking him to come and live with her in a small lakeside house near Tryon; in a tactful, Highland Hospital style, she explained that she had abandoned him only because, after their idyllic stay in Cuba, he would have to go to a hospital to have his lungs treated—as he indeed did.

Back in Hollywood after his treatment, Scott sent her a deeply tender letter. In May he seriously considered bringing her to California for a month. But the wretched Cuban trip was their last chance to try to return to the close relationship they had not had for years. A few weeks later he made it up with Sheilah, and his thoughts turned to other things. In fact, the early summer of 1939 was the last time he would ever see his wife and daughter. Only his affectionate, nostalgic letters, made more poignant by distance, preserved feelings that the divergences in their lives threatened to stifle.

In the same period another break with the past, harsher and more final, separated Fitzgerald from Ober. We recall the agent's advice to Fitzgerald when his M-G-M contract expired and money grew tight again. Ober rightly feared that Scott would again be caught up in the infernal cycle of advances and debts. This is just what did happen when Fitzgerald's meager savings disappeared, exhausted partly by the costly medical care he needed after every bender. Late in June 1939 he wired a request for a five-hundred-dollar advance on two inferior stories that were finding no buyers. Ober cabled him the money and wrote him a letter of warning, which he could not bring himself to mail. "I think," the letter said, ". . . it would be a great mistake for us to get back into the position we were in. I think it is bad for you and difficult for me. . . . In any case, I think I ought to let you know that I cannot start loaning you money which means my borrowing money which is expensive and which is a thing I do not like to do."[3]

Two weeks later Fitzgerald again asked for money. Ober refused. Fitzgerald then sent a long telegram to Perkins asking for a loan of six hundred dollars, mentioning his agent's defection, the deplorable state of his own health since his return from New York and the fact that he was flat broke. Another cable went to Ober on July 13, reproachful and insistent on an advance "so that I can eat today and tomorrow." This too was refused. On July 18 Fitzgerald wrote a long letter to Ober thanking him for all he had done for him and Scottie in recent years, but firmly announcing that he was terminating the services of the man who had represented him since 1919. Throughout his career Fitzgerald had relied on Ober, and the loss of the sense of security the agent's constant efforts must have given him had to have been a severe blow. "When Harold withdrew from the questionable honor of being my banker," he later remarked to Perkins, "I felt completely numb financially and I suddenly wondered what money was and where it came from. There had always seemed a little more somewhere and now there wasn't."[4]

So Fitzgerald entered the summer of 1939 sick, poor and with most of his emotional ties cut. He lived like a hermit in Encino, working in bed while a record-breaking heat wave made the air irrespirable, dictating notes and plans for his novel, writing the first publishable stories he had turned out since his arrival in Hollywood in 1937, "The Lost Decade" and "Design in Plaster." Beginning in September, he would write two or three short short stories a month for *Esquire* built around a small-time, alcoholic scriptwriter named Pat Hobby, a weak and contemptible character who lived from hand to mouth and could never land a steady job. Like everything Fitzgerald sold to *Esquire*, the stories brought in little money—two hundred fifty dollars at first, then three hundred. Little as this was, it did restore his confidence that he could live by writing. And in projecting a ridiculous image of an erratic and irrecoverable alcoholic, he was also trying to propitiate fate, to achieve what his wretched double could not do, to see himself clearly and laugh at his own degradation and so to overcome it.

Fitzgerald's professional problems now, as during his time with M-G-M, intruded into his relationship with Sheilah. A few days after rejections from both the *Post* and *Collier's*, which had once fought for his stories, he picked up two tramps on Ventura Boulevard and took them home to Encino for dinner. When Sheilah got there, she found him drunk, distributing his ties, shirts and Brooks Brothers suits to the filthy, bearded hoboes, with whom Scott seemed perfectly at ease. She told them to return the clothes they were trying on and suggested that it was time they left. Scott demurred: "Why should they go, Sheilah? I told you they're my friends. . . . Don't talk like that to my friends. . . . *You* go. These are my friends. Old friends."[5]

She threatened to call the police. This was language the tramps understood. They ostentatiously laid the clothes on a chair and nonchalantly disappeared. Scott did not react immediately. Sheilah heated some soup and served it to him, hoping food would dilute the alcohol. But he just sat in his chair, grumbling helplessly that his friends had been badly treated, that he had never been so insulted in his life. Suddenly he leaped up, rushed to the table, grabbed up the soup plate and hurled it against the wall. Sheilah began cleaning up the mess; as she headed for the kitchen to dispose of the broken crockery, he stepped in front of her and slapped her as hard as he could. Drawn to the noise, a nurse who happened to be in the building came in and tried to calm him. "Oh, you think she needs protecting, eh?" Fitzgerald screamed. "You think she's something worth protecting? . . . She's right out of the slums of London . . . her name's not Sheilah Graham, it's Lily Sheil, Lily Sheil!"[6]

When the nurse tried to step between them, he kicked her in the shin. She ran out; Sheilah tried to follow her, but he again blocked the door. "You're not going," he said. ". . . I'm going to kill you." She sat down without showing how frightened she was, knowing that if she lost her head, the situation could become really dangerous. Never taking his eyes from her, Fitzgerald searched for his revolver. But when he went into the kitchen and fumbled through drawers there, she phoned the police and, before he could stop her, gave them the address and asked for help. He let her leave then. All through the night the phone rang in her North Hayworth Avenue apartment. She answered it the first time; it was Scott. After that she let it ring. The next morning at dawn she received a threatening letter from him addressed to Lily Sheil Graham.

A few days later, after withstanding a siege of telephone calls and death threats, she received a contrite letter from him that dimmed the memory of those terrible days: "I'm glad you no longer can think of me with either respect or affection. People are either good for each other or not, and obviously I am *horrible* to you. I loved you with everything I had, but something was terribly wrong. You don't have to look far for the reason—I was it. Not fit for any human relations. I just *loved* you—you brought me everything. And it was very fine and chivalrous—and you."[7]

She tried to drive him out of her mind; she began going out again, rediscovering the pleasure of being courted, happy, she told her friends, because she had "returned to circulation." But she was not rid of Scott. He paid a visit to her apartment in her absence; a few evenings later, while dressing to go out, she looked in vain for the silver fox jacket he had given her two years before. Obviously, he had taken it. Furious, she reported the theft to her insurance agent, who contacted Fitzgerald. He admitted having taken the fur, but he contended that it was his and that he had merely lent it to Miss Graham. Under threat of arrest, he agreed to return it to her. It would take a few days, however: he had sent it to Scottie as a Christmas present.

This time Sheilah was determined to break off her affair with Scott once and for all, to wipe out all trace of it. She began by tearing out of Scott's books all the title pages on which he had written dedications to her. His theft of the fur jacket, on top of everything else that had happened, seemed the worst thing he had done. "*I don't want to see his name again, I don't want to hear his name again, I don't want to be reminded of him,*" she declared. "I hated this man. He had betrayed me. He had betrayed my most secret confidences—my name, the orphanage—my background. He had struck me; he had threatened to kill me, he had tried to make me lose my job; and most infuriating of all, he had stolen my precious silver-fox jacket, the first real fur I ever had, so dear to me that I dared not even lean back in it!"[8]

She did not see him again for five weeks. To her relief, she returned to an uneventful life woven of parties, first nights, dinner dances. Her self-confidence returned, and she now joined in conversations with an intellectual maturity that won approval from the men whose culture and talent she respected. She was popular in Hollywood society, and her column, "Hollywood Today," now syndicated in sixty-five newspapers across the country, had made her influential. From no one, however, did she get the kind of searching and critical attention Scott paid her.

He sent her roses, and she didn't refuse them. Frances went to see her the following day, ostensibly to return a suitcase full of personal items, and said that Scott had stopped drinking and was hard at work on the second chapter of his novel. Sheilah listened coldly. She did not know that this visit was part of Fitzgerald's strategy; when Frances returned to Encino and told him that she had seen the roses on Sheilah's desk, his face brightened and he exclaimed, "I've got her!"[9]

When he called her one Saturday evening and asked to see her the next morning, she did not have the heart to refuse. He took her up into the Hollywood hills overlooking Los Angeles, where they had a long, quiet, friendly talk. He was sure he was going to write a good book. He spoke sensibly about his drinking problem, tracing it to its source and analyzing its effects. The forgetfulness he sought in liquor, he said, was worse than the reality he was trying to forget. He had sworn never to touch the stuff again and he solemnly assured her that he would keep his promise. She could help him regain his balance. He needed her. This was what she wanted to hear, what she wanted to believe.

With lucidity and humility, he also reviewed his position in the film world. He was capable now of being ironic about his illusions, even to Scottie. "I'm convinced," he told her, "that maybe they're not going to make me Czar of the Industry right away, as I thought 10 months ago. It's all right, baby—life has humbled me—Czar or not, we'll survive. I am even willing to compromise for Assistant Czar!"[10]

Just when he thought he would never work in a studio again, that he was blacklisted, when he tried to exorcise the spectacle of his disgrace by identifying with Pat Hobby, he was given an incredible break. Lester Cowan, an independent producer, had bought the screen rights to "Babylon Revisited." He offered a pittance, nine hundred dollars, for the rights, but hinted that Fitzgerald would write the screenplay himself. Up to then, except for *Infidelity*, Scott had always worked on other writers' often inferior products, sometimes having to follow them as faithfully as though they had been Holy Writ. "Do you know," he wrote to Perkins, "that in the *Gone with the Wind* job I was absolutely forbidden to use any words except those of Margaret Mitchell; that is, when new phrases had to be invented one had to thumb through as if it were Scripture and check out phrases of hers which would cover the situation?"[11]

Now, he exulted to Zelda, he could "write as I please upon a piece of my own and if I can make a reputation out here (one of those brilliant Hollywood reputations which endure all of two months sometimes) now will be the crucial time."[12] This, he said, seemed the last life buoy Hollywood was going to throw him.

Fitzgerald completed a first draft of the script, 146 pages long, on May 29, then spent two more months on it. The second version, cut to 130 pages, was ready July 30, under the title *Cosmopolitan*. In ten weeks of work over a period of four months he had earned $4,500 at the rate of $450 a week, an almost insulting salary in Hollywood. True, he did not have to show up at the studio every day and could work alone in Encino.

With the screenplay ready, the search began for a director and a cast; at one point there was some question of giving the lead to Shirley Temple. Nothing came of it and the film, like so many others, was temporarily shelved. It is to be noted in passing that Cowan later sold the script to M-G-M for $100,000 and that the film, completed in 1954, was released under the title *The Last Time I Saw Paris*, borrowed from Elliot Paul.

Never mind: for Fitzgerald, who had sold his story to *The Saturday Eve-*

ning Post in 1931 for $4,000, the money Cowan paid him was a godsend that kept him going all spring. In a curious way his screenplay in some ways echoed the novel it had temporarily interrupted. Like Stahr in the book, the movie's Wales is a hardworking captain of industry threatened by his associates. Each is a widower, haunted by his wife's memory, whose zest for life is restored by a poor girl's love. None of this figured in "Babylon Revisited." The extrapolations simply mirror Fitzgerald's emotional and professional cares in the last years of his life.

His financial situation was less desperate than it had been the year before. Although his income in 1940 would be about what it had been in 1939—some fourteen thousand dollars—his expenses had dropped sharply. Sobriety paid: since his reconciliation with Sheilah, his medical bills had plummeted. Not seeing Zelda may also have helped steady him. After a year's campaigning, she had finally been allowed to leave the hospital. Four years and one week after entering Highland, she rode a bus alone to Montgomery to live with her mother. Fitzgerald hesitated a long time before agreeing to the arrangement, which considerably reduced his expenses; he offered to give her a monthly allowance of $120, half of which would go to Mrs. Sayre for Zelda's maintenance.

His rent went down, too. After his eighteen months in Encino, Sheilah found him an apartment near hers, on the top floor of a three-story building at 1403 North Laurel Canyon, which cost $110 a month, about half what he had been paying until then. He took possession in mid-June, after a two-week visit with Sheilah to the San Francisco World's Fair. This was a new turning in his life, and before leaving for San Francisco, he explained his attitudes in a letter to Perkins. Europe was at war; that very day he had heard a radio report of the fall of Saint-Quentin, northwest of Paris, to the Germans. He thought of France and of André Chamson, of the past from which the war had now cut him off so brutally. At the time he was writing a nostalgic essay about his generation, the one formed in the First World War. "I have never loved any men as well as those who felt the first springs when I did," he wrote, "and saw death ahead, and were reprieved—and who now walk the long stormy summer step in step with me. If my generation was ever lost it certainly found itself. It is staunch by nature, sophisticated by fact—and rather deeply wise. And in this tragic year, so like another year, I keep thinking of a line of Willa Cather's, 'we possessed together the precious, the incommunicable past.' "[13]

He was nevertheless obliged to recognize that he had fewer and fewer friends. Only Murphy and Perkins had unreservedly supported him in the previous five years. "It's funny what a friend is," he remarked in a letter to Perkins. "Ernest's crack in 'The Snows,' poor John Bishop's article in the *Virginia Quarterly* (a nice return for ten years of trying to set him up in a literary way) and Harold's sudden desertion at the wrong time, have made them something less than friends. Once I believed in friendship, believed I *could* (if I didn't always) make people happy and it was more fun than anything. Now even that seems like a vaudevillian's cheap dream of heaven, a vast minstrel show in which one is the perpetual Bones."[14] For even Bishop, whose literary enterprises Fitzgerald had always backed, seemed to have gone over to the enemy and taken up Hemingway's line. The *Virginia Quarterly* article referred to in the letter was published in 1938, and Fitzgerald just happened across it two years later; it said he had been expelled from Princeton and, again, that he sought the company of the rich.

His break with the past added importance to Fitzgerald's estimate of his status as a writer. In his letter to Perkins he again paraded his grievances: "I wish I was in print. It will be odd a year or so from now when Scottie assures her friends I was an author and finds that no book is procurable. It is certainly no fault of yours. . . . Professionally, I know, the next move must come from me. Would the 25-cent press keep *Gatsby* in the public eye—or *is the book unpopular?* Has it *had* its chance? . . . But to die, so completely and unjustly after having given so much! Even now there is little published in American fiction that doesn't slightly bear my stamp—in a *small* way I was an original."[15]

Fitzgerald was also concerned about the war in Europe. He followed its progress on maps, argued with Sheilah about Britain's ability to resist the Germans, was delighted at the British evacuation from Dunkerque. He turned back to Spengler, conceding the rightness of his notion of "the world as spoil" and his prophecy of "gang rule," but he recognized the basic irony of his position: "Poor old Spengler has begotten Nazis that would make him turn over in his grave."

He questioned Perkins about Hemingway's opinions: "How does Ernest feel about things? Is he angry or has he a philosophic attitude? The Allies are thoroughly licked, that much is certain, and I am sorry for a lot of people. As I wrote Scottie, many of her friends will probably die in the swamps of Bolivia."[16] The letter alluded to, written on June 7, goes at length into the causes and possible consequences of the war, the sheepishness of American communists and, as indicated, the possibility of an invasion of South America.

The decline of the West, France's defeat—all this was still a distant echo of his private battle. In his personal theater of operations the stakes were also high. "I am not a great man," he told Scottie, "but sometimes I think the impersonal and objective quality of my talent and the sacrifices of it, in pieces, to preserve its essential value has some sort of epic grandeur."[17] Instead of adopting a heroic posture, he identified himself in his novel with Thalberg, in whom he saw the last of the great individualists, a man who made himself by talent and force of will alone.

The Last Tycoon is written around this exceptional man's tragic struggle and the circumstances specific to the United States in the 1930s. It illustrates Fitzgerald's conviction, one he had held for twenty years, that life is too tough for people. He believed, he told his daughter, "that life is essentially a cheat and its conditions are those of defeat, and that the redeeming things are not 'happiness and pleasure' but the deeper satisfactions that come out of struggle."[18]

In September Darryl Zanuck, the boss at Twentieth Century, hired Fitzgerald at a salary that seemed high after the miserable sum Cowan had paid him. The engagement, which brought him over seven thousand dollars, lasted until October 11. His assignment was to adapt Emlyn Williams's *The Light of Heart* to the screen. Was this an exercise in black humor for Zanuck, who had met Fitzgerald several times in France when the writer was at the top of his fame? The story Fitzgerald was being asked to adapt concerned a has-been, alcoholic actor struggling to support his crippled daughter. Scott was replaced on it by Nunnally Johnson, whom he had once advised to leave Hollywood forever.

In letters following his replacement, he announced to Zelda that he was resuming work on his novel and would try to finish it in two months—mid-December—while living on the money he received from Zanuck. "My room is covered with charts like it used to be for *Tender Is the Night*, telling the different movements of the characters and their histories. However, this one is to be short, as I originally planned it two years ago, and more on the order of *Gatsby*."[19] And, four days later: "I am deep in the novel, living in it, and it makes me happy. It is a *constructed* novel like *Gatsby*, with passages of poetic prose when it fits the action, but no ruminations or sideshows like *Tender*. Everything must contribute to the dramatic movement."[20] Another note to Zelda late in November affirmed that the novel "will, at any rate, be nothing like anything else as I'm digging it out of myself like uranium—one ounce to the cubic ton of rejected ideas. It is a novel *à la Flaubert* without 'ideas' but only people moved singly and in mass through what I hope are authentic moods."[21]

Five days after sending that last letter he was taken ill at Schwab's drugstore. The following morning he consulted his doctor, who told him he had experienced a cardiac spasm and prescribed rest, forbidding him to climb the three flights of stairs to his apartment. Sheilah immediately installed him in a ground-floor room in her apartment on North Hayworth Avenue, and he went on working, sitting up in bed. In a letter to Zelda on December 6 he minimized the incident: "No news except that the novel progresses and I am angry that this little illness has slowed me up. I've had trouble with my heart but never anything organic. This is not a major attack but seems to have come on gradually and luckily a cardiogram showed it up in time. . . . Everything is my novel now—it has become of absorbing interest. I hope I'll be able to finish it by February."[22]

Most of his time he spent in bed now, writing on a table he had made in Encino during his convalescence. "The cardiogram shows that my heart is repairing itself but it will be a gradual process that will take some months. It is odd that the heart is one of the organs that does repair itself."[23]

In the last letter he wrote to his wife, dated December 19, 1940, he regretted not being able to give her even a modest Christmas present. He urged her to say nothing to Scottie, who was expected in California on a year-end visit, about the strain that paying for her studies at Vassar would entail.

Fitzgerald did come out of his isolation occasionally. On Friday the thirteenth he had spent the evening with Nathanael West and his bride, Eileen. He thought West's latest novel, *The Day of the Locust*, was better than Schulberg's *What Makes Sammy Run?*, which had also been bought for the movies. Scott and West had become friends, and West had spent a pleasant evening at the Encino house along with the Hacketts and Elliot Paul, in whose honor Scott sang "The Last Time I Saw Paris."

A week later, on Friday, December 20, he finished the first episode in chapter 6 of *Tycoon*, in which a drunken Stahr is knocked down by the union leader he had taunted. Fitzgerald's doctor was to come by that evening to take an electrocardiogram. Absorbed in his work, resenting the interruption, Scott asked Sheilah to call the doctor and postpone the visit until the following day. He wanted to go out after dinner to celebrate his completion of a section that had given him a good deal of trouble. Sheilah had invitations to the premiere of a film comedy, *This Thing Called Love*, starring Melvyn Douglas and Rosalind Russell. As they left the showing, Fitzgerald staggered and leaned on her arm. "I feel awful," he told her. "Everything started to go as it did in Schwab's. . . . I suppose people will think I'm drunk."[24] She walked him slowly out to the car, pretending that they were deep in conversation. He was very pale, but he refused to see a doctor immediately, since he was to be examined the next day in any case. So he drove calmly home, feeling better by the time he got there, took a sleeping pill and fell asleep at once.

In the morning Sheilah brought him his breakfast in bed. He worked a while on his chapter 6, then dressed and helped Sheilah write a letter that had to be done tactfully: she was sending an evening dress she had worn only once, along with the silver fox jacket of dolorous memory, to Scottie for Christmas. Scott told her what to say to avoid wounding his daughter's pride. Then Sheilah made sandwiches and coffee while he read newspaper accounts of the tripartite agreement just signed by Germany, Italy and Japan; now, he thought, the United States will have to get into the war. If his book made money, he would imitate Hemingway and go to Europe as a war correspondent.

Scott settled into his chair by the fireplace and began to read an article on the Princeton football team in an alumni magazine Miss Kroll had brought him. Sheilah curled up on the sofa with a biography of Beethoven. Out of the corner of her eye she saw Scott suddenly stand up, reach for the chimney and slide noiselessly to the floor. He lay on his back, his eyes closed, his breathing ragged. Sheilah thought wildly about what to do: open his shirt collar? feed him brandy? His doctor would be here at any moment, she thought, but time passed with no sign of him; no one answered his phone. She called another physician, then ran to fetch the janitor. He bent over Fitzgerald's prostrate form and found no heartbeat. Francis Scott Fitzgerald was exactly forty-four years, two months and twenty-seven days old. His death certificate gave the time of death, as declared by Frances Kroll, as 5:15 P.M. December 21, 1940. Cause of death: coronary occlusion.

Fitzgerald had made a will before going to Hollywood. It began, "Part of my estate is first to provide for a funeral and burial in keeping with my station in life."[25] Later, probably in 1939, when he was no longer earning a steady income from M-G-M, he had crossed out the word "funeral" with a pencil and written in "the cheapest funeral," adding, "without undue ostentation or unnecessary expense." Of the $700 he had in cash when he died, $613 went to the undertaker. Among the other effects he left were a trunk of clothes, a smaller trunk full of souvenirs, a carton of photographs and notebooks, four crates of books, two wooden tables, a lamp, a radio. . . . The life insurance against which he had so often borrowed would provide for Zelda and Scottie.

Fitzgerald's body was laid out in the back room of the William Wordsworth funeral parlor on Washington Avenue. Friends, screenwriters, actors, a few producers paid their respects. One left a macabre description of the made-up face that he said resembled a store dummy "in technicolor": "not a line showed on his face. His hair was parted slightly to one side. None of it was gray. Until you reached his hands, this looked strictly like an A production in peace and security. Realism began at the extremities. His hands were horribly wrinkled and thin, the only proof left after death that for all the props of youth, he actually had suffered and died an old man."[26]

Dorothy Parker, who had known Fitzgerald in his wild years and in his anguish, was among those who lingered longest at his bier. Her eyes fixed on his face, she repeated the words that were said over Gatsby's grave: "The poor son-of-a-bitch." She felt sorry for Sheilah. At a Christmas party she gave, she saw how upset Sheilah was and left her guests to shepherd her to her bedroom and make her lie down. Mrs. Parker stayed with her and wept with her.

Fitzgerald had wanted to be buried beside his Maryland ancestors in tiny St. Mary's Catholic Cemetery in Rockville. His coffin was shipped to Baltimore by train. A few days later Sheilah, to whom Scottie had made it clear that her presence would not be welcome at the funeral, left Hollywood for New York with the idea of returning to Britain. In the train she met Sidney

Perelman, who had been with her and Fitzgerald at the Wests' dinner party on Friday the thirteenth. He was escorting the bodies of his sister and brother-in-law—Eileen and Nathanael West—who had been killed in an automobile accident the day after Scott's death.

The bishop of Baltimore refused to allow Fitzgerald to be buried in consecrated ground: Scott's books were considered immoral; besides, he had not received last rites. So the body was buried in the nearby Rockville Union Cemetery; an Episcopalian minister, less doctrinaire than his Catholic colleague, officiated. Some thirty relatives and friends were at the graveside, in the rain, at dusk on December 27. Here again, someone could have quoted one of the few things said at Gatsby's burial: "Blessed are the dead that the rain falls on."[27]

With Scottie, Ceci and Rosalind, who represented the family—Zelda had not felt up to making the trip—the mourners included two Princeton friends, Fowler and Biggs; the two men who had done the most to further Fitzgerald's career, Perkins and Ober; as well as the Murphys and the Turnbulls. Wilson could not attend, but he wrote the same day to Zelda: "I have been terribly shocked by Scott's death. . . . Though I hadn't seen much of him of recent years, we had a sort of permanent relationship, due to our having known one another at college and having started writing at the same time. It has brought so many things back—the day when you and he arrived in New York together—and I have been thinking about you a lot these last few days. I know how you must feel, because I feel myself as if I had been suddenly robbed of some part of my personality—since there must have been some aspect of myself that had been developed in relation to him."[28]

Zelda seemed not to have been as shattered by her husband's death as might have been feared. In fact, as had happened when her father died, it was months before she felt the blow. Then she had to return to Highland for a while. She continued to write and paint, was subject to spells of mysticism, lived apart from the world. When she had first entered Highland Hospital, Fitzgerald had defined their relationship in a letter to Sara Murphy: "In an odd way, perhaps incredible to you, she was always my child (it was not reciprocal as it often is in marriages). My child in a sense that Scottie wasn't, because I've brought Scottie up hard as nails. . . . Outside of the realm of what you called Zelda's 'terribly dangerous secret thoughts' I was her great reality, often the only liaison agent who could make the world tangible to her."[29] He had finally conceded that she would never again be well. "How strange," he mused, "to have failed as a social creature—even criminals do not fail that way. They are the law's 'Loyal opposition,' so to speak. But the insane are always mere guests on earth, eternal strangers carrying around broken decalogues that they cannot read."[30]

Zelda did not attend Scottie's marriage in February 1943 to Lieutenant (j.g.) Samuel J. Lanahan in New York, but she was uprooted by the birth of her first grandchild three years later. She would occasionally leave her mother in Montgomery and spend a few days in New York with Scottie, or in Asheville for treatment.

In November 1947, shortly before her second grandchild was born, she had to return to the hospital. Six months later, on the night of March 10–11, the hospital's main building, in which she and thirty other patients were housed, caught fire. Miss Ella's flaming dress, the fire at La Paix, the tortured figures in Zelda's paintings—all these seemed to prophesy these last moments. Locked in her room on the top floor, she and nine other women died in the flames. Her body was identified through a dental examination.

Scottie buried her beside Scott in the Union Cemetery, on the slope of a tree-shaded hill. Until a few years ago the common grave was marked by a simple headstone that read:

Francis Scott Key
Fitzgerald
September 24, 1896–December 21, 1940
Zelda Sayre
his wife
July 24, 1900–March 10, 1948

In 1975 St. Mary's Cemetery, by then absorbed into the suburbs of Washington near an expressway junction, was officially declared a historic monument. Fitzgerald's wish was then realized: his daughter obtained permission to transfer his and Zelda's remains to this enclave of history where for three centuries his ancestors had blended with the dust of Maryland.

Moved by an ecumenical spirit, the cardinal archbishop of Baltimore received the lost sheep into the bosom of the Church. His message of religious reconciliation also showed shrewd understanding of the quality of Fitzgerald's imagination: "F. Scott Fitzgerald came out of the Maryland Catholic tradition. He was a man touched by the faith of the Catholic Church. There can be perceived in his work a Catholic consciousness of reality. He found in this faith an understanding of the human heart caught in the struggle between grace and death. His characters are involved in this great drama, seeking God and seeking love. As an artist he was able with lucidity and poetic imagination to portray this struggle. He also experienced in his own life the mystery of suffering and, we hope, the power of God's grace."[31]

For a fairer perspective, we should translate this theological language into terms more accessible to a spirit whose realm was the earth—substitute "seeking holiness," perhaps, for "seeking God," or "a state of grace" for "God's grace." The message of Fitzgerald's life and work would gain in truthfulness, and perhaps in grandeur. For if, as E. M. Cioran maintained, his was "a Pascalian experience without a Pascalian mind," it was also testimony to the limitations of a man who, after long years of mundane frivolity, struggled and sacrificed without the help of faith to achieve self-renunciation. And who acceded in the process to the supreme dignity of those who acknowledge defeat but go on fighting.

BIBLIOGRAPHY:
FITZGERALD'S POSTHUMOUS GLORY

One of the most striking phenomena of American literary history after World War II is certainly the extraordinary enthusiasm that developed for F. Scott Fitzgerald both as a man and as a writer. The man who died at the age of forty-four in poverty and almost total oblivion is far more celebrated now than he was in the decade preceding the Great Depression.

Fitzgerald was famous then, but for reasons that often had nothing to do with literature. After the success of *This Side of Paradise* in 1920, it was the man more than the novelist who made the headlines. He was a celebrity, true, but not even his first book made the best-seller list. Compared with the performance of the really popular books of the period, the sales of *This Side of Paradise* (44,000 copies the first year) seem low. Five years later *The Great Gatsby* was considerably less successful (under 20,000), and *Tender Is the Night*, the last of Fitzgerald's novels published in his lifetime, was a relative failure (fewer than 13,000 copies sold). In 1939 he collected thirty-three dollars in royalties and his books were almost impossible to find.

Despite the glowing newspaper reviews his books received, most of the major American critics maintained a certain reserve toward them because they were unwilling to take seriously a novelist who cashed in on his talent by writing sentimental stories for *The Saturday Evening Post*. Only his peers, such illustrious forerunners as Edith Wharton, Gertrude Stein and T. S. Eliot, and respected contemporaries, such as Edmund Wilson, John Dos Passos and Ernest Hemingway, seemed to see in him a writer following a new vein that was to be reckoned with in American letters. And in *The Autobiography of Alice B. Toklas* Miss Stein did, after all, predict that Fitzgerald would be read when many of his well-known contemporaries were forgotten.[1]

In testimony to this esteem was a "memorial" raised to him in the pages of *The New Republic* (February 17, March 3 and 17, 1941) shortly after his death, partly to protest the hostile and unfair obituaries that had appeared in the newspapers, but also to pay tribute to his talent and intellectual probity. Like most of Fitzgerald's contemporaries, newspapermen had forgotten the novelist and remembered only the stereotype of Fitzgerald as spokesman for the Roaring Twenties and as a youthful dandy dazzled by the rich and sapped by alcohol. For the first time, then, authoritative voices asserted the primacy of the writer over the public figure. Some months later, Stephen Vincent Benét added his condemnation of the Fitzgerald myth. "This is not a legend," he said, "this is a reputation—and, seen in perspective, it may well be one of the most secure reputations of our time."[2]

It was thanks to the loyalty and devotion of a small group of friends and admirers that his work was rescued from oblivion. In the forefront of these are the Princetonians, Fitzgerald's biographers and critics: Henry Dan Piper, Arthur Mizener and Andrew Turnbull, and his fellow student Edmund Wilson. It was through Wilson that the unfinished manuscript of, and the notes for, *The Last Tycoon* were published in 1941; in 1945, under the title *The Crack-Up*, he edited a collection of previously unpublished letters, notes and essays. In the same year Dorothy Parker pulled together a body of Fitzgerald's out-of-circulation works—*The Great Gatsby, Tender Is the Night* and some of his short stories—and had them issued in *The Portable F. Scott Fitzgerald*, with a preface by John O'Hara.

The second phase of this renascence opened a few years later. In 1951 four other publications helped draw popular and critical attention to Fitzgerald's works and personality, which had figured the previous year in Budd Schulberg's roman à clef *The Disenchanted*. These were Arthur Mizener's widely read biography of Fitzgerald; a collection of critical articles edited by Alfred Kazin; a volume of twenty-eight stories (ten of them previously unpublished) put out by Malcolm Cowley; and a new edition, also arranged by Cowley, of *Tender Is the Night*, which used the author's notes and plans to tighten the book.

Not until 1960, however, were all of Fitzgerald's novels made available in a new hard-cover series issued by Scribner's beginning in 1958, five novels and three volumes of short stories, to which *The Pat Hobby Stories*, most of them never before published, were added in 1962. Scribner's also published other works, *Afternoon of an Author* (essays and stories) in 1958 and *The Letters of F. Scott Fitzgerald* in 1963. In 1965 the Rutgers University Press brought out *The Apprentice Fiction of F. Scott Fitzgerald*, fifteen stories Fitzgerald wrote in his teens.

The many critical studies that have appeared since 1951 were stimulated by these issues: in the ten years from 1961 to 1971, no fewer than seventeen books and seven collections of articles were devoted to Fitzgerald. In 1967 *The Critical Reputation of F. Scott Fitzgerald*, a monumental 400-page bibliography compiled with precision and skill by Jackson R. Bryer, appeared at the right moment to inventory this flood of studies and show the breadth and diversity of the reactions aroused by Fitzgerald. Bryer prepared an exhaustive catalog of everything written about Fitzgerald over a period of forty-five years, a total of 2,261 titles, including 1,033 reviews, 644 critical articles, 192 books wholly or partly devoted to his work, 73 theses and unpublished memoirs, to cite only the items written in English up to 1965. The corpus has grown considerably in the past fifteen years; in addition, previously written but unpublished works have appeared since 1965. Fitzgerald's novels have sold in the hundreds of thousands, and a number of motion pictures have been made of his works (three different versions of *Gatsby* alone). In short, the Fitzgerald industry is thriving.

It is not limited to the United States, either: the same process has developed in France, in similar stages. *Gatsby*, translated (atrociously) into French in 1926 and virtually unnoticed at the time, has since then been reissued—in the same translation—by five different publishers. *Tender Is the Night* appeared in 1951 and *The Last Tycoon* in 1952, in equally dismal translations. New translations began appearing in 1963, only three of them tolerable; between then and 1967, for example, Gallimard and Laffont issued *This Side of Paradise, The Beautiful and Damned* and four volumes of Fitzgerald's stories. In 1977 Julliard published *Éclats du Paradis (Fragments of Paradise)*, which combined material by Scott and Zelda Fitzgerald.

WORKS BY F. SCOTT FITZGERALD

Flappers and Philosophers. New York: Charles Scribner's Sons, 1920.

This Side of Paradise. New York: Charles Scribner's Sons, 1920.

The Beautiful and Damned. New York: Charles Scribner's Sons, 1922.

Six Tales of the Jazz Age. New York: Charles Scribner's Sons, 1922.

The Vegetable, or, From President to Postman. New York: Charles Scribner's Sons, 1923.

The Great Gatsby. New York: Charles Scribner's Sons, 1925.

All the Sad Young Men. New York: Charles Scribner's Sons, 1926.

Tender Is the Night. New York: Charles Scribner's Sons, 1934.

Taps at Reveille. New York: Charles Scribner's Sons, 1935.

The Last Tycoon. An Unfinished Novel. Together with *The Great Gatsby* and Selected Stories. New York: Charles Scribner's Sons, 1941.

The Crack-Up. With other Uncollected Pieces, Note-Books and Unpublished Letters. Edited by Edmund Wilson. New York: New Directions, 1945.

The Stories of F. Scott Fitzgerald. With an introduction by Malcolm Cowley. New York: Charles Scribner's Sons, 1951.

Tender Is the Night. With the Author's Final Revisions. New York: Charles Scribner's Sons, 1951.

Afternoon of an Author. A Selection of Uncollected Stories and Essays. Princeton, N.J.: Princeton University Library, 1957.

The Pat Hobby Stories. New York: Charles Scribner's Sons, 1962.

The Letters of F. Scott Fitzgerald. Edited by Andrew Turnbull. New York: Charles Scribner's Sons, 1963.

The Apprentice Fiction of Francis Scott Fitzgerald. 1909–17. Edited by John Kuehl. New Brunswick, N.J.: Rutgers University Press, 1965.

Thoughtbook of Francis Scott Key Fitzgerald. Princeton, N.J.: Princeton University Library, 1965.

Dear Scott/Dear Max: The Fitzgerald-Perkins Correspondence. Edited by John Kuehl and Jackson R. Bryer. New York: Charles Scribner's Sons, 1971.

F. Scott Fitzgerald in His Own Time: A Miscellany. Edited by Matthew J. Bruccoli and Jackson R. Bryer. Kent, Ohio: Kent State University Press, 1971.

As Ever, Scott Fitz-. Letters between F. Scott Fitzgerald and his literary agent, Harold Ober, 1919–40. Edited by Matthew J. Bruccoli. Philadelphia and New York: J. B. Lippincott Co., 1972.

F. Scott Fitzgerald's Ledger. A facsimile. Introduction by Matthew J. Bruccoli. Washington, D.C.: NCR/Microcard Editions, 1972.

Bits of Paradise. 21 uncollected stories by F. Scott and Zelda Fitzgerald. Edited by Matthew J. Bruccoli. Foreword by Scottie Fitzgerald Smith and preface by Matthew J. Bruccoli. New York: Harcourt Brace Jovanovich, 1973.

The Notebooks of F. Scott Fitzgerald. Edited by Matthew J. Bruccoli. New York: Harcourt Brace Jovanovich, 1978.

The Price Was High. The last uncollected stories of F. Scott Fitzgerald. Edited by Matthew J. Bruccoli. New York: Harcourt Brace Jovanovich, 1979.

BIOGRAPHICAL SOURCES

BIOGRAPHIES OF F. SCOTT AND ZELDA FITZGERALD:

Bruccoli, Matthew J. *Some Sort of Epic Grandeur: The Life of F. Scott Fitz-gerald*. New York: Harcourt Brace Jovanovich, 1981.

Koblas, John J. *F. Scott Fitzgerald in Minnesota: His Homes and Haunts*. St. Paul, Minnesota: Minnesota Historical Society Press, 1978.

Mayfield, Sara. *Exiles from Paradise*. New York: Delacorte Press, 1971.

Milford, Nancy. *Zelda*. New York: Harper & Row, Publishers, 1970.

Mizener, Arthur. *The Far Side of Paradise*. Boston: Houghton Mifflin Co., 1951.

Smith, Scottie Fitzgerald, Matthew J. Bruccoli and Joan P. Kerr, eds. *The Romantic Egoists: A Pictorial Autobiography from the Scrapbooks and Albums of F. Scott and Zelda Fitzgerald*. New York: Charles Scribner's Sons, 1974.

Turnbull, Andrew. *Scott Fitzgerald*. New York: Charles Scribner's Sons, 1962.

MEMOIRS AND SECONDARY SOURCES:

Allen, Joan. *Candles and Carnival Lights*. New York: New York University Press, 1978.

Baker, Carlos. *Ernest Hemingway: A Life Story*. New York: Charles Scribner's Sons, 1969.

Bruccoli, Matthew J. *Scott and Ernest: The Authority of Failure and the Authority of Success*. New York: Random House, 1978.

Callaghan, Morley. *That Summer in Paris*. New York: Coward-McCann, 1963.

Chamson, André. *La Petite Odyssée*. Paris: Gallimard, 1965.

Cowley, Malcolm and Robert, eds. *Fitzgerald and the Jazz Age*. New York: Charles Scribner's Sons, 1966.

Dos Passos, John. *The Best Times*. New York: New American Library, 1966.

Goldhurst, William. *F. Scott Fitzgerald and His Contemporaries*. Cleveland and New York: World Publishing Co., 1963.

Graham, Sheilah. *College of One*. New York: Viking Press, 1967.

——. *The Real F. Scott Fitzgerald: Thirty-five Years Later*. New York: Grosset & Dunlap, 1976.

—— and Gerold Frank. *Beloved Infidel: The Education of a Woman*. New York: Henry Holt & Co., 1958.

Hemingway, Ernest. *A Moveable Feast*. New York: Charles Scribner's Sons, 1964. New York: Penguin Books, 1966.

Latham, John Aaron. *Crazy Sundays: F. Scott Fitzgerald in Hollywood*. New York: Viking Press, 1970.

Sklar, Robert. *F. Scott Fitzgerald: The Last Laocoön.* New York: Oxford University Press, 1967.

Stein, Gertrude. *The Autobiography of Alice B. Toklas.* New York: Random House, 1933.

Tomkins, Calvin. *Living Well Is the Best Revenge.* New York: Viking Press, 1971.

Wilson, Edmund. *The Shores of Light.* New York: Farrar, Straus & Giroux, 1952.

———. *The Twenties,* ed. by Leon Edel. New York: Farrar, Straus & Giroux, 1975.

I am limiting mention here to a few of the most significant and useful works available. Even a selected bibliography of recollections published concerning Fitzgerald would far exceed the possibilities of this list. I would nevertheless like to mention five especially revealing articles:

THURBER, JAMES. "Scott in Thorns," *The Reporter,* April 17, 1951.

KING, FRANCES KROLL. "Footnotes on Fitzgerald," *Esquire,* December 1959 (by Fitzgerald's secretary in Hollywood).

SCHULBERG, BUDD. "Old Scott: The Mask, the Myth and the Man," *Esquire,* January 1961 (on Hollywood and the Dartmouth carnival).

COWLEY, MALCOLM. "A Ghost Story of the Jazz Age," *The Saturday Review,* January 25, 1964 (Fitzgerald at La Paix).

HEARNE, LAURA GUTHRIE. "A Summer with F. Scott Fitzgerald," *Esquire,* December 1964 (on Fitzgerald's love affair in Asheville in 1935).

Among the works on Fitzgerald's life, I am first of all indebted to the biographies by Mizener (1951) and Turnbull (1962); they have been extremely useful despite certain errors and gaps. Many publications have appeared since then to cast light on hitherto obscure aspects of Fitzgerald's life, especially Nancy Milford's richly documented *Zelda,* which gave me valuable details on the writer's relationship with his wife. Calvin Tomkins's study of Gerald Murphy enabled me to highlight the important role the Murphys played in the Fitzgeralds' lives in France.

In the twenty years I worked on Fitzgerald, I visited most of the places he lived and interviewed a number of people. Some of the places have changed, some of the houses he lived in have vanished. I was fortunate enough to see Rockville, the Fitzgerald family cradle, before it fell victim to urban development. My first visit in Maryland, in 1960, was to the Fitzgeralds' grave. But when I went to see the Garden of Allah in Hollywood a few months later, I found that it had just been torn down. I narrowly missed seeing La Paix before it disappeared; thanks to a tip from Andrew Turnbull, who had been warned by Baltimore *Evening Sun* reporter John Sherwood, I managed to visit the house in September 1961, on the eve of its demolition. Two small panels from the study in which Fitzgerald wrote *Tender Is the Night* thus escaped the wreckers; I can see them in a corner of my office as I write these lines.

From St. Paul to Hollywood via Buffalo, New York, Montgomery, Great Neck, Ellerslie, Baltimore and Asheville, I have seldom failed to find witnesses willing to recount their memories of the Fitzgeralds, even though those memories were often blurred by time or adulterated by recollections of things read. Fitzgerald's personality incites to sensationalism, inflation, extrapolation when the facts seem too routine. So great is the power of the Fitzgerald legend that it is sometimes difficult to separate truth about him from apocrypha.

Luckily, recent works—biographies of, and letters by, his contemporaries—allow for more accurate cross-checking and chronology than was once possible. To cite only one example, Carlos Baker's minutely documented biography of Hemingway makes hash of a fanciful story by Aaron Latham in which Fitzgerald supposedly sheltered Hemingway in his Malibu Beach retreat and supported him while he completed *For Whom the Bell Tolls*.

I therefore used uncorroborated recollections with the greatest caution, preferring to rely on confirmed sources that are generally considered impartial. Among the people who knew Fitzgerald well and whom I had the privilege of interviewing, I shall list only those whose names appear in this book: Sylvia Beach, Lucie and André Chamson, John Dos Passos, Lubow Egorova, Sheilah Graham, Edouard Jozan, Sara Mayfield, Esther Murphy Arthur, Gerald Murphy, Dwight Taylor, Alice Toklas, Andrew Turnbull, Edmund Wilson. I take this opportunity to repeat my gratitude for the help they so generously gave me. I would also like to thank Scottie Fitzgerald Smith for the details she was kind enough to supply about her childhood in Paris. Matthew J. Bruccoli, through his publication of so many of Fitzgerald's unpublished writings, considerably lightened the last stages of my work, when I was constantly having to verify the notes I had taken at Princeton.

In this connection I want particularly to express my gratitude to Alexander Clark and Wanda Randall of the Princeton University Library's Rare Book Department. From my first visit there in 1959, they unfailingly helped me in my research with exemplary kindness and efficiency. Thanks to their unflagging patience, I was able to examine all of the immense Fitzgerald collection, including manuscripts, notebooks, files, press clippings, letters, bills, prescriptions, contracts, even passports whose immigration stamps clarified a number of previously obscure points.

NOTES

(The initials FPP used in these notes stand for the unclassified Fitzgerald Princeton Papers.)
(Works by Fitzgerald have no author attribution.)

CHAPTER 1

1. Henry Dan Piper, *F. Scott Fitzgerald: A Critical Portrait* (New York: Holt, Rinehart & Winston, 1965), p. 6.
2. *The Apprentice Fiction of Francis Scott Fitzgerald* (New Brunswick, N.J.: Rutgers University Press, 1965), p. 67.
3. Ibid., p. 68.
4. *The Letters of F. Scott Fitzgerald* (New York: Charles Scribner's Sons, 1963), pp. 419–20.
5. Preface to *Etchings of Historic Maryland Homes* by S. Donovan Swann, in *F. Scott Fitzgerald in His Own Time: A Miscellany* (Kent, Ohio: Kent State University Press, 1971), p. 158.
6. *Apprentice Fiction*, p. 68.
7. Interview in the New York *Post*, September 25, 1936, in *Fitzgerald Miscellany*, p. 296.
8. Ibid.
9. *Tender Is the Night* (New York: Charles Scribner's Sons, 1934), p. 203.
10. *Apprentice Fiction*, p. 63.
11. *Letters*, p. 503.
12. Press excerpt in Fitzgerald Scrapbook.
13. *The Great Gatsby* (New York: Charles Scribner's Sons, 1925), p. 169.
14. *Letters*, p. 531.
15. Letter from Mgr. Dowling, June 3, 1921, in FPP.
16. *F. Scott Fitzgerald's Ledger* (Washington, D.C.: NCR/Microcard Editions, 1972), p. 165.
17. *Letters*, p. 456.
18. *The Stories of F. Scott Fitzgerald* (New York: Charles Scribner's Sons, 1951), p. 69.
19. *Fitzgerald Miscellany*, p. 141.
20. *Ledger*, p. 14.
21. Ibid., p. 21.
22. Ibid., p. 169.
23. Ibid., p. 160.
24. Piper, *Fitzgerald*, p. 11.
25. Letter dated July 18, 1907, in FPP.
26. Andrew Turnbull, *Scott Fitzgerald: A Biography* (New York: Charles Scribner's Sons, 1962), p. 37.
27. *Letters*, p. 419.
28. Ibid., p. 541.
29. Letter dated September 15, 1936, in *Letters*, p. 199.

CHAPTER 2

1. "A Night at the Fair," in *Afternoon of an Author* (Princeton, N.J.: Princeton University Library, 1957), p. 23.
2. "He Thinks He Is Wonderful," in *Taps at Reveille* (New York: Charles Scribner's Sons, 1935), p. 49.
3. *The Crack-Up* (New York: New Directions, 1945), pp. 233–34.
4. *This Side of Paradise* (New York: Charles Scribner's Sons, 1920), pp. 15–16.
5. *Thoughtbook of Francis Scott Key Fitzgerald* (Princeton, N.J.: Princeton University Library, 1965).
6. *This Side of Paradise*, p. 73.
7. Ibid.
8. Ibid., p. 101.
9. *Ledger*, p. 165.
10. "The Freshest Boy," in *Taps*, p. 25.
11. *This Side of Paradise*, p. 30.
12. *Fitzgerald Miscellany*, p. 4.
13. "Author's House," in *Afternoon*, pp. 234–35.
14. *This Side of Paradise*, pp. 26–27.
15. Ibid., p. 26.
16. FPP.
17. *This Side of Paradise*, p. 26.
18. *Fitzgerald Miscellany*, p. 134.
19. *Times Literary Supplement*, October 31, 1958, p. 632.
20. *Ledger*, p. 155.
21. Ibid.
22. Ibid.
23. *Apprentice Fiction*, p. 68.
24. Manuscript of *The Romantic Egoists* in FPP.

CHAPTER 3

1. *Afternoon*, p. 108.
2. *The Romantic Egoists* (New York: Charles Scribner's Sons, 1974), Chap. 1, p. 13.
3. *The Romantic Egoists*, p. 33; *This Side of Paradise*, pp. 20–21.
4. *This Side of Paradise*, p. 20.
5. Christian Gauss, "Edmund Wilson," *Princeton University Library Chronicle*, February 1944, p. 41.
6. *This Side of Paradise*, pp. 46–47.
7. *Afternoon*, p. 93.
8. *This Side of Paradise*, p. 57.
9. John Peale Bishop, *Collected Essays* (New York: Charles Scribner's Sons, 1948), p. 394.
10. Edmund Wilson, "Woodrow Wilson at Princeton," in *The Shores of Light* (New York: Farrar, Straus & Giroux, 1952), p. 312.
11. Ibid.
12. Edmund Wilson, "Prologue, 1952: Christian Gauss as a Teacher of Literature," in *Shores of Light*, p. 6.
13. Ibid., p. 15.
14. Ibid., p. 5.
15. Ibid., p. 15.
16. "Princeton," in *Afternoon*, p. 75.
17. *Ledger*, p. 163.
18. *This Side of Paradise*, pp. 55–56.
19. Turnbull, *Fitzgerald*, p. 52.
20. Ibid.
21. *Letters*, p. 88.

22. Wilson, *Shores of Light*, p. 27.
23. *Letters*, p. 348.

CHAPTER 4

1. Bishop, *Essays*, p. 400.
2. *This Side of Paradise*, p. 27.
3. *Gatsby*, p. 6.
4. "Princeton," in *Afternoon*, p. 94.
5. *This Side of Paradise*, p. 46.
6. *Afternoon*, p. 15.
7. *Ibid.*, pp. 94–95.
8. *This Side of Paradise*, pp. 47–48.
9. *Crack-Up*, p. 70.
10. "The Bowl," *The Saturday Evening Post*, January 21, 1928.
11. Ibid.
12. Ibid.
13. Letter from Wilson, August 28, 1915, in FPP.
14. "My Lost City," in *Crack-Up*, p. 24.
15. Letter to Arthur Mizener dated November 7, 1947, in Arthur Mizener, *The Far Side of Paradise* (Boston, Houghton Mifflin Co., 1951 and 1965), pp. 52 and 112.
16. *Nassau Literary Magazine*, January 1916, pp. 318–19.
17. *Crack-Up*, p. 76.
18. This quotation and the one that follows are from Fitzgerald's Scrapbook, in FPP.
19. Letter dated January 19, 1916, in FPP.
20. *Letters*, p. 63.
21. Scrapbook, in FPP.
22. *Crack-Up*, p. 25.
23. *Ibid.*, p. 76.
24. *Afternoon*, p. 109.
25. Letter from Fay dated June 6, 1918, in *This Side of Paradise*, p. 236.
26. *Letters*, p. 320. The letter is undated, but must have been written before the end of October 1917.
27. *Ibid.*, p. 321.

CHAPTER 5

1. *This Side of Paradise*, p. 172.
2. "Who's Who—and Why," in *Afternoon*, p. 105.
3. FPP.
4. Letter to Wilson dated January 10, 1918, in *Letters*, pp. 323–24.
5. *This Side of Paradise*, p. 224.
6. FPP.
7. Letter to Charles Scribner, May 6, 1918.
8. *The Beautiful and Damned* (New York: Charles Scribner's Sons, 1922), p. 320.
9. *Ledger*, p. 172.
10. Ibid.
11. *Ibid.*, p. 173.
12. Ibid.
13. FPP.
14. Zelda Fitzgerald, "Caesar's Things," an unpublished novel, Chap. 4, p. 30, in Nancy Milford, *Zelda* (New York: Harper & Row, 1970), p. 34.
15. *Letters*, p. 454.
16. *Crack-Up*, p. 25.
17. FPP.
18. *Afternoon*, p. 110.
19. *Crack-Up*, p. 85.
20. "Who's Who—and Why," in *Afternoon*, p. 110.

21. Milford, *Zelda*, p. 39.
22. Ibid., p. 41.
23. Ibid., p. 42.
24. Ibid., p. 43.
25. Ibid.
26. *Ledger*, p. 173.
27. Milford, *Zelda*, p. 45.
28. Ibid., p. 47.
29. Ibid., p. 50.
30. *Letters*, p. 189.
31. *Stories*, pp. 151–52.
32. Interview in the St. Paul *Daily News*, March 5, 12 and 19, 1922, in *Fitzgerald Miscellany*, pp. 250–51.
33. FPP.
34. Letter dated March 18, 1918, in FPP.
35. Fay died in the "flu" epidemic on January 18, 1919.
36. Letter to F. Scott Fitzgerald dated August 17, 1918, in FPP.
37. Elizabeth Beckwith Mackie, "My Friend Scott Fitzgerald," in *Fitzgerald/Hemingway Annual* (Washington, D.C.: NCR/Microcard Books, 1970), p. 23.
38. Ibid., p. 17.
39. *Crack-Up*, p. 86.
40. Milford, *Zelda*, p. 55.
41. Ibid., p. 57.
42. The reference is to Wells's novel *Kipps: the Story of a Simple Soul*, published in 1905. (Translator's note.)
43. Letter to Perkins dated January 1920, in *Letters*, p. 141.
44. Turnbull, *Fitzgerald*, p. 104.
45. Milford, *Zelda*, p. 61.
46. Ludlow Fowler to Arthur Mizener, in Mizener, *Far Side of Paradise*, p. 120.
47. Milford, *Zelda*, p. 62.
48. Burt Struthers, quoted by Turnbull, *Fitzgerald*, p. 105.
49. Zelda Fitzgerald, *Save Me the Waltz* (Carbondale and Edwardsville: Southern Illinois University Press, 1960 [1932]), p. 35.

CHAPTER 6

1. "Early Success," in *Crack-Up*, p. 88.
2. Burton Rascoe, *We Were Interrupted* (Garden City, N.Y.: Doubleday & Company, Inc., 1947), p. 20.
3. December 31, 1920, in *Letters*, p. 145.
4. Elizabeth Stevenson, *Babbitts and Bohemians: The American 1920s* (New York: The Macmillan Co., 1967; Collier Books, 1970), pp. 125–26 and 148.
5. *As Ever, Scott Fitz* (Philadelphia and New York: J. B. Lippincott Co., 1972), p. 36.
6. Ibid., p. 34.
7. *Tales of the Jazz Age* (New York: Charles Scribner's Sons, 1922), p. 158.
8. "The Swimmers," in *The Saturday Evening Post*, October 19, 1929.
9. *Crack-Up*, p. 60.
10. Ibid., p. 27.
11. Alexander McKaig, "Diary," entry for April 12, 1920; this and the following excerpts from the diary are taken from Turnbull, *Fitzgerald*.
12. Edmund Wilson, *The Twenties* (New York: Farrar, Straus & Giroux, 1975), p. 47.
13. Ibid.
14. Ibid.
15. McKaig, "Diary," entry for September 11, 1920.
16. Wilson, *Twenties*, p. 55.
17. McKaig, "Diary," entry for September 11, 1920.
18. Edna St. Vincent Millay, "First Fig," *A Few Figs from Thistles* (New York: Harper & Brothers, 1923).
19. Wilson, *Twenties*, p. 51.

20. Gauss letter to F. Scott Fitzgerald dated November 14, 1930, in FPP.
21. *Crack-Up*, p. 28.
22. Dorothy Parker to Nancy Milford, in Milford, *Zelda*, p. 67.
23. Ibid.
24. Ibid.
25. *Crack-Up*, p. 41.
26. Milford, *Zelda*, p. 70.
27. G. J. Nathan, "Memories of Fitzgerald, Lewis and Dreiser," in *Esquire*, October 1958, p. 148.
28. Ibid.
29. Ibid.
30. Ibid.
31. Ibid.
32. McKaig, "Diary," entry for October 13, 1920.
33. "The Cruise of the Rolling Junk," in *Motor*, April 1924, pp. 55 and 68.
34. Letter to Charles Scribner, August 12, 1920.
35. Milford, *Zelda*, p. 74.
36. Lawton Campbell to Nancy Milford, in Milford, *Zelda*, p. 78.
37. *Dear Scott/Dear Max: The Fitzgerald-Perkins Correspondence* (New York: Charles Scribner's Sons, 1971), p. 32.
38. *Beautiful and Damned*, p. 389.
39. *Crack-Up*, pp. 27–28.
40. C. Lawton Campbell, "The Fitzgeralds Were My Friends," an unpublished memoir, in Milford, *Zelda*, p. 81.

CHAPTER 7

1. *Crack-Up*, p. 42.
2. *Ledger*, p. 175.
3. F. Scott Fitzgerald to Edmund Wilson, June 1920, in *Letters*, p. 326.
4. *Ledger*, p. 175.
5. *Letters*, pp. 326–27.
6. Edmund Wilson to F. Scott Fitzgerald, July 5, 1921, in FPP.
7. Wilson, *Twenties*, p. 82.
8. *Letters*, p. 148.
9. Ibid., p. 327.
10. Ibid., p. 153.
11. Milford, *Zelda*, p. 183.
12. F. Scott Fitzgerald to Frances Fitzgerald, June 14, 1940, in FPP.
13. H. L. Mencken, "The National Letters," in *Prejudices: Second Series* (New York: Octagon, 1920).
14. To Harold Ober, December 19, 1919, in *As Ever, Scott Fitz*, p. 7.
15. *Letters*, pp. 326–27.
16. *Bookman*, March 1920, p. 81, in *Fitzgerald Miscellany*, p. 121.
17. *This Side of Paradise*, p. 224.
18. *Fitzgerald Miscellany*, p. 247.
19. *Crack-Up*, p. 14.
20. *Beautiful and Damned*, p. 56.
21. *Dear Scott/Dear Max*, p. 40.
22. *Beautiful and Damned*, p. 142.
23. *Ledger*, p. 176.
24. Ibid.

CHAPTER 8

1. *Ledger*, p. 176.
2. "Under Fire," a review of Thomas Boyd's *Through the Wheat*, the New York *Evening Post*, May 26, 1923, in *Fitzgerald Miscellany*, p. 144.
3. *Dear Scott/Dear Max*, p. 271.

4. Ibid., January 18, 1922, p. 51.
5 Milford, *Zelda*, p. 93.
6. Zelda's Scrapbook.
7. *Letters*, p. 329.
8. Zelda Fitzgerald to Fowler, December 22, 1921, in Milford, *Zelda*, p. 85.
9. *Letters*, p. 334.
10. Bishop, *Essays*, pp. 229–30.
11. "Friend Husband's Latest," the New York *Tribune*, April 2, 1922, reprinted in *Fitzgerald Miscellany*, pp. 333–34.
12. F. Scott Fitzgerald to Max Perkins, July 18, 1922, in FPP.
13. June 20, 1922, in *Dear Scott/Dear Max*, p. 61.
14. "Winter Dreams," in *Stories*, p. 145.
15. Wilson, *Shores of Light*, p. 30.
16. Ibid., p. 31.
17. *Letters*, pp. 330–31.
18. Letter to Wilson, January 1922, in *Letters*.
19. "A Table of Contents," *Tales of the Jazz Age*.
20. Ibid.
21. Wilson, *Shores of Light*, p. 32.
22. *Gatsby*, p. 114.
23. Fitzgerald's Scrapbook, in FPP.
24. Milford, *Zelda*, pp. 93–94.
25. Ibid., p. 94.
26. Ibid., p. 97.
27. Turnbull, *Fitzgerald*, p. 139.
28. Letter dated October 13, 1922, in Turnbull, *Fitzgerald*, p. 133.
29. "How to Live on $36,000 a Year," *The Saturday Evening Post*, April 5, 1924, cited in *Afternoon*, p. 119.
30. Burton Rascoe, *We Were Interrupted* (New York: 1924), pp. 223–26.
31. Wilson, *Shores of Light*, p. 149.
32. Ibid., pp. 151–52.
33. Clifton Fadiman, "Ring Lardner and the Triumph of Hate," *The Nation*, March 22, 1933, p. 316.
34. "Ring," in *Crack-Up*, p. 38.
35. Ibid., p. 35.
36. Turnbull, *Fitzgerald*, p. 135.
37. Milford, *Zelda*, p. 99.
38. Turnbull, *Fitzgerald*, p. 136.
39. James Gray, the St. Paul *Dispatch*, March 2, 1926.
40. B. F. Wilson, "F. Scott Fitzgerald," *The Smart Set*, April 1924, p. 33.

CHAPTER 9

1. *Gatsby*, p. 74.
2. Letter to Max Perkins, December 20, 1924, in *Letters*, p. 173.
3. *Gatsby*, p. 172.
4. Ibid., p. 91.
5. "Early Success," in *Crack-Up*, p. 87.
6. Ibid., p. 29.
7. Edmund Wilson to F. Scott Fitzgerald, May 26, 1922, in FPP.
8. G. J. Nathan, *The Theater, the Drama, the Girls* (New York: 1921), p. 16.
9. *The Vegetable, or, From President to Postman* (New York: Charles Scribner's Sons, 1923), title page.
10. Mencken, "On Being an American," in *Prejudices: Third Series*.
11. "How to Live on $36,000 a Year," in *Afternoon*, p. 118.
12. Ibid., p. 120.
13. To Edmund Wilson, October 7, 1924, in *Letters*, p. 341.

14. "How to Live on $36,000 a Year," in *Afternoon*, pp. 114–15. All succeeding quotes in this chapter are from the same source, pp. 114–27.
15. Matthew 25:14–30.

CHAPTER *10*

1. "How to Live on Practically Nothing a Year," in *Afternoon*, p. 131.
2. *Ledger*, p. 178.
3. To Max Perkins, before April 15, 1924, in *Letters*, p. 162.
4. To Max Perkins, June 18, 1924, in *Letters*, p. 164.
5. To John Jamieson, April 15, 1934, in *Letters*, p. 509.
6. FPP.
7. See note 3.
8. *Letters*, p. 163.
9. *Gatsby*, pp. 111–12.
10. "Author's House," in *Afternoon*, p. 233.
11. *Gatsby*, p. 99.
12. Ibid., p. 2.
13. Ibid.
14. Ibid.
15. Henry James, *Stories of Writers and Artists* (New York: New Directions, 1944), pp. 331 and 336.
16. Cited in *The Price Was High* (New York: Harcourt Brace Jovanovich, 1979), p. 48.
17. Cited in *Fitzgerald Miscellany*, p. 128.
18. *Beautiful and Damned*, p. 309.
19. *Gatsby*, p. 40.
20. Ibid., p. 23.
21. Ibid., p. 182.
22. Ibid., p. 114.
23. Ibid., p. 120.
24. Ibid., p. 17.
25. Manuscript of *Gatsby* in FPP.
26. *Gatsby*, p. 5.
27. Ibid., p. 162.
28. Ibid., p. 42.
29. Ibid., p. 123.
30. Ibid., p. 25.
31. Ibid.
32. *Tender*, p. 12.
33. "Absolution," in *Stories*, p. 171.

CHAPTER *11*

1. *Gatsby*, p. 92.
2. Ibid., p. 34.
3. Ibid., p. 23.
4. To Max Perkins, August 27, 1922, in *Letters*, p. 166.
5. *Gatsby*, p. 158.
6. Ibid., p. 160.
7. Vasili Kandinsky, *Du spirituel dans l'art* (Paris: Denoël-Gonthier, 1969), pp. 122–24. The book exists in English under the title *Concerning the Spiritual in Art and Painting in Particular* (New York: Dover Books, 1970).
8. *Gatsby*, p. 23.
9. Edmond and Jules de Goncourt, *Journal* (Paris: Denoël-Gonthier, 1936), Vol. 1, p. 306.

10. *Afternoon*, p. 69.
11. *Taps*, p. 125.
12. *Tender*, p. 136.
13. Ibid., pp. 135–36.
14. Ibid., p. 136.
15. "Three Acts of Music," *Esquire*, May 1936.
16. *Gatsby*, p. 112.
17. Ibid.
18. *Gatsby* manuscript in FPP.
19. *Gatsby*, pp. 99–101.
20. *Crack-Up*, p. 18.
21. *Gatsby*, p. 151.
22. Ibid.
23. *Crack-Up*, p. 13.
24. Ibid., p. 16.
25. *Gatsby*, p. 40.
26. *Gatsby* manuscript in FPP.
27. *The Last Tycoon* (New York: Charles Scribner's Sons, 1941), p. 95.

CHAPTER 12

1. Zelda Fitzgerald, *Save Me the Waltz*, p. 72.
2. Milford, *Zelda*, p. 104.
3. Zelda Fitzgerald, *Save Me the Waltz*, p. 72.
4. "How to Live on Practically Nothing a Year," in *Afternoon*, p. 144.
5. Zelda Fitzgerald, *Save Me the Waltz*, p. 79.
6. Ibid., p. 80.
7. *Gatsby*, p. 12.
8. Ibid., p. 118.
9. "How to Live on Practically Nothing a Year," in *Afternoon*, p. 148.
10. Zelda Fitzgerald, *Save Me the Waltz*, p. 84.
11. Ibid., p. 89.
12. *Ledger*, p. 178.
13. Ernest Hemingway, *A Moveable Feast* (New York: Penguin Books, 1966), p. 129.
14. Milford, *Zelda*, p. 114.
15. Fitzgerald, "Notebooks in FPP."
16. *Ledger*, p. 178.
17. Milford, *Zelda*, p. 174.
18. Zelda Fitzgerald, "Caesar's Things," Chap. 7, p. 5, in Milford, *Zelda*.
19. Ernest Boyd, *Portraits, Real and Imaginery* (London: 1924), p. 220.
20. *The Notebooks of F. Scott Fitzgerald* (New York: Harcourt Brace Jovanovich, 1978), note 765, p. 106.
21. *Letters*, p. 166.
22. Raymond Radiguet, *Le Bal du Comte d'Orgel* (Paris: Club Français du Livre 1951), p. 207. The book exists in an English translation by Violet Schiff, *Count d'Orgel Opens the Ball* (London: The Harvill Press, 1952). The translation given here is W. R. Byron's from the French edition.
23. *Letters*, p. 168.
24. *Tender*, p. 15.
25. The farm girl whose visions of the Virgin Mary turned Lourdes into a pilgrimage site. (Translator's note.)
26. "The Adjuster," in *Tales of the Jazz Age*, p. 142.
27. John Wheeler to Paul Reynolds, December 4, 1924, in *As Ever, Scott Fitz*, p. 70, note 4.
28. To Harold Ober, January 26, 1925, in *As Ever, Scott Fitz*, p. 74.
29. Ibid., p. 73.
30. Letter to Howard Coxe, April 15, 1934, in FPP.
31. *Crack-Up*, p. 58.

32. To Bishop, April 1925, in *Letters*, p. 357.
33. Ibid., p. 356.
34. To Max Perkins, December 20, 1924, in *Letters*, p. 173.
35. To Max Perkins, January 24, 1925, in *Letters*, pp. 175–76.
36. Max Perkins to F. Scott Fitzgerald, November 20, 1924, in *Dear Scott/Dear Max*, pp. 82–83.
37. Max Perkins to F. Scott Fitzgerald, February 24, 1925, ibid., p. 94.
38. Ibid., p. 101.
39. Ibid., p. 272, note 33.
40. To Edmund Wilson, May 1925, in *Letters*, p. 342.
41. *Ledger*, p. 179.
42. July 14, Bastille Day, is the French counterpart of America's Independence Day. (Translator's note.)
43. Malcolm Cowley, *Exile's Return* (New York: W. W. Norton & Co., 1934), p. 38.
44. Ibid.
45. *Stories*, p. 388.
46. The title can be roughly translated as The Tomboy. (Translator's note.)
47. "How to Waste Material—a Note on My Generation," *The Bookman*, May 1926.
48. *Letters*, p. 167.
49. Glenway Wescott, "The Moral of Scott Fitzgerald," in *Crack-Up*, p. 324.
50. *Letters*, p. 184.
51. Ibid., p. 170.
52. Ibid., p. 196.
53. Ibid., p. 198.
54. Ibid., p. 200.
55. *Fitzgerald/Hemingway Annual*, p. 12.
56. Ibid., p. 11.
57. *Letters*, p. 298.
58. Letter of April 6, 1934, in *The Papers of Christian Gauss*, ed. Katherine Gauss (New York: Random House, 1957), p. 218.

CHAPTER 13

1. Hemingway, *A Moveable Feast*, pp. 107–8.
2. Ibid., p. 112.
3. Ibid.
4. Ibid., pp. 132–33.
5. Gertrude Stein to F. Scott Fitzgerald, May 22, 1925, in *Crack-Up*, p. 308.
6. Gertrude Stein, *The Autobiography of Alice B. Toklas* (New York: Random House, 1933). Modern Library edition, 1955, pp. 218–19.
7. Edith Wharton to F. Scott Fitzgerald, June 8, 1925, in *Crack-Up*, p. 309.
8. T. S. Eliot to F. Scott Fitzgerald, December 31, 1925, in *Crack-Up*, p. 310.
9. To Christian Gauss, April 23, 1934, in *Letters*, p. 385.
10. Turnbull, *Fitzgerald*, p. 153.
11. To Max Perkins, August 28, 1925, in *Dear Scott/Dear Max*, p. 120.
12. *Tender*, pp. 6, 16.
13. Calvin Tomkins, *Living Well Is the Best Revenge* (New York: Viking Press, 1971), p. 39.
14. *Ledger*, p. 178.
15. *Crack-Up*, p. 58.
16. "Autobiographical Sketch," March 16, 1932, quoted in Milford, *Zelda*, p. 251.
17. Milford, *Zelda*, pp. 124–25.
18. To Sara Murphy, August 15, 1935, in *Letters*, p. 423.
19. Gerald Murphy to F. Scott Fitzgerald, September 19, 1925, in FPP.
20. *Letters*, p. 488.
21. To Max Perkins, December 27, 1925, in *Letters*, p. 195.
22. Ibid., p. 193.
23. Ibid., p. 488.

24. Carlos Baker, *Ernest Hemingway: A Life Story* (New York: Charles Scribner's Sons, 1969), p. 222.
25. Hemingway, *A Moveable Feast*, p. 158.
26. To Max Perkins, *Letters*, p. 200.
27. To Harold Ober, April 26, 1926, in *As Ever, Scott Fitz*, p. 89.
28. *Crack-Up*, pp. 89–90.
29. Ibid., p. 90.
30. To John Peale Bishop, June 1926, in *Letters*, p. 359.
31. *Tender*, p. 32.
32. Tomkins, *Living Well*, p. 125.
33. Ibid.
34. Ibid., p. 127.
35. Gerald Murphy to Ernest Hemingway, July 13, 1926, in Baker, *Hemingway*, p. 222.
36. John Dos Passos, *The Best Times* (New York: New American Library, 1966), p. 152.
37. Turnbull, *Fitzgerald*, p. 161.
38. Grace Moore, *You're Only Human Once* (New York: Arno, 1944), pp. 108–9.
39. Milford, *Zelda*, p. 121.
40. To Ernest Hemingway, September 24, 1926, in *Letters*, p. 297.

CHAPTER 14

1. FPP.
2. Ernest Hemingway to F. Scott Fitzgerald, December 21, 1935, in FPP.
3. Ernest Hemingway to F. Scott Fitzgerald, December 15, 1925, in FPP.
4. Tomkins, *Living Well*, p. 141.
5. *Crack-Up*, p. 325.
6. Ernest Hemingway to F. Scott Fitzgerald, September 13, 1929, in FPP.
7. Ernest Hemingway to F. Scott Fitzgerald, September 4, 1929, in FPP.
8. Turnbull, *Fitzgerald*, p. 168.
9. To Max Perkins, August 10, 1926, in *Letters*, p. 207.
10. Milford, *Zelda*, p. 128.
11. Fitzgerald Scrapbooks, cited in *Fitzgerald Miscellany*, pp. 272–73.
12. New York *World*, April 3, 1927, in Fitzgerald Scrapbooks, cited in *Fitzgerald Miscellany*, p. 276.
13. G. J. Nathan, "The Golden Boy of the Twenties," *Esquire*, October 1958, pp. 148–49.
14. To Frances Fitzgerald, July 1937, in *Letters*, p. 16.
15. Zelda Fitzgerald to Carl Van Vechten, May 27, 1927, in Milford, *Zelda*, p. 133.
16. "Looking Back Eight Years," in *College Humor*, June 1928, p. 37.
17. Turnbull, *Fitzgerald*, p. 173.
18. Ibid., p. 175.
19. Milford, *Zelda*, pp. 134–35.
20. To Ernest Hemingway, November 1927, in *Letters*, p. 301.
21. Wilson, "A Weekend at Ellerslie," in *Shores of Light*, p. 375.
22. Zelda Fitzgerald, *Save Me the Waltz*, p. 98.
23. André Chamson, *La Petite Odyssée* (Paris: Gallimard, 1965), p. 46.
24. Ibid., pp. 50–51.
25. "The Swimmers," in *The Saturday Evening Post*, October 19, 1929.
26. To Max Perkins, July 21, 1928, in *Letters*, p. 211.
27. Chamson, *La Petite Odyssée*, p. 48.
28. Ibid.
29. Mizener, *The Far Side of Paradise*, p. 147.
30. James Joyce to F. Scott Fitzgerald, July 7, 1928, in FPP.
31. *Crack-Up*, pp. 20–21.
32. *Ledger*, p. 182.
33. Max Perkins to F. Scott Fitzgerald, November 13, 1929, in *Dear Scott/Dear Max*, p. 154.

34. To Max Perkins, March 1, 1929, in *Letters*, p. 213.
35. *Crack-Up*, p. 50.
36. Zelda Fitzgerald to F. Scott Fitzgerald, in Milford, *Zelda*, p. 168.
37. Ibid., p. 261.
38. Sheilah Graham, *The Real F. Scott Fitzgerald* (New York: Grosset & Dunlap, 1976), pp. 30, 120.
39. Morley Callaghan, *That Summer in Paris* (New York: Coward-McCann, 1963), p. 150.
40. Ibid., p. 156.
41. Ibid., p. 186.
42. Zelda Fitzgerald, "Autobiographical Sketch," March 16, 1932, cited in Milford, *Zelda*, p. 250.
43. Ibid., p. 183.
44. *Dear Scott/Dear Max*, p. 159.
45. Callaghan, *That Summer*, p. 204.
46. Ibid., p. 205.
47. Ibid., p. 191.
48. Ibid., p. 205.
49. Ibid., p. 213.
50. Ibid.
51. Ibid., p. 217.

CHAPTER 15

1. *Letters*, p. 215.
2. November 5, 1929, in *Letters*, p. 216.
3. *Crack-Up*, p. 19.
4. Sara Murphy to F. Scott Fitzgerald, autumn 1929, in FPP.
5. FPP.
6. Callaghan, *That Summer*, p. 246.
7. Ibid., pp. 246–47.
8. Dos Passos, *The Best Times*, p. 203.
9. "Autobiographical Sketch," in Milford, *Zelda*, pp. 251–52.
10. *Crack-Up*, p. 52.
11. Milford, *Zelda*, p. 158.
12. Turnbull, *Fitzgerald*, p. 192.
13. To Dr. Oscar Forel, June 8, 1930, cited in Milford, *Zelda*, p. 171.
14. Ibid., pp. 171–72.
15. Ibid.
16. Ibid., p. 191.
17. Ibid., p. 176.
18. Ibid., p. 170.
19. Ibid., p. 173.
20. Ibid., p. 181.
21. Ibid., p. 152.
22. Ibid, pp. 182–83.
23. Ibid., pp. 183–84.
24. Ibid., p. 178.
25. To Harold Ober, November 30, 1930, in *As Ever, Scott Fitz*, p. 172.
26. To Max Perkins, September 1, 1930, in *Letters*, p. 224.
27. To Max Perkins, July 30, 1934, in *Letters*, p. 251.
28. To Thomas Wolfe, April 2, 1934, in *Letters*, p. 508.
29. "One Trip Abroad," in *Afternoon*, p. 205.
30. To Harold Ober, December 1930, in *As Ever, Scott Fitz*, p. 174.
31. *Letters*, p. 588.
32. "Babylon Revisited," in *Stories*, p. 388.
33. *Tender*, p. 203.
34. *Apprentice Fiction*, p. 67.

35. To Dr. Oscar Forel, January 29, 1931, in Milford, *Zelda*, p. 186.
36. To Harold Ober, December 1930, in *As Ever, Scott Fitz*, p. 174.
37. "On Your Own," unpublished, collected in *Price*, p. 327.
38. "Flight and Pursuit," in *Price*, p. 319.
39. Harold Ober to F. Scott Fitzgerald, May 19, 1931, in *Bits of Paradise* (New York: Charles Scribner's Sons, 1973), p. 176.
40. Milford, *Zelda*, p. 188.
41. *Crack-Up*, pp. 52–53.
42. Ibid., p. 52.
43. Ibid., p. 53.
44. Ibid.
45. Ibid.
46. Ibid.
47. Tomkins, *Living Well*, p. 138.
48. Gerald Murphy to F. Scott Fitzgerald, December 31, 1935, in FPP.
49. Milford, *Zelda*, p. 191.
50. *Crack-Up*, p. 54.

CHAPTER 16

1. *Crack-Up*, p. 32.
2. Ibid.
3. Ibid.
4. Ibid., p. 54.
5. FPP.
6. To Harold Ober, December 1931, in *As Ever, Scott Fitz*, p. 181.
7. To Dr. Oscar Forel, April 18, 1932, in Milford, *Zelda*, p. 209.
8. To Dr. Adolf Meyer, April 10, 1933, in FPP.
9. To Dr. Oscar Forel, April 18, 1933, in Milford, *Zelda*, p. 209.
10. Ibid., p. 215.
11. To Dr. Mildred Squires, March 14, 1932, in FPP.
12. Zelda Fitzgerald to F. Scott Fitzgerald, March 1932, in Milford, *Zelda*, p. 220.
13. Ibid., p. 221.
14. Zelda Fitzgerald's Scrapbooks.
15. To Dr. Mildred Squires, March 1932, in Milford, *Zelda*, p. 222.
16. *Ledger*, p. 186.
17. Ibid.
18. Matthew J. Bruccoli, *The Composition of Tender Is the Night* (Pittsburgh: University of Pittsburgh Press, 1963), p. 76.
19. Ibid.
20. Ibid., p. 80.
21. Ibid. For "Pincio" read "Paris."
22. "One Hundred False Starts," in *Afternoon*, pp. 158–59.
23. Ibid., p. 172.
24. *Ledger*, entry for November 1932, p. 187.
25. To Max Perkins, January 19, 1933, in *Letters*, p. 230.
26. To Edmund Wilson, March 1933, in *Letters*, p. 345.
27. Turnbull, *Fitzgerald*, p. 230.
28. Zelda Fitzgerald to John Peale Bishop, in Milford, *Zelda*, p. 258.
29. Zelda Fitzgerald to Max Perkins, October 1932, in Milford, *Zelda*, p. 269.
30. Ibid., p. 199.
31. Ibid., p. 215.
32. To Zelda Fitzgerald, spring 1932, in Milford, *Zelda*, pp. 254–55.
33. To Edmund Wilson, February 1933, in *Letters*, p. 345.
34. *Letters*, p. 440.
35. To Max Perkins, March 4, 1934, in *Letters*, pp. 247–48.
36. Milford, *Zelda*, p. 267.
37. Ibid., p. 268.

38. Dos Passos, *Best Times*, pp. 209–10.
39. Malcolm Cowley, "A Ghost Story of the Jazz Age," *Saturday Review*, January 25, 1964, pp. 20–21.
40. Mizener, *The Far Side of Paradise*, p. 250.
41. Ibid.
42. *Crack-Up*, p. 55.
43. Max Perkins to F. Scott Fitzgerald, in *Dear Scott/Dear Max*, p. 190.
44. To Max Perkins, March 11, 1935, in *Letters*, pp. 259–260.
45. To Harold Ober, December 8, 1934, in *As Ever, Scott Fitz*, p. 209.
46. *Romantic Egoists*, p. 199.

CHAPTER *17*

1. To Max Perkins, November 8, 1934, in *Letters*, p. 253.
2. April 9, 1934, p. 12.
3. Milford, *Zelda*, p. 290.
4. James Thurber, "Scott in Thorns," in *The Reporter*, April 17, 1951.
5. Ibid.
6. *Romantic Egoists*, p. 200.
7. *Ledger*, p. 188.
8. Ibid.
9. *Crack-Up*, pp. 57, 62.
10. Milford, *Zelda*, p. 303.
11. Ibid., p. 305.
12. Mizener, *The Far Side of Paradise*, p. 255.
13. To Gertrude Stein, November 23, 1934, in *Letters*, p. 517.
14. December 29, 1934, in *Letters*, p. 518.
15. *Ledger*, p. 189.
16. *As Ever, Scott Fitz*, p. 218.
17. *Ledger*, p. 189.
18. Laura Guthrie Hearne, "A Summer with F. Scott Fitzgerald," *Esquire*, December 1964, p. 161.
19. *Notebooks*, notes 550–51, pp. 78–79.
20. Hearne, "Summer," p. 161.
21. Ibid., p. 162.
22. In seducing Sophie de Coulanges in the eighteenth-century novel *Les Liaisons dangereuses* by Choderlos de Laclos. (Translator's note.)
23. Hearne, "Summer," p. 236.
24. Ibid.
25. Ibid., p. 254.
26. Ibid., p. 258.
27. To James Boyd, August 1935, in *Letters*, p. 528.
28. To Harold Ober, September 5, 1935, in *As Ever, Scott Fitz*, p. 224.
29. *Taps*, p. 297.
30. To Laura Guthrie Hearne, September 23, 1935, *Letters*, p. 531.
31. December 12, 1935, in *As Ever, Scott Fitz*, p. 233.
32. *Notebooks*, pp. 260–61.
33. "Sleeping and Waking," in *Crack-Up*, p. 67.
34. "Afternoon of an Author," in *Afternoon*, pp. 224, 228.
35. "The Lost Decade," in *Stories*, pp. 471–72.
36. Ibid., p. 164.
37. *Crack-Up*, p. 82.

CHAPTER *18*

1. *Crack-Up*, p. 84.
2. Carl Van Doren, *The Viking Portable Library* (New York: Viking Press, 1945), pp. 91, 95.

3. In his edition of *The Crack-Up*, Edmund Wilson reversed the titles of the last two essays. The order of their publication in *Esquire* proceeded from "The Crack-Up" to "Pasting It Together" and finally "Handle with Care." This is the order used here.

4. *Crack-Up*, p. 69.

5. May 8, 1935, in *Letters*, p. 523.

6. *Crack-Up*, p. 71.

7. Ibid., pp. 72–73.

8. Ibid., pp. 73–74.

9. *Gatsby*, p. 124.

10. *Crack-Up*, p. 74.

11. Ibid., pp. 79–80.

12. E. M. Cioran, "Physionomie d'un effondrement," *Profils*, October 1952.

13. *Nouvelles Litteraires*, December 30, 1965, p. 11.

14. *Crack-Up*, p. 77.

15. Ibid.

16. Ibid., pp. 77–78.

17. Ibid., pp. 75–76.

18. Ibid., p. 79.

19. Ibid., pp. 80–81.

20. Ibid., p. 81.

21. Ibid., p. 84.

22. Ibid., p. 83.

23. To Beatrice, September 1935, in *Letters*, pp. 529–30.

24. May 28, 1934, in *Letters*, p. 307.

25. May 10, 1934, in *Letters*, p. 307.

26. April 8, 1935, cited in Malcolm Cowley's introduction to *Tender Is the Night*, 1951 edition, p. xi.

27. April 15, 1935, in *Letters*, p. 261.

28. FPP.

29. Baker, *Hemingway*, p. 305.

30. Stein, *Autobiography*, p. 216.

31. December 21, 1935.

32. Ernest Hemingway, "The Snows of Kilimanjaro," *Esquire*, August 1936, pp. 195, 200.

33. Ibid., p. 28.

34. July 1936, in *Letters*, p. 311.

35. September 19, 1935, in *Letters*, p. 267.

36. September 15, 1935, in *Letters*, p. 543.

37. New York *Post*, September 25, 1936, in *Fitzgerald Miscellany*, p. 294.

38. Baker, *Hemingway*, p. 376.

39. Edmund Wilson, "Letters to the Russians About Hemingway," *The New Republic*, December 11, 1935.

40. Turnbull, *Fitzgerald*, p. 282.

41. Marjorie Kinnan Rawlings to Arthur Mizener, in Mizener, *The Far Side of Paradise*, p. 291.

42. Turnbull, *Fitzgerald*, p. 282.

43. November 8, 1940, in *Letters*, p. 312.

44. FPP (notes for *The Last Tycoon*).

45. April 18, 1927, in *Letters*, p. 300.

46. *Crack-Up*, p. 79.

47. *Letters*, p. 309.

48. Ibid., p. 229.

49. *Crack-Up*, p. 177.

50. *Letters*, p. 430.

51. December 24, 1938, in *Letters*, p. 281.

52. *Crack-Up*, p. 181.

CHAPTER *19*

1. April 24, 1925, in *Letters*, pp. 180–81.
2. January 10, 1935, in *As Ever, Scott Fitz*, p. 216.
3. July 1937, in *Letters*, pp. 16–17.
4. *Crack-Up*, p. 78.
5. *Tycoon*, p. 11.
6. Ibid., p. 80.
7. Milford, *Zelda*, p. 314.
8. Aaron Latham, *Crazy Sundays: F. Scott Fitzgerald in Hollywood* (New York: Viking Press, 1970), p. 104.
9. Anthony Powell, "Hollywood Canteen," in *Fitzgerald/Hemingway Annual*, 1970, p. 76.
10. *Tycoon*, p. 80.
11. July 19, 1937, in *Letters*, p. 274.
12. Lillian Hellman, *An Unfinished Woman* (Boston: Little, Brown, 1967), pp. 67–68.
13. Ibid.
14. Sheilah Graham and Gerold Frank, *Beloved Infidel: The Education of a Woman* (New York: Henry Holt & Co., 1958), p. 175.
15. Ibid., p. 182.
16. Latham, *Crazy Sundays*, p. 127.
17. Ibid., pp. 8–9.
18. Ibid., p. 123.
19. November 27, 1937, in FPP.
20. *Letters*, p. 19.
21. Mizener, *The Far Side of Paradise*, p. 300.
22. Graham and Frank, *Beloved Infidel*, p. 205.
23. Latham, *Crazy Sundays*, p. 133.
24. *As Ever, Scott Fitz*, p. 342.
25. Latham, *Crazy Sundays*, p. 187.
26. Ibid., p. 121.
27. Ibid., pp. 123–24.
28. January 20, 1938, in *Letters*, p. 563.
29. February 9, 1938, in *As Ever, Scott Fitz*, p. 350.

CHAPTER *20*

1. February 1938, in *Letters*, p. 22.
2. March 4, 1938, in *Letters*, pp. 275–76.
3. N.d., in FPP.
4. Latham, *Crazy Sundays*, p. 159.
5. March 11, 1938, in *Letters*, p. 427.
6. Bob Thomas, *Thalberg—Life and Legend* (Garden City, N.Y.: Doubleday & Company, Inc., 1969), p. 210.
7. Spring 1938, in *Letters*, p. 29.
8. March 11, 1938, in *As Ever, Scott Fitz*, p. 359.
9. March 4, 1938, in Milford, *Zelda*, pp. 316–17.
10. *Letters*, p. 27.
11. July 7, 1938, in *Letters*, p. 33.
12. June 1938, in *As Ever, Scott Fitz*, p. 365.
13. Graham and Frank, *Beloved Infidel*, p. 256.
14. Powell, "Hollywood Canteen," p. 77.
15. December 13, 1940, in *Letters*, p. 291.
16. February 25, 1939, in *Letters*, p. 284.
17. To Perkins, April 23, 1939, in *Dear Scott/Dear Max*, p. 245.
18. "Financing Finnegan," *Esquire*, January 1938.

19. Graham and Frank, *Beloved Infidel*, p. 217.
20. Ibid., p. 188.
21. December 24, 1938, in *Letters*, pp. 281–82.
22. January 4, 1939, in *Letters*, p. 283.
23. January 11, 1939, in *As Ever, Scott Fitz*, p. 381.
24. To Harold Ober, January 1939, ibid., p. 381.
25. Budd Schulberg, "Old Scott: The Masque, the Myth and the Man," in *The Four Seasons of Success* (Garden City, N.Y.: Doubleday & Company, Inc. 1972), p. 95.

CHAPTER 21

1. Frances Kroll King, "Footnotes on Fitzgerald," *Esquire*, December 1959, pp. 149–50.
2. Graham and Frank, *Beloved Infidel*, p. 278.
3. June 21, 1939, in *As Ever, Scott Fitz*, p. 394.
4. December 19, 1939, in *Letters*, pp. 286–87.
5. Graham and Frank, *Beloved Infidel*, p. 294.
6. Ibid., p. 296.
7. Ibid., pp. 300–1.
8. Ibid., p. 303.
9. Ibid., p. 305.
10. *Letters*, p. 48.
11. February 25, 1939, in *Letters*, p. 284.
12. May 11, 1940, in *Letters*, p. 116.
13. "My Generation," *Esquire*, October 1968, pp. 119–23.
14. May 20, 1940, in *Letters*, p. 288.
15. To Max Perkins, May 20, 1940, in *Letters*, p. 289.
16. To Max Perkins, June 6, 1940, in *Letters*, p. 289.
17. October 31, 1939, in *Letters*, p. 62.
18. October 5, 1940, in *Letters*, p. 96.
19. October 19, 1940, in *Letters*, p. 127.
20. October 23, 1940, in *Letters*, p. 128.
21. November 23, 1940, in *Letters*, p. 131.
22. Ibid.
23. To Zelda Fitzgerald, December 13, 1940, in *Letters*, p. 132.
24. Graham and Frank, *Beloved Infidel*, p. 327.
25. FPP.
26. Frank Scully, *Rogue's Gallery* (Culver City, Calif.: Murray & Gee, 1943), pp. 268–69.
27. *Gatsby*, p. 176.
28. Milford, *Zelda*, pp. 350–51.
29. March 30, 1936, in *Letters*, pp. 425–26.
30. To Scottie Fitzgerald, December 1940, in *Letters*, p. 100.
31. Quoted by Joan M. Allen, *Candles and Carnival Lights: The Catholic Sensibility of F. Scott Fitzgerald* (New York: New York University Press, 1976), p. 144.

BIBLIOGRAPHY

1. See Chapter 13, note 6.
2. S. V. Benét, "Fitzgerald's Unfinished Symphony," *The Saturday Review of Literature*, December 6, 1941, p. 10.